D1405144

FACTS AND JUDGMENTS

FACTS AND JUDGMENTS

A New Approach to College Writing

BY George R. Cerveny NEW YORK UNIVERSITY

HARCOURT, BRACE AND COMPANY hb NEW YORK

[e·12·49]

PRINTED IN THE UNITED STATES OF AMERICA

PREFACE

THE FIRST aim of *Facts and Judgments* is to free college teachers of English composition from some of the burden of explaining how to write, leaving more class time for the sort of discussion and criticism that will stimulate student papers. A second aim is to put students directly, and willingly, to the task of expressing themselves by taking some of the mystery out of the nature of thought and its communication.

Facts and Judgments contains two types of materials: technical discussion and illustrative readings. The first concern of the technical matter is to make a workable distinction between fact and judgment; the second is to describe the essay patterns into which facts and judgments fall. The illustrative readings have been carefully selected to follow the distinctions made in the text. If the book succeeds in its aims, the result will be shown in student papers mature in purpose, form, and content, and in class time that the creative teacher can use to draw from his students the priceless qualities of individuality and confidence.

Chapter 1 makes some preliminary remarks on the nature of language and on the communication of meaning. The chapter is intended to give the students notice that they themselves are the chief sources of the ideas and experiences they will use for their writing projects.

Chapter 2 is concerned with the distinction between writing which aims to communicate facts and that which aims to communicate judgments.

Chapter 3 describes the techniques of writing several types of factual essays: directions, summaries, scientific description, classification, formal reports, and factual narration. Each type is illustrated with an essay taken from professional sources, but selected for student appeal. The essays are good examples of language put to its task in a working world, and they clearly illustrate the techniques they are meant to illustrate. They are, furthermore, illustrative of kinds of writing the student, liberal arts major or professional, must attempt as he goes through college.

Chapter 4 explains the techniques of handling judgments. The patterns that such writing falls into, from the simple structure with one central judgment to be established to the complex and highly generalized essay, are thoroughly described and illustrated.

The essays in the reading section of the book illustrate the patterns discussed in the text. Many collections of readings are arranged by types of subject matter; but since writing skill, and not subject matter, is the important aim of writing courses, the arrangement of the essays in *Facts and Judgments* follows the plan of the text and illustrates techniques. The essays do, however, provide stimulating discussion topics suitable to student abilities and interests. The essays were selected on the principle that technique can best be taught in connection with subject matter which the student can grasp without unusual difficulty—hence the essay on working one's way through college in preference, say, to an article on cartel economics.

An appendix contains abundant material on library research and documentation.

Because *Facts and Judgments* has in it more writing problems than any student can complete in one term, it is not expected that the teacher should work straight through from problem to problem, but that he should use appropriate sections to establish the differences between essays of fact and those of judgment, and then move back and forth as the interests and needs of the class require, working from the simple patterns in either type to the more complex. The arrangement of the book will facilitate such flexible planning. The book is adaptable, moreover, to class or to individual work; but its function is to free the teacher as much as possible from the duty of explaining how to write, leaving him more time to discuss what has been written and to stimulate individual activity. The teacher and class can act as a critical audience only if there is time for it left over from outright instruction and only if everyone knows what is being attempted. The effort of the book is to supply some of the time and to provide a common, technical background.

Facts and Judgments abandons the conventional patterns of word, sentence, paragraph, and whole theme, and assumes at all times that a finished essay is to be written. This is in line with a growing practice in composition teaching. All the details applicable to an essay problem are worked out for that problem as it is developed. The repetition involved in this scheme is not a burden; rather it buttresses good learning. Handbook and workbook materials are so easily available to students and teachers who need them that they are not included in this book.

The plan and much of the materials of *Facts and Judgments* are new; but even though I have had to give the materials by lecture and on mimeographed sheets, they have been carefully tested on all types of college students: freshmen and graduates; incompetent, average, gifted. Nothing I have found or devised has given me and my students the sense of power and control over our work that these materials have. Much language theory is at hand nowadays, but little of it can be directly used to stimulate student writing. The theory is too abstract to serve as a good stimulus; and it does not concern essay patterns except as an application after the patterns have been solved, a fact that bedevils the teacher who wants to use the theory and at the same time get writing from his students. Modern theories of language are well established, and I have used whatever I have needed; but I received my first teachable insight into the classifications in this book from a student who balked at learning a technique I had been taught, but which was wrong. I am glad to acknowledge my debt to all the students who rebelled against dogma that did not make sense to them. I owe T. C. Pollock's *The Nature of Literature* for some of the distinctions in my first chapter. I owe, also, my colleagues for much direct and indirect help. They know my gratitude.

G. R. C.

FOREWORD TO THE STUDENT

IF YOU are a freshman, there is no doubt that you are entering your course in college composition with zeal and a sense of excitement over the future. We can say this confidently because you are young and because you have not yet learned from the upper classmen to assume a blasé indifference to scholarship. The upper classmen will get at you soon enough; but for the moment you are earnest, curious, a little apprehensive, and secretly determined to do a good job if you can. Perhaps you have the idea that writing is the work of a genius and that authors live in a world of their own, drinking wine, smoking a great many cigarettes, and flirting with girls with somewhat messy hair. Or perhaps you have concluded that your world is too grubby and that you are too ordinary to have either the need or the ability to write. You are going to be a chemist or a farmer or a teacher. You expect to read, you have a feeling of dread that some day you will be called upon for an after-dinner speech; but you do not expect to write. Writing, you may think, is for novelists and for journalists; so you wonder what value college composition has for you and why your adviser put it in your schedule with the remark that everybody has to take it.

You did not ask why, but you wondered and you looked a little uneasy. The question would have been fair, and the reply might have been one of several. Your grammar, spelling, and punctuation are not good enough. Certain of your mental traits need discipline. Your esthetic qualities need development. These are good reasons for taking a course in college composition, but they are oblique. They suggest grammar for the sake of grammar, discipline for the sake of discipline, or self-expression for the sake of some vague personality development. You should be told, however, what these reasons add up to: that you are in college composition because a deliberate attempt is going to be made to increase your intellectual power by increasing your language skill. Even though you may not write much after you leave college, you will read and reflect. Your life will have to include mental activity. What you are after now is help in developing a good mind. Such a mind is one able in discrimination, prompt in seeing relationships, mature in judgment, and skillful in communication. The most important goal of college composition is not good grammar, decent spelling, and acceptable punctuation. It is efficient, adult intellectual power, without which grammar, spelling, and punctuation have little meaning. Intellectual power and language skill are closely bound. You are in college composition to develop them both.

We should consider for a moment the workaday world of yours and your natural assumption that writing has only a small part in it. Look first into the immediate future. You will be in college, if all goes well, four years and perhaps an extra one to get an advanced degree. You will take approximately five courses a semester and have to write two examinations for each, one long paper, and several short ones. As a guess, six thousand words, not counting notes, per semester per course should be your minimum average. That will add up to more than two hundred thousand words for your first degree. You will write two plump books in the next four years; and if you go on for a master's degree, you will write a third one! They might as well be good books.

It is possible that you will not write much in the years after college, but you should not be too quick to assume it. Thousands of books are published every year in this country; and by far the greater number of them belong in the professional areas where you study in college: history, literature, law, chemistry, sociology, agronomy, medicine, teaching, engineering. A weekly, monthly, quarterly, yearly stream of magazines and journals, most of them with professional aims, complements the stream of books. The world needs professional books and journals; and responsible persons, usually those who are succeeding in life, write them. Success brings with it an obligation to write, and you should be reluctant to cut yourself off from that future responsibility. To do so is to mark yourself for failure even while you are preparing for your career. There is no sense in that.

Even though you are sure you will never write, you undoubtedly see the need of intellectual power. Writing, as an act, is a problem in communication from you to others; but before you can communicate with others, you must first communicate with yourself. You must hold an organized round-table in your mind, where you discuss and arrange your judgments and their supporting data. Skill in this sort of intimate conversation is part of what is meant by intellectual power. The skill can be developed by a systematic program of writing jobs set up in ascending complexity. As you move from job to job, you will increase your knowledge of what is meant by thinking, and of how to think, as well as get the strength that comes only from practice. This is the process that faces you as you begin college composition. The process is going to make demands upon your patience and your good humor. It is going to set limits on your labor that may irk you intensely. Self-expression is one of the goals toward which you will strive, but your method of reaching it will be rigorous. It has to be, for writing is hard work. You cannot construct sentences easily until you have practiced often, just as you cannot play a good game of tennis until you have gone through the training required for each separate skill. Illustrations that will illumine your meaning or convince your reader that your judgments are sound do not appear by magic just when you need them. They must be hunted down like game in a forest or like accessories for a new dress.

At rock bottom, thinking consists of making and supporting conclusions. To make and support conclusions you will have to be able to recognize the relationship, and the difference, between objective facts and your judgments drawn from the facts. *Facts and Judgments* is aimed at specific training in handling the materials of thought; in it writing techniques have been classified, not arbitrarily, but after careful analysis of many pieces of writing, so as to provide such training. The book makes distinctions and emphases which professional writers use as a common practice. Philosophers can and do argue over the distinctions, but the distinctions are used even in the argument. It can be argued, for example, that measurements are judgments. We are going to assume that they are facts. They are close enough to factuality, anyhow, so that skyscrapers and bridges can be built with a high degree of stability. When bridges do collapse, it is not because the engineer judged incorrectly the length of a foot: it is because the engineer drew wrong conclusions from his figures or made an error in calculation. The classification of writing techniques usual in college composition texts—exposition, argument, description, and narration—

is ignored, though the terms have some usefulness and are applied as convenient.

Once skill in handling facts and judgments is acquired, skill with all your writing will follow. This is a promise to the student who loves to write. To the practical fellow who demands a statement of profits before he invests, it is a promise that when his future employer calls on him for a report, his employer will get a good one.

CONTENTS

Part Three: Illustrative Readings

Part One
Some Preliminary Understandings

1. ON COMMUNICATING MEANING

WHAT is a word? Is it a symbol—sound or written sign? Is it a meaning? Is it symbol and meaning, the two *one* in the same way that husband and wife are said to be one? What, furthermore, is a symbol? And what is meaning?

These are questions difficult to answer, but the answers are preliminary to our actual program of writing. We have meanings—that is, something to say—buzzing through our heads all the time we are awake and much of the time we are asleep. Some of the meanings are the simple, every-day "Please, may I have the butter?" sort of thing. Others are complex abstractions such as Emerson's remark, "History is the lengthened shadow of one man." We have to get these meanings expressed. Community life is possible only if we can express them. Our personal happiness, also, depends largely on our success in communication, for a large part of our frustrations rise from misunderstandings caused by failure to make ourselves clear.

Words, of course, are not our only means of communication. Signs, such as we make with our hands or faces, carry meaning. All of us depend, probably more than we realize, on gesture and grimace. The scowl is a universal sign of displeasure. The uplifted hand, palm outward, to the American Indian meant the sign of friendship. The driver of an automobile now interprets it as an order to stop. The scowl and the gesture are examples of a kind of language that reaches a high level of art in some of the dance forms, where complex and subtle meanings are expressed. A musician uses patterns of sound to communicate his meanings. A painter uses patterns of color and line. The medium of communication that concerns us is words. Our meanings are those that support the life of our community and of our special interests. Like all artists, we have to whip our meanings and our patterns into control. If we are to be efficient, we must know how to present our words so that our readers understand *our* meanings. Our readers should get from our words what we intend our words to convey, otherwise misunderstandings arise, even among persons of good intentions. The task of efficient writing will be easier if we know something about words and how they convey meaning. The "meaning of meaning" is our goal now.

Consider the following stanza from Lewis Carroll's poem:

'Twas brillig, and the slithy toves
  Did gyre and gimble in the wabe.
All mimsy were the borogroves
  And the mome raths outgrabe.

What do the words *toves, gimble, wabe, mimsy,* and *mome* mean? Almost nothing. The stanza as a whole does have some meaning, for we get an idea of animals cavorting in a forest; but such words as *toves* and *mimsy* are nearly meaningless because we do not know the objects or qualities they stand for. Carroll did not want to communicate meanings; rather he was trying to arouse in his reader a feeling of delight in the nonsense, the rhythm, and the rime. The words, then, though they do arouse feeling, do not communicate much meaning of a conventional sort.

Let us take another poem, this time the whole of it:

I wandered lonely as a cloud
That floats on high o'er vales and hills,
When all at once I saw a crowd,
A host of golden daffodils,
Beside the lake, beneath the trees,
Fluttering and dancing in the breeze.

Continuous as the stars that shine
And twinkle on the milky way,
They stretched in never-ending line
Along the margin of a bay;
Ten thousand saw I at a glance,
Tossing their heads in sprightly dance.

The waves beside them danced, but they
Outdid the sparkling waves in glee—
A poet could not but be gay

In such a jocund company.
I gazed—and gazed—but little thought
What wealth the show to me had brought:

For oft when on my couch I lie
In vacant or in pensive mood,
They flash upon that inward eye
Which is the bliss of solitude;
And then my heart with pleasure fills,
And dances with the daffodils.

Most of us, if we know and like growing flowers at all, respond to the poem in two ways. First, we have an experience, sometimes called a vicarious experience in that it is supposed to be second hand. We do not just visualize Wordsworth wandering lonely as a cloud. *We ourselves wander.* We are delighted and made warm and gay by the poem in the same way we would be by the actual field. The words and their patterns take the place of the color and motion of the flowers. A new set of stimuli is substituted for that of the actual field, but the reaction to the stimuli provided by the words is similar to the reaction to an actual field. Second, though the poem does give us an experience, it also communicates meanings. We are informed of certain factual matters: the color of the flowers, their number, their action in the breeze. We are also told the judgments Wordsworth made as to the value of the experience.

Carroll's stanza gave us an experience, but it did not communicate much conventional meaning. Wordsworth's poem gave us an experience and meaning. Good fiction and poetry must reckon with experience and meaning. Though we shall have plenty of opportunities to try emotional tone in our writing, we shall be concerned chiefly with meanings.

The subject matter of meanings is as wide in range as all the universe. We find it everywhere, in reports, directions, descriptions, arguments. The illustrative papers we will read throughout *Facts and Judgments* begin with an excerpt about grizzly bears, a set of directions for getting meat out of a lobster, and a description of a "State of Maine" lumber camp. Some of the full-length essays in the reading section of the book are concerned with fact only, others with judgment. One of the latter argues that America is undergoing an artistic renaissance. Another declares that we should mark up our books. Another declares that blind workers are better in many ways and on certain jobs than sighted workers. All of these essays and excerpts have the one basic purpose of communicating meaning. They are intellectual. They tell us about their subjects. If they cause us to respond emotionally, it is to make their meanings more palatable.

Communication of meaning involves three elements, tabulated here so that they may be easily examined:

1. A person with a meaning he wishes to communicate
2. The symbols and their pattern that carry the meaning: *cat, haste,* $\pm$, H_2O, $\sqrt{\ }$, *complex, sister, I am hungry*
3. A person who receives the communication

The first and last of these are personal, and to explain them the whole system of psychical and physical features that are summed up by the word *mind* would have to be analyzed and accounted for. We do not need to attempt it. The middle element, the symbols and their organization into patterns such as phrases and sentences or mathematical equations, is a social instrument that every individual absorbs from his environment. We find French in France, Italian in Italy, English in England and America, Brooklynese in some sections of Brooklyn. The grammar, spelling, pronunciation, idiomatic usage, and conventional meanings associated with the symbols are part of the middle element; and they, too, are learned from the environment.

When words communicate meanings, they do so as symbols associated in our minds with objects or concepts. We must keep the fact of association clear: the symbol and the objects or concepts are different things. The word *cat* is not a cat. We cannot stroke the word. It cannot purr, scratch, lap milk, or catch mice. Furthermore, whatever meaning the word *cat* has for us is rooted in our experience. Only as we have experienced cats, directly, or indirectly by reading or hearing about them, can the symbol have meaning. The symbol H_2O, to use another type of example, is not the combination of gases known as water. It is only a symbol associated in our minds with water. A thirsty man would die if all he had to drink was a page written full of H_2O*'s*. Here again the meaning of the symbol is dependent upon our experience with the object it stands for. Is there not, for instance, a difference in the meaning of H_2O and *water?* We associate laboratories with H_2O. With water we associate swimming!

We must illustrate still further the connection of meaning and experience. Suppose someone says to us: "One of the reasons for the inefficiency of the first turbine engines is that the designers imperfectly understood the principle of adiabatic expansion." Or he says: "Miss Jones, of the physics department, uses mathematical conceptions with a heuristic power unequaled by her colleagues." Hardly anyone in a general audience can get a full communication of meaning from these sentences. Assuming that we know what a turbine engine is, do we know what *adiabatic* is? And do we know what is meant by *heuristic?* Before these symbols can be used to communicate meaning to us, we must have had experience with the objects or concepts that go with the symbols. To know *adiabatic* we must study it as a theory and apply it practically to turbine construction. To know *heuristic* we must experience the power it names. Not until we have had the experience, directly or indirectly, can we get any communication from the symbols. The meaning is in our heads, not in the words.

Some words get a long way from our experience. We have, let us say, a romp with a certain four-legged object we call Grishkin (our friend's dog). This particular four-legged object is, we are told, a member of the class of objects called *Pomeranian.* The Pomeranian class is a member of a large class known as *dog.* Here we have spaniels, hounds, terriers, etc. Each of these terms stands for increasingly larger numbers of the four-legged objects and increasingly complex concepts about them, and each term takes us further from Grishkin. To illustrate this, read the following table from the bottom up:

Organism
Animal
Mammal
Placental
Quadruped
Canine
Dog
Pomeranian
Grishkin

The table clearly reveals two points: (1) each higher term summarizes more and more individual objects; (2) the concepts get more and more remote from the place where we actually experience the objects.

The further up the table we go the higher our level of abstraction is and the further from actual experience we are. When we use these high-level abstractions we are in a realm of short-hand symbols that sum up vast areas of experience but do not point to any specific items of experience. They generalize rather than particularize. The danger in using them, as we shall see in a moment, is that the reader may not call to his mind the experiences the writer had in his. In such circumstances meaning is not communicated with clarity.

Abstraction is a function of intellect. We notice, for instance, that some animals feed their young by a system of glands and suckling. Grishkin does it. A bear we watched did it. Pigs do it. When we have recognized that some animals do and some do not, we have abstracted a meaning that includes a whole class of objects and we can classify the objects on the basis of that meaning. It is easy then to find or invent a symbol that stands for that class, in this instance, *mammal.* Thenceforward we may speak of mammals, but without calling attention to specific instances by way of illustration. We drop the specific and cling to the abstraction, because we have in mind the concept of all animals with such characteristics as form the class. Grishkin and the time when we saw her suckling her offspring drop into the background.

The older and more intellectual we grow the more we may get away from experience—that is, the more abstract we are likely to become. The concept associated with the term *vegetation,* as an example, is far from the specific corn, wheat, daisies, grass, and heather that we crush with our boots as we cross fields. Except as a mental process we cannot experience vegetation. We experience only the individual plants from which we abstract the concept. Our ears respond to the corn leaves rustling in the wind. Our backs ache because corn and pig-weed grow in close companionship. Our tongues bathe in the juices of corn kernels, butter, and salt. A time comes, however, when the efficiency of our thoughts requires that we stop using concepts of individual plants. We need a large unit of experience summed up by a single word. When we discover the relationship of all plants, we apply a label, such as *vegetation.* We may even reach the place in our classification when Grishkin and a specific corn plant are grouped together as organisms.

We cannot abandon experience for verbal excursions among high-level abstractions without running the risk of failure to communicate. The term *vegetation* will seldom cause confusion; but what can a reader take from such terms as the following: *truth, beauty, democracy, progressive education, rights of man, occupational therapy, romanticism?* Their meaning, whatever it is, is rooted in experience; and if a reader is to understand the writer who uses them, the experience must be made known somehow. Keats' lines

> "Beauty is truth, truth beauty,"—that is all
> Ye know on earth, and all ye need to know

compounds abstractions and confounds generation after generation of college students who try to find out what Keats meant. The difficulty is that students rarely have had the experience that will give the clue or the illumination by which the meaning may be found or seen. The lines are just "so many words" until experience, real or vicarious, gives them meaning. "Democracy," says the high-level abstractionist, "is the noble association of all mankind in the highest forms of equality. In it all men are free, all men are equal, all men are brothers." Hearing this, another man writes a check on the former's bank account. The indignant abstractionist loses his money. The equally indignant forger, protesting that words mean what they mean, is escorted by a policeman to jail. Democracy obviously has limits, and the person who speaks of it is obliged to make clear what he thinks the limits are. The limits vary, of course, according to the person and the situation. It is this variability that makes high-level abstractions dangerous as communicators of meaning.

If all this seems made up to fit the occasion, examine the following quotation from a book review, looking for high-level abstractions:

> A good many readers of this book [*Teacher in America*] will envy Professor Barzun for having written it. They have been planning to write one

like it themselves. I confess I am among the envious. Unfortunately, the deans, to whom it might be a breviary, will be too busy in successive committee meetings to glance at it, and the educationists will not be able to comprehend it, since it is written with wit and grace and not in the jargon they use as a substitute for English. The teachers will read it, and there are, one hopes, still more teachers than educationists abroad in the land.

Professor Barzun begins by making an essential distinction. What is wrong with our schools is not the "failure" of education but poor and aimless teaching. . . .[1]

This excerpt will puzzle the uninitiated reader. The abstractions by themselves do not clearly communicate the distinctions in the author's mind. What does he mean by deans, educationists, and teachers; education and teaching? Clearly he differentiates these terms; but is not a dean an educationist? It would seem that anyone concerned with administering schools is. And is not a teacher also an educationist? Furthermore, is teaching not a function, or part, of education? If it is, how can one say that education has not failed, but that teaching has? Surely, the uninitiated will think, they fail together. The author has distinctions in *his* mind, and they are good ones; but he does not make his distinctions clear to *all of us*. If he had written only for experts in the theory and practice of education (or is the word teaching?), the terms he uses might not require elaboration, though even experts have trouble getting together on meanings.

It is apparent that many of our words need help if they are to convey our meaning to a reader. The following illustrations will show us some ways of buttressing an abstraction so that it fulfills its function.

An abridged dictionary says of a gyroscope that it is "an instrument consisting of a flywheel capable of rotating about an axis which is arranged to move freely in one or more directions." As a communication of the meaning of a gyroscope this fails. It does not touch the function of the instrument, the method by which it operates, or the ordinary experience most of us have had with forms of gyroscopes. An author who knows the difficulty in making clear the meaning of such a complex principle as that of the gyroscope wrote the following:

[1] From a New York *Times* book review, Feb. 25, 1945, by Willard Thorp. Reprinted by permission of the author and The New York *Times* Book Review.

A child rolling a hoop is rolling a form of gyroscope. As long as the hoop revolves fast enough, it will remain upright.

A boy spinning a top is spinning a gyroscope. Given sufficient speed of rotation, it stays erect; when it slows down, it falls over.[2]

Now we begin to comprehend the gyroscope! As you would see if you were to read the book, the author uses statements that are abstract; but he also links the statements with the experience of the readers. If he were writing for engineers, he would not need to mention hoops and tops. He might call attention to the complicated forms of the gyroscope, such as the ship stabilizers or the gyroscopic compass. His rule is to link his abstractions with the experience of his readers, and on their level of understanding.

A writer describing river steamboating as follows would communicate almost nothing:

In crossing a sandbar the pilot would select the most promising chute and proceed by the trial-and-error method. If the vessel moved more and more slowly, finally coming to a dead standstill, warping was tried. If there were no trees, the order was "Plant a deadman!" When the boat rested too solidly on the bottom for the warping method to work, "sparring" was tried in an attempt to dislodge it. If the craft could not be sparred over the sandbar, the crew was "blue" indeed, for "double tripping" was the last resort.

Many of these terms need explaining; and in the original, shown below, they were explained. The author's method was to describe each process named by the abstract terms. He first made the statement containing the term. Then he followed up immediately with description. Here is the original:

In crossing a sandbar the pilot would select the most promising chute and proceed by the trial-and-error method. One of the deckhands was kept at the bow on the forecastle sounding the channel. In case no channel was found by direct trial, the pilot went out in a yawl and sounded the entire river over the shallow portion, sometimes spending hours in diligent search for the deepest water. Having settled on the best place, he began the long, laborious task of getting the boat over it. . . .

[2] From *The Star Finder,* by Henry M. Neely. New York: Smith and Durrell, Inc., 1943.

If the vessel moved more and more slowly, finally coming to a dead standstill, warping was tried. If there was a tree on the bank, a line was made fast to it and the other end was slowly drawn in by the capstan. By this means the boat was pulled over the bar. If there were no trees, the order was "Plant a deadman!" This consisted of digging a hole three or four feet deep on the prairie and burying a log with a line attached to the middle to serve as a fixture to be used in place of a tree for warping. So the boat pulled itself out of the mud by its own bootstraps.

When the boat rested too solidly on the bottom for the warping method to work, "sparring" was tried in an attempt to dislodge it. The spars were two poles like masts shod with sharp iron points, held erect, one on each side of the bow; when the boat stuck, the ends of the spars were lowered to the river-bed. By means of block and tackle operated by a small donkey-engine, commonly called the "nigger," the front end of the boat was raised a foot or more off the bottom. The paddles were then put in motion at full speed, and with luck the vessel was jumped over the bar. The order to start the engine was, "Go ahead on the nigger."

If the craft could not be "grasshoppered" over the sandbar, the crew was "blue" indeed, for "double tripping" was the last resort. This was the simple process of lightening the boat by unloading half the freight on the bank, steaming over the bar, unloading the other half, returning for the first half, passing over the bar again, loading up and proceeding. Sometimes the passengers were requested to get out and walk in order to lighten the boat for the passage of rapids or sandbars.[3]

It is always possible that a reader will not have had enough experience to make direct communication possible. The communication may then be made indirectly by showing how the unknown object or idea is similar to a known object or idea. An author trying to make known the meaning of the term *essay* wrote as follows:

The essay is the rainbow of the literary arts, stretching in its vast arch from somewhere to anywhere. It has taken all knowledge, all thoughts, all arts, all science, to be its province, examining all of them, exhausting none of them. It touches and blends with the ultra-violet of the scholarly treatise and sweeps through every color and mood to the infra-red of poetry. It may be as formal as a minuet, as gay as a jog. It may cut through data to a

[3] From *Vanguards of the Frontier,* by Everett Dick. Reprinted by permission of D. Appleton-Century Co., Inc.

conclusion as coldly and impersonally as a surgeon's scalpel, and it may be as intimate and personal as a love lyric. The essay is all-embracing.[4]

The following excerpt gets its meaning made clear in illustrations:

What is meant by vocabulary? Just what the word signifies. Does *enervating* mean *soothing, exciting, distressing, invigorating,* or *weakening?* For most well-educated persons the choice is between *invigorating* and *weakening.* Fifty-two per cent of the college graduates measured by the Laboratory choose *invigorating* as the synonym; only sixteen per cent choose *weakening,* the dictionary definition. Does *stilted,* in the phrase: "His *stilted* manner," mean *irresolute, improper, cordial, stiffly formal,* or *vicious?* A majority of educated persons mark *stiffly formal,* but more than a third select *irresolute.* Answers to the meaning of *scurrilous,* in the phrase: "*scurrilous* rogue," divide themselves more or less evenly between *hurrying, desperate, abusive, frantic,* and *diseased,* with *desperate* the most popular. For *peremptory,* a majority mark *decisive,* but many choose *persuasive, uncertain,* and *angry. Pleasant,* the fifth choice, is not so popular. *Linguist* and *glutton* are equally enticing as synonyms for *polyglot.* For *refulgent,* in: "A *refulgent* smile," *repellent* is most alluring, and *very bright* next, with *mischievous, flattering,* and *sour,* all following closely in popularity. For *monograph* forty per cent choose *soliloquy* and less than twenty per cent *treatise* and *epitaph* each.

The word *vocabulary,* as used in this book, signifies a knowledge of the dictionary meaning of just such words as *enervating, stilted, scurrilous, peremptory, polyglot, refulgent,* and *monograph.*[5]

The meaning of the term *vocabulary* is surely clear. The illustrations make it unmistakable.

An example of a brief, but useful, illustration is found in the following sentence:

A galvanometer is an instrument, such as the battery indicator found on the panel of an automobile, used for detecting the existence and measuring the intensity and direction of an electric current.

When a brief explanation or illustration is all one needs to keep an abstraction from soaring away from contact with experience, the

[4] From *The Revised College Omnibus* edited by James Dow McCallum. Copyright, 1939, by Harcourt, Brace and Company, Inc.

[5] From *English Vocabulary Builder,* by Johnson O'Connor. Reprinted by permission of the author.

explanatory material may be inserted into the sentence containing the abstraction. The insertion, unobtrusive, yet efficient, lies in wait for the reader without interfering with the main thought of the sentence. The two following sentences illustrate the technique:

Parasites, animals or plants that live at the expense of other animals or plants, sometimes destroy themselves by destroying their hosts.

Modern household economy has found use for the thermostat, an instrument which, in response to temperature changes, controls the operation of machines such as the oil-burning furnace or the mechanical refrigerator.

Though this discussion has not been very long, it has been concerned with a difficult subject: the high-level abstraction *language*. Trying to practice what we were preaching, we have used a constant flow of ordinary experience with language and of familiar illustrative materials. If we have been successful, these points about language are clear:

Words may be used as stimuli to communicate experience.

Words may be used as symbols to communicate meanings.

Meaning is rooted in experience.

Words become meaningful by association with experience.

Some of our words are so abstract—that is, they serve as shorthand summaries of vast amounts of experience—that they need help if they are to communicate precise meanings.

To help abstractions communicate fully we tie them to specific experience, descriptive elaboration, or illustration.

Exercises

A. Explain why the following sentences do not make their full communication of meaning. The difficulties vary with the sentences—and in some instances will vary with the student. Seek to show what has caused the failure by showing how the symbol and the pattern have lost or confused the meaning.

1. He said flippantly, —A mí no me importa.
2. My father's profession is teaching, which I will be some day.
3. I have thought that some professors were queer, but before the term was

over, I changed my mind because I began to understand his point of view. I don't say they aren't, but he will have to be very queer for me to call him really queer.

4. Our inventions are much more numerous than other countries.

5. The tub has a heavy canvas cover with a hole in it for the patient's head, which laces with rope to metal hooks on the sides of the tub.

6. When we try to consider all phases of intellect as a whole, we should not lose sight of the fact that all individuals are not endowed with the same span of reasoning or growth, although intellect may be varied, that is, from the point of view which may interest a person. In some cases intellect may be brought about in one or two specific fields—thus lacking to give the person the full benefits of all their powers of learning and reasoning.

7. You'd think all was dodo belonging to him how he durmed adranse in durance vaal. (James Joyce)

B. The following sentences have been adapted from newspaper and magazine sources. What do you think each means? Be ready with your interpretation. Ask other persons to interpret the sentences. Do the interpretations differ?

1. All that we ask for our workers is economic protection.

2. Philosophically, Dreiser's stories are a mixture of economic determinism, realism, and sentimental romanticism.

3. The common man of America has reached the highest standard of living he has ever known anywhere.

4. If William F. Stanley is put in the Cabinet, free-enterprise in America will die.

5. Education must take the burden of teaching Americanism to our young people.

6. Collectivism is leading us right down the road to serfdom.

7. The world needs most of all a return to religion.

C. Find in your textbooks examples of definitions. Analyze them for the methods used to make the meanings clear. Be ready to discuss in class how successful the definitions are in telling you what is meant. Suggest ways of improvement if you can think of any. Tell the class what experience you may have had which reveals the meanings of the terms.

D. Write sentences which have insertions that explain the meaning of each of the following terms. Keep the main part of each sentence from being itself a definition.

Passover	Percolator
Narwhal	Pentecost
Libido	Bass viol
Sagebrush	Ball bearing
Sharpie	Hellbroth
Klipspringer	Social work
Mineralogy	Kindergarten

E. Read the excerpt below. It attempts to explain the meaning of the term *induction*. The method is to call attention to a piece of inductive reasoning all of us have made. After you have read the excerpt, write in a similar way an explanation of one of these terms, or of one that you select yourself: oral hygiene, weather forecasting, social work, home economics, geometry, navigation, range finding.

. . . Suppose you go into a fruiterer's shop, wanting an apple. You take up one, and on biting it you find it is sour; you look at it and see that it is hard and green. You take up another one, and that too is hard, green, and sour. The shop man offers you a third; but before biting it you examine it and find that it is hard and green, and you immediately say that you will not have it, as it must be sour like those you have already tried.

Nothing can be more simple than that, you think; but if you will take the trouble to analyze and trace out into its logical elements what has been done by the mind, you will be greatly surprised. In the first place, you have performed the operation of induction.[6]

F. The following article explains the term *actuary,* the title of a very important person in an insurance company. Read it carefully to see if the term is sufficiently clear and to see how the author presented his explanation. After you have studied the article write a similar explanation of the title of any work that you know well: stenographer, building superintendent, garage roustabout, waitress, night clerk, postman. You may, if you wish, use a variation of the title of the essay below, for it will help you define your writing problem.

[6] From *On Our Knowledge of the Causes of the Phenomena of Organic Nature,* by Thomas Henry Huxley.

Say, Mr. Clark—What Is *an Actuary?*

Suppose you were being shown through the Home Office of a life insurance company and came to a door lettered "Actuary." Perhaps you might be puzzled as to the meaning of the word.

Of course, if you turned to the dictionary, you would learn there that an Actuary is "one whose profession is to calculate insurance risks and premiums."

This definition is correct, as far as it goes. But it falls far short of picturing the true scope of an Actuary's activities.

Nowadays his profession is highly specialized. It is a profession in which a man may hope to gain recognized standing only after years of intensive study and training. For he must have a thorough knowledge of the three complicated factors on which life insurance premiums are based . . . Mortality, Interest, and Expense.

For example, in order to arrive at premium charges which will be both safe and fair, the Actuary must make detailed analyses of the past and present death rates among different groups of people. From these studies, he is able to compile mortality tables which provide an amazingly dependable yardstick for his guidance in computing premiums.

The Actuary must also take into account the interest rate which the company may reasonably undertake to earn on the investments it makes for the benefit of its policyholders.

And in a mutual life insurance company, such as Metropolitan, the Actuary prepares data which enable the Board of Directors to determine the annual divisible surplus which will be returned to the policyholders in the form of dividends.

Another of the Actuary's duties, together with the legal staff, is to draw up the policy forms issued by the company.

He keeps running records of such important matters as mortality . . . the ages and occupations of people insured . . . the company's experience on outstanding policies. He also assembles data needed for the preparation of the Annual Statement, which is submitted to the proper state authorities, and forms a public record of the year's activities.

In short, an Actuary might be defined as the "engineer" who helps design the "product" a life insurance company offers . . . and then figures out what the policyholders should reasonably pay for the benefits provided by their contracts.[7]

[7] Reprinted by permission from an advertisement of the Metropolitan Life Insurance Company.

G. If your instructor is willing, select from your class two committees of about five or six members. Have each committee take one of the following books for an oral, class report: *Language in Action,* by S. I. Hayakawa; *The Folklore of Capitalism,* by Thurman W. Arnold. Each committee should explain to the class the main points of the book it reports on and provide concrete illustrations gathered from the book or from such sources as newspapers and magazines. At least a month should be allowed for preparation of the reports.

2. DISTINGUISHING BETWEEN FACTS AND JUDGMENTS

THE preliminaries are over, and we can begin our specific techniques. Our first step is to divide our writing materials into two classes: (1) verifiable facts and (2) judgments or conclusions drawn from facts. This is a rough, but necessary division. Our control over our writing depends upon how well we control the two classes: facts on one side; judgments (conclusions, themes, propositions, opinions, hypotheses, laws, call them what we wish) on the other. For instance:

FACTS: A catalogue of books available in the adult department of the Middletown library, issued in 1893, showed in useful arts (technology, advertising, salesmanship, etc.) 91 books as against 1,617 in the adult department of the library in 1924; in fine arts 45 as against 1,166; in history 348 as against 2,867; in biography 132 as against 1,396; in sociology 106 as against 1,937; in literature 164 as against 2,777; in science 89 as against 585; and so on through the other classifications.[1]

JUDGMENT: The Middletown library expanded greatly during the years between 1893 and 1924.

We must keep this division clear. Is it facts we intend to communicate, or is it judgment drawn from facts? Do we say of a table, to cite another instance, that it is twenty-six inches square on top, thirty inches high, made of solid birch, and finished with rubbed wax; or do we say that the table is unusually beautiful? The first statement is factual. It is objective. Any person using standard scales of measurement can verify every fact given. The second is a judgment. It is subjective. Other persons may or may not be willing to accept it. The best we can do is to explain why we think as we do. After we have given the facts which convinced us, others can decide for themselves how correct they think our judgment is. The judgment about the Middletown library is also personal, but it is so well backed up with facts that we must accept it.

[1] From *Middletown*, by Robert S. Lynd and Helen Merrell Lynd. Copyright, 1929, by Harcourt, Brace and Company, Inc.

A writer discussing the library or the table needs to know if he is describing them factually or is judging them. If the purpose is to describe, to give the verifiable facts, the problem works out simply. He examines the library or the table for the facts, divides them into appropriate groups, and sets them down in the best prose he has suitable for the occasion. If the purpose is judgment, he examines all the facts and makes up his mind what he thinks. He then writes out his judgment and offers the facts and arguments which support him, ignoring everything that is irrelevant or not helpful. If the facts he ignores are destructive of his judgment, he must, to be honest and safe, make the necessary revision.

To say there are two types of material is to imply two purposes in our writing: (1) to communicate facts and (2) to communicate judgments. This is only a beginning, for the two may be variously combined. First we must be sure that the division of material and purpose is understood. Because illustration is a good method of explanation, putting us on the experience level, suppose we look now at two examples of each. The first two will show authors presenting and supporting judgments. We are to notice that each author has one central judgment, italicized here to help us locate it, and that all the following details are used to attest the truth of the judgment. It is as if the authors thought of keeping their readers from asking, "Why do you believe that?"

What will a grizzly do if he suddenly meets up with a man on his own stamping grounds? You can get plenty of opinions on that, most of them different, from men who have had some experience hunting the big beast. Some years ago I read a magazine article in which the writer claimed he could chase all the animals in North America with a buggy whip and a tin whistle.

I have reason to doubt that statement—not because it may be difficult, in this automobile age, to obtain a good buggy whip—but because I've spent practically 365 days a year in grizzly country for the last twenty-seven years. And I know of several occasions when the best buggy whips would have been a poor line of defense.

Take the case of Tom Meanie. In the late winter of 1925 Tom was working his trapline about twenty miles north of my place in British Columbia. He shot a moose for meat, and then left it for a week. Later he and a helper returned to spring the traps, and Tom sent his friend down a side line to pick up traps while he went over to the carcass to get meat. Never expecting a bear to be out that early, he took only an ax to chop off the frozen flesh.

From what we could reconstruct from his tracks later, he got within thirty-five yards of the moose carcass when a large grizzly ran out to meet him. That's the place where Tom's body was found. The bear had struck him and driven him down through the snowshoe trail to his knees; then he had fallen backward. The first blow seemed to have taken off half his skull and practically all his face; the second savage swipe removed the rest of the scalp.

The bear ran away and never returned directly to the body, although it came back and circled it several times before the police came in a week later.

I and my son Edward have had meet-ups with grizzlies, when tin whistles would have been pretty poor weapons. Back in 1933 Edward, also working a trapline, was on his way home for Christmas, when about a mile and a half from the house he saw an animal moving in the twilight. At first he thought it was a wolverine, but when he came within 150 yards he discovered it was a young grizzly. He started to whistle to scare it away, but the whistle had no terrors for the bear. Getting his scent, it started for him on the jump. Ed hollered and banged on a tree with a stick he carried to knock snow from his snowshoes, but the little battler came on with increased speed.

Ed decided it was time to clear the decks for action, so he unslung his .30/30 and when the bear was twelve feet away, he fired. The bullet struck the grizzly in the chest, passed through its heart, and killed it instantly.[2]

Are we not convinced? Do we not believe that a buggy whip and a tin whistle are insufficient weapons with which to face a grizzly? The author certainly has reached that conclusion. He wants to do more than give us objective facts about bears. He wants to interpret his facts, to show their meaning to him, to make, that is, a judgment. Accordingly he gives us his judgment and then presents some factual data for support.

The next example of judgment and support comes from the WPA guidebook, *Idaho.*

[2] From "Grizzlies Are Bad Actors," by J. B. Hooker. *Outdoor Life,* November, 1941. Reprinted by permission of *Outdoor Life.*

Much of Idaho for the sensitive person is lonely today with the memory of the vigorous and turbulent life of towns and cities where there is now only desolation and a handful of ruins. Where once there were thousands of persons there may now be only a few shacks or there may be nothing but a stone or a tree and the indefinable loneliness of something that is dead. For Idaho in one perspective is an area of ghost towns or of spots where not even the ghost remains. . . .

There is what once was Springtown just west of the present Hansen Bridge. In the eighth decade of the last century it sprang into existence on the rim of the Snake River Gorge. Today there are only the ruins of some mud huts in which Chinese miners are said to have lived while they feverishly panned gold. There was Bullion a few miles west of the present town of Hailey: it had two general stores, a post office, a hospital, many dwelling houses, and nobody knows how many saloons. Today nothing remains. Or Oro Grande, situated on the west side of Loon Creek, had as many as five stores, and a saloon for every store. The gold here was exhausted in about a year, the gulch abandoned and sold to the Chinese who trailed the more enterprising hordes and reworked what they left; and now the site of this town is indistinguishable from the country which surrounds it. Vienna at the base of the Sawtooth Range had almost a thousand persons in it and was the largest of the mining towns in this region. The last resident left it in 1892. One of its competitors, Sawtooth City, flourished for many years, but when, in 1897, the postmaster resigned there was an exodus, with only five persons remaining in possession of everything in sight. These weathered one more season and then left Sawtooth City to loneliness and the snow. Up north in the Panhandle, Eagle City was once the capital of the Coeur d'Alenes and so thriving and ambitious a place that extensive improvements were made, and town lots, inviting newcomers, lay almost the length of a mile. Today Eagle City is not even shown on a map. And there were Galena and Kingston, Florence and Gem—or Moose City which once had nine thousand persons. Today it can be reached only by horseback in a journey of three days over the Bitterroot Divide, and where once was a city of nine thousand, only one decaying log cabin stands now.[3]

Through the vanishing of these towns, and through the use of words that carry the atmosphere (*lonely, desolation, abandoned, exodus, de-*

[3] From *Idaho: A Guide in Word and Picture,* edited by Vardis Fisher. Published by The Caxton Printers, Ltd., Caldwell, Idaho. Used by special permission of the copyright owners.

caying) the author makes and establishes his judgment that much of Idaho is filled with the memory of vigorous and turbulent life in the cities that did not live.

Judge and support: that is the intention, and that is the formula. Every detail goes under the censorship of the judgment. Every detail works its way by supporting the judgment. It makes no difference whether one is judging ideas, physical objects, or events; whether one's supporting evidence is idea, fact, or narration. The intention is to set out the judgment and its supporting particulars. All of the particulars are subordinate in the same way that pillars are subordinate to the deck of a bridge—they hold up the judgment. The descriptive label we are going to use for such writing as this is *thematic,* a word coming from the Greek *thema,* meaning proposition. The judgment is a proposition, or theme, which is to be established. One of the chapters which follow contains a full discussion of methods of supporting themes.

What happens when the writer is working with the other of the two purposes: reporting factually, that is, reporting for the sake of giving verifiable details and not for the sake of making a point? The two following examples, one a description of a process and the other an informal description of a typical object, will answer the question.

To open lobsters and remove the meat, take off the large claws, small claws, and separate the tail from the body. Tail meat may sometimes be drawn out whole with a fork; more often it is necessary to cut the thin shell portion (using scissors or a can opener) in the under part of the tail; then the tail meat may always be removed whole. Separate the tail meat through the center and remove the small intestinal vein which runs its entire length; although generally darker than the meat, it is sometimes found of the same color. Hold the body shell firmly in the left hand, and with the first two fingers and thumb of the right hand draw out the body, leaving in the shell the *stomach* (known as the lady), which is not edible, and also some of the green part, the *liver*. The liver may be removed by shaking the shell. The coral, a red spongy substance sometimes found in the female lobsters, is edible and highly prized for its brilliant color. The sides of the body are covered with the *lungs;* these are always discarded. Break the body through the middle and separate the body bones, picking out the meat that lies between them, which is some of the sweetest and tenderest to be found. Separate the large claws at the joints. If the shells are thin, with a knife cut off a strip down the sharp edge, so that the shell may be broken apart and the meat removed whole. Where the shell is thick, it must be broken with a mallet or hammer. Small claws are used for garnishing. The shell of the body, tail, and lower parts of the large claws, if not broken, may be washed, dried, and used for serving of lobster meat after it has been prepared. The portions of lobsters which are not edible are the *lungs, stomach* (lady), and *intestinal vein*. Lobster meat may be purchased in cans.[4]

There is here no judgment which the writer intended to support, though occasionally one is put in parenthetically. The reader may reach one of his own and decide to buy lobster in cans; but that is not the purpose in the writer's mind. The writer thinks of a hungry man with a lobster. The man wants information: what are the edible parts of a lobster? how get the meat out of a lobster? All that the writer does is to present the facts that solve the problem. They are presented, and the man has lobster for lunch. Nobody makes judgments except the fellow who concludes that lobster is not worth so much trouble; and he does it without any prompting from the writer, who wants only to describe a process and to give some information on what parts of the lobster to eat. The facts are not meant to support anything. Whatever judgments get into the article are in the nature of an aside.

Giving directions is only one of many writing tasks requiring facts without the control of a theme. The following excerpt illustrates another. It is an informal description of a typical object. Such description as this sometimes is called *scientific description,* to distinguish it from *literary description;* and its purpose is to be factually informative.

. . . The "State of Maine" lumber camp, which became the typical frontier type, had but one building about thirty by forty feet with sidewalls scarcely two feet above the ground. The walls were built of logs, and the roof was made of shakes covered with evergreen boughs or clay. The building was so low inside that for one-third of the width it was impossible for a man to stand erect. The door was at the south, and in the center of the building was an enclosure a foot high and about eight feet square filled

[4] From *The Boston Cooking-School Cook Book,* 1936, by Fannie Merritt Farmer. Reprinted by permission of Little, Brown and Company.

with stone or sand. Here was built the fire. In the roof above this open fireplace was the smoke-hole, a large square opening which was supposed to allow the smoke to escape. To facilitate this purpose, shakes split from pine logs were put up under the roof around the opening, extending down in such a way as to form a large wooden funnel to catch as much of the smoke as possible. For further assistance to the draft, sometimes a mud and stick chimney was built on top of the roof, but in most camps this was dispensed with. In some places a hole in the roof eight feet long and three feet wide sufficed without a funnel. The open fire served for heating, part of the cooking, and even lighting, for there were no windows in the low sides of the building.

Along one side of the room was a field bed extending the full length of the building. The men slept with their heads toward the low side walls. Between the logger's feet and the fire at the foot of the bed was a long flat beam called the "deacon's seat." This was one of the unique institutions of a lumberman's camp. On it the logger mounted upon stirring out of his neighborly bed after the night's rest. Here he sat to dress, and again at night it was his last stepping-place before he crawled under the covers. In a jolly row the lumberjacks sat on it before the blazing fire telling stories and cracking jokes to while away the time of the long winter evening. On this seat the logger made his bargain with the boss and received his pay. When in after years his mind turned back to those logging days, the "deacon's seat" occupied a central place.

At the end of the building opposite the door was a projection containing a stove and a pantry. This was the domain of the cook. Across the same end, but not set apart by a partition, was the dining-room, furnished with some rough wooden tables and benches made of split logs. Here the meals were served. Around these tables, during spare hours when the men were not in bed, they sometimes spent their time smoking and talking. In this apartment was to be found a grindstone, much used by the men in keeping their tools in shape but never mentioned by a recruiting officer for the lumber camp. Many hands, when hiring out, never suspected it was part of their duty to keep their axes in order. There, too, was a wash sink, a water-barrel, and various other items of equipment. On one side of the low room was the wood supply and general stowaway.

Near the central log fire hooks and wires were arranged on which to dry wet clothes. A visitor to a Rum River camp in 1867 was given a buffalo robe and allowed to sleep by the fire. Looking up toward the roof, he thought he was in a stocking factory or moccasin store because of the countless footwear hanging around the roof in the vicinity of the fire.

The next morning all were gone, only to reappear again in the same spots at night. The apparel of the logger included heavy socks and rubbers, a mackinaw, and a wool cap.

The so-called field bed, as we have seen, extended the entire length of the building along one side, allowing about two feet for each man. Usually the bed consisted of a plentiful supply of small spruce or hemlock boughs with a log at the head for a pillow, or longer boughs without the log were sometimes used. Often, however, the men folded up their coats and used them for pillows. The entire bed was covered with a single bedspread two inches thick. The men slept "spoon-fashion," all lying on the same side. When one got tired of lying in one position, he would shout, "Spoon!" and everyone would turn over.[5]

Such writing as is illustrated by the process and the factual description may be thought of as bread-and-butter prose. It is often matter-of-fact, almost pedestrian, although it need not be, for the more the writer is an artist the more will he sound imaginative overtones; and the more he is skilled as a thinker, the more precise, and thrilling because of his precision, will he be in his presentation. What the writer wants in this type of essay is a body of verifiable facts. If he uses judgments, such as that about the uniqueness of the deacon's seat, they are put in more or less parenthetically. A popular audience finds that they add flavor to the facts. If the audience is composed of technical readers, the judgments are ruthlessly excluded, and the resulting prose is as factual in its way as a blue print is in its.

We need a name for factual writing; and because there is precedent, we shall call it by the descriptive label *informative*. This limits the word to a narrower use than is generally allowed it, but the restriction need not confuse us if we remember that informative writing is meant to give us only a body of verifiable facts, avoiding all effort to establish judgment.

Because there are times when the thematic purpose and the informative are combined, one possibility should be mentioned as forewarning: the use of informative material in one section of an essay, and the elaboration of a related theme in another. This will be fully explained later. It is mentioned here as a warning to the student not to pick up a literary magazine and expect of every article in it such a

[5] From *Vanguards of the Frontier*, by Everett Dick. Reprinted by permission of D. Appleton-Century Co., Inc.

clear division as he now has in mind. Some of the articles will be sharply thematic or sharply informative; but some will not.

Sources of thematic writing are likely to be the magazines and books that go in for controversy. Informative essays will appear most often in handicraft and industrial magazines and books, in textbooks, and in all magazines or books that are scientific or are devoted to a profession or branch of commerce. Newspapers, except, perhaps, during political campaigns and apart from the editorials, are preponderantly informative.

Know the purpose. Is it thematic? Is it informative?
Thematic writing presents judgments *plus* supporting facts.
Informative writing presents facts.

Exercises

A. The following sentences, taken from Thoreau's *Walden,* are thematic or informative. Be prepared to tell them apart. If you find a word or phrase which seems to be thematic in character though the remainder of the sentence is informative, point it out for class discussion.

1. The Fitchburg Railroad touches the pond about a hundred rods south of where I dwell.
2. A lake is the landscape's most beautiful and expressive feature.
3. It is time that villages were universities, and their elder inhabitants the fellows of universities, with leisure . . . to pursue liberal studies the rest of their lives.
4. I have thus a tight shingled and plastered house, ten feet wide by fifteen long, eight-feet posts, with a garret and a closet, a large window on each side, two trap-doors, one door at the end, and a brick fireplace opposite.
5. No man ever followed his genius till it misled him.
6. From exertion come wisdom and purity; from sloth ignorance and sensuality.
7. Above all, as I have implied, the man who goes alone can start today; but he who travels with another must wait till that other is ready, and it may be a long time before they get off.
8. As I sit at my window this summer afternoon, hawks are circling about my clearing; the tantivy of wild pigeons, flying twos and threes athwart my view, or perching restless on the white-pine boughs behind my house, gives

a voice to the air; a fish-hawk dimples the glassy surface of the pond and brings up a fish; a mink steals out of the marsh before my door and seizes a frog by the shore; the sedge is bending under the weight of the reed-birds flitting hither and thither; and for the last half-hour I have heard the rattle of railroad-cars . . . conveying travelers from Boston to the country.

9. Ancient poetry and mythology suggest, at least, that husbandry was once a sacred art; but it is pursued with irreverent haste and heedlessness by us, our object being to have large farms and large crops merely.

10. As I came home through the woods with my string of fish, trailing my pole, it being quite dark, I caught a glimpse of a woodchuck stealing across my path, and felt a strange thrill of savage delight, and was strongly tempted to seize and devour him raw. . . .

11. The mass of men lead lives of quiet desperation.

12. I finally left Walden September 6th, 1847.

B. Write five thematic sentences and five informative, putting each set under a proper heading.

C. The following excerpts are all thematic. Be prepared to point out which sentence, or sentences, in each makes the theme statement developed by the author.

1. We trust it is not unpatriotic to say that in the matter of finding good names for fighting planes the British have it all over us. Picking here and there in Hanson W. Baldwin's recent little article, we learn that the British call a certain American machine Lightning and we call it Lockheed P-38. A plane which we call Consolidated B-24 they call Liberator. They say Catalina where we say Consolidated PBY-5. As for their own machines, who has failed to be thrilled by the mere sound—Tornado, Whirlwind, Spitfire, Defiant? On the other hand, think of Americans going forth to battle for freedom and human rights in Consolidated PBY-5's.[6]

2. Like other New England towns, which seemed on the surface so harmoniously blended of the good, the true, and the beautiful, Gardiner had its share of self-willed individualists, who escaped from the picture and sat themselves on the frame. There was Peg-leg Talbot, the disreputable "tin-knocker," who repaired stoves; Wash Benjamin, who had a mistress down the road and cursed the Episcopal Church every chance he had; Squire

[6] Editorial. From The New York *Times,* March 12, 1941. Reprinted by permission of The New York *Times.*

Whitmore, who was so close that he kept only one hen which, he said, could lay all the eggs he and his sister would want to eat. The Squire was a sight to see, letting a pail down from his carriage when he wanted to descend, or putting a paper-bag over his beaver hat when it rained. John Walsh was his match. He was the town's handy-man, who, asked by the Squire to view his portrait, pointed out that it was untrue to life in that the Squire's hand was shown in his own pocket and not in some other man's.[7]

3. The statistics on the reading of comic books are astounding, the more so when one recalls that the first comic magazine appeared only in 1933. A recent survey, by the Market Research Company of America, on the reading of comic books throughout the country reveals that comic books have as large if not a larger public than have the comic pages of the newspapers, a public estimated at seventy million.

Of children 6 to 11, 95 per cent of boys and 91 per cent of girls read comic books regularly. Of adolescents 12 to 17, 87 per cent of boys and 81 per cent of girls are regular readers. Regular readers among adults number 41 per cent of men and 28 per cent of women between the ages of 18 and 30, 16 per cent of men and 12 per cent of women 31 and over (with another 13 per cent of men and 10 per cent of women occasional readers).

Paul W. Stewart and Associates, Inc., questioned the entire population of Hudson, New York, on their reading of comic books. They found that they were regularly read by 93 per cent of children between 8 and 15, by 72 per cent of boys and girls of the ages of 16 and 17, by 27 per cent of adults 18 to 34, and by 10 per cent of adults over 35. These figures conform closely to those for the country as a whole. Indeed, the National Market Research Company survey found only slight variations in the reading of comic books from one part of the country to another. . . .

The size of the comics' public is equaled only by the avidity and absorption with which that public follows the adventures and misadventures of its favorite characters. When Milton Caniff, two years ago, staged the death of Raven Sherman in "Terry and the Pirates," 1,400 letters of sympathy poured in, a number accompanied by floral offerings.

A Pennsylvania paper, which did not subscribe to the strip, carried the story of "Raven's" death as a news item. Caniff was interviewed on the radio, so he could explain why "Raven" had to die. On the day "Raven" was buried in the hills north of Chungking, 450 students of Loyola Uni-

[7] From *Edwin Arlington Robinson: A Biography,* by Hermann Hagedorn. By permission of The Macmillan Company, publishers.

versity of Chicago paid tribute to her by gathering on their campus, facing east for a minute of silence.[8]

D. Analyze the following excerpt from a news report to decide the author's basic purpose. Is he interested in communicating judgments or facts?

On Oct. 11, while the enemy was still trying to figure out what had hit him to the northward, the airplanes of one carrier group swept over the northern part of Luzon, main island of the Philippine Commonwealth, while the other carrier forces were refueling. That strike cost the Japanese ten to fifteen airplanes destroyed on the ground. Enemy opposition was inconsequential.

Three times, in as many days, the United States forces had struck at three different and widely separated strongholds of the enemy. On the fourth day, Oct. 12, a fleet appeared in the enemy's own backyard, off the island of Formosa, from which the aerial attack against the Philippines had been launched by the Japanese nearly three years before. Our objectives were the twenty-five to thirty first class military airfields on Formosa, the airplanes based there, and, of course, any other military establishments on shore and the enemy shipping in the harbors.

Our fleet maneuvered in the vicinity of Formosa for three days, Oct. 12, 13 and 14. Fifty-five enemy vessels of all kinds were certainly destroyed and thirty-two were probably sunk, while approximately 396 airplanes were destroyed in the air or on the ground. On the last day, and on Oct. 16, Formosa was additionally the target of United States Army B-29's, flying from China.[9]

E. Go through the articles of a magazine, popular or professional, to find a clear example of thematic or informative writing. It may be the whole article, or it may be an excerpt. Bring the example to class and be ready to show why you have classified it as you did.

[8] From "The Comics—There They Stand!" by Harvey Zorbaugh. *Journal of Educational Sociology,* December, 1944. Reprinted by permission of the author and the *Journal of Educational Sociology.*

[9] From Navy Communiqué No. 554, November 17, 1944.

Part Two
Techniques

3. THE INFORMATIVE ESSAY

TEACHERS, lecturers, publishers, manufacturers, and governmental agencies, like stokers sweating over roaring furnaces, shovel information into the world's maw, feeding an imperative hunger for facts: "How do I get the meat out of a lobster?" "What shall I do about the Japanese beetle?" "Tell me how to improve my bridge game." "What is Smith's new house on the hill like?" "How does a salmon spend its life?" "Tell me about your visit to Alaska." "Teach me gardening." "What preparation should I make for a career in forestry?" "What happened after you left college?" Who? What? How? Where? When? Because informative writing gets its creative motive from human curiosity and from sheer human necessity, nothing can interrupt for long its production; and as life gets more complex, the demand and production increase. We *want* to know about the expedition to Mount St. Elias. We *have* to know how to prevent the spread of pear blight.

Informative writing, as we discovered in Chapter 2, is concerned with communicating verifiable facts. Judgments sometimes get in, but incidentally. Frequently they are found in beginning or closing remarks, or in transitions. The factual purpose, however, is the controlling purpose; and the author succeeds in so far as that purpose is held to. The pilot is not very informative who comes back from a mission over enemy territory and reports to his intelligence officer as follows:

> Below me was the field and on it a big bunch of planes. I made several passes at the field, firing as I went over. I saw some of the planes burst in flames.

The intelligence officer wants facts, such as these:

> When I reached the field, I counted ten fighter planes parked on the south edge of the runway. I made two strafing runs over the planes; and I saw five of them smoking heavily as I left, my gas and ammunition low.

The phrases "big bunch of planes" and "some of the planes" are too loose to be factual. They tell the officer what the pilot thought, or guessed; but they do not contain real information. Most military planes carry cameras because the pilot is ordinarily too busy to make trustworthy notes of the facts of an engagement or other mission during its critical moments. Within its mechanical limits, the camera is objective. It records facts. A picture of an airstrip shows the kind and the number of planes on it at the time the shutter snapped. Informative writing does exactly the same. A reader who can sketch, for instance, can go through the description that we read in Chapter 2 of the "State of Maine" logging camp and draw a scaled picture of the main features of the building. The facts are in the description.

The amount of factual material in an informative essay depends on the circumstances and the intention of the writer. A little later we shall read the story of wheat harvesting, done in panoramic size. The facts in the story are sufficient only to give a general knowledge of the growth and harvesting of wheat. They are not specific enough so that a novice farmer can use them to plant and cut his own grain. The article will satisfy curiosity. It will not teach us to raise wheat. If a novice attempted to use it as an agricultural guide, he would be as frustrated as a cook who takes up a recipe and reads that she is to put "some butter in a bowl and mix it with flour." How much butter? How much flour? The writer must tell according to his purpose. If he expects us to make a cake, he tells exactly the amounts of materials we are to use. It is, to cite another example, factual to say, "We gave the children their lunch." It is not, however, always factual enough. If the writer is supposed to be giving an informative account of a day in a kindergarten, the reader will want to know what food the children ate. The trained writer anticipates the demand and provides the details.

> At twelve-thirty we gave the children a lunch of vegetable soup, bread and butter, a pint of milk, apple sauce, and an oatmeal cooky.

All the facts consistent with the circumstances are now in the sentence.

Informative writing presents the facts clearly. Because clarity depends in part on the amount of experience and knowledge a reader brings to an essay, a careful writer arranges his language and his explanatory material to fit his estimate of the readers who are to be informed. In setting out directions for making a table, for instance, he may use undefined technical terms and ideas only if his readers can understand them. If he thinks his readers are trained in woodworking, he may write as follows:

> Two battens are used to re-enforce the top and to provide anchors for the legs.

The experienced woodworker will understand the term *batten*. But if the readers are inexperienced, the language must be revised. Perhaps the author can translate the term *batten* and write:

> Two strips of wood are used to re-enforce the top and to provide anchors for the legs.

A too technical language is a common fault of experts addressing a general audience. The expert, full of his subject and familiar with his terms because of daily contact with them, too easily assumes that his readers are equal to him. We must constantly ask ourselves if our readers can follow us. If simpler language and more explanation are called for, we should provide them.

A violation of clarity more insidious than the use of over-technical language occurs when we garble a statement or when we omit significant facts. A determined reader can find out what words mean if they are correctly used; but who can be certain of the following direction: "Mix a coat of shellac with 60 per cent of turpentine"? A coat of shellac is that shellac which has been spread on a surface. Is one supposed to mix turpentine on the shellacked object? Perhaps the author meant: "Mix enough shellac for a coat with 60 per cent of turpentine." The statement about the turpentine is not absolutely clear, either. Does it mean that the volume of turpentine mixed with the shellac is 60 per cent of the volume of shellac and that the two together are to make the coat? Probably it does; but the reader cannot be sure and must proceed at the risk of wasting expensive materials or of ruining a treasured panel or floor. The reader who comes across the following statement: "Fold the paper once through the middle each way and then cut as shown by line C in Figure 1," expects to find line C clearly drawn and labeled. The directions fail if the drawing fails. The reader who is asked to turn to Appendix B and examine Table 6 will feel betrayed and angry if he cannot find Appendix B clearly distinguished from the other appendices and if the tables are not numbered. Clarity is difficult, and to be sure of it we must accept the labor of checking and testing all our facts and all our statements concerned with them.

Though informative writing is factual, it need not be colorless. Color, however, must never interfere with the facts. The author of a formal, line-of-duty report is writing a record of his actions. His purpose is not to entertain the superior for whom the report is written, but to get all the facts into the report, where they can be studied at the proper time. Style is a factor, surely; but in a formal report the style should be even, straight as the facts. Any attendant drama or excitement is revealed between the lines, rather than in the lines. The report of the pilot who radioed to his base, "Sighted sub; sank same," is an extreme example of the laconic quality of formal reporting. Not many reports would be cut so crisp as this is. The quietness of the following paragraph is typical of what is usually expected:

At 1 P.M., the 17th, in latitude 45-00, longitude 46-26, a small berg was passed close aboard, water 47°, a fall of 1°. This berg floated about 10 or 15 feet above the water and was hardly 200 feet in length. Its top was furrowed and gullied through in many places, and appeared on the point of breaking up. As it pitched in the swells the seas broke in sprays on the bluff ends, while others swept unbroken through the gullies across its top. Considerable trash ice was floating to leeward. Though our track had been in latitude 45, nothing was seen of the bergs near which the *Seneca* had been lying two days before. Fog set in, engine was stopped at 3 P.M., and vessel drifted.[1]

This is narrative, but it is passionless. Any feeling of the author's has been carefully held back. Now read a bit where the feeling has been heightened by the use of words that suggest excitement:

You plant winter wheat under the hot sun of late summer, in soil plowed when the summer drought has relaxed under a gentle rain. You watch, and

[1] From *Reports of Vessels on Ice Patrol in the North Atlantic Ocean,* R.C.S. Bulletin No. 1, Treasury Department, 1913.

the planted grain sends up eager green shoots until the field, the hills, the whole expanse of the plains is green as a new lawn in some townsman's dooryard. It grows and sends down roots to fortify itself against the winter. Frost nips it and sleet pelts it and snow comes to cover it with a December blanket. And when the March thaw sets in, there is your wheat, green and eager, thrusting through the bedraggled crust of dying winter.

April, and it is reaching toward the white-clouded sky. May, and it is knee-high, high enough to hide a hungry rabbit. June, and the heads are long and fat as a farmer's finger, bearded heads that hold the fattening grain. June, and you watch the sky and hold your breath and mutter a prayer each time the clouds pile up on the horizon.[2]

In the first excerpt the narrative runs along without emotional pressure. It is a bare recital of facts meant for study later. The men who read and write such reports are just as human as the man who wrote the dramatic story of wheat, but their purposes differ. The former is written for the advancement of a governmental function—that of making safe the sea lanes. The latter is written to advance general knowledge and to entertain. The tone of informative writing varies between the austerity of pure science and the emotional warmth of entertainment. The author must estimate the needs he attempts to serve and dress his facts accordingly; but if he uses color, he must not let it blur his facts, for his main purpose in writing informatively is to communicate them.

As we shall see later, an author has a variety of methods of presenting themes to a reader. Informative writing gets its variety from differences in subject matter. A set of directions is informative. An objective description and a classification are informative. A summary is informative. So is factual narrative. Though each of these may be treated from a thematic approach, they seldom are. As informative prose they form the bread-and-butter writing staple of the working world and are found everywhere. Our intention now is to describe and illustrate the special techniques of several informative problems. They differ greatly enough so that we need training in each. First is the writing of directions.

[2] From "Harvest Time," by Hal Borland. The New York *Times* Magazine, July 23, 1944. Copyrighted by Hal Borland, 1944. Reprinted by permission of The New York *Times* and Willis Kingsley Wing.

DIRECTIONS

The motive for writing directions is to tell a reader how he can do something. The manufacturer of an automobile sends with the car a booklet of directions for its operation. The manufacturer of macaroni prints on the box a recipe for making macaroni au gratin. The teacher of nursing skills provides each student with directions for every skill the nurse must have: making beds, sterilizing instruments, bathing patients, using the hypodermic needle. In every instance the person who knows tells the person who does not know. The reader is in the dark, and he wants light. The function of a writer of directions is therefore to set out clearly all the necessary information—every item of it. He will follow, or at least seek the objectives of, some such plan as this:

First, he will indicate at the onset just what the directions are for. If for a handicraft object, cooking, or something similar, and if the directions are to be filed in a notebook or drawer, or are to be printed in a technical magazine, the title may be sufficient indication of the purpose. If the directions are to be written as a finished essay, it is useful to include in the opening paragraphs as well as in the title a remark that shows the purpose. If the writer depends entirely on the title and begins the essay with the first step of the process, he runs the danger of abruptness. A little easing into the subject matter is a psychological aid to the reader.

Second, whenever materials are needed, the writer should list them before he begins describing the steps of the process. All the materials and their exact amounts should be given. Directions that do not require materials, such as how to find one's way across a city or how to operate an outboard motor, naturally do not contain such a list; and directions such as those for preparing buns need not include standard kitchen equipment. Only those materials that go into the object and the tools peculiarly essential to its making are needed for the list.

Third, he will divide the process into its steps, arranging them in the order they are to be performed and presenting each with the utmost clarity and fullness. Because drawings, maps, charts, etc., help a reader understand difficult steps, they may be used as appropriate, referred to in the text, generally by label, and placed, if possible, neatly on the page where the reference is made. If all the drawings and text are on one page, as is often true in magazines and newspapers, the drawings may be grouped. If the drawings are easy to identify, labels may be omitted. The directions and drawings in the essay "Buoyant Hollow Aquaplane," page 170, came originally from a handicraft book; and the drawings were grouped in one plate. The drawings in the essay "How to Cast a Fly," page 176, were spread out and labeled because they show step by step how fly casting is performed.

Fourth, the writer of directions should put transitions between steps to show clearly that a new step is about to begin. To do this he may use such devices as enumeration: *first, second, third;* or (a), (b), (c); or transitional phrases: *having completed the frame, we next make the top . . . When finished with the top, we start the drawers . . .* etc. It is imperative that the steps be kept distinct. Paragraphing between steps is often a useful device.

Fifth, he will provide a suitable ending. He may omit a formal conclusion if space economy requires it; but if he does, he should make an effort to show that the last step in the process is clearly the last; otherwise a concluding remark is needed. If the directions are written as a finished essay, a concluding remark may provide a graceful ending.

Sixth, he will use a consistent and suitable style. The language of directions should be simple, because the reader is always one who does not know how to make the object or to achieve the aim he has in mind. Technical vocabulary should be on the expected level of the reader, never higher. Every directive statement should be consistently imperative or declarative. The two types should not be mixed, either in the same sentence or in the same set of directions. For instance:

> The bathroom should be warm and make sure that there are no drafts.

Here we have a sentence that starts as a declarative and ends as an imperative. It should perhaps be written in one of the following ways:

> Make sure that the bathroom is warm and without drafts.
> The bathroom should be warm and without drafts.

"Cookbook" style frequently causes trouble for the young writer, for it is easy to imitate unconsciously. Note in the following that the articles have been omitted:

Soak gelatine in cold water, dissolve in boiling water, and add sugar, fruit juices, sherry, and salt. . . . Put mold in pan of ice water and pour in just enough of mixture. . . .

Such a style is suitable for recipes if space is at a premium. It is not, however, pleasant to read; and if the purpose includes some literary charm, the style must be more acceptable, as in this excerpt from an editorial:

First, of course, one tries out two or three slices of salt pork which have a few streaks of lean marbling the white goodness. Then the nut-brown, crisp slices are cut into small cubes and, together with the tried-out fat, placed in the bottom of the kettle sitting in one of the middle-row holes.[3]

Whether the purpose is strictly utilitarian or whether the purpose includes pleasure in the reading, the writing of directions is an art. Directions are an immediately practical form of expression, but even so they give a satisfactory scope for trying out one's skill with words. Indeed, they test one's skill to the utmost.

The following set of directions is of the kind we come upon every day in our general reading. The aim is practical.

Start a Flying Club

Introductory paragraphs. The author implies his purpose.

Learning to fly is fairly simple. The big problem is how to pay for it! The day hasn't yet arrived when you can go to the nearest junkyard and pick up a "model T" that is in safe flying condition for a ten-spot, and the day probably will never come in our normal lifespan. Airplane operations costs are above the average pocketbook when considered in terms of owning a plane or even renting one individually. A group of fellows owning a plane together is the cheapest way to fly.

Flying clubs usually operate best where the entire group lives within a short distance of where the plane is based. Of course, there are always those who are willing to travel quite a distance on a day off from school or work to fly the club plane, but the fairest way to run a club is on a

[3] From "Corn Chowder." The New York *Times,* January 13, 1945. Reprinted by permission of The New York *Times.*

flight schedule. In this way, each person's time is allotted in sequence and everyone knows ahead of time when the ship will be available to him. Fellows who are really bitten by the urge to fly and are willing to co-operate with the rest of the gang naturally make the best club members, but a strong-minded operations manager can keep the "playboys" in line.

The directions begin. The first step: organizing the club.

Suppose we deal briefly with the organization, itself, first. Before a ship can be purchased, the purchasing power must be there. A group of ten to twenty usually works best. The smaller the group, the more time can be allotted to each member, but on the other hand there should be at least ten to break the costs down to reasonable figures. A group such as this would not need many executive members; a president or chairman, a treasurer, an operations manager and a maintenance man should suffice. The president should be someone who has the happy faculty of keeping a meeting going along without letting it become a shambles because everyone wants to talk at once. A strong leader is the main requirement for the success of any organization.

The operations manager has one of the worst headaches. If possible, this fellow should be of the serious type, for on his shoulders falls the job of checking the plane over, determining when it is ready to fly, and generally governing the club's flying activities. If no one in the club has sufficient experience for this job, perhaps a pilot or one of the fellows in the airport manager's office might be convinced that he can be a help by taking a job. Common sense on the part of the rest of the gang will make his work easier.

Maintenance is something that can't be stressed too much. The ship has to be checked over constantly. We don't mean that it has to be taken apart after every flight; too much tinkering can have bad results. One man should be responsible for the plane's condition. If nobody in the group has a mechanic's license, it would be a good idea to approach one of the mechs at the field about the idea of keeping a fatherly eye on the crate and giving it the government-required, periodical inspections. A clear understanding of simple mechanical maintenance will usually induce any group to co-operate. Pyralin should be covered up when the ship isn't in use. Discoloration is rather rapid when the ship is left out in the sun without a cover over the windshield—and cracked, dirty or discolored pyralin has been the cause of more than one accident.

The second step: financing the plane. Note the indirect transition.

Probably the first thing any group choruses at their first meeting is "How quickly can we get a ship?" The enthusiasm is good, but first decide how much you can afford to spend. A good used plane in the 50 to 65 horsepower class will cost from $800 to $1,000. When we say "good" we don't necessarily mean a nice, shiny paint job. The job of buying a plane is not one for the amateur; don't be hesitant about asking advice from men who work on planes every day. A licensed mechanic or pilot can probably tell you more about a plane in a half an hour than you could discover in a week. The log books for the planes, if they have been kept properly, can tell a story all their own.

If the club buys a plane from an established aircraft dealer, arrangements can usually be made to finance the purchase with one-third down and the balance divided up into twelve equal payments due monthly for a year. In the event the club decides to bid on one of the surplus training planes the government is selling, cash for the bid price must be paid. In a private sale sometimes cash is asked, and sometimes the owner can work out terms for you somewhat similar to the standard methods of financing. The club must decide how much money it is willing to put up as initiation fees, and then the decision to pay cash or to finance the ship should be made. If $800 is decided to be the maximum price to be paid, each of ten club members will have to ante up $80. If the plane is financed, $266 is required for a down payment or about $27 each member. The monthly payments will be about $50 per month, but this does not include insurance. Insurance of the airplane itself is required when financing the payment of the plane, but it is a good idea even when cash is paid.

The inserted "box" summary provides a complete view of expenses per member.

EXPENSES PER MEMBER FOR 10-MEMBER CLUB

Cost per flying hour:	
Gas, 5 gals, @ 25c	$ 1.25
Oil, 1½ gals, per 20 hrs.	.20
Overhauls, 200 and 500 hours	.60
Sinking fund	.45
Total	$ 2.50
Monthly dues to cover operations:	
Hangar rent @ $30 per month	$ 3.00
Insurance at $250 per year	2.00
Depreciation, 15% first year	1.00
Total	$ 6.00
Private Pilot's License:	
Dues for 4½ months	$ 27.00
Solo, 35 hours	87.50
Instruction, 10 hours @ $1.00	10.00
Total	$124.50

Figures prepared by the Aero Insurance Underwriters show that a plane in the class we've chosen can be insured for about $250 per year. This insurance works as follows: (a) $50 deductible for windstorm and land damage (the insurance company pays all damage costs over $50—the first $50 is paid by the owner); (b) crash insurance where the owner pays one-third and the other two-thirds is paid by the insurance company. In a 10-man club, this $250 will work out to $25 per year, or a little over $2 per month per man.

The third step: instruction expenses. Again the transition is indirect.

Now you have a plane. It sits out at the airport, all nice and shiny. Everyone wants to fly—right now! Has anyone thought of who is to do the instructing? The government requires that a properly licensed instructor engage in the gentle art of knocking air sense into students' heads.

The instructor's fee usually runs from $1 to $2 on your plane and your gas. That fee is for instructing only; he'll satisfy himself that the plane is air-worthy, instruct and sign log books, but don't expect him to service the plane, too.

The fourth step: Note the transition from instruction expense to operating expense.

Since no one has yet found a plane engine that will run on water instead of gas and oil, suppose we investigate the cost of running the ship so that a fair charge can be made per hour of flying. The simplest way to handle the instructor's cost is to make this the responsibility of each member taking instruction. Let him make the payment to the instructor when he takes his flight time. Gas, oil and servicing can be arranged for on a monthly basis with the manager of the airport or hangar. Five gallons of gas is a fair estimate per hour, since the plane has to be warmed up and a large amount of taxiing will be done during instruction periods. A gallon and a half of oil every twenty hours is about right, but other items should come out of the operating costs. Periodic overhaul of the engine and plane is not paid for with soap coupons. Money must be laid aside for these items as the club goes along, so that the treasurer can write a check for the mechanic and still say, "hello," at the local bank. The engine will require a top overhaul every 200 hours or so, and the 500-hour mark means a complete overhaul. A major overhaul of a four-cylinder engine usually costs in the neighborhood of $150 to $200. The top overhaul at 200 hours costs about $75. Over a period of 500 flying hours, this means about 60c per flying hour. Another item which you should have is a "sinking fund." The idea of a sinking fund is to keep a small amount of extra cash rolling in for unexpected "incidents" that will occur every so often.

The last step: arranging programs for meetings.

As with most clubs, meeting nights offer ideal times for instructive programs. Mechanics, preferably those holding Airplane and Engine licenses, make ideal instructors. If a clubroom can be equipped with a blackboard, or if a school classroom can be obtained for meetings, the instructor's job will be easier. A licensed pilot can start the "course" by giving a brief summation of what knowledge is demanded of a student before he can obtain his license. The club leaders can obtain interesting and instructive material and even movies from manufacturers. Your best bet along these lines is to write to the Public Relations men of the differ ent lightplane manufacturing companies and the engine companies, too.

Conclusion: how to meet people interested in a club.

Many times fellows want to fly—may even want to start clubs, but do not know how to go about it. If you are interested, why not approach other fellows whom you see regularly at the local airport—or even insert a small advertisement in the local paper. A sure way to reach others with the same idea would be to post a notice at the local airport. The manager will undoubtedly give you a space on the bulletin board or let you leave a notice in some convenient spot.[4]

Exercises

A. Revise the following excerpts, making them consistently declarative or imperative:

1. Put your left hand under Scotty's chin, and hold him while he is in his bath. Doing this you will keep him from drinking his soon very dirty water. Your right hand with the soapy wash cloth will give him a good rubbing.

2. The first step is to cut out a strip of material following the measurements indicated in Figure 1. Next, cut a piece of material as indicated in Figure 2.

3. The first step is to brush your hair for several minutes, and bend over while you do it.

4. Don't let lumpy brown sugar interfere with your cooking plans. Instead, a method of softening the lumps is to pour the sugar into an open bowl and then to put a damp cloth over the bowl. Let it stand for ten minutes.

5. Remove the sheet from the line while it is slightly damp, and then it is to be folded crosswise in quarters.

B. Subjects for directions are innumerable. Home economics, shop, art, and science teem with activities that the novice must learn. Sport, agriculture, manufacturing, and the professions offer endless varieties of useful processes. Select one that you know well and write a set of directions in the general pattern of "Start a Flying Club."

C. Write a set of directions suitable for filing or for publishing in a cookbook or handicraft magazine. Use "cookbook" style.

[4] "Start a Flying Club," by Ed Yulke. *Mechanix Illustrated Magazine,* July, 1945 Reprinted by permission of Fawcett Publications Incorporated.

D. Study the sets of directions in the reading section of this book and be ready to discuss them in class. Make note of style, introductory paragraphs, transitions from step to step, and of concluding remarks. Point out any obscure places if you find them.

SUMMARY

Our next informative problem is the summary, a prose statement of the essential facts and judgments contained in a full essay or book. The aim is to draw from the original only the fundamentals. The writer of a summary keeps himself strictly objective. His opinions of the work he is summarizing are completely censored, for he wants only to communicate in a brief form what another author has said. It is this feature that makes the summary the purest of the informational types of writing. No judgment whatever from the summarizer is allowed. Naturally in a condensation the overtones of mood and the subtleties of thought of the original will be left behind or damaged; but despite this loss a summary has many values, all of them springing from compactness and objectivity. The summary puts the core of thought in an essay or book out in the light where it can be examined easily. It permits the reader to compile notes he can use in his own writing. It saves the time of many men who are too busy to do all their own reading. It is, finally, of great value to the student who must train himself in the discipline of good reading and accurate reporting as part of his preparation for creative thinking.

A summary involves two distinct steps: (1) reading, (2) writing.

Reading. It is not likely that a young reader can go through an essay or book just once and produce a good summary. Several readings are necessary. The first one can be used for an overview and a start in the discovery of the important items. The second can be used to isolate the divisions and sub-divisions of the work and to note the relationships of each part to the whole. The third reading, and perhaps last, can be used to find the development of each of the sections. The readings may be telescoped just as soon as skill is at hand with which to do it.

The following outline of directions will help in getting at and keeping account of the materials that belong in a summary.

1. Look for and copy in a notebook or underline in the text or label in the margin the author's own statement of his purpose. If the author does not make a specific statement, determine what his purpose is and make a note of it.

2. If the essay or book is thematic, label, underline, or copy in a notebook a statement of the theme. If the essay develops several themes, locate each.

3. If the essay is thematic, note the methods of development—that is, the types of data the author uses to support his theme or themes. Label or copy some of the data. (See Chapter 4, "Finding Material to Support the Theme.")

4. If the essay is informative, discover and label the divisions of the subject. Make a rough outline. Fill in the outline with some of the facts from each division. Distinguish illustrative materials from whatever is being illustrated.

5. Look for and note transitional statements.

6. Look for and note the author's summaries, if any are present.

7. If the author is developing an argument, number his points where he begins them, between the lines or in the margins. Circle key passages.

8. Do not mark any book that is not your own. When you use a book or magazine belonging to a library or a friend, depend entirely on notes.

Writing. The following directions are useful as a guide to the writing of a summary. They are not offered arbitrarily as the only procedure, but as suggestions.

1. Use the title of the essay or book being summarized as the title of the summary. At the bottom of the first page of the summary place a footnote identifying the source of the original work: author, title, place of publication, date of publication.

2. Indicate, directly or indirectly, within the first paragraph that you are writing a summary. To do this indirectly, you may refer to the author and the title or you may use a direct or indirect quotation with an appropriate reference to the author. (See below the summary of "Our Widening American Culture.")

3. Keep almost all of the summary in your own words. Use quotations sparingly, and always with quotation marks. To show dele-

tions within a quotation use three dots (. . .) at the points where the deletions occur.

4. Keep your personality out of the summary. Do not adopt a tone which distorts the original in any way. Do not permit any omissions that twist the author's meaning. Do not emphasize anything that the author treated as subordinate. Do not criticize. If you need to make any comment of your own, place it within brackets [ ].

5. Write in a prose style in keeping with that of the original.

As an illustration of the technique of summarizing read the essay "Our Widening American Culture," page 117, and the analysis that accompanies it; then read the summary of the essay that is placed here.

Our Widening American Culture *

The author's main point. Note reference to the author by quotation and use of his name.

We Americans, says Frederick Lewis Allen in "Our Widening American Culture," are failing to see that a flowering of art, in native forms, is all about us. In spite of the large amount of bad taste still undeniably present the country "is making cultural progress in a new exciting way."

The author's point about the democratic spread of art is made here and supported by some of his data.

Culture, the author goes on to say, does not mean an effete dilettantism with tested art objects. It means a genuine and democratic appreciation of the creative elements in modern life and an interest in their production. Millions of Americans are now sensitive to musical beauty and stirred to creative energy. Sixty Yale bowls would hardly seat the listeners to Toscanini's weekly radio broadcasts, four and a half millions of them; and there are 35,000 school orchestras *making* music. In books, the standards of current best sellers are higher by far than were those of 1910. A comparison of Steinbeck's *The Grapes of Wrath* with Harold Bell Wright's *The Winning of Barbara Worth* shows the difference. Furthermore, says Mr. Allen, there are now 26 magazines circulating over a million, whereas 50 years ago there were none. Nothing in Europe touches this mass interest in reading. Turn to the fine arts:

The footnote acknowledgment and direct statement that this is a summary.

* A summary: Frederick Lewis Allen, "Our Widening American Culture," *The Saturday Review of Literature,* June 29, 1940.

an exhibit of Italian Masters at the Museum of Modern Art drew in 73 days 277,794 people!

Intermediate summary and transition remark. The author's point about new art forms made and supported with his data.

These figures show how wide is the democratic base of our culture and attest its growth. Changes have also been made in art forms. The movies, and their subdivision the animated cartoons, are new. Photography is new, and exceedingly popular. Landscape architects and engineers are producing beauty along our highways unbelievable a few years ago. Manufacturers and sales experts have worked together to make both the factory and the kitchen functionally good in design. Cities and villages are in themselves museums of beauty, and the crowds who admire window displays are unconscious critics of a new art form.

Concluding summary: the main point repeated.

America is maturing in art. Whether or not its peaks of creative skill are higher than before, it is certain that the groundswell is upward.

Exercises

A. Read the essay "How to Mark a Book," on page 398. Prepare for class discussion your ideas on what is important in the essay. If you disagree with anything, be ready to tell in what ways and why, but keep your disagreements distinct from your statements of what the essay says. Discuss the structure of the essay. Show what items should be included in a summary if you were asked to write one.

B. Write a summary of one of the essays in the reading section of this book.

SCIENTIFIC DESCRIPTION

Sooner or later we all have to write or speak objectively about a specific object or class of objects. The traveler who wishes to describe factually what he has seen, the engineer who wants to tell the exact details of something he has built, the mechanic who has to report on a new machine—all must describe with but one aim: to inform. They are coolly observant. They take measurements and note materials. They want a sort of prose blueprint. They are therefore after such details as are physically or measurably part of the object. Literary artists wish to evoke experience and a mood; but writers of scientific description want to communicate above all else the physical details of the object they are scrutinizing. They are scientific in their approach, though they need not be formal. Their emotional responses to the object they are describing are held in check except, possibly, as incidental elements in the introductory and concluding remarks.

Of the technical points involved in scientific description the first is naturally the beginning. The beginning—frequently only a sentence or two—indicates the object to be described. The writer may often be content simply to give the name of the object or to state his intention.

The second technical point is the division of details. They are put into their natural compartments. A description of a room, for example, may use the principle of contiguity and divide the room into planes: foreground, middle ground, and background. The details of each plane can then be filled in. The room may, on the other hand, be described by beginning on one side and going around it wall by wall, finishing with the floor and ceiling. Such is the principle of contiguity: the writer moves from one place to the next. Any other natural grouping of details may be used. In one group could go the details of wall and window decorations and specifications; in another, furniture; and in still another, building materials used within the room. Almost any object has appropriate dividing points. The writer determines what they are and concentrates on the groups one by one. If the object is so small or so well unified that it cannot be broken up, all one needs do is to present the details in convenient order. To help control the reader's mental image of the object being described, we may use a technique sometimes called "the frame of reference." The frame is a general idea of the outline or shape of the object. It is given before the grouping of details is begun. Note the following:

> This rolling home of the herder was a common farm wagon with a wide-bottomed bed covered with a rounded top of canvas.[5]
>
> Two points ran out as the horns of the crescent, one of which—the one to the westward—was low and sandy . . . ; the other is high, bold, and well wooded, and has a mission upon it, called Santa Buenaventura, from which the point is named. In the middle of this crescent . . .[6]

[5] From *Vanguards of the Frontier,* by Everett Dick.

[6] From *Two Years Before the Mast,* by Richard Henry Dana.

The general image of a wagon with a canvas top and of a crescent-shaped bay helps the reader to hold his picture together as he moves from detail to detail.

A third technical problem is transition. Each shift from one group of details to another should be obvious to the reader. Paragraph breaks sometimes are enough for this. A phrase or clause may be sufficient, such as, *behind the stove we see the shelves,* or *on the back wall is,* or *the materials of the floor are.* Transitions are necessary to keep everything orderly in the reader's mind.

When the subject of scientific description is a machine, the principles of its operation are properly included in the description. The general method here is first to explain the principles and then to trace their operation from part to part of the machine.

Scientific description ranges from the informal to the formal in tone and in technical level. If the audience is technical and the purpose a strict account of the facts, the writing level is kept appropriate. A popular audience requires a low level of technicality and much illustration and elaboration of difficult points. The rule is to suit the manner of presentation to the circumstances of purpose and audience.

Scientific description may deal with a class of objects or with a particular object. In the first we assume that all the objects within the class are composed of similar details. We assume a type. The country store is a type. The city drug store is a type. The village wit is a type. The gasoline engine is a type. When we describe a typical object, we use the details which are found in all such objects.

When we describe a particular object, our aim is to individualize it. All houses, for instance, have certain details in common; but the house at 120 Cedar Street has details that make it different from any other house in the world. The unique details individualize the house, and they are therefore emphasized in the description.

The two descriptions that follow deal with objects that belong to a general class. The tone of the sheep wagon selection is informal, and we are told what we would find if we should examine any such wagon we happened upon. The author describes all sheep wagons, not a particular wagon owned by Bill Jones of Red Rock, Wyoming. The description of the herring in the second selection is slightly formal in tone, though not technical. We are told what we could expect to find in the structure of any fish, as exemplified by the herring.

The Sheep Wagon

The object named and the purpose to describe implied. Note the "frame of reference." Details are grouped here around the idea of the main structure of the wagon.

Since a herder accumulated many personal effects, it became no small task to strike the tent, load the accumulation into the wagon, and pitch the camp again. Furthermore, a tent was not any too satisfactory as a protection in stormy weather. As a result of these conditions, the sheep wagon evolved and became the standard by the turn of the century. This rolling home of the herder was a common farm wagon with a wide-bottomed bed covered with a rounded top of canvas. The canvas was usually of several thicknesses, making the abode warm in winter and cool in summer. A double floor also aided in insulating the domicile. Herders often lived in these vehicles all winter in a latitude where the mercury goes down to forty below zero. In the back end was a window, and in the front end a little to one side was a doorway with a door made in two halves, permitting the door to be open at the top with the bottom closed.

Transition to the inside of the wagon. Details grouped here around the interior of the wagon. Note transition phrases.

The visitor stepped on the wagon tongue and, grasping the sides of the door, hoisted himself into the doorway of the wagon. On one side he saw a stove with the pipe extending through the roof. Behind the stove was the dish cupboard. At the back end was a bunk built crossways of the wagon leaving plenty of room beneath for the dogs. A table on hinges could be folded up against the wall when not in use. Trapdoors, shelves, and lockers were ingeniously arranged in benches, on the walls, and in the bottom of the wagon in such a way as to accommodate the maximum amount of plunder in the minimum amount of space. These living-quarters were cool in summer, but on the coldest winter evening with a sizzling hot fire the herder could sit in his cozy wagon and laugh at the fiercest arctic blast. Through the window in the back he could look out at night and see how the sheep were behaving. A rope enabled him to open the window to any desired

Details here show how the wagon operated as a home.

The general tone is of rude comfort. Note the use of words and ideas that build the tone.

point. The wagon was swept out occasionally, and, as one herder remarked, scrubbing and dusting were done everytime the Republicans swept the Solid South. An old black coffee pot, a skillet, a Dutch oven, and a few pans supplied the herder's culinary needs, and the food was served on tin dishes and eaten with iron "silverware." [7]

Fish

The subject and purpose announced here.

The general arrangement of details is from the head to the rear of the herring.

Here the details are concerned with fins.

If anyone wants to exemplify the meaning of the word "fish," he cannot choose a better animal than a herring. The body, tapering to each end, is covered with thin, flexible scales, which are very easily rubbed off. The taper head, with its underhung jaw, is smooth and scaleless on the top; the large eye is partly covered by two folds of transparent skin, like eyelids—only immovable and with the slit between them vertical instead of horizontal; the cleft behind the gill-cover is very wide, and, when the cover is raised, the large red gills which lie beneath it are freely exposed. The rounded back bears the single moderately long dorsal fin about its middle. The tail-fin is deeply cleft, and on careful inspection small scales are seen to be continued from the body, on to both its upper and its lower lobes, but there is no longitudinal scaly fold on either of these. The belly comes to an edge, covered by a series of sharply-keeled bony shields between the throat and the vent; and behind the last is the anal fin, which is of the same length as the dorsal fin. There is a pair of forelimbs, or pectoral fins, just behind the head; and a pair of hind-limbs, or ventral fins, is situated beneath the dorsal fin, a little behind a vertical line drawn from its front edge, and a long way in front of the vent. These fins have bony supports or rays, all of which are soft and jointed. . . .

The mechanism of the mouth treated here.

The mouth of the herring is not very large, the gape extending back only to beneath the middle of the eye, and the teeth on the upper and lower jaws are so small as to be hardly visible. Moreover, when a live herring opens its

[7] From *Vanguards of the Frontier*, by Everett Dick. Reprinted by permission of D. Appleton-Century Co., Inc.

mouth, or when the lower jaw of a dead herring is depressed artificially, the upper jaw, instead of remaining fixed and stationary, travels downward and forward in such a manner as to guard the sides of the gape. This movement is the result of a curious mechanical arrangement by which the lower jaw pulls upon the upper, and I suspect that it is useful in guarding the sides of the gape when the fish gulps the small living prey upon which it feeds.[8]

Exercises

A. Write an informal, scientific description of a typical object: village store, corner gas station, small farm, comic book, city apartment, summer hotel, or any such object you are familiar with. Select a tone that is appropriate to the object and build it up with words and ideas that convey it.

B. Write an informal scientific description of any specific object you can find worth your study. Put into a notebook all the facts you can discover, and turn your notes in with the finished description. Suggested subjects are the following: local building, book, furniture, fireplace, street lamp, workbench, doorway, gun, pump, automatic signal, electric-eye, well-driller, hoist.

C. Write a scientific description of a formal nature, using terminology as technical as you can command with accuracy, and selecting a typical representative of a class of objects. Do not use a textbook account for your facts. Any laboratory or museum should be full of specimens you can study. If none there suits your interest, you can go out into the fields, woods, or factories near you and select a specimen for close observation.

D. Prepare for class recitation a discussion of the essay "The First Robot Bomber," page 179. The questions that accompany the essay will provide material for study.

CLASSIFICATION

A somewhat complicated variant of scientific description is a form known as classification. By classification is meant the systematic separation of related items within a general group. The general, that is, family group, is broken into its parts; and each part is described. We

[8] From "The Herring," by Thomas Henry Huxley.

do not describe schools, but kindergarten, primary school, grammar school, junior high, high, college, and university—the types within the group term school. Animals, to use another example, may be classified as carnivorous or herbivorous, according to whether or not they feed on flesh or grass. The aim of the classifier is to distinguish each item from the others within the group. His descriptive method is the same as when he is doing scientific description. The series of informative problems that we are now studying is a classification. The general class of writing is the informative; the specific types are directions, summary, scientific description, classification, and—still to be described—the formal report and factual narration.

Classification is valuable as a way of making the world orderly for our short-sighted eyes. Without it modern science and technology would hardly be possible. Victory over the many fevers that man is subject to depends on their classification and the use of the appropriate cure for the type of fever the patient has. The forester must type his lands before he can plan their effective control. The miner who fails to type his coal will fail to market it to his best advantage. The scholar patiently seeking the answers to his many riddles will have to retrace himself endlessly unless he can classify his facts and record them suitably. Even the young college student will find that his work becomes less difficult if he can classify it into types and learn it type by type. People who depend upon intuitive flashes sometimes look upon the classifier as a dry grind, a poor hack who sifts the dust of life and arranges it in graded heaps. But let the intuitionist's wife feed him field corn for dinner when he wants Golden Bantam, or give him a penoe when he wants whitefish, and he will see that the classifier is building ladders to new worlds and distant heavens which his intuition but dimly perceives—and which his comfort and even his life demand.

The first step in classifying is to determine the basis for dividing the group into its parts. There must be no overlapping of the types, except where combinations exist. We may, for instance, divide men on the basis of color: black, white, red, yellow, and the combinations or mixtures that do exist; or we may divide on the basis of nationality, naming the man by his country; or we may divide on the basis of occupation; or by physiological differences—male, female; or by psychological differences—introvert, extrovert; or by any of many other principles of division. *Once the principle is decided upon, the division is completed on it.* One does not start with nationality and jump to psychology. One may use both, but only after completing the first.

It should be emphasized that an object may belong to more than one classification. The individual man may be classified as an American, a lawyer, a republican, a husband, a Californian. In each classification different characteristics of the man are revealed. It is therefore clear that no one classification tells all there is to know about its types. The snap-categorizing of persons as communists, tories, shanty-Irish, bohunks, etc., tells us nothing about the persons as students, fathers, or business men. We should constantly remember that the details presented in a classified description are selected on the basis of the principle by which the group is split into its parts, and that only details which fit the principle are used.

Having selected a principle of division and having selected the types which he wishes to describe, the writer's next step is to treat the types one by one. His emphasis is on the details which distinguish the types from each other. If the author needs to establish relationships, he may note similarities; but it is the distinction he is after. His aim is the better manipulation of each type within the group. This means he must know all the individualities of each. When he wants to grow and eat Golden Bantam, the characteristics of the seed, the special methods of planting and cultivating it, and the correct way to cook it are the important facts.

The work of the classifier is therefore analytical: he begins with a general group; he finds its elements, using a consistent principle throughout; he describes each element to show its distinctive qualities or physical make-up.

An important possibility in handling classifications remains to be pointed out: Within each main division, for instance, within the divisions wood-flooring and tile-flooring, there may be other types. The type itself may be a general term containing types. Such secondary classification is not hard to keep orderly. The secondary types are kept in the section of the essay given to the group in which they belong, and a transitional statement is put at the place where the switch to and from secondary types is made. A writer eager to do justice to himself and his subject will find that an outline is useful. It would look somewhat as follows:

Classification of Floors

I. Wood floors
 A. Strip
 B. Plank
 C. Block
II. Tile floors
 A. Asphalt
 B. Ceramic
 C. Quarry
 D. Rubber
 E. Cork

Here floors are divided into two main types, and then each is further divided into its types. No doubt there are types of strip floors, etc., so that if one wanted to he could further divide the secondary types into tertiary types.

Classification is by all odds one of the important activities of men who want to keep on being men. Even the poet, who often gets impatient with the scientist, uses types of rimes, meters, verses, stanzas, and poems. Perhaps the classifier should not work only for the sake of classification, but for some use to which it can be put, eating mushrooms, perhaps, after the poisonous, non-poisonous grouping has been made. Classify we must, however, whether for its own sake or for the sake of some practical end, because civilized life requires it.

The classification of avalanches that follows is interesting for the information it contains and for the qualities of style which enliven what might have been a bare recital of facts.

Avalanches

The purpose announced and the first type named.

There are several sorts of avalanches, which have to be distinguished, and which are worthy of separate descriptions. One is called *Staub-Lawine,* or Dust-Avalanche. This descends when snow is loose and has recently fallen. It is attended with a whirlwind, which lifts the snow from a whole mountainside and drives it onward through the air.

The chief characteristic of the avalanches is brute force. Note how the author builds up the impression with modifiers, verbs and illustrations.

It advances in a straight line, overwhelming every obstacle, mowing forests down like sedge, "leaping (as an old peasant once expressed it in my hearing) from hill to hill," burying men, beasts, and dwellings, and settling down at last into a formidable compact mass without colour and without outline. The snow which forms these Staub-Lawinen is dry and finely powdered. When it comes to rest upon the earth, it immediately hardens into something very like the consistency of ice, wrapping the objects which have been borne onward by its blast tightly round in a firm implacable clasp. A man or horse seized by a Staub-Lawine, if the breath has not been blown out of his body in the air, has it squeezed out by the even, clinging pressure of consolidating particles. A human victim of the dreadful thing, who was so lucky as to be saved from its clutch, once described to me the sensations he experienced. He was caught at the edge of the avalanche just when it was settling down to rest, carried off his feet, and rendered helpless by the swathing snow, which tied his legs, pinned his arms to his ribs, and crawled upward to his throat. There it stopped. His head emerged, and he could breathe; but as the mass set, he felt the impossibility of expanding his lungs, and knew that he must die of suffocation. At the point of losing consciousness, he became aware of comrades running to his rescue. They hacked the snow away around his thorax, and then rushed on to dig for another man who had been buried in the same disaster, leaving him able to breathe, but wholly powerless to stir hand or foot. This narrative reminded me of an anecdote told by Haydon the painter, who nearly sacrificed a Negro's life by attempting to take an entire cast of the man's body at one moment from the feet to the chin. When the plaster-of-Paris began to set, the Negro could not breathe, and he was only saved from asphyxiation by Haydon's tearing down the mould of brick in which he had been placed.

Transition to the second type.

Another sort of avalanche is called the *Schlag-Lawine,* or Stroke-Avalanche. It falls generally in spring time, when the masses of winter snow have been loosened by warm winds or sodden by heavy rainfalls. The snow is not whirled into the air, but slips along the ground, following

Descriptive details.

the direction given by ravines and gullies, or finding a way forward through the forest by its sheer weight. Lumbering and rolling, gathering volume as they go from all the barren fells within the reach of their tenacious undermining forces these "slogging" avalanches push blindly onward till they come to rest upon a level. Then they spread themselves abroad, and heap their vast accumulated masses by the weight of pressure from behind up into pyramids and spires. They bear the aspect of a glacier with its seracs, or of a lava-stream with its bristling ridges; and their skirts are plumed with stately pine-trees, nodding above the ruin they have wrought. Woe to the fragile buildings, to the houses and stables, which they meet upon their inert grovelling career! These are carried with them, incorporated, used as battering-rams. Grooving like the snout of some behemoth, the snow dislodges giants of the forest, and forces them to act like ploughs upon its path. You may see tongues and promontories of the avalanche protruding from the central body, and carried far across frozen lakes or expanses of meadow by the help of some huge pine or larch. The Schlag-Lawine is usually greyish-white and softer in substance than its more dreadful sister, the Staub-Lawine—that daughter of the storm, with the breath of the tornado in her brief delirious energy. It is often distinguished by a beautiful bluish colour, as of opaque ice, in the fantastically-toppling rounded towers which crown it; whereas the Staub-Lawine looks like marble of Carrara, and presents a uniform curved surface after it has fallen. Though the Schlag-Lawine closely resembles a glacier at first sight, practised eyes detect the difference at once by the dulled hue which I have mentioned, and by the blunted outline of the pyramids. It might be compared to a glacier which had been sucked or breathed upon by some colossal fiery dragon. Less time has gone to make it; it is composed of less elaborated substance, it has less of permanence in its structure than a glacier; and close inspection shows that it will not survive the impact of soft southern winds in May. In extent these Schlag-Lawinen are enormous. I have crossed some which measured a thousand feet in breadth and more than sixty

Note how the characteristic of brute force is handled here.

The two types are contrasted to help show their differences and their own qualities.

feet in depth. All road-marks, telegraph-posts, parapets, etc., are, of course, abolished. The trees, if trees there were upon their track, have been obliterated. Broken stumps, snapped off like matches, show where woods once waved to heaven. Valleys are made even with the ridges which confined them. Streams are bridged over and converted into temporary lakes by the damming up of water.

The third type. The author chose to treat it as a distinct type and as a related or secondary type; and with less skillful handling the result might have been confusing.

A species of the Schlag-Lawine may be distinguished, to which the name of *Grund-Lawine,* or Ground-Avalanche, shall be given. There is no real distinction between *Schlag-* and *Grund-*Lawine. I only choose to differentiate them because of marked outward differences to the eye. The peculiarity of a Grund-Lawine consists in the amount of earth and rubbish carried down by it. This kind is filthy and disreputable. It is coloured brown or slaty-grey by the rock and soil with which it is involved. Blocks of stone emerge in horrid bareness from the dreary waste of dirty snow and slush of water which compose it; and the trees which have been so unlucky as to stand upon its path are splintered, bruised, rough-handled in a hideous fashion. The Staub-Lawine is fury-laden like a fiend in its first swirling onset, flat and stiff like a corpse in its ultimate repose of death, containing men and beasts and trees entombed beneath its stern unwrinkled taciturnity of marble. The Schlag-Lawine is picturesque, rising into romantic spires and turrets, with erratic pine-plumed firths protruding upon sleepy meadows. It may even lie pure and beautiful, heaving in pallid billows at the foot of majestic mountain slopes where it has injured nothing. But the Grund-Lawine is ugly, spiteful like an asp, tatterdemalion like a street Arab; it is the worst, the most wicked of the sisterhood. To be killed by it would mean a ghastly death by scrunching and throttling, as in some grinding machine, with nothing noble or impressive in the winding-sheet of foul snow and débris heaved above the mangled corpse.

Note the slanting of the details to build up the dominant impression.

The last type, also secondary but treated as independent.

I ought to mention a fourth sort of avalanche, which is called *Schnee-Rutsch,* or Snow-Slip. It does not differ materially from the Schlag-Lawine except in dimension, which is smaller, and in the fact that it may fall at any time and in nearly all kinds of weather by the mere detachment of some trifling mass of snow. The Schnee-Rutsch slides gently, expanding in a fan-like shape upon the slope it has to traverse, till it comes to rest upon a level. Small as the slip may be, it is very dangerous; for it rises as it goes, catches the legs of a man, lifts him off his feet, and winds itself around him in a quiet but inexorable embrace. I once saw a coal-cart with two horses swept away by a very insignificant Schnee-Rutsch while standing at my window in the Hôtel Belvedère at Davos-Platz. The man and one horse kept their heads above the snow and were extricated. The other horse was dead before he could be dug out. There is a Davos proverb to the effect that "a pan of snow may kill a man"; and certainly the incident which I have just mentioned, occurring on a public road in Davos-Platz, and close beneath the windows of one of its chief hotels, corroborates the proverb. While crossing the higher passes in sledges, where the road is often carried at a vast altitude along precipitous slopes, with a width of less than five feet for the vehicle to move upon, a snow-slip of this kind may cause very serious accidents. Yet I ought not to speak ill of Schnee-Rutschen, for I have started them myself upon the declivities of the hills above Davos, and have ridden down on them to my great delight, feeling the snow surge and swell beneath me like a horse or wave, until our breathless descent was over, and stood nine feet above the level ground which brought us to quiescence. These, however, were tame, carefully chosen, carefully-calculated snow-slips, far different from such as leap upon the traveller unaware, and flick him, as a towel flicks a fly, from precipice into river-bed.[9]

Again note the slanting of details and of the illustration.

This remark seems to weaken the impression of brute force, but note how the last sentence recovers the idea.

Exercises

A. Read, beginning on pages 183 and 188, the essays "The ABC's of Hats" and "Types of Forest Fires." Prepare for class discussion an analysis of the writing techniques shown by the essays, basing your analyses on the questions that accompany the essays.

B. Write an informal essay classifying and describing the types within a general group. You can type streets, shop windows, whistles, trains, radio

[9] From *Our Life in the Swiss Highlands,* by John Addington Symonds. By permission of The Macmillan Company, publishers.

announcers, advertisements, newspapers, villages, mountains, streams, teachers, books, class assignments, novels, salesmen, fish, games, furniture—anything. Select a dominant tone or characteristic that you can emphasize by use of the proper words and illustrative materials. Avoid "smarty" attitudes.

C. Prepare a formal classification. Suitable subjects abound in all scientific and professional fields. The applied and descriptive sciences are prolific with subjects: hybrid corn, bivalves, pine trees, plant fungi, drugs, engines, radios. Literature, music, painting, nursing, and commerce contain many interesting possibilities of classification. Take enough time to find accurate details by first-hand investigation and by library research. Use illustrations where they will help reveal the characteristics of your types.

FORMAL REPORTS

Any informative essay is, of course, a report, for it communicates verifiable facts—that is, it reports on them. The distinction we need to make now between all informative writing and the *formal report* rests on the context within which the formal report functions. The term implies a tone we are familiar with, that of objectivity, of impersonal seriousness; but the most important factor in the context of formal reports is their connection with the activities of an organization. The reports are commonly made of meetings, investigations, committee work, and line-of-duty activity; and they are tasks assigned to one or more members of an organization as part of its work.

Some illustrations will help us to see just what a formal report consists of and how it is similar to other types of informative writing and how it differs. Let us say that a fraternity delegate from a local chapter attends the national meeting of his group. When he returns, he is expected to bring with him a report of the activities of the meeting, for the chapter that sent him wants official and accurate information in order to keep local functions in line with national policy. The information that the delegate brings will be about such matters as dates and place of the meeting, summaries of the important speeches, motions carried or lost, recommendations and plans for the future. The report will have some of the characteristics of factual narration, for it is in part a running account of what happened at the meeting. It may also have characteristics of the summary, for there are likely to be speeches to report on. For a typical report of an investigation we may imagine a group of students who want to set up a co-operative association designed to cut their living costs at college. They know of a co-operative at another college and they want information on how it functions. To get the information they delegate one or more persons to visit and investigate the established co-operative. The delegation compiles such facts as the scheme of organization, marketing techniques, housing plan, arrangements for dividing and rotating housekeeping tasks, costs per member, saving per member, and social benefits. When the delegation comes back to its own organization, it reports this information as the final act of the investigation. Such a report as this may well include some scientific description, for the delegation will probably study the living quarters of the co-operative: kitchen, dormitories, storage space, social rooms. For an illustration of a committee report we may take such a group as the English Club and a decision to install an alcove where the members can find popular magazines and current books. A committee will be selected to furnish and operate the alcove. At the end of a set period and as part of its duties the committee will make a formal report of its work: costs, books available, turn-over, and general recommendations for the future. Because line-of-duty reports form a running account of the performance of a task, they are narratives, and because their narrative structure is typical and simple enough to be easily understood, it will help us if we reserve this particular kind of formal report for discussion and illustration in the section given to factual narration, soon to follow. Such illustration as we have used, however, is enough to show that the formal report does overlap other types of informative writing and that its special distinction is its connection with the activities of an organization.

As is true in writing directions, the title of the formal report may be sufficient introduction. If it is not, the first line or two may be used to state the purpose and the limitation. If the report is long and complicated, an introductory letter addressed to the officer who receives the report may accompany it and give what explanation is required. Since the chief purpose of the report is to be factual, the technique is to group the facts in their proper subdivisions. The nature of the subject will suggest the groupings. If the report is of a meeting, the facts will naturally fall into the types of activities; and the order in which the groups are arranged will most likely be the order in which they occurred. If the report is of an investigation or of committee work, the problems themselves will determine the groups of facts and their order.

As the task of reporting a meeting is the one most likely to fall to college writers, we shall illustrate this section with a report of a section meeting of an American Hospital Association convention. The speakers at the meeting were themselves making reports of investigations they had conducted. The report is therefore a "report of reports." Students who like to ponder the intricacies of classification will be interested in observing to what extent the report is also a series of summaries.

The subject and circumstances of the report stated.

A Report of the First Meeting of the Tuberculosis Section of the American Hospital Association. The Problem:

TUBERCULOSIS AMONG NURSES AND HOSPITAL PERSONNEL

Report of the first speech of the meeting. The facts are grouped according to the speeches made at the meeting.

Mrs. Elizabeth S. Keltzsch, Personnel Director of Milwaukee County Institutions, Wisconsin, discussing tuberculosis as a compensable disease, reported that in Wisconsin tuberculosis has been a compensable disease for twenty years. Although the number of claims filed in Wisconsin has not been great, the experience there has been such that hospitals are increasingly studying the hazards involved in connection with giving care to tuberculosis patients and are setting up better measures of control, particularly more rigid preëmployment examinations and education of personnel in aseptic technic.

Report of the second speech of the meeting.

Dr. Grant Cunningham, Director, Division of Industrial Hygiene, Ontario Department of Health, discussed "blanket" arrangements for compensation (in effect, health insurance) and factors which have bearing on the incidence of active tuberculosis among workers, particularly selection of employees and the conditions in specific occupations which lead to their overcrowding on the job or elsewhere. The value of blanket provisions for compensation, he indicated, lies in the potential liability imposed on employers to make enquiries into the hazards existing in particular occupations and to set up measures for controlling them.

Report of the third speech of the meeting.

Mrs. Lorna Doone Mitchell, Director of Nursing, Sea View Hospital, Staten Island, New York, in a very interesting paper reported on studies made at Sea View Hospital on the incidence of active tuberculosis in the graduate nurse staff. Sea View is a hospital for tuberculosis patients and has a graduate nursing staff largely made up of Negro nurses. She summarized the findings from the study as follows:

Note the transition statement.

1. In a study of 1,041 graduate nurses applying for positions at Sea View Hospital, the x-ray evidence of tuberculosis was 1.34 per cent.

2. The incidence of x-ray evidence of pulmonary tuberculosis in 930 Negro nurses was 1.47 per cent.

3. There were no cases of pulmonary tuberculosis found in 111 white graduate nurses examined in the same manner.

4. Over a period from January 1, 1930, to July 1, 1939, the occurrence or development of pulmonary tuberculosis was as follows:

Again note the transition.

(a) In a group of 1,027 graduate nurses (Negro and white) the occurrence or development of pulmonary tuberculosis was 3.52 per cent.

(b) In a group of 916 Negro graduate nurses, the occurrence or development of pulmonary tuberculosis was 3.6 per cent.

(c) In a group of 111 white graduate nurses, the occurrence or development of pulmonary tuberculosis was 2.8 per cent.

5. Nursing in a tuberculosis institution is not as dangerous as we are led to believe. This is shown by the 96.48 per cent of the 1,027 graduate nurses who did not develop tuberculosis.

6. Tuberculosis developing in nurses while working in

a tuberculosis hospital is an occupational disease because of the greater frequency of occurrence of tuberculosis among them than occurs in a similar group of women living under average normal conditions.

Among factors important in helping to prevent active tuberculosis infections, Mrs. Mitchell cited: educational programs to make nurses "technic conscious"; the intelligence of the group; non-employment of nurses having a history of active tuberculosis; a good living regime which includes outdoor exercise, prevention of overfatigue, interests that take the nurse away from the hospital, maintenance of good technic.

Report on the fourth speech.

The paper by W. H. Oatway, Jr., M.D., Wisconsin General Hospital, Madison (read by A. J. Hockett, M.D., Touro Infirmary, New Orleans), in describing a program for safeguarding hospital personnel, pointed out the need to find sources of infection and that the only new factor in the employee's life is the patient.

Report on the fifth speech.

Mrs. Ellen Stahlnecker, Superintendent of Nurses, Herman Kiefer Hospital, Detroit, Michigan, described the regime at the Herman Kiefer Hospital for safeguarding hospital personnel from tuberculosis. The hospital is a communicable-disease hospital with a large tuberculosis unit. Prospective employees have a thorough preëmployment physical examination including chest x-rays and tuberculin tests and come to the hospital several days in advance of final employment to be taught the technic of self-protection and to visit wards of the hospital.

Of a staff of 375 graduate nurses, from July, 1938, to June, 1939, only two had active tuberculosis. Employees at Herman Kiefer have a forty-hour week; two weeks vacation with pay after one year; fifteen days sick leave; and are urged to take leaves of absence in addition to vacation after two years. Since employees live away from the hospital, a graduate nurse visits all employees reporting off duty for illness. No charge is made for medical service or physical examination and an educational program is conducted to teach the employees to protect themselves.

Dr. H. McLeod Riggins, New York City, reported on a ten-year study among nurses at Bellevue Hospital, New

Report on the sixth speech. Note that the author's method is to begin each speech or paper with its author's name. The name signals a change from speech to speech.

York City, and a five-year study at Lenox Hill Hospital, New York City. He showed that the frequent periodic chest x-rays conducted on student nurses made it possible to detect active tuberculosis in its minimal stages when prognosis is hopeful, whereas in graduate nurses who are responsible for their own health check-up, active tuberculosis when detected was found to have progressed to a more advanced stage and hence was less amenable to treatment.[10]

Exercises

A. Write a report of what happened in one of your class meetings, using a set of notes in which you kept an account of the assigned lesson, who spoke, what was said, special activities, and the new assignment. (This is part of the work required of you as your share of the partnership you hold with the school faculty.)

B. Keep a set of minutes of the next club meeting you attend. Work the minutes into a full report.

C. Prepare a report on the progress of a project you are interested in. Assume that you are the chairman of a committee working out the project and that you are making a regular report to a superior officer.

D. For a project of some length prepare a report on the activities of an organization you belong to engaged in such work as game conservation, the forestry plantation, a civic music program, co-operative marketing, etc. Or write up a report of a field trip conducted for the purpose of investigation: geology field trip, forest or river inspection, industrial exploration, visit to a school, etc.

FACTUAL NARRATION

A. The General Process

The general process is a narration in that it tells the story, step by step, of the way in which something is generally done. It uses specific

[10] "A Report of the First Meeting of the Tuberculosis Section of The American Hospital Association." *The American Journal of Nursing,* Vol. 39, pp. 1259-1260, November, 1939. Reprinted by permission of *The American Journal of Nursing.*

events only to illustrate a generalized process or to provide human interest material. The general method of launching all ships may be illustrated by the story of how the *S.S. Peacock* was put in the water at Norfolk on July 4, 1940. The details of that launching help to tell the general story of all launching. It is the story of all launching that the reader wants, not just the story of putting the *S.S. Peacock* afloat. The general process is therefore a factual account of how something is generally done. How are caissons sunk? How is glass made? How is a permanent wave put in hair? How are horses groomed for a race? How does a baker make his bread? How is air transportation managed? How do dining-car operators get a meal ready?

The general process differs from directions in at least one major respect: directions are meant to be followed as a means of accomplishing a desired act: making a cake, grinding the valves in a gasoline motor, building a log cabin. The cake, the ground valves, and the cabin are the ends desired. In the general process, however, the end is simply satisfied curiosity and a feeling of being "in the know." The directions for casting a fly make it possible for the reader to cast flies; but knowledge of the general process by which lost airplanes are found by a radio direction-finding system does not equip the reader to operate the system. All that the general process does is outline the system in such a way that the reader understands the principles and the methods by which the steps are worked out. The reader is informed about the operation, but not taught to operate.

The general process differs from specific narrative in ways suggested by the latter's name. Specific narrative tells the story of your first day at the university, of your grandmother's trip to the Great Plains in 1880, of the forest fire that nearly burned Menominee, of the cruise of the *Miami* on ice patrol. It is concerned with specific events rather than with a generalization of how things are done.

Because all factual narrative is concerned with things and places as well as with events, a great deal of description is often used along with the details of the event. The description may be formal or informal, depending upon the tone selected for the story. It may convey no emotional impression or a strong one. It does, however, always aim to communicate facts. The technique of scientific description, as given earlier in this chapter, is part of the equipment of the person who would write either the general process or the specific narrative.

The basic structure of the general process is a chronological, step-by-step description, with the steps filled in with enough detail to make them clear. The elaboration of the steps may give the writer a chance to spread himself with anecdote and tone. If the writer wants to build up a dominant tone, he must first decide what it is and then select words and details that contribute to it. Underneath the tone, however, is the factual material of the process itself. If the material is lost sight of, the purpose of the essay is unfulfilled.

Subject matter for the general process is found wherever there are people doing things and wherever nature is performing her acts. This means that thousands of subjects lie all around us. We have only to select a process, become thoroughly familiar with it, arrange the chronology of the steps in outline, fill in the steps with enough detail to make them clear, and tone the whole as desired. Because the general process is more often informal than not, a freer use of judgment is permitted than for most informative writing. Judgment should not, however, interfere with the informative purpose. Where it is used it should guide and interpret the information and help the tone: "hot sun," "gentle rain," "destined to bring to this nation and its armed forces a direction-finding service that has since shepherded hundreds of lost planes to safety."

The following essay describes the general process of wheat raising. The panoramic spread of the western wheat plains and the clattering movement of harvesting machinery set the tone.

Harvest Time

The title and the first paragraph give the only clue to the subject, an indirect clue.

The machines clatter across the skyline and a shimmering cloud of dust and fine golden chaff fills the air like a haze. Into the slow-rolling trucks flows the stream of wheat—new wheat shredded from clipped heads that this morning rippled in the July breeze like a golden surf.

To the north that golden surf still stretches away beyond the horizon, hill after low hill, until it is a green surf of wheat not yet fully ripened under the late Dakota sun. To

The setting in which the story of wheat occurs. Note how the author achieves a feeling of great space and of the slow movement of the harvest from south to north.

the south, farther than the eye can see, the hills are already shorn of their grain, ripened with the north-moving season, ripened and harvested and hauled away to the bulging bins in a million farmyards, to the tall elevators beside the spider-web tracks of steel where it flows with its surf hiss into railroad cars. Stubble stands on those southern fields, the stubble of clipped fields; and the harvest moves north with the season.

North from the plains of Texas, where blue-bonnets waved so brightly only a few weeks ago. North, as the buffalo once flowed north in a brown flood, as the trail herds spilled north in a horn-rattling, hoof-clicking stream. North, from the Staked Plains, across the Canadian River and the Cimarron and the Arkansas, across the Smoky Hill and the Republican and the Platte, north across the Niobrara and the westward-reaching forks of the Missouri.

The names of the rivers, and of the Indians in the following paragraph, lend space and glamor to the harvest.

The Kiowa, the Cheyenne, the Pawnee, the Arapaho, the Dakota followed the buffalo north, and the hard-riding Texans followed the trail herds. And now the sweating sunburned men of truck and combine follow the wheat harvest north across the sunburned plains.

The harvest moves north, the reaping that will bring bread to a hungering world. And in the fields of stubble when the harvesters have passed are the crisscrossed tracks of an army, the wheel tracks of a thousand vehicles; and over the land still hangs the golden haze and the new wheat smell and the smoke of hot oil and burned gasoline, simmering in the summer heat. But it is a peaceful army, an army of those who gather the grain that men and women and little children may eat.

Background history of wheat in America.

Wheat, the golden seed of a tall, slim grass that came out of western Asia in the forgotten past. Wheat that has been sickled and scythed and cradled and bound and headed and combined. Wheat that has been trodden out and flailed and threshed in the maw of a thundering machine. Wheat that has been ground in stone metates and between the groaning stones of little water mills and between the whirling steel rollers of giant flour factories. Wheat for bread.

In the hills of New Mexico they grew *el trigo Sonoreno*

the soft wheat that the Spaniards brought to the Mexico of Montezuma; but the yield was poor. And one day Don Nazario Gonzales, who lived at La Cienega, not far from Santa Fe, shot a wild goose and found in its crop seven grains of a strange, hard wheat that came from beyond the horizon, none knew where. Don Nazario planted those seven grains of hard, dark wheat, and from the heads they bore he gathered the seed to plant a patch twice as big as his garden. And thus came the hard wheat of bountiful yield to New Mexico, from the crop of a goose from beyond the horizon.

On the high flatlands of Dakota a family named Karski built house, barn and fence and planted a hopeful field; and in one corner of that field the old grandmother sowed a handful of wheat she had brought from the Ukraine. It grew and throve in the Dakota soil, and thus came the hardy Russian wheat to the high flatlands of the upper Missouri.

Grasshoppers brought winter wheat to Kansas. In the summer of 1874 the grasshoppers came in swarms and sun-darkening clouds to the new lands along the Arkansas River where farmers had watched their first sod corn sprout and spread its green bayonets. When the grasshoppers had passed by, the land was as barren as when the plow had first turned the soil. And one among the settlers said that wheat planted now might make a crop for next year, so they sent East for winter wheat and pledged their future to pay for it. And Kansas, in 1875, harvested wheat where the grasshoppers had passed by.

First step: planting the winter wheat.

You plant winter wheat under the hot sun of late summer, in soil plowed when the summer drought has relaxed under a gentle rain. You watch, and the planted grain sends up eager green shoots until the field, the hills, the whole expanse of the plains is as green as a new lawn in some townsman's dooryard. It grows and sends down roots to fortify itself against the winter. Frost nips it and sleet pelts it and snow comes to cover it with a December blanket. And when the March thaw sets in, there is your wheat, green and eager, thrusting through the bedraggled crust of dying winter.

The fall and winter phase in the story of wheat.

Spring phase and the period of crisis in which nature works.

April, and it is reaching toward the white-clouded sky. May, and it is kneehigh, high enough to hide a hungry rabbit. June, and the heads are long and fat as a farmer's finger, bearded heads that hold the fattening grain. June, and you watch the sky and hold your breath and mutter a prayer each time the clouds pile up on the horizon.

Facts about one of the dangers that face growing wheat.

You watch for the green tinge that means hail in those clouds, the muddy darkness and swirling scud that mean wind; wind and hail, that can sweep across a field in less time than it takes you to walk out to the barn, and leave a tattered waste of broken stems and beaten ground and hopelessness. One swath of hail across the wheatlands can wipe out a score of farmers in one chilling hour. So you watch the clouds and mutter a prayer, and you stare helplessly out across that sea of bronzing green.

You and the earth and the weather have grown this wheat. You plowed the soil a year ago, you and all the other middle-aged farmers and boys not even as tall as a tractor wheel and girls with wheat-colored hair and lonely laughter. You plowed the ground and sowed the seed, and the rains came and sprouted it. And in letters, written by lamplight, you told the boys, so far away, how green were these October hills.

Facts about more of the dangers.

All through the winter you watched it, hoping for snow, for moisture that would be stowed away there for the roots. And through the spring you watched for chinch bugs and Hessian flies. You watched for smut and rust as its stems grew tall and the heads appeared and began to fill. Then the scorching sun drove away the clouds when it most needed rain to plump the heads, and you watched the brown withering creep up the stems as it "fired" at the edges of the field. Rain came at last, and the heads filled, and the beards began to glow with gold. And you knew you had a crop, a harvest. And you watched then for hail.

Second step: harvesting the wheat.

And now the harvest. The machines move in. The clatter of the sickle bar is a song that rises high above the roar of the motors. The golden heads are cut, in an endless swath, and swept back into the thundering combine, there to yield their kernels of breadstuff. Chaff and straw spew out in a gleaming spray, to scatter with the wind, and the grain itself comes pouring into the trucks like a stream of fine nugget gold.

The harvest moves north.

The harvest army creeps across the field and behind it grows the expanse of stubble, the shorn land with its stiff, headless straw crisscrossed by the tracks of a thousand wheels. The harvest moves north, ever north: May in southern Texas, June in Oklahoma, July in Kansas and Nebraska, August in Dakota and Montana. North across the empire of wheat.

Details of the size of the harvest, its economic value.

The golden grain grows in almost every spot where Americans till the soil, but here in this short-grass land, an empire 400 miles from east to west and 1,000 miles from south to north, wheat covers the hills as once the buffalo covered them. Wheat and grass, bread and beef. You could set down here that German Reich which first heiled Hitler and still have room to graze half a million steers. You could haul in all the grain cars on all the American railroads and fill them with this land's wheat and still have it heaped along the tracks, waiting for more cars. Count out half a billion dollars and you still have not tallied up the worth of this wheat on the market.

Wheat, from horizon to blue horizon, a golden surf of ripened wheat. And this is only the heartland, the inner empire, of wheat. Box the compass from here and you will find wheat somewhere on the horizon—a billion bushels of it last year, as much again when this harvest is tallied up.

The essay begins to end. Note the incomplete sentences.

Grass from a forgotten valley somewhere in ancient Asia. A few hard grains from the crop of a wild goose, come from nobody knows where. A handful of seed from a Ukrainian field.

A recapitulation of the first paragraph of the essay.

The machines clatter across the skyline and the mounded trucks roll away to the towering elevators beside the spider-web tracks of steel. The harvest moves north with the season.[11]

[11] "Harvest Time," by Hal Borland. The New York *Times* Magazine, July 23, 1944. Copyrighted by Hal Borland, 1944. Reprinted by permission of Willis Kingsley Wing and The New York *Times*.

Exercises

A. Go over the essay "Harvest Time" with special attention to the style. How does the writer get his panoramic effect? Does he use too many sentences beginning with "and"? Why does he use incomplete sentences? Make a list, two dozen or more words in length, of the most effective verbs you find in the essay. Make a similar list of modifiers. What is the contribution these words make to the tone of the essay?

B. Write a general process. For a subject you need only open your eyes and choose, but look first at the places where you have worked long enough to get familiar with what goes on. A telegram is sent and delivered. A woman goes into a beauty parlor and comes out with a permanent wave. A customer goes into a restaurant and eats a good dinner. A jeweler cuts a diamond. A department store puts on a super-sale. A furrier makes a "mink" coat out of muskrat pelts. How are these things done? Bricks, tires, hats, glass, matches, books, paper, and vitamin flour all get made. How? A farmer goes in for soil conservation. How? A radio program is broadcast. How? Vegetables reach a big, city market. How?

C. Read the general process essays, beginning on page 190, and be ready to discuss in class their technical aspects and your interest in their information.

B. Specific Narration

The most important characteristic of the second type of factual narration is that it tells the story of a particular event or series of events. It is specific. We do not generalize a process; instead we take from the present or the past something that happened to us or to others and write its record. The cruise of the *Miami* from June 15, 1913, to July 1, 1913; the struggle to prevent the burning of Menominee, Michigan, in October of 1871; a horseback excursion away from home—these are the events of specific narration. By telling these stories we become historians, for we are concerned with truth. We tell what happened, where it happened, and to whom it happened. If we wish, we interpret the event and reveal its significance: its causes and its consequences. We may write with the cold factuality and logic of the formal historian, or we may write with the emotional appeal of the creative artist. We may write of some minor, personal occurrence; or we may write of something as vast as the Crusades. Whichever event or tone we select, it is history we write, for we tell a true story.

An occurrence is made up of a series of minute details with consecutive relationship. One follows the other. One leads to the next. Put together in the telling they form a total impression in the same way that a motion picture film, made up of a great many "still" pictures, gives the impression of motion. Note the following, item by item:

> After climbing the stairs for several minutes, we reached the top and entered Madison Square Garden itself. I stopped from fatigue from the stairs and from amazement. It seemed miles across to the other side—miles and miles around the open space to section 18 and the stairs going down to the first row. I looked around when I was seated. I looked to my right and then around those miles of heads to where I had started from—a complete circle of dark hats and dark suits, all alike and inert.
>
> It wasn't until later that I became conscious of the noise around me. It was made by all the people there, but was blended into one voice. It wasn't loud at all, but was low and murmuring. It was like the sound of the ocean: you do not hear it until you try to hear it consciously. It was the sound that accompanies every big event at the Garden.
>
> Soon the atmosphere became heavy. A thick blue pall of smoke hung mid-air over the floor. I could not see the other side, for the smoke. No one watched the smoke or the people, only the movements of the players. I must watch them, too; and I turned my attention to the orange rectangle and the baskets at each end.[12]

To do this sort of thing we need only to observe closely, remember (or put in our notebooks), and later select for recording the most meaningful details. The details will concern the setting, the people, the action, and the significance of everything to the persons in the story and the person telling it. The details depend strongly upon direct sensory impression: taste, sight, smell, touch, and hearing. Though general and abstract material almost certainly will appear, the emphasis is on the concrete and specific. We should select verbs that name the specific action and carry sensory stimuli. The verb *say* is weak in its stimuli and in accuracy. How was the speech said? Was it muttered? whispered? whimpered? or screamed? The verb *walk* is similarly weak. Did the person scramble? meander? hobble? or

12 Jean Beneker. A student paper.

sprint? Concrete and specific detail give a realistic impression of the setting, the actors, the action, and the explanation of the whole. It is generalizing to say, "We ate a good dinner." If it is an impression of reality we want, it is more effective to say, "We ate a dinner of chicken broth, apple salad, lamb chops, mashed potatoes with melted butter, green peas, coffee, and almond cake." To say that the temperature was 18° below zero is accurate enough for a formal report, but it does not make one feel cold. If we step into the drifts, choke with the cold air in our lungs, freeze our ears, beat against the wind, and cry with misery, all through the medium of words, we get the reality of 18° below zero. If we are writing a formal account of an event such as a tour of duty, our tone will of course be impersonal and we will seek to make our facts as precise as possible. Accuracy and exactness will be our aim.

What occurrences are suitable for use in specific narration? Few events are really dull. An interpreter with insight enough to penetrate routine and habit and with independence to consider his opinions as important can show us the significant details and cause us to be interested in almost any event. The mere fact of time's passing ought to fill everybody with suspense for the outcome of the slightest action. The mere fact that the slight event has somewhere, sometime, a bearing on the crises of our lives ought to fill us with eager attention. We need to be jarred awake, to be jostled into a state of living, of reaching out into the world around us with every sense probing for material that bears on our goals. The writer who can jar us does not need to ask for an interesting event. He takes what comes his way and shows us his true reaction to it. For the student, however, this is no better than being told that the way to write is to write. He still wants specific advice. Let him begin with his own interests. Desires he struggled to satisfy; travels that excited him; events at the office, shop, school, or out in the fields that caught at his attention are likely to be interesting to all of us, for mankind has a remarkable community of interests. The young writer can begin with himself: the things he wanted and got, or failed to get; the events of the day that caught at him out of all the rest that slipped by unnoticed; what he liked and disliked. The events we recall from the past probably were significant; they stuck to us because they meant much. After we have learned to write personal narrative, we can go on to other forms: stories told us by our parents about their early struggles, biographies of people we are studying in school, news stories of local events, historical accounts of happenings from the past.

The pattern for most specific narration is chronological. The event is broken into its major scenes whenever it has them, the scenes are arranged in the order of their occurrence, and the details of each scene filled in. The beginning of the story provides enough orientation so that the reader knows, or has at least a clue to, the author's purpose and story thread. The following paragraph illustrates how orientation may be secured by direct statement:

> When the romance began to fall off the race horses, I looked around for a new interest and there was none within my old range. I had about exhausted the resources of the world within a quarter of a day's ride of home. My circle must be widened; I must go off for all day. What held me? Not my parents; they let me go wild. Not my pony: he was a tough little cayuse. The noonday meal was the stake I was tied to. If I could ride away out into the country till noon, eat there somewhere, and ride back in the afternoon, I could cover miles and miles, see new things, new people. The problem was where to eat and feed my pony.[13]

The largest part of any narrative is concerned with what happened and with the details of setting; but perhaps the most important technique in handling details is transition in time and place. Changes in time and place need to be indicated if the reader is to keep everything orderly in his mind. The best method of carrying the reader from one time or place to another is that of transitional phrases and sentences: *The following week he phoned. . . . We entered Port Washington just as it was getting dark*. Such remarks as these keep the stream of details flowing evenly.

The ending of the narration may be abrupt or it may be a summarizing glance backward that lets a reader out of the story the way the closing of a door lets a visitor go free of his visit. The following is an ending that summarizes:

[13] From *The Autobiography of Lincoln Steffens*. Copyright, 1932, by Harcourt, Brace and Company, Inc.

I left Bozeman in the spring of 1917 to enter the University of Minnesota in the autumn as a graduate student. I have never been back, but I shall go some day to render tribute where tribute is due. From time to time I see certain of my friends who taught there with me and laugh with them about pining for pins. Occasionally one of my former students appears in one or another corner of the country. The principal of the Irving school, to whom I owe more than I can ever repay, is now on the faculty of Montana State College as a teacher of economics. I feel sure she understands with me that in the liveliness, rigor, and fun of the Irving School we gained resources incalculable for graduate study and for college teaching.[14]

The following factual narrative is also a formal report on a tour of duty. The characteristics of factual exactness and impersonality are typical of this sort of writing.

U. S. Revenue Cutter *Miami,*
Great Banks of Newfoundland,
Latitude 43-35, Longitude 52-54,
July 1, 1913

Orientation of the reader by formal statement of the subject.

Subject: Report of third cruise on ice patrol.

SIR: On June 15 radio communication was established between the two patrol vessels and our 8 A.M. position was reported to the *Seneca,* lying at the time to the eastward of the banks in latitude 45, near a grounded berg, which had afterwards broken in two, forming two distinct bergs, which were drifting to the northeastward. At noon same day vessels exchanged noon positions and Capt. Johnston appointed a meeting for next day on parallel 45. Vessels met at 5 A.M. the next day and lay to until 6 A.M.; the senior officer delivering to me diagrams of bergs sighted and reported to date and copies of ice reports forwarded from the *Seneca.* That vessel, upon being relieved soon afterwards, stood to the westward. The *Miami* stood to the eastward for those waters in which search was to be made, in accordance with department's radiogram of the 9th instant.

[14] From *A Goodly Fellowship,* by Mary Ellen Chase. By permission of The Macmillan Company, publishers.

A day-by-day account of the cruise. Most of the transitions are made by indicating changes in date.

Scientific description. Note the exactness of the details, here and in succeeding paragraphs.

At 1 P.M., the 17th, in latitude 45-00, longitude 46-26, a small berg was passed close aboard, water 47°, a fall of 1°. This berg floated about 10 or 15 feet above the water and was hardly 200 feet in length. Its top was furrowed and gullied through in many places, and appeared on the point of breaking up. As it pitched in the swells the seas broke in spray on the bluff ends, while others swept unbroken through the gullies across its top. Considerable trash ice was floating to leeward. Though our track had been in latitude 45, nothing was seen of the bergs near which the *Seneca* had been lying two days before. Fog set in, engine was stopped at 3 P.M., and vessel drifted.

Transition.

The 18th, 19th, 20th, and 21st the *Miami* cruised along latitude 44-45 to longitude 42-15, then south to latitude 43-15, then west to longitude 45-45, then north and east to latitude 43-15, longitude 45-10, when vessel stopped at dark to drift until daylight the morning of the 22d. Up to this time no bergs had been sighted and none had been reported by steamers crossing the rectangle between parallels 43 and 45 and meridians 42 and 46. These tracks had covered every quarter of the zone. On the evening of the 21st, the *Cambrian* reported a berg in latitude 44-30, longitude 45-25. Up to date, this is the only berg in the rectangle since the three reported in southeastern corner the first week in June, which have not been reported again, though that locality is crossed several times each day by the many vessels using the lanes to the English and Irish Channels.

Transition.

The 22d came in foggy; but partly clearing before 8 A.M., got under way and stood for reported position of berg sighted by *Cambrian* the night before. After standing to within 10 miles of position of berg, engine was stopped and vessel allowed to drift. A dense fog had set in which made further search for the time useless. The *Cambrian* had reported the drift of this berg as south-southeast, as the smaller pieces lay to the north-northwest. This is not always proof of the line of drift of the berg, as the wind at the time was moderate southeast, and the small pieces are likely to be blown and washed to leeward. Wind shifted to southwest, blowing fresh, attended with moderate sea. Weather continued so until 6 A.M., when fog cleared, and vessel stood to the northward. Noon position by observation on the 22d placed the vessel in latitude 45-30, showing a drift of over 60 miles to the northward since the 21st. We had been set beyond the range of radio communication with vessels on the lanes to the southward. Course was set to the southeastward, to get into warmer water, where chances of fog are less, radio communication could be re-established, and the search continued.

The *Cambrian* found a south-southeast drift at the time of sighting berg on the 21st; between the 21st and 23d the *Miami* found a drift of 60 miles to the north-northeast, wind having shifted to southwest. From this I was persuaded that this berg must have been set to the northward of forty-fifth parallel; but with search frequently interrupted by fog among variable currents, whose drift can only be determined by observations, lacking in thick weather, ship possibly influenced by surface current while berg is drifting with a cross or counter undercurrent, all make plotting of positions and forecasting of drift of ice most uncertain.

Transition. On the 23d cruised to southeastward to latitude 44-30, longitude 43-30; and on the 24th to the southwestward to latitude 43-50, longitude 45-00. The track of the *Miami* and those of the many vessels reporting by radio had brought all of rectangle under observation except the extreme western edge, the berg sighted by the *Cambrian* being the only berg in the rectangle since those sighted by the *Winifridian* on June 9 in extreme southeast corner.

Transition. The 25th began with light westerly breezes and partly cloudy. Observations had accurately fixed position the day before, so I planned to drift for several days in the hope of getting some line on set of current when not confused with vessel's leeway. This plan was interrupted at 11 A.M. by a radiogram from the *Columbia* reporting passing a berg eight hours earlier in latitude 44-01, longitude 45-05, which should have been within sight of the *Miami,* but was not. We cruised in that vicinity for four hours until fog set in. The wind coming out from southeast backing into and blowing fresh from the east, *Miami* lay to and drifted to the westward. We have found that the east winds hold on and may increase after sunset; the west winds moderate and lull soon after sunset. This day, standing to the westward in latitude 44, longitude 45, water dropped from 58° to 40° at the condenser, 56° to 42° at the surface. Vessel drifted all the 26th.

At 11 P.M., the 25th, disconnected portions of a radiogram from the *Seneca* were received, seeming to refer to her departing for New York and the discontinuance of patrol. All efforts to obtain confirmation proved unsuccessful. At 9.05 P.M., the 26th, received following radiogram from senior officer, quoting telegram from department: "Search rectangle between meridians 41 and 42, parallels 42 and 43-30. If you find no large icebergs, discontinue patrol and return to New York; *Seneca* ordered New York."

Transition.

Got under way at 1.30 A.M., the 27th, and stood to the southeastward to complete search as directed. Arrived in those waters the 28th, where a thorough search was made. Sea was smooth, sky and atmosphere clear with light northerly breeze. Here we found the finest weather since leaving Key West in March; water 58°, atmosphere, dry bulb 58°, wet bulb 54°. No bergs could have been set across the tracks on the lanes without being reported. Seven steamers reported courses through eastern rectangle on the 27th and five on the 28th. If any bergs had gotten across in foggy weather, their existence would have been a short one in such temperatures. Here the most satisfactory service of the *Miami's* part of the patrol was rendered, the ships reporting their courses, positions, and conditions. With information thus collected, there was no reservation in answering the queries of ships coming into the rectangle with the information gathered from those that had just passed out. At 4 P.M., the 28th, having searched the waters prescribed and found no ice therein, course was set for the banks, with Halifax in view as port of destination; but with St. Johns close at hand if reduced coal supply and strong westerly winds should make a visit to latter port the choice of alternatives.

Summary of the findings resulting from the cruise.

Only three bergs were sighted and reported during the last two weeks of patrol, that sighted by *Miami* in latitude 45-00, longitude 46-26, on the 17th; that by the *Cambrian,* the 21st, latitude 44-30, longitude 45-25; that by the *Columbia,* the 25th, latitude 44-01, longitude 45-05. These three positions are on a line bearing southeast true and running through the position of the bergs sighted by the *Niagara* on May 29 and supposed to have drifted about 120 miles farther to the south and east, where they were sighted by the *Winifridian* a week later, a daily rate of about 15 miles per day. If the three bergs sighted the 17th, 21st, and 25th had been one and the same berg, it would have shown the same set and rate, 15 miles per day southeast. The trend of the drift swings in a broad curve more to the eastward as it reaches lower latitudes, a resultant of the cold current setting approximately south, prevailing westerly winds, and the warm Gulf current setting to the north of east.

Summary continued.

While a sharp drop in temperature does not necessarily indicate the presence of ice in vicinity, it does show that vessel is entering a cold current from the north, which, from its direction of flow, is likely to bear bergs and from its lower temperature likely to be accompanied with fog, further increasing the dangers of ice.

Summary continued.

Scientific description of a berg in successive stages of its life.

Of the bergs sighted during the *Miami's* patrol, great difference was noted between those sighted in April, May, and June as to size and general appearance. The first sighted, April 23, looked as if freshly carved from its glacier; its walls nearly perpendicular; its top flat, smooth, and as white as a field of snow; and with but little erosion at water line. It gave the appearance of a berg in its first stage. On the 26th it was again observed after breaking across its top, one part tilting over about 45° and what had been its wall becoming the top of a new berg, producing a saddle-shaped outline, which after further melting would give a double-peaked effect—a berg in its second stage, such as sighted May 16. The immersed part of this berg, after melting faster than the part above water, would again roll over and bring what had been the edge of fracture uppermost, presenting a wedge-shaped berg, such as sighted May 22, showing the two old water lines at which it had previously floated—a berg in its third stage. The berg sighted June 17 was peaked and gullied in many places and was rapidly breaking up. Though by far the smallest berg observed, it was accompanied by a much greater quantity of small ice in its vicinity. These stages illustrate how easily an observer might mistake same berg for as many different bergs sighted at intervals of several weeks.

Ending.

The *Miami* reached the Great Banks this day, July 1. The weather since the 28th of June has been average, as good as could be expected, and the expenditure of coal has been kept within such limit that a trip to St. Johns will not be necessary, so course was set for Halifax, Nova Scotia.[15]

A. L. Gamble,
COMMANDING.

It is said that every person has at least one good novel in him. If that is true, it is because the events that befall us form story materials. The following autobiographical narrative is one example that the theory is true. It is a reminiscence of boyhood and tells the kind of story that is common to all of us: an adventure of youth.

The Neely Farm

The first paragraph tells the reader the nature of the story: a problem to solve.

When the romance began to fall off the race horses, I looked around for a new interest and there was none within my old range. I had about exhausted the resources of the world within a quarter of a day's ride of home. My circle must be widened; I must go off for all day. What held me? Not my parents; they let me go wild. Not my pony; he was a tough little cayuse. The noonday meal was the stake I was tied to. If I could ride away out into the country till noon, eat there somewhere, and ride back in the afternoon, I could cover miles and miles, see new things, new people. The problem was where to eat and feed my pony.

15 From *Reports of Vessels on Ice Patrol in the North Atlantic Ocean,* R.C.S. Bulletin No. 1. Treasury Department, 1913.

Indifferent attempts to solve the problem.

I tried nowhere at first. I rode half a day, dismounted on the edge of a vineyard, and ate grapes, but there is no grass when grapes are ripe; my pony had to nibble stubble. That was not enough for him, and the grapes were too much for me. I came home with a stomach-ache. My mother, who did not understand a boy at all, said it was the grapes, and she proposed that I take my lunch with me. "Your father does," she argued. Yes, but teamsters, scouts, knights, and vaqueros did not carry a lunch—and I wasn't going to. When my mother insisted and made up a lunch parcel for me I hid it in the stable or ditched it. I would not be weak. I would "find" myself, as my kind of people did.

I consulted the bridge-tender about it. He said I might share his meal whenever I wished, and his fare was good regular food: ham and eggs with black coffee and brown sugar. He could not provide for a horse, however, and the bridge was not far enough out of town. I used his hospitality only for breakfasts when I rose early and could get out to his place by six-thirty A.M.

First real attempt to solve the problem. Note the use of dialogue.

I made friends with Ah Hook, a Chinese farmer a little farther out. He was hostile at first. Having a patch of melons and another of peanuts, he was suspicious of a boy.

"What for you come catchem eat here?" he asked. "What for you no go home?"

I explained, "Too far," and he asked, "What for you go too far?"

That was an easy question. I had to see what was beyond. He laughed.

"Melican boy, he go lookee see—what? No ting, no ting. China boy, he no go lookee see. He know all-leadee, notting, allee samee."

I answered that: "What for you Ah Hook come allee way China lookee see—Sacramento?"

"Me no come lookee see Sacramento," he replied. "Me come catchem dollar, go home China."

"Yes," I argued, "you come catchem dollar to catchem eat allee samee me."

Ah Hook liked that. He chuckled and surrendered.

"All li," he said. "All li, you come eatee lice here."

The attempt fails. This paragraph also makes the transition to the next attempt.

And I did once or twice, and Ah Hook put up my pony to feed with his old skeleton of a horse. But his bill of fare was always the same "lice" and tea, both made Chinese fashion, and I didn't like rice. I had to find another road-house.

As my custom was, I made a business of the search, and I turned the business into a game. My youngest sister has turned this trick into a philosophy. "Why work?" she says whenever anyone complains of the labor of something. "Make a game of your job and then—play."

I played that I was a fugitive from justice in search of a friend, but I became so absolutely a hunted criminal that I was too cautious. I ran away from the people who might have helped me. I found nothing, and another day was wasted because I was after an enemy and forgot that it was actually a friend I wanted. I avoided everybody. The next Saturday I was more sensible. I was the trusted scout of a general who sent me out to find a base, an advance post where he could quarter and supply his troops; and he ordered me to hunt till I got what we must have.

Details of setting.

Riding up on a low eminence on the Stockton road, I folded my arms and reconnoitered, and I saw several places that would do. I was judging by appearances; I preferred neat farms. The Duden Farm was spick and span. It was small, but all the buildings were painted; the fences were well made and the fields well tilled. Mr. Duden had a blacksmith's shop on the corner of the main road and a cross road. There he himself always worked; his sons kept the farm. That was an objection. Country boys had an uncomfortable way of looking a city boy contemptuously up and down, asking technical questions, and laughing at the answers. I was desperate, however; the troops must be provided for; the general was a fine chief but a martinet. I considered the Duden place.

Riding on to the blacksmith's shop, I stopped and stared at Mr. Duden. He looked up from his anvil, asked me if I wanted my pony shod, and when I said I didn't, he went on with his work, hammering red-hot irons and spattering the sparks all over everything, even his leather apron and—to my wonder—his own bare, hairy arms. It was a fascinating sight. I wouldn't mind being a blacksmith who shod horses. The glowing splinters burned black spots on the floor, but they didn't burn Mr. Duden. Why? I asked him.

"They know me," he answered, but he did not look up. He went on beating the red-hot irons, ducking them sizzling into water and poking them back in the open fire, just as if I wasn't there. I rode on, therefore, and the Dudens lost for a year or two the chance to know and feed me.

This attempt fails.

The Duden place was five miles out. Two miles farther there was a cross road that led left to Florin, a railroad station, now the center of a Japanese colony which has been written about many times as an example of the failure of the whites to hold land against the cleverest of the yellow races. In my day the farms were almost ranches in size and the houses few. There was no building between Duden's and the cross road, none beyond for miles. It was all open fields of wheat, shining hot in the sun. You could see the heat radiating like white flames over the land. I turned down the Florin road because I saw off to the left of it an oasis, a white cottage, with a flying windmill in a small, fenced garden of young trees, and near it a big, unpainted barn. Pretty good. A lane opened off the road; I jogged along it between the yellow wheat and the great, light green vineyard irrigated by windmills, up to the house. I saw that there were flowers in the garden, kept fresh by tiny streams of water, carried all through and around it by a perfect little system of ditches. The whole place was neat, cool, shady, and quiet; and not a sign of a human being till I arrived opposite the cottage gate. There I saw, with a start, a woman standing, wiping her hands on her apron and staring hard at me. It was Mrs. Neely.

Details of setting.

Final attempt begins.

Mrs. Neely was the New England wife of William Neely, a tall, straight, gentle man from Mississippi. This I learned later, and indeed a good deal of what I have to tell now of her and me is her story, told afterward to my mother, and all mixed up hopelessly with my own recollections. But I can see still the picture of her at our first meeting; I can feel the straight line of her tight,

Mrs. Neely described. Her actions and her conversation provide the best indications of her character traits.

silent lips, and the gleeful, dancing look out of her watching, inquiring eyes. She drove all thought of my troops out of my head.

"How de do?" I began anxiously.

"How do you do?" she answered.

"I'm Lennie Steffens," I explained, "and I'm looking for some place where I can get lunch for us when I'm off on long trips in the country."

"Us?" she repeated. "Who are us? You don't mean you and your pony?"

"Yes," I said, "and my father says it's more important to feed my pony than me, but he can eat grass, if you have no hay."

"Oh, we have hay," she answered, "but why should we feed a boy and a horse whenever they happen along?"

"I don't know," I said, and I didn't. I was often asked the question; I had even asked it myself; and I never could answer it.

"Where do you and your pony live?" she questioned. "And what do you two do for a living? What are you doing now 'way out here?"

I told her where I lived. I could not tell her what I did for a living, except that I went to school. And as for this trip, I had explained that, but I repeated a little more fully. I was hunting for a place where I could always be sure of regular meals when I was out on the Stockton road.

"Does your mother let you range the country wild like this? And your father! Do they know where you are today?"

"No." I blushed for them. "They don't know where I am today. They hardly ever know till I get back. But they don't mind. They let me go anywhere I want to, as long as I am with my pony."

"Umph, I see," she said. "They trust the pony." And she called, "Jim, Jim."

A man stuck his head out of the barn. "Hallo?" he answered.

"Here, Jim," she said. "Come and take this useless boy's good-for-nothing pony; put him in the barn and feed him. Hay, no barley. And you"—she turned to me—"you climb down off that horse and come with me."

Shift in place.

Jim came and took the pony with a wondering look at me. I went with Mrs. Neely, who led me to her kitchen and bade me "wash up." She said I was dirty. She went on with her cooking, and when I had washed, we had a long talk. I don't remember what it was all about, but I do recall her interest in my sisters, who did not interest me. They weren't boys and could be used, so far as I had discovered, only on rainy days, when they served pretty well as brakeman and better still as passengers on a train of chairs or a steamboat. Yes, and she asked me about school, which bored me. The only good thing I could tell her about school was that Friday was a short day, closing at two o'clock instead of three, and there was no school from then till Monday. Two days and a half free. In order to use them, however, I had to find places where I could stop and feed up.

She saw, she said. "And when you decide that we will do for one stopping place, you will go on and look for others farther out."

"Ye-e-e-s," I agreed. I had not thought so far ahead as that, but the moment she mentioned it, I could see it would be well to have other stations. Also I could see that Mrs. Neely could understand—some things; which is very important to a boy, whose life is one long search for people who have some insight; intelligence is so rare, especially among grown-ups.

Shift in time.

Dinner was a long time preparing. I thought Mrs. Neely would never stop putting things on the table—wonderful things: cakes and jams, honey and milk and pickles. Long after there was enough even for me she kept baking and cooking and pulling things out of cupboards, cellars, and the oven. And I wasn't the only impatient one. Before she was ready Jim came up to the house.

"Always first—to meals," Mrs. Neely said uncomfortably, but Jim answered her back. "It's late," he said. "That noon train went by long ago." Her reply was a blast on a horn that brought Mr. Neely up to the door. Both men wiped their boots carefully on the door-mat outside the kitchen door, and that made me notice that the house was very clean.

Note how these details characterize the persons of the household.

I was introduced to Mr. Neely as "a good-for-nothing boy who has come here on a useless pony for a square meal for both, and he proposes, if the board is satisfactory, to come often, whenever he is passing by—at meal times."

"Then," said Mr. Neely, "I hope you have a good dinner for him." He said this charmingly, with a polite bow to me, and he gave me a warm handshake. I liked Mr. Neely right then and there. Of Mrs. Neely I could not be sure; she was queer. As for Jim, Mr. Neely's brother—I ranked him where Mrs. Neely put him, at the foot of the table; he was just a regular fella.

Shift in place and time.

"Yes," Mrs. Neely repeated when the men had washed up and we were seated at table, "I have done my best, as you see, with the cooking of this first—a sample meal. For I infer from what he tells me that he won't come to us again unless he is suited, though he says his father says it is more important that Jim feed his pony well." It was true that I had said all that; only the way Mrs. Neely said it made me feel very uneasy. It was always a puzzle to me why people took what I said and gave it a twist that made it sound preposterous or ridiculous.

I was hungry, however. So were the other men, and the food was not only abundant, it was good. I had chanced upon the best cook in the county; so I ate; we all ate, all but Mrs. Neely, who kept at me with questions, funny questions. How was the election going to go? Who would be our next President? What was playing at the theater? And the opera? (Sacramento had no opera.) When would the next ball be? What were the latest fashions? I didn't answer the questions; didn't have to; nobody did. We just ate and ate, and she asked questions without waiting for answers till I was full, very full, and then Mrs. Neely got me started telling the story of my life—to come. That seemed to interest them all; they sat around listening to what I was going to be, until Mrs. Neely said it was time to go to work. Then Mr. Neely shook hands with me, said good-bye, and told me to come again whenever I wanted to.

"That settles it so far as we are concerned," said Mrs. Neely. Mr. Neely was head of the house, and if he said

I might come again, I could be sure of a welcome from her.

"But how about you?" she asked me. "Do you want to come again? Does the board suit you?"

I told her it did; I was very sincere on that point, and she was glad. She liked to have a visitor now and then from the great world; liked to hear the news. She complained that some visitors, especially boys, did not know much, had no idea what was going on; and some boys were a lot of trouble, banging around and breaking fences and things, making noises that scared the cattle and fowls. I wasn't like that. She was pleased that I was different. And she seemed to have a grievance against a boy that came, not by himself, but with a horse that had to be fed and cleaned. What would I do with a boy like that? What could such a boy expect? To be taken in and coddled and—I was troubled. It sounded just like me, this part, and Jim grinned. She turned on him and drove him out. "You go on to your work," she commanded angrily, and when he obeyed and was gone, she grabbed and squeezed me.

"You darling," she said, "you darling," and she kissed me, several times, hard, the way my mother did till I had to put a stop to the practice. I couldn't stop Mrs. Neely. I saw what looked like wetness in her eyes, and besides, all of a sudden she pushed me out of the house and slammed the door.

Shift in place.

Jim was waiting for me. He took me to the barn. He kept snickering a suppressed laugh while he showed me that the pony had fed well. He put on bridle and blanket, boosted me upon the pony.

"Now, boy," he said, "you come often. We get better meals when you do. The Missis doesn't strain herself every day the way she did today. And Will, he likes you."

Abrupt ending, but on a note of triumph and complete solution of the problem.

"But how about Mrs. Neely?" I asked. "Does she really want me to come?"

"Want you?" Jim exclaimed. "*Want* you! She has wanted a boy like you all her life."[16]

[16] From *The Autobiography of Lincoln Steffens.* Copyright, 1932, by Harcourt, Brace and Company, Inc.

Exercises

A. Write a formal report of some action of yours concerned with a duty. Keep it impersonal and exact. Keep all changes in time and place perfectly clear. If you wish, invent a superior officer who requires the report of you.

B. Stories of personal experience are so intimate that assigned topics are useful only as suggestions. Examine the following to see what they call to your mind of your past. Take something from your past that interests you and write it up. Use a first person approach and let the reader get the details of setting, action, and people through your eyes.

1. My First Day at the University
2. I Plan and Cook a Dinner for Guests
3. My Trip Alone Up Haystack Mountain
4. I Learn to Milk a Goat
5. The Story of My Library Research Paper
6. My Class Takes a Field Trip
7. Two Youngsters Visit a Night Club for the First Time
8. I Wait on Tables in a Summer Hotel
9. I Am Interviewed for a Job
10. Hitch-hiking Home
11. Chainman on a Surveying Crew
12. I Get a Dog
13. The Plain Facts about My Operation
14. Holiday by Myself
15. Confirmation
16. My Worst Day as a Forest Ranger
17. The River Floods Its Banks
18. Storm on the Bay
19. I Prowl Through Frenchtown After Midnight
20. Summer in a Steel Mill
21. Planting Trout on the South Fork
22. A Day's Adventures as a Sales-lady
23. Initiation
24. A Vacation Adventure
25. Dinner at a Logging Camp

C. Write a diary of each day's events for a week, having as your aim a record of the kind of life you are leading. After the week is up, go through the entries to edit the non-essentials, the repetitions, and the style. A record of your impressions of your life will form an interesting part of the diary, but keep the objective facts well in the foreground.

D. Read as assigned by your instructor the narratives that begin on page 209, and prepare for class discussion the analysis that accompanies each.

The techniques of informative prose vary with the type. There are so many types that our discussion has been long. Even so, we have treated only the most common and useful of them. The purpose of informative prose, we discovered, is to communicate facts accurately and with degrees of objectivity that depend upon our readers and our intentions. We examined directions, the summary, scientific description, classification, formal reports, and factual narration. Knowledge of these and fair skill in writing them are required of every educated person. It is not easy to write them well, and anyone who can do it has a valuable tool at his command. Informative prose is more than a tool, however: at its best it is an art that satisfies the creative urge of many talented persons. History and biography are art forms of the highest type. News writing at its best requires talent and skill. All writing—not just the informative—demands sharp observation, analytical skill, language ability, and creative insight; but to these must be added one more item if an educated person is to fill his highest place: the ability to reach sound judgments and to communicate them. The next chapter, "The Thematic Essay," has for its aim this important skill.

4. THE THEMATIC ESSAY

THERE is, as we have seen, a division of labor between informative and thematic writing. The first communicates to us such facts as how meat is got from a lobster, how wheat is grown on the great plains of the West, how loggers built their bunkhouses in the old timber-boom days; it tells us what happened at a committee meeting or during the exploratory expeditions of early travelers. Informative writing is often lively and inspiring, but its main intention is a factual account. Thematic writing, however, has a different burden. Its aim is judgment. It examines the facts revealed by the informer, reflecting upon them, and reaches conclusions. It goes, therefore, beyond informative details. After examining the details and coming to conclusions, its purpose is to communicate the conclusions and to reorganize the details in such a way that the conclusions are seen to be reasonable.

Everyone is always making judgments. Sometimes the judgments are careless, based on prejudice or skimpy evidence. Sometimes they are entirely sound, having their sources in unassailable evidence. Our effort as writers is to be as sound as we can. Suppose we look at some illustrative judgments in order to become more aware of them as a function in life and as a principle in thematic writing.

A hunter—for instance the grizzly bear expert whose comment we read in Chapter 2—recalls a remark about American big game. The remark does not fit his experience with grizzly bears. He runs through the details of his experience, reflecting on them, and draws his conclusions, in this instance that because grizzly bears really are dangerous, buggy whips and tin whistles are poor weapons to carry in grizzly country. Another man examines the ghost towns of Idaho and draws from his data the conclusion that Idaho is lonely with the memories of once turbulent and now vanished cities.

We can use other obvious illustrations. A jury sitting on a trial must come to a collective judgment. The lawyers present the facts; the jury ponders them and comes to a decision—a judgment. A student reading a novel, perhaps Norris's *The Pit,* sees evidence of literary naturalism and concludes that Norris belonged, at least in so far as one novel indicates, to a particular school of writers. The evidence is there on the pages of the novel, revealed by the author's treatment of his subject matter. A scientist observes certain facts during an experiment, say with floating objects. He forms an hypothesis, which is only a tentative conclusion, and then experiments further until he can reject his early judgment or confirm it and call it a theory or a law. A mathematician starts with a proposition he wishes to establish if he can. He may use direct evidence, such as blocks or drawings; or he may use the subtleties of higher mathematics; or he may use other propositions that have already been proved. No matter who it is, the hunter or the mathematician, the aim is a judgment which can stand firmly.

The value of a judgment is its use in human activity. Action resulting from deliberation is based on some judgment or other. The hunter needs to know what to carry with him for safety. The jury and the judge want to use facts and the machinery of government and law to the best interest of society. The student wants to understand Norris in order to build up critical skill or as an aid in writing original novels. The scientist and mathematician, apart from the noble aim of truth for truth's sake, know that their judgments are essential to civilized living. The horrible necessity for spies is the result of a need for information on which to base judgments that determine success or failure in the crucial enterprise of war. Methods of reforestation, of soil control, of river and harbor improvement, of disease elimination, of slum clearance, of public safety can be determined only on a basis of judgment and fact. The movies we see and the books we read, when we have a choice, the college we attend, the profession we enter, the car we buy all await the judgment that clears the way for action. This may be giving many of us more credit than we deserve, but the credit surely is one we all should seek if we claim to control our actions.

A judgment may be named by many terms. We have been using some of them here for the sake of familiarity: theme, opinion, conclusion, hypothesis, law, proposition. Though each of them has some distinctive elements in its meaning, the meanings have in common the element of being a judgment drawn from data. Writing that is concerned with judgments we have called *thematic*. The *theme* is the judgment the author develops.

For the next page or two let us examine themes used by contemporary writers. The themes, though they may look a little complicated at first glance, are not really formidable. Each is an author's considered judgment. The part that the author developed, that is, for which he had data, is italicized. Here is the first:

Down where the spur track makes a V with the highway U. S. 20, Gopher Prairie still stands, *but Main Street has disappeared.*[1]

The next one states a theme that has been used by many modern writers:

All I have tried to say is that you and I, and Americans generally, have each a personal standard of honorable conduct. *Under prevailing conditions, largely economic, it is frequently impossible to live within striking distance of that standard.*[2]

The following excerpt also contains a popular theme:

The creative writers of our democracy have a new duty, which is only an old duty that many of them had forgotten: not to write propaganda for the democratic way of life, not to crusade for reform, not to advance with clashing arms upon the foe—*merely to show us citizens the best in human life by contrast with the worst, the heroic as well as the abject, the noble as well as the sordid. They must give us again what will make us proud to be man, a sense of our dignity and an awareness of our responsibility.*[3]

One more will be enough, this time a recent announcement from the age-long series on the theme that the theater is dying:

The Broadway stage today presents a strange paradox. It is feeding on a rich diet of standing room only, *yet is starving to death.* It is at least a

1 From "Main Street Twenty Years After," by Bernard DeVoto. *Harper's Magazine,* November, 1940.

2 From "The Luxury of Integrity." *In The Nemesis of American Business,* by Stuart Chase. Published by The Macmillan Company.

3 From "Nihilism. Literature, and Democracy," by Louis Halle, Jr. *The Saturday Review of Literature,* December 14, 1940. Reprinted by permission of *The Saturday Review of Literature.*

quarter of a century since the houses have been so packed, *yet the theatre is on its way out.*[4]

These are the judgments that have concerned authors so much that they organized their supporting data into essays. The judgments are not to be shied from. A certain formality accompanies them, but that is only because their authors wanted to be sure to say exactly what was to be defended. The repetition in two of them is for the purpose of emphasis and of catching the experience of as many readers from as many angles as possible and of giving the readers time to grasp the thematic implications.

We are now ready for the major problems in thematic writing. There are two: (1) finding support for the theme, (2) organizing support for the theme.

FINDING MATERIAL TO SUPPORT THE THEME

A constant purpose of the thematic writer is to show the reasonableness of his judgment. He does this by presenting his evidence. He may find it necessary to explain some of his terms or to tell why he is interested in the subject, but his chief purpose is to set forth the basic theme support. This is not to say the writer argues. He may; but he may also be only describing a certain section of his world, physical or abstract, and his interpretation of it. No matter which it is, he has a theme and its supporting particulars put together in such a way as to show their connection. Material that does not reveal the truth of his theme is ignored as not useful, even though it may have some connection with the general subject. To put it in would be to destroy the unity of the theme and its supporting data and thus to blur the meaning.

What, from the point of view of an author, do supporting particulars consist of? The answer will almost solve the problem of what to say and relieve us of a common embarrassment when we have a thematic problem to work out, and the answer is easy. The most useful types of particulars are the following:

[4] From "The Theatre Has Swallowed a Tapeworm," by George Freedley. *The Saturday Review of Literature,* August 14, 1943.

1. Detail: descriptive and statistical
2. Illustration: anecdotes and examples
3. Experiment
4. Authority
5. Reason

When the particulars have been gathered and interpreted and the essay is ready to be written, the most frequent practice is to begin with a statement of the theme and to follow with the particulars. This order is generally followed, also, when the essay is made up of a series of themes. The theme may, however, find a place within the particulars or at the end of them. It may even be left out, but only if the particulars can be relied upon to cause the reader to frame it without a direct statement.

Detail

We shall consider two kinds of details: *descriptive* and *statistical.*

DESCRIPTIVE DETAIL

Before we attempt to say what a descriptive detail is, let us read a simple example of a judgment supported by simple details. This procedure is sound, for it gives us an illustration, putting us on the experience level.

Spring is in the air. The neighbor's children have appeared with marbles and roller skates, and their father says he has put out the furnace fire. The department stores, Grinnell's, Coyle's, and Winston's, have filled their windows with bathing suits, hoes and rakes, and lawn chairs. Four invitations to weddings came last week. The garage man has announced his $2.98 tune-up special. Grandma Williams has told her story of sulphur and molasses. The sun, friendlier now than two weeks ago, hangs in the kitchen window longer in the afternoon and is bright enough so that it glares on the sink. Baseball, vacations, sailing, strawberries, and the State Fish and Game Bureau make talk during the dinner hour. The signs are here. Spring has come.[5]

The descriptive detail, as can be seen, is a small part of a whole object. The doorknob is a detail of the door. Decorations are details of

[5] William Bleakley. Student paper.

the knob. A scale is a detail of a fish. The colors are details of a watch face. In the excerpt above all the details are part of spring: they are what spring is. We get our descriptive details primarily through sense experience: sight, smell, taste, touch, and hearing (to use the popular concept of what the senses are); but we may get them after our minds have used the original sense material and developed it into abstractions. We see *red* in the sunset, but we may think *color*. Either word in the right context may serve as a useful detail. The first is close to our original sense impression. The second is farther away. In general, *the words that are close to the senses will serve us best as descriptive details.* Even when our problem is thoroughly abstract, it is well to go to the senses for help. Especially is this true when we are writing for general readers. The learned philosopher may use his abstractions with his colleague at will, but it is only because the two of them have previously labored through much concrete material and have summed it up in their abstractions. They know what is meant. We do not; and because we do not, the details close to our experience are very helpful.

When we use details to support a judgment, the problem is to select the right ones. The solution is accurate and thorough observation, notebook in hand. The judgments probably come to us during our first observation. They may come quickly, or they may not come until long after all the data about a subject have been gathered and we have pondered over them carefully. The judgment comes to us as we see relationships among the details. The relationship is their meaning. The theme is a statement of the meaning. We look at a change in the details of our locality and we conclude that spring is coming, or summer, or autumn. Once we have the theme, we go back over the details for the most revealing and use them in the essay for support.

The next excerpt, written by a scientific observer, has more literary skill than our first one, and a more complex judgment; but the technique is the same. The theme is comparative, and as a result the details are paired. Because the comparison involves time, the pairing is arranged in a before and after pattern.

Now a gradual change took place in the looks of our salmon. In the sea he was plump and round and silvery, with delicate teeth, in a symmetrical mouth. Now his silvery color disappeared, his skin grew slimy, and the scales sank into it; his back grew black and his sides turned red—not a healthy red, but a sort of hectic flush. He grew poor; and his back, formerly as straight as need be, now developed an unpleasant hump at the shoulders. His eyes—like those of all enthusiasts who forsake eating and sleeping for some loftier aim—became dark and sunken. His symmetrical jaws grew longer and longer, and, meeting each other, as the nose of an old man meets his chin, each has to turn aside to let the other pass. And his beautiful teeth grew longer and longer, and projected from his mouth, giving him a savage and wolfish appearance.[6]

Though the author here has an artist's interest in details, as we can see from his way of presenting them, his main purpose is the scientific judgment that salmon change in appearance when they leave the sea to ascend their home rivers. He, or an assistant, procured salmon caught in the sea and in the river and compared them. The details followed as a matter of observation. The essay from which the excerpt is taken is meant for popular reading; hence its tone and its lack of technical vocabulary. If the essay had been technical, exact measurements would have been used: for "he grew poor," we might have found, "He lost three pounds for every hundred miles up the river."

The next excerpt uses the first and last sentences for the thematic statement. The first implies "death" by using the phrase "icy wind of loneliness." The last uses the word itself as the climax toward which the details lead.

. . . *Within, the houses breathed an "icy wind of loneliness,"* a characteristic phrase of Miss Wilkins herself. The clock had often gone dead, and no one could make it tick any longer. The parlour and the kitchen were the only rooms that visitors saw; and the kitchen was the scene of all the life,—that is, the social life,—which the house admitted. The parlour was commonly used for funerals only, and it sometimes had no carpet on the floor. There stood the shabby haircloth rocker and sofa, shabby alike from age and excess of care; for the haircloth had been house-cleaned through so many seasons that its holes represented much beside its years. A clove-apple, a nautilus shell shared the shelf with bits of china. Perhaps there were two or three pieces with lavender sprigs, each one an heirloom of incalculable value, as precious as a rajah's ruby to the members of the household. Framed coffin-plates hung on the walls, together with funeral-wreaths

6 From "The Story of a Salmon," by David Starr Jordan.

that had sometimes been woven from the hair of five generations. A great-grandsire's hair had provided the acorns, a grandmother's curls had yielded the leaves, and the lilies had come from the tresses of an aunt, which had turned a greenish yellow in her last illness. Uncle Abijah's hair had produced the poppies; the rosebuds were souvenirs of Lois. On the mahogany table lay Mrs. Hemans and Mrs. Sigourney, bound in red and gold, and perhaps a photograph-album with views of the Holy Land or pictures of uncles and cousins who had died or gone West. *Death pervaded the air, and what remained of life seemed to have reached a state of fossilization.*[7]

STATISTICAL DETAIL

The statistical detail is a number. We count the separate items we are working with and arrange the figures to reveal their meanings. Is there a switch of population from the country to the city? The census takers count the persons involved, make comparisons with earlier counts or as the result of questions asked of the persons, and reach conclusions. Has the fire department campaign to reduce false alarms been effective? Counts are taken and compared. Is a local outbreak of disease becoming so dangerous that state health authorities should be called in? A count will tell us. The person who writes up the results makes the appropriate judgment and then uses his figures to support it.

Tabulations and graphs are ways of handling statistical details to get at their meaning. Also, as any student knows who has looked into a book on statistics or has taken a course in them, many formulae have been devised for wringing the truth out of numbers. The formal tabulation and graph are within our reach, for we have all had some experience preparing them or studying them; and of course we can all use informal citation, the casual dropping of figures into an essay, to buttress a point.

As an example of formal statistical detail the following item is interesting. The judgment of the author, supported by the figures, is that English teachers vary in their estimate of student writing. (This problem would make an excellent student essay. After interviewing classmates and teachers, or after a class discussion, some conclusions help-

[7] From *New England: Indian Summer,* by Van Wyck Brooks, published by E. P. Dutton & Co., Inc., New York, copyrighted by Van Wyck Brooks.

ful to the teacher and to the students might be reached.) Note that the excerpt does not contain a statement of the judgment.

Hudelson showed variation in the judgments of seventeen English teachers in one school who had been satisfied with their ability to judge composition merit subjectively. The range of their judgments on seventeen themes on a percentage basis of scoring was 0-35, 35-60, 40-70, 70-83, 30-70, 30-60, 0-30, 30-75, 45-80, 30-60, 40-75, 48-80, 45-80, 50-83, 50-85, 27-50, and 45-80. To indicate further the serious injustice to pupils done by such wide divergence, Table XLI presents the percentage marks of ten teachers in the same school on eight compositions.

TABLE XLI

PERCENTAGE SCORES GIVEN TO EIGHT THEMES BY TEN TEACHERS IN THE SAME SCHOOL

Theme	*Teachers*										*Average*	*Average Deviation*
	A	B	C	D	E	F	G	H	I	J		
1....	55	88	71	80	60	90	86	85	90	70	77.5	±10.8
2....	70	89	78	90	83	94	85	85	92	79	83.6	± 6.7
3....	40	84	85	76	50	95	82	70	75	65	72.2	±12.7
4....	80	94	75	92	80	88	91	90	95	90	87.5	± 5.5
5....	75	87	79	90	70	70	81	79	85	75	79.1	± 5.3
6....	40	92	72	86	75	92	80	80	60	75	75.2	±10.8
7....	25	75	50	42	30	45	40	40	30	35	41.2	± 9.4
8....	30	75	62	38	40	45	45	35	45	40	45.5	± 9.2

Theme 3 received a score of 40 from one teacher and a score of 95 from another. Teacher B, a very liberal marker, would have "passed" all eight pupils: Teacher A would have given failing marks to six pupils. These two instructors were teaching different sections of the same composition course. Six teachers would have "passed" with an average score of 83 the pupil who wrote Theme 3, while four teachers would have caused him to fail with an average score of 56.[8]

With the figures for the two sets of papers and teachers before us, the judgment that the teachers vary in their marking is irrefutable. No one can deny it. The judgment stands, supported by figures.

[8] From *Summary of Investigations Relating to Grammar, Language, and Composition,* by R. L. Lyman. Reprinted by permission of The University of Chicago.

The following informal essay was written by a physical education student who was challenged on the difficulty of his course of study. To support his opinion that physical education students had to work hard in order to finish the course he went after the figures and marshaled them firmly. He had learned a technique for thematic writing as thoroughly as he had no doubt learned a technique for advancing a ball on the basketball court. He did not use graphs or tabulations, though under formal circumstances he could have.

The average student's and even professor's conception of the teacher training program in Physical Education revolves mainly about the intricacies of "raising arms upward overhead" and the fundamentals of shooting baskets. To them, that is all the knowledge that one needs in order to receive a Bachelor of Science degree in Physical Education. Unlike their curriculum, be it Social Studies, Business Education, or English, here is a snap course, a course in which all you do is wear a gym outfit, play ball and rest your cortical cells.

Nothing could be further from the truth than this interpretation of the teacher training program in Physical Education. Concerned as we are with those things near home, let me by briefly analyzing the program as given by New York University attempt to reveal why those students and professors are in error.

Like other courses, Physical Education, or Curriculum 24 as it is known, requires 128 points for successful completion. Of these 128 points, only 20 are in classes where the prospective educator wears a gym outfit! Surprised? In addition to these 20 points, we have only 6 more directly connected with the teaching and coaching of sports. This leaves us with 102 points that range from the structure of man to the philosophies of Aristotle and Plato.

Broken down numerically and by subjects, Curriculum 24 presents a true picture of the wide ramifications and diversities of the Physical Education program of teacher training. The embryo teacher must complete 12 points of English: written, spoken, and literary; 10 points of Social Studies and 12 points of Sociology, Psychology and Philosophy. He must undergo 3 points of Statistics, 4 points of Secondary Education, 8 points of Camping Activities and 2 points of First Aid. Does this appear like a snap course thus far?

Budding physical educators are also required to teach Health and Hygiene, observe and attempt to correct abnormal conditions of their pupils, supervise and administer playgrounds and recreation centers and become cognizant of the culture of the times. In addition they must take

18 points of Science, Physiology and Anatomy, courses which I dare any medical student to call "snap" courses.

All this must be mastered in addition to the other 26 points of games, coaching, running intramurals programs and the actual teaching of classes before one can become a physical educator in Curriculum 24.

Not everyone passes this "snap" course. As a freshman in 1938, I entered the university with a class of 138 aspiring physical educators. Today as the class of '41 we number 43! A loss of 95 students over a three year period testifies to the selectivity of Curriculum 24.

I should like to see the belittlers of my field take a course in Curriculum 24. The carnage would be terrific.[9]

Illustration

An illustration is a particular expression or instance of a truth. The Latin source of the word, *illustrare,* means "to light up"; and an illustration, therefore, is said to throw light upon one's meaning. It illumines.

Out of all the anecdotes that reveal a great man's trait, for instance, one is selected and told; and the trait stands illuminated. Out of all the examples that prove that the sea builds up land, for another instance, one or more are described; and the truth stands clear. The illustrations have point; they are aimed at understanding the theme, the judgment. Often they begin with some such phrase as *for example* and *for instance.* The phrase ties the illustrative material to the theme by forming a transition from one to the other, thus keeping the reader aware of the shift.

Illustration may be used to explain meanings as well as to support judgments. We saw how meanings are made clear by illustration when we studied Chapter 1. Composition books, for instance, are filled with them. A point is made about writing technique, and then illustrated. Our purpose here, however, is to show how illustrations help support a judgment.

The types of illustration we shall examine are two: *anecdotes* and *examples.*

[9] Dave Malachowsky. Student paper.

ANECDOTES

An anecdote is a short narrative or sketch used to make a point. It tells of an occurrence. Anecdotes are usually true—we are not speaking of fiction, where the illusion of truth is sufficient—because the validity of the point is lost if the particulars supporting it are known to be invented.

The following anecdote finds its source in personal experience:

Winds are advertisements of all they touch, however much or little we may be able to read them; telling their wanderings even by their scents alone.

. . . As an illustration of this, I may tell here that I breathed sea-air on the Firth of Forth in Scotland, while a boy; then was taken to Wisconsin, where I remained nineteen years; then, without in all this time having breathed one breath of the sea, I walked quietly, alone, from the middle of the Mississippi Valley to the Gulf of Mexico, on a botanical excursion, and while in Florida, far from the coast, my attention wholly bent on the splendid tropical vegetation about me, I suddenly recognized a sea-breeze, as it came sifting through the palmettos and blooming vine-tangles, which at once awakened and set free a thousand dormant associations, and made me a boy again in Scotland, as if all the intervening years had been annihilated.[10]

The following excerpt is composed of three anecdotes which, because the stories cover a long period of time, might be called sketches. They have anecdotal flavor and structure, and they illustrate a judgment that the author considers very important.

Many years ago there lived in the city of Boston a small boy whose days were spent in a singularly wearisome way. At the age of ten, when most boys are dividing their time between school and play, he was busy all day boiling soap, cutting wicks for tallow candles, filling candle molds, and otherwise drudging as assistant to his father in the soap and candle business. It was a business in which the father took an honest pride, and in thus apprenticing his youngest son to it, he did so with the expectation of giving him full charge and ownership in later years.

As it happened, though, the son's mind was filled with thoughts of

[10] From *The Mountains of California,* by John Muir. Reprinted by permission of D. Appleton-Century Company, Inc.

other things than soap and candles. He worked faithfully enough at the kettles and wicks and molds; but he worked with such scant enthusiasm and such little skill that his father soon perceived that he would never become an expert candle-maker. Bitterly disappointed, he nevertheless appreciated the folly of compelling his son to persist in an occupation manifestly uncongenial to him. To another and much older son he one day said:

"Will you take Ben into your printing shop? He will never be a successful chandler, but he may be a fair printer. At any rate, I wish you would give him a chance."

Into the printing shop, accordingly, young Ben went, somewhat against his will, for the handling of inky type seemed to him only a trifle less unpleasant than dealing with greasy molds. But he presently made the important discovery that through typesetting he was in a position both to gain knowledge for himself and to make knowledge available for other people by putting it into print. Forthwith he became interested in printing as he had never been in candle-making; also, he became fired with a desire to learn all he could about as many subjects as possible, and he developed, besides, an ambition to turn author and see his own thoughts take form on the printed page.

Behold him, then, sometimes sitting up the whole night long poring over Plutarch's *Lives, The Spectator,* Locke's *Essays,* and kindred works of information and literary power. Behold him in the fervor of his zeal turning vegetarian at the age of sixteen, because the greater cheapness of his meals would allow him more money for books. Behold him scribbling and rescribbling in the effort to give clear expression to the ideas forming in his mind as a result of his wide reading and hard thinking. Finally, behold him timidly slipping under the door of his brother's newspaper office an unsigned essay written in a disguised hand—an essay so good that, on publication, its authorship was variously ascribed to leading writers of the day.

Thereafter he toiled more industriously than ever—printing, reading, thinking, writing. Ere he was thirty he was widely known, and long before his death he was acclaimed on two continents as one of the wisest of men. We of today, looking back from the vantage point of more than a century later, feel that the praise of his contemporaries was not misplaced. For the whilom candle-maker who thus rose to eminence was none other than Benjamin Franklin, philosopher, scientist, diplomat, and apostle of America's freedom.

Take, similarly, the history of an English lad born some twenty years after Franklin died. More happily circumstanced, being the son of a successful physician, this boy was given all the advantages of a good schooling. But he did not seem to draw much profit from his lessons. In fact, as he himself has told us, both his father and his teachers were inclined to regard him as "rather below the common standard in intellect." To make matters worse from the father's point of view, he showed a marked distaste for the tasks of the schoolroom, and an equally marked fondness for vagabondage.

Gun in hand, he would roam for hours through verdant lanes or across the open country. "You care for nothing but shooting, dogs, and rat-catching, and you will be a disgrace to yourself and all your family," his father once predicted, mournfully. As the boy grew older, his propensity for idling seemed only to increase. In spite of this, hoping against hope that he would yet settle down to serious things, his father entered him at the University of Edinburgh, with the idea of fitting him for the practice of medicine. "It is no use," the boy frankly avowed, after a few months at Edinburgh. "I hate the work here, and I cannot possibly be a physician." So earnest were his protests that he was transferred to Cambridge University, on the understanding that he would study to be a clergyman.

At Cambridge, as good fortune would have it, he entered the natural history class of an eminent and enlightened scholar, Professor Henslow, who sent him into the woods and fields to make collections of plants and insects. Free again to roam under the clear blue skies, but this time with a lofty purpose set before his mind, a passion for achievement took possession of him. The boy whom other teachers had found dull and lazy proved himself, under Professor Henslow's inspiring guidance, a marvel of industry and mental vigor. There was no longer any thought of the "last resort" plan of putting him into the ministry. He would, he assured his now delighted father, devote his whole life to the study of nature's laws.

Thus it came about that, when his college days were over, he eagerly accepted an opportunity to accompany a government exploring expedition. During the long voyage in Southern seas he accumulated a remarkable collection of specimens. What was far more important, he brought back with him to England, after five years' absence filled with hardships, a mass of new ideas regarding fundamental principles in natural science—ideas which, being masterfully scrutinized and sifted, were afterwards to make him world-famous as Charles Darwin, originator of the doctrine of evolution.

Again, there was born in the German city of Salzburg, about the middle of the eighteenth century, a bright-eyed boy, the son of a Court musician.

As was inevitable by reason of his father's vocation, this child, from the hour he first opened his eyes and ears to the world about him, daily heard melody from violin, clavier, and harpsichord. Before he was three years old it was noticed that he not only seemed to take great delight in listening to music, but also that he often attempted with his little fingers to strike harmonious intervals on the clavier. His father, amused but impressed, offered to give him lessons; joyfully, the child accepted, and at once a start was made.

Thenceforth music dominated his waking thoughts. The toys of childhood were cast aside, and in their stead he played with the keyed and stringed instruments to which his father gave him ready access. Increasingly he astonished all around him with his unusual skill. By the time he was four he could play several minuets on the harpsichord; at five he was able to play the violin so well that he once assisted his father and a celebrated violinist in rehearsing six trios which the latter had recently composed.

Modest, unassuming, bending his every effort to progress in the art which had so fascinated him, the youngster passed in quick succession from one notable feat to another. On all sides the prediction was heard: "If this boy keeps on as he has begun, he will be one of the world-masters of music." Those who are familiar with Mozart's marvelous compositions for church, opera-house, and concert-room know well that the prediction was amply fulfilled.

Now, I have recalled these beginnings of the careers of Franklin, Darwin, and Mozart because they strikingly illustrate a profound psychological truth the significance of which can scarcely be over-estimated. It is a truth, to be sure, that has long been partially recognized. But its full meaning has not been—and could not be—appreciated until quite recently. Only within the past few years has scientific research effected sundry discoveries which make its complete recognition possible and of supreme importance—of such importance that practical application of the principles involved would make for an immediate and stupendous increase in human happiness, efficiency, and welfare.

Stated briefly, the truth in question is that success in life, meaning thereby the accomplishment of results of real value to the individual and to society, depends chiefly on sustained endeavor springing out of a deep and ardent interest in the tasks of one's chosen occupation.[11]

[11] From "The Importance of Being Interested," by H. Addington Bruce. *The Outlook*, July 18, 1914. Reprinted by permission of the author.

The stories of Franklin, Darwin, and Mozart were drawn from the author's reading. The story that follows comes from the author's personal experience. Something happened to him. He reflected upon its meaning. He then arranged the meaning and the happening in such a way that the meaning—the judgment—is apparent to his readers. Again, the statement of the judgment is kept for the end of the story.

Somehow or other in my later years at Berkeley, two professors, Moses and Howison, representing opposite schools of thought, got into a controversy, probably about their classes. They brought together in the house of one of them a few of their picked students, with the evident intention of letting us show in conversation how much or how little we had understood of their respective teachings. I don't remember just what the subject was that they threw into the ring, but we wrestled with it till the professors could stand it no longer. Then they broke in, and while we sat silent and highly entertained, they went at each other hard and fast and long. It was after midnight when, the debate over, we went home. I asked the other fellows what they had got out of it, and their answers showed that they had seen nothing but a fine, fair fight. When I laughed, they asked me what I, the D.S. [damned-stinker], had seen that was so much more profound.

I said that I had seen two highly-trained, well-educated Masters of Arts and Doctors of Philosophy disagreeing upon every essential point of thought and knowledge. They had all there was of the sciences; and yet they could not find any knowledge upon which they could base an acceptable conclusion. They had no test of knowledge; they didn't know what is and what is not. And they have no test of right and wrong; they have no basis for even an ethics.

Well, and what of it? They asked me that, and that I did not answer. I was stunned by the discovery that it was philosophically true, in a most literal sense, that nothing is known; that it is precisely the foundation that is lacking for science; that all we call knowledge rested upon assumptions which the scientists did not all accept; and that, likewise, there is no scientific reason for saying, for example, that stealing is wrong. In brief: there was no scientific basis for an ethics. No wonder men said one thing and did another; no wonder they could settle nothing either in life or in the academies.

I could hardly believe this. Maybe these professors, whom I greatly respected, did not know it all. I read the books over again with a fresh eye, and with a real interest, *and I could see that, as in history, so in other branches of knowledge, everything was in the air.* And I was glad of it.[12]

Though in this excerpt the last two paragraphs are an elaborate discussion of the point of the anecdote, the italicized parts make the clinching statement.

Anecdotes form a body of priceless material for the writer. They are quick to capture interest and therefore they make good beginnings. They lift dull and stale pages into lively reading. They create emphasis where a point is likely to slip by unnoticed. All this in addition to their main function of illumination and support of the judgment.

EXAMPLES

The example, as the term is used here, is meant to be any illustrative material distinct from the anecdote—that is, the example tells no story. The sports reporter might say that there are many brilliant shortstops in the big leagues this year, and then back up his judgment with suitable examples. The travel writer might say that there are mountains in the New World as magnificent as those in the Old, and then bring into his essay those he had in mind. The agricultural reporter might say that nowadays farmers have excellent labor-saving machines for harvesting crops, and then point out several that support his assertion.

Examples may be of different types. They may be objects, concrete or abstract. They may be case studies, such as a social worker gathers. They may be graphs and pictures. At times the example is given only a brief description. At other times the description is elaborate and lengthy.

The following excerpt contains several scantily developed examples:

The work of the sea, as we have seen, is constructive as well as destructive. It is stated that on one portion of the coast of England (the estuary of the Humber) about 290 square miles have been added to the coast, while on another (Fens of Lincolnshire), the area of the land has been increased more than 1000 square miles. It is stated that for every square mile washed away from portions of this coast, three square miles have

[12] From *The Autobiography of Lincoln Steffens.* Copyright, 1932, by Harcourt, Brace and Company, Inc.

been added on others. Moreover the sea-built land is on the whole, richer than that which was destroyed. A telegraph pole erected at a point on the English coast in 1873 was 300 feet inland in 1902. At Atlantic City, New Jersey, portions of the sand reefs are being built out while others are retreating. Hotels have had to be moved forward so as to be kept near the sea. The history of the town of Rye, England, is instructive as showing that the land may be attacked by the sea at one time and later be increased at the same point by the same agent. This town was once destroyed by the sea, but the site is now two miles inland.[13]

Here is another set of examples used to show the truth of a theme:

Gardiner was no centre of intellectual ferment but it read books and talked about them; and even wrote them. Caroline Swan's green haunt of the Muse was merely one of many gardens in the area cultivated for a century. Across the lane from Miss Swan, Laura E. Richards, daughter of Julia Ward Howe and of Samuel Gridley Howe, teacher of the deaf and blind, was pouring out a flood of girls' stories, and of nonsense rhymes which had the enchanting ripple and irrationality of the Bab Ballads. On Lincoln Street, not far from the Robinsons, lived Kate Vannah, half Irish by blood and all Irish by temperament, a poet and successful composer; a handsome, vain, amusing soul, bursting with personality. "Why have I never married? My dear, I was too eager after 'em!" Gertrude Heath, mellow and lovable, a homeopathic physician like Dr. Schumann, was a painter and illustrator, writing stories for *St. Nicholas* and finding a public for her sentimental or humorous verse. There were others, casual laborers in the literary vineyard, contributing now and again to this magazine or that; and others, who led lives of quiet study for no end except self-improvement, like old Sarah Whitmore, who, having mastered Latin and Greek, took up the study of Hebrew in middle life so that she might read the Old Testament, as well as the New, in the original. Her brother Nathaniel, a skinflint out of Horatio Alger, would quote Horace as he borrowed the broom from the office next to his own. In Farmingdale, just across the Cobbossee, a group of music-lovers gathered periodically to listen to a string quartette and mix good music with excellent wine. There was a club at whose meetings ladies in tight-fitting waists and bustles read papers on current events.[14]

[13] From *Geology: Physical and Historical,* by H. F. Cleland. Reprinted by permission of the American Book Company.

[14] From *Edwin Arlington Robinson: A Biography,* by Hermann Hagedorn. By permission of The Macmillan Company, publishers.

Experiment

An experiment is a test set up under controlled conditions to discover unknown facts upon which to base a judgment or to verify known facts and judgments. The experimenter reserves a definite judgment until the experiment is finished; then he concludes—that is, makes up his mind. If he has properly done his work, he is justified in his conclusions, for the experiment has pointed to them. Should he at any time later wish to defend his conclusions, a recapitulation, either on paper or in the laboratory, will help him. What he does is to write out fully the complete description of the experiment so that anyone qualified may repeat it in a laboratory, or he himself performs the experiment before qualified observers. Experiments range, of course, from the very simple to those so complicated that only a few persons can follow them and realize their implications. The young student will probably deal with simple experiments.

The two following selections are taken from a high school text in physics. They illustrate the connection between the experiment and the judgment drawn from it.

All freely falling bodies have the same acceleration. In Galileo's time people still believed that heavy objects fell faster than light objects. They believed, in other words, that the speed of a falling body depended upon its weight. But Galileo maintained that all bodies, if unimpeded by the air, fell the same distance in the same length of time. He insisted that the only thing that caused some objects—like pieces of paper or feathers—to fall more slowly than pieces of metal or coins was the resistance of the air. To convince his doubting friends and associates, he caused balls of different sizes and materials to be dropped at the same instant from the leaning tower of Pisa. They saw the balls start together and fall together, and they heard them strike the ground together. Some were convinced. But others, distrusting the evidence of their senses, returned to their rooms to consult the books of the old Greek philosopher Aristotle.

Later, when the vacuum pump was invented, the truth of Galileo's view was confirmed by dropping a feather and a coin in a vacuum tube.

We place a piece of metal and some light object, like a bit of paper or pith or a feather, in a long tube and pump out the air. When we suddenly invert the tube, the two objects fall side by side from the top to the bottom. If we open the stopcock, letting the air in again, and repeat the experiment, we find that the metal falls to the bottom first.[15]

Galileo's judgment concerning falling bodies is thus supported, first by his experiment and later by ours.

Every time our water pipes freeze and burst we get a convincing parallel demonstration of the following judgment and supporting experiment:

That the expansive force of water in freezing is enormous can be seen from the following experiment:

We fill a cast-iron bomb with cold water (free from air), close the hole with a screw plug, and put the bomb in a box of ice and salt (or, better, "dry ice"). When the water in the bomb freezes, the pressure inside increases more and more, and the bomb eventually explodes.[16]

We do not always need to describe in complete detail the experiment which supports our judgment. Most writing problems do not require it. We say enough to indicate the nature of the experiment, and that is all. A general background, a partial description is sufficient. If anyone is interested in finding out more detail, footnotes, bibliography, or general indication in the text of the sources show where to go.

All of us have come in contact with experiments in some way, reading about Archimedes floating in his bath or about Mendel studying peas, watching agents of the government set up test plots for the control of white pine blister rust or the corn borer, and performing for ourselves experiments in school laboratories or at home in the basement. All the material of such experimental activity is good evidence of the truth of certain judgments. The writer's aim is to tell according to his purpose as much as he needs of the experiment to support his judgment. If he wishes complete demonstration of truth, he will give a complete description. If he wishes only a general demonstration, a partial description is all he will give.

[15] From *Elementary Practical Physics,* by Newton Henry Black and Harvey Nathaniel Davis. Reprinted by permission of The Macmillan Company, publishers.

[16] *Ibid.*

Authority

The judgments of other persons may be used to support our own judgments. We can speak of the other persons as "our authorities." By this is meant only that backing supplied by, or from, someone who is an expert has the validity of his expertness and reputation. We are not saying that because someone in a position of authority says a thing is so, it is so and must be accepted. By every means we should test our authorities and reject them as soon as we find a good reason to question their judgment. To use authority, we simply go to the source and directly or indirectly quote what we find, giving the authority's name and being certain that none of the material is twisted or stated so fragmentarily that the authority is misrepresented.

Authority is good supporting material, and we can often call upon it. The two following are examples. In the second the exact sources of the borrowed support are meticulously given. In the first the authority's name is enough.

If we compare the general susceptibility of men and women to agreeable odors, apart from the question of sexual allurement, there can be little doubt that it is most marked among women. Groos pointed out that even among children little girls are more interested in scents than boys, and the investigations of various workers, especially Garbini, have shown that there is actually a greater power of discriminating odors among girls than among boys. In America Alice Thayer showed that girls are considerably more influenced by odor in their likes and dislikes than are boys. Marro went further and in an extended series of observations on girls before and after the establishment of puberty, he found reason to believe that girls acquire an increased susceptibility to odors when sexual life begins, although they show no such increased powers as regards the other senses. It may be added that some women acquire a special olfactory hyperaesthesia during pregnancy. Even in old age, as Vaschide's experiments showed, women preserve their olfactory superiority over men. On the whole, it would appear that, as Van de Velde and various other gynecologists now agree, women are more affected, and more frequently affected, than are men by olfactory impressions.[17]

[17] From *Psychology of Sex*, by Havelock Ellis. By permission of Random House, Inc.

The second illustration is from a letter to a newspaper, apropos of the exchange of United States destroyers for bases in the western Atlantic. The letter has the formality of legal discussion.

> The United States has consistently adopted this [see italics at the end of excerpt] attitude in practice, long before the adoption of Hague Convention XIII. For instance, Secretary of State Day wrote to Ambassador John Hay in London, June 25, 1898, as follows: "It is a grave offense against the law of nations for a neutral government to sell a man-of-war to a belligerent."
>
> Moreover, the same edition of Oppenheim relied upon by Professor Sack states in another and more appropriate section (Section 321): "If a State remains neutral, it violates the impartiality by furnishing a belligerent with troops or men-of-war." This is so commonplace as hardly to require corroboration, were it not challenged by the present action. For instance, George Grafton Wilson (International Law, 9th ed., New York, 1935, p. 328) says: "The neutral State may not furnish to a belligerent any assistance in military forces, supplies of war, loans of money, or in any similar manner." And in support of this statement, Wilson quotes the English authority, William E. Hall (International Law, 8th ed., by Pearce Higgins, London, 1924, p. 711): "The general principle that a mercantile act is not a violation of a state of neutrality is pressed too far when it is made to cover the sale of munitions or vessels of war by a State."
>
> *In other words, a private citizen of a neutral State, in the absence of municipal law to the contrary, is free to engage in war-vessel trade at his own risk, while a neutral State itself may never engage in war-vessel trade with a belligerent.*[18]

A type of authority nowadays popular is that of the "little man," sometimes called the "man in the street." Writers wanting to interpret trends or to explain the significance of some event like to interview ordinary persons and to use their opinions as the basis of a judgment. This is sound procedure if enough persons are questioned and if they are questioned about matters where their experience and judgment count. In a democracy the public mind is made up of many conflicting minds brought finally into harmony by the principle of majority rule. The average citizen is therefore an authority. What he

[18] From a letter to The New York *Times,* by Herbert Wright, Dec. 15, 1940. Reprinted by permission of the author's estate and The New York *Times.*

thinks is important, and a writer is justified in going to him for backing.

The following excerpt, written by sociologists, contains two judgments regarding the influence of automobiles on family life. Though the authors switch, at the end of each paragraph, from authority to statistics, we are to note especially how they use authority.

Many families feel that an automobile is justified as an agency holding the family group together. "I never feel as close to my family as when we are all together in the car," said one business class mother, and one or two spoke of giving up Country Club membership or other recreations to get a car for this reason. "We don't spend anything on recreation except for the car. We save every place we can and put the money into the car. It keeps the family together," was an opinion voiced more than once. Sixty-one per cent of 337 boys and 60 per cent of 423 girls in the three upper years of the high school say that they motor more often with their parents than without them.

But this centralizing tendency of the automobile may be only a passing phase: sets in the other direction are almost equally prominent. "Our daughters [eighteen and fifteen] don't use our car much because they are always with somebody else in their car when we go out motoring," lamented one business class mother. And another said, "The two older children [eighteen and sixteen] never go out when the family motors. They always have something else on." "In the nineties we were all much more together," said another wife. "People brought chairs and cushions out of the house and sat on the lawn evenings. We rolled out a strip of carpet and put cushions on the porch step to take care of the unlimited overflow of neighbors that dropped by. We'd sit out so all evening. The younger couples perhaps would wander off for half an hour to get a soda but come back to join in the informal singing or listen while somebody strummed a mandolin or guitar." "What on earth *do* you want me to do? Just sit around home all evening!" retorted a popular high school girl of today when her father discouraged her going out motoring for the evening with a young blade in a rakish car waiting at the curb. The fact that 348 boys and 382 girls in the three upper years of the high school placed "use of the automobile" fifth and fourth respectively in a list of twelve possible sources of disagreement between them and their parents suggest that this may be an increasing decentralizing agent.[19]

[19] From *Middletown*, by Robert S. Lynd and Helen Merrell Lynd. Copyright, 1929, by Harcourt, Brace and Company, Inc.

Reasons

Reasons may be used to support a theme. The only tricky element in their use is that each reason is a new judgment requiring its own support and finding it in details, illustrations, experiment, and authority, whichever is appropriate. Each of the reasons properly supported is part support of the main theme.

The structure can be illustrated with a simple outline. Let us suppose someone asks you if four years of college are worth the effort. You immediately organize in your mind your answer, perhaps something like this:

(Theme) Yes, four years of college are worth the effort.
- A. (Because) They add greatly to one's wisdom.
- B. (Because) They give one professional training.
- C. (Because) They give one a permanent circle of friends.
- D. (Because) They provide an available route to prestige.

You can see at a glance that each of the reasons is itself a judgment concerning *part* of the worth of college. Each supports the main judgment, but each needs its own support. You need to present some evidence that college will add to one's wisdom and that it will provide an available route to prestige. If you can support your reasons, you support your main theme that college is worth the effort it costs. If you were to write out your argument, you would probably use the first paragraph to state your main point and follow it with a series of paragraphs, each given to a reason and its supporting data. The first half of the essay "*Pro* and *Con*—Abolish Football?", page 283, is a good example of a major theme supported by reasons. "Mr. Pro" has four reasons to support his judgment that football should be abolished as a major sport in college. Each of his reasons is in turn supported by data. If you are curious about the technique, or about the future of football, glance at the essay. The reasons are in italics and can be quickly found.

Detail, illustration, experiment, authority, and reason—these are the particulars with which to support and elaborate our judgments. These are the materials with which we build our thoughts. Properly brought to bear upon a theme, they attest its truth, for they are the particulars of the truth, its substance. In order to weaken or destroy the judgment, we must first attack the particulars. Failing in that, the judgment stands.

The communication of the judgment to a reader is the author's purpose. He is not interested in facts for their own sake but for the sake of the light they throw on his judgment. The facts he uses make his judgment convincing and clear. That is their purpose. This means that he sifts all the extraneous items from among the facts and then selects for exhibit from the items remaining those which are the most convincing and clear. If the data are properly chosen, they convince by their self-evident relationship to the judgment. They communicate meaning accurately because they limit it to specific and verifiable matter on or close to the experience level of the writer and the reader.

Data are often used in combinations. Rarely does an author depend upon only one kind. Sometimes details are used as a kind of cement between blocks, say, of anecdote or authority. The procedure is a good one; but we may need to be warned that an indiscriminate mixture may cloud the lucidity of the data. A theme ultimately depends upon the self-evident significance of its data. Any confusion among them is likely to cause a fatal blur. Prevention of confusion is a problem in the construction of the essay—its architecture, its frame or outline. We need methods of arranging judgments and their support so that the best results are obtained. Some of the methods are described in the next section of this chapter, "Organizing the Thematic Essay."

Exercises

A. Analyze the essay "Plenty of Grass in Parks," page 245, for its theme and the types of data used to support it. Study the questions on technique that follow the essay and be ready to discuss them in class.

B. Analyze the essay "The Cat: Vicious Predator or Harmless Pet?", page 273, for its theme and the types of data used to support it. Study the questions on technique that follow the essay and be ready to discuss them in class.

C. State the most likely types of data to support the following judgments and see if you can think up some specific items that you can present orally. If you feel like it, use one of the themes and your data for a short paper.

1. Carelessness is expensive.
2. A fool and his money are soon parted.
3. Co-educational schools serve good purposes.
4. A union of all the democracies is a step for peace.
5. Forest fires menace the abundant life.
6. Dew does not fall.
7. School children nowadays have schools different from those of their grandparents.
8. O. Henry was a clever writer.
9. Some of Dreiser's novels are written in a naturalistic vein.
10. Winters are not the hardship that they used to be.
11. Eroded land can be reclaimed for efficient use.

D. Prepare a series of short essays, each containing one theme supported by one of the following types of data. Draw on your own resources of experience and study for the themes and the data.

1. Detail: descriptive or statistical
2. Illustration: anecdote or example
3. Experiment
4. Authority
5. Reasons (Support the reasons with data)

ORGANIZING THE THEMATIC ESSAY

Thematic essays fall into several distinct organizational patterns. A knowledge of them will not solve all the difficulties that rise whenever we sit down to compose an essay involving judgment, but it will go a long way toward solving the most pressing of them. The pattern is the basic architecture of the essay, the scheme or arrangement set up to present the judgment and their support. The three patterns described here are common—and indispensable. No writer interested in communicating judgment can get along without them. Anybody capable of making judgments can master them. Each is now described in turn and illustrated with a complete essay accompanied by an analysis for minute study.

First Pattern

Scattered through the body of our daily reading, perhaps a fifth of it, are essays which have one central judgment to communicate, *and only one*. The judgment is the key to the entire essay. Everything in the essay bears on the judgment. The author considers his subject, reaches one conclusion, and uses all his material to establish that conclusion. All the details, illustrations, experiments, authorities, and reasons are aimed at the one conclusion. Often, of course, it is necessary to make definitions, to set limits, to clear away negative aspects of the theme, or to provide other background; but even this is theme support in that it clears the ground for direct data.

The following essay makes one central point—italicized where it is stated most clearly. The point, once it is stated and the ground cleared, is split into halves. Each half is supported in turn. The theme of each half is a reason for believing the central theme. The essay therefore has a structure like that discussed above under reasons.

Theme: This country is making cultural progress in a new and exciting way.

I. Millions of Americans are becoming more sensitive to beauty and are stirring with creative energy.

II. Many new arts have sprung up.

When each of the secondary themes has been supported with proper data, the main theme is also supported. The whole is supported part by part.

Our Widening American Culture

Main theme first stated here.

Under pressure of more dramatic affairs, we Americans are, I believe, failing to notice a salient—and cheerful—fact about our country: the flowering, or at least the budding, of an American culture of which we may well be proud.

Explanation of the author's point of view.

This flowering is unlike any previous one in history. We must not expect to see duplicated here what happened in the Athens of Pericles or the Florence of the

Medici, or, for that matter, in nineteenth century England or France. For the essence of what is happening in America is that it is new, that it takes unprecedented forms, and that it is manifold.

Negative aspects of the point of view.

I realize that anybody who speaks in such terms as these may seem to be—in the expressive phrase of the day—sticking his neck out. In the American culture of 1940 one can find plenty of evidences of undisciplined or corrupt taste. Listen to some of our radio programs; read the concentrated pap which passes for fiction in many of our magazines for the millions; sit through some of the Class B pictures at the movies; or look at the monotonous suburban developments and devastated regions which lie at the edges of our American cities, and you may well wonder what in heaven's name I am talking about.

Theme stated positively.

Nevertheless I stand by my guns. I think this country is making cultural progress in a new and exciting way.

Definition of the key word in the theme.

To most people "culture" may suggest a gentleman sitting in his library with a volume of Montaigne in his hand, a glass of old port at his elbow, and a quotation from the original Greek on his lips—familiarity with, and appreciation of, old and tested things. But culture may also mean the natural feeling for beauty that went into the building of old New England houses and Pennsylvania barns—a sense of order and graciousness, whether cultivated or instinctive, and whether accompanied by wide learning or not. And any culture is sterile which is not animated by the creative impulse. The periods which we think of as the great flowerings of culture were periods not merely of appreciation but, preëminently, of production; indeed, any culture is sterile which is not animated by the devouring curiosity of the discoverer and the fierce energy of the experimenter.

In these latter aspects American culture is showing special progress. Whereas no other cultural flowering in history has involved more than a small fraction of the population, *today millions of Americans are becoming more sensitive to beauty, and in them creative energy is stirring.*

First supporting reason. Followed by transition to data: statistics and illustrations.

Look, for example, at music—from that same radio that brings us so much shoddy entertainment. Toscanini's weekly symphony concert is enjoyed by an audience of four and a half million. It would take 60 Yale Bowls to seat this astronomical number of listeners. Walter Damrosch's NBC music appreciation hour is heard each week by several million. Have any such opportunities for the masses to hear good music ever before existed—and been taken advantage of? And it has all come about in the past 15 years. Incidentally, the highly intelligent "Information Please," which recently won an award by *The Saturday Review of Literature* for distinguished service to American literature, is said to be heard by 12,000,000 members of that radio public which we used to be told had 13-year-old minds!

More data: statistics and illustrations. Note transition.

Participation in the *making* of music has sharply increased, too, even though the piano is no longer a standard household ornament. Note some 35,000 school orchestras. Note how many of our school and college glee clubs have become choruses singing fine music. Recently I heard the madrigal club of a small West Virginia college lead off, not with "The Bullfrog on the Bank," standard fare 30 years ago, but with the classic chants of Palestrina. The extraordinary growth of such institutions as the Berkshire Music Festival is another agreeable sign of our musical times.

Transition. More data: illustrations.

Next, consider reading. It is true that book sales have shown little increase during the past generation. But there can be small doubt that the books which now sell most widely represent, on the average, a considerably higher level of quality. There is a world of difference between the solid fiber of John Steinbeck's "The Grapes of Wrath" (the leading fiction best seller of 1939) and the sentimental gush of Florence Barclay's "The Rosary" (which topped the lists in 1910 and 1911, against stiff competition by Harold Bell Wright's "The Winning of Barbara Worth"). We must remember, too, that the book as a form of entertainment must now compete with the radio and the movies; while the book-reading public is now underpinned—and presumably reduced—by a gigantic magazine-reading public.

Fifty years ago there was not a single magazine in the

United States with a circulation of a million. Now there are twenty-six. Many of the most popular periodicals are full of literary marshmallows and shy at ideas which might possibly offend a perceptible number of readers or advertisers; yet I think it is safe to say that if we take these magazine as a group, and think how many good things are to be found in them, they offer a creditable exhibit of mass reading. There has been nothing in Europe to compare with this vast magazine public; and those European magazines which have long been famous for their high quality—such, for instance, as *Punch*—have had tiny audiences by any American standard.

Transition. More data: illustrations and statistics.

Turn to the fine arts. Popular magazines like *Life* are now reproducing paintings by old masters and contemporary Americans. "A Treasury of Art Masterpieces" (price $10) is a recent best-seller. There has been a notable increase in the sale of good color reproductions of masterpieces for home decoration. Our museums are becoming active agencies for adult education, and their turnstiles are clicking. The recent Picasso exhibit at New York's Museum of Modern Art was attended by 99,503 people during its fifty-one days; the Italian masters, at the same museum, were seen in seventy-three days by 277,794 people —an astonishing record.

Transition. More data: statistics and illustrations.

Remarkable, too, is the growth in educational opportunity. If many of our universities have elephantiasis—and also foot-ballitis—this is because the number of students in American colleges and universities has increased ten-fold since 1900. The inspiring fact that millions of Americans have wanted a higher education for their children has put a heavier load on the educational machinery than it could carry without creaking here and there. Yet our professional schools have been strikingly improved; American medical education, for example, has been revolutionized for the better in the past fifty years. And those new patrons of education and science, the great foundations, are contributing hundreds of millions both to lift the standards of teaching and research and to seek out young talent and give it the chance it deserves. I have heard it stated, by people who should know, that there is now small chance that any young man of authentic scientific genius, whether in Pennsylvania, Georgia, or South Dakota, will go unassisted if he needs assistance.

More ***data.***

Do not forget what the WPA has done for men who had not sold a picture for years—and were given post-office murals to paint; for half-starved musicians who found themselves playing to big audiences in WPA orchestras. Call this boondoggling if you will; but does it not represent a new conception of the responsibility of the public to see that potential artists have a chance to be artists, no matter what their circumstances?

Summary: a repetition of the first secondary theme. Followed by a statement of the second: another reason for believing in a flowering of culture.

Yes, the democratic base of our culture has been widened.

I should also like to remind you how many new arts have sprung up beside the seven arts of tradition. Let us forget for a moment the traditional assumption that one measures the state of a culture chiefly in terms of such familiar vehicles as books, plays, paintings, sculpture, architecture, and music. Let us assume that other vehicles may offer a means of expressing the impulse to create and enjoy beauty, and let us look about us.

First ***new art.***

New arts? One thinks immediately of the movies, which after a long period of high technical competence and singular evasion of reality are now showing signs of growing up: witness that documentary masterpiece, "The River," and such recent pictures as "Rebecca," "The Grapes of Wrath," and "Wuthering Heights." One thinks with even more assurance of that remarkable subdivision of the movies, the animated cartoon drama, realizing that in Disney we have an artist using a medium which hardly existed twenty years ago.

Second new art.

Note the remarkable increase of interest in photography; hundreds of thousands of people, old and young, are taking pictures—and developing them in their own darkrooms, in the true spirit of the amateur in the arts.

Third ***new art.***

Drive over the magnificent parkways in the outskirts of our cities, and see how engineer and landscape architect have joined hands to create majestic avenues in peculiarly 20th-century style. Look at our new bridges and dams, works of art as well as of utility. Is there any one of us who looks at, let us say, the George Washington Bridge without a lift of the heart at the extraordinary beauty, especially at night when the great sweep of its cables is picked out with lights?

To look at some of the photographs in Walter Dorwin Teague's new book, "Design This Day" (such as the pictures of New York's Bronx-Whitestone Bridge, with its clean, undecorated, soaring arches, or of a new Texaco gas station) is to feel that this is the sort of thing we Americans do best, this is where our own peculiar genius has full play.

Fourth new art. Do not the incredible effects achieved in lighting the New York World's Fair demonstrate the exciting possibilities of another virtually new art—that of lighting with color?

Fifth new art. Think of the strides made in applying the principles of functional design. No automobile manufacturer decides upon his new model nowadays without anxious consideration of the way purchasers will react to the grace and sweep of its lines. And I wonder if until the past decade a designer ever planned a railroad train as a harmonious unit, as some new streamliners were planned.

Note the gay use of color in the equipment of a modern kitchen. Look at some of Frank Lloyd Wright's or Albert Kahn's factories; why, even factories and their machinery —or the best of Woolworth's glassware—are being built as if intended to be looked at! The packaging of goods has been revolutionized. Little by little we are re-learning that useful things can be beautiful, learning that millions of people like them to be beautiful. Pull out a pile of magazines of twenty years ago and lay them beside their counterparts of today; in type and format the advance has been remarkable. Their improvement has extended to books and even to the designing of letterheads; if you occasionally receive, as I do, a letter from an office which has not changed its letterheads within the memory of the oldest employee, you will wonder who could ever have hit upon such an absurd combination of discordant types.

Sixth new art. We see, too, the beginnings of an art essentially new to America in town and regional planning. The overall design in New York's Rockefeller Center and our beginning attempts—as at Radburn, New Jersey—to lay out villages on new patterns for the motor age are steps toward the development of new techniques for harmonizing and rationalizing the work of architects, landscape architects, engineers, and what we might call social engineers. Contrast the ramshackle hodgepodge of old-style amusement parks with the efficient beauty of Jones Beach, Long Island, where 100,000 people may park their cars and bathe and picnic without traffic jams or overcrowding and, miraculously, without littering the oceanside!

Seventh new art.

I live in New York near an avenue of department stores whose windows provide an ever-changing spectacle of bold patterns in color and light and ingenious, imaginative compositions; and as I stroll up this avenue at night, I notice how many other strollers are enjoying the show as one might enjoy a visit to a gay museum. A generation ago nobody dreamed of arranging the round-eyed manikins in shop-windows with an eye to color harmonies and compositional effects.

It never occurs to most people who revel in the shop-window effects of 1940 that they are rendering art judgments. They think they are outside the sacred enclosure of the arts. But they are inside it all the time. For the fences have been moved.

Beginning of the end. Summary and explanation.

Very rapidly we Americans are getting away from the Colonial attitude. Already it is a long time since we took it for granted that American novels should be respectable imitations of the best English works. It is several years since most of our literary *emigrés* returned from Montparnasse to discover that America was a good place to write in and about. Now we know we have our own traditions in a literary sense, we are grown up. And we are beginning, too, to be far less subservient in other arts. If we still make pseudo-Venetian furniture in Grand Rapids, still design bank buildings to look like Parthenons, we are apparently approaching the end of this phase. Our new streamlined trains are not Byzantine, or Louis XV, or Dutch Colonial.

I do not say that this national culture independence is wholly good. The classicist will hasten to remind us that there is little to be gained by throwing away the past—and of course he is right. And we want no tariff walls against the best modern products of foreign civilizations. Our American culture must not try to walk alone, without benefit of the past or of the contributions of its neighbors. Yet what is to grow in our soil must be what is adapted to that soil. We may compare, we may learn, but I am glad we are coming to build for ourselves. For that is the only way in which anyone can build greatly.

One closing word: if I have said little about the peaks of our cultural landscape, if I have dodged the question whether our finest products in arts and letters are better today than they used to be, or better than they are elsewhere, this, I must confess, is because I would prefer to dodge a question on which there would inevitably be endless wrangling. One may be conscious, as one drives across country, that one is climbing on to rising ground, and yet lack the surveyor's instruments to judge the precise altitude of the surrounding summits. I prefer to focus your attention upon the undeniable groundswell of the land all about us.

Repetition of the central theme.

Whether or not the very finest things that we produce are better than they used to be, we Americans are a distinctly more mature people, a more culturally enlightened people, than we were a generation ago; and we appear to be better off for the participation of the millions in cultural things that were once considered chiefly the affair of the few.

Whenever I hear anybody lamenting a supposed lack of authentic contemporary American masterpieces, I am tempted to quote to him those familiar lines of Arthur Hugh Clough's:

> In front the sun climbs slow, how slowly!
> But westward, look, the land is bright! [20]

[20] "Our Widening American Culture," by Frederick Lewis Allen. *The Saturday Review of Literature,* June 29, 1940. Reprinted by permission of the author, *The Saturday Review of Literature* and *The Reader's Digest.*

Exercises

A. Prepare a class discussion of the following essays: "Plenty of Grass in Parks," page 245, "Grizzlies Are Bad Actors," page 257, and "The Blind Do It *Better*," page 262. Your interest will be mainly in the theme and data, but note also any definitions, transitional devices, or other structural elements that you find. Note how the authors keep their supporting data focused on the theme.

B. Write an essay, of about a thousand words, in which you support one central theme. Underline your first statement of the theme. In the margin of the manuscript label the types of support you use. Suggested themes follow. Select one of them if you wish, or use one that you think of yourself. It is best that you write on a topic with which you are already familiar, but you may draw on any source for additional material.

1. "Strip and get out" is a disastrous logging method.
2. Classical literature depends heavily upon magic and superstition for material.
3. Milk deliveries in small towns should be made from a central milkshed.
4. Advertising is sometimes deliberately misleading.
5. The study of etymology teaches one history and mythology.
6. Football should not be abolished as an intercollegiate sport.
7. Intramural sports have values that intercollegiate sports cannot supply.
8. Swimming pools may spread dangerous diseases.
9. Examinations are not popular teaching instruments.
10. Digest magazines do not keep their readers up to date in essential literature or in current events.
11. Much can be said against the elective system of education as practiced by most colleges and universities.

Second Pattern

In the essay, "Our Widening American Culture," the author used his whole space to establish one central theme. After examining his subject, he found a judgment that was so important to him that he wanted to spend all his energy on it. He might, however, have reached several judgments parallel in type. If he had, his essay would have been concerned with a series of themes, each a minor theme that could have been left out without marring the value or lucidity of those left in. His whole essay, apart from the beginning and the concluding remarks, would have been a succession of theme developments.

The important new element introduced by this pattern is the series of themes. The methods of development are the same as before: details, illustrations, experiments, authorities, and reasons. Because the essay space has to be divided into several sections, each theme is generally given a relatively short development; but an elaborate study, such as a treatise, could use long and complex developments.

The following essay, an evaluation of experience in factory work, provides us with a good case study of judgments in series. The author has several points to make about American factories and the men who work in them. After his opening remarks, he presents his points one by one, supporting each as he comes to it. The phrasing of the last two paragraphs clearly reveals that the author intends to evaluate his experience, that is, to reach conclusions about it. He could have indicated this intention at the start of the essay. Most authors would have.

For purposes of compression the essay as reprinted here has been abridged, but the structural pattern has not been interfered with. Each of the parallel themes has been italicized for accurate identification.

In an American Factory

Preliminary material concerned with getting the job and with the factory setting.

When one gray, foggy morning in the beginning of 1937 I got off the train in Cleveland, I became dismayed at the thought of what lay before me. I did not know a soul in this city. I had never done physical work before. I wanted to return to New York where I had friends. But there was no more money for another train fare and no way out. As I stood in the cold, damp mist I felt weak for a moment.

"Which is the way to the X Company?" I asked a passer-by. He pointed to a waiting trolley car.

Rolling along the dingy, interminable avenue, I began to whistle. The morning sun pierced through the torn rags of dirty fog, and slowly a feeling of glory descended upon me. I was following the old trail that for forty years before me had been trodden by those countless thousands of immigrants from Yugoslavia who had helped to build America. With a few borrowed dollars in my pocket I was on my way to work in an American factory. "It's a great thing," I said to myself.

It was bitter cold and a heavy snowfall set in as I walked through the gloomy, smoky industrial district to put on overalls for the first time. The huge plant, covering two blocks, all in steel and concrete, was run by electricity. Passing through enormous rooms, I saw countless machines swinging their metal arms through the air like fantastic octopuses, hissing furiously, and drowning in their roar the voices of men. Over them were bending rough, athletic-looking workers, with rolled-up sleeves and black caps, their faces grim and smeared with oil and grease, their eyes intent.

The so-called "turret lathe" was manufactured in this shop. This is a machine which in its turn makes tools and machine parts. You can fabricate almost anything with it, from automobile parts to bullets.

The factory itself was spotless. I had seen orderly European shops, but they had not gleamed with such beautiful cleanliness.

I was assigned to the second shift. Through underground passages I was led to the Assembly, another huge room where the finished parts of turret lathe machines were put together, tested, and taken apart for shipment. The workers cast curious glances at the newcomer. They were amused at my clumsy attempts to punch the clock and showed me a vacant locker along the left wall where I changed clothes. Then, at four o'clock, the note of the factory bell sounded in my ears, and our shift started off like a regiment toward the machines in the center. Holding our tool boxes in our hands, we waited in line for the foreman to assign us our jobs.

First of the series of themes. Supported with details of rough work.

I did rough work on that first night. I swept the floor and picked up waste and dirt with my bare hands. I carried heavy machine parts in my arms or on my shoulders. I screwed big pipes together. A compassionate worker showed me how to hold a file, and with it I smoothed off the edges of five push-button plates. Within fifteen minutes my hands were blistered, my arms impregnated with black metal dust and machine oil, and my mouth full of grease. When I was through at midnight the muscles of my feet, legs, fingers, hands, arms, and back ached terribly. I dragged myself home and slept like a dead man. "How do you feel?" the foreman asked me as we washed up the following night. I shrugged my shoulders. He winked at another worker and laughed: "It'll do him good; in three weeks he'll have muscles like Popeye the Sailor."

Second theme. Supported with details.

The factory reminded me of a European dictatorial state, where bureaucrats plan and order and citizens work and obey. The board of the Company was the government, and the workers were the people, ruled through a centralized hierarchy of officials and controlled by a mechanized system of registration, bookkeeping, time cards, and punch clocks. Like citizens of authoritarian states, we did our individual assignments without knowing their purpose or the general plan of work. I met a worker whose specialty was to assemble gear boxes to the turret lathe machines and who had no idea what the machines were for. The foreman was our supreme visible authority. With his superiors we could not communicate. And the president, with his board members and directors, sat high above us like an invisible, unapproachable god. Watchmen were stationed inside and outside the building to let nobody in or out except on a special permit. We even had our numbers. Mine was 1941.

Third theme. Supported with details and an ironic comment.

I was struck by the contrast between the American worker's political freedom and the rigid regimentation of his forty-hour week. The French worker cannot conceive a personal freedom which does not include a certain leisureliness at work. So he must work six days a week if the production is not to lag and the production costs to rise. The American worker pays for his two free days by straining his energies under a mechanized discipline during the other five. A German-American worker, who previously had been employed in an automobile plant, said to me: "What are you talking about? This machine shop is a fine place to work. On my last job, after we'd won the sit-down strike, the Company made us punch our cards even when we went to the toilet!" I have often wondered whether the willingness of the American worker to submit to such regimentation might not be due, not only to his sense of efficiency but also to a general American trait. In spite of their fundamental belief in the democratic form of government, Americans show a certain predilection for personal rule and the "one man" system in their group and business activities. In no other free country are the significant terms "chief" and "boss" so frequently heard.

Fourth theme. Supported with illustrations.

We were only twenty in our group in the Assembly Room, but we were of fourteen different nationalities: Serbs, Slovenes, Croats, Italians, Hungarians, Rumanians, Czechs, Germans, Poles, Swedes, Englishmen, Scotchmen, Irishmen—even Americans. When, later, I was transferred to other departments, I found Slovaks and Lithuanians in addition. Of course only the older men were foreign-born. The young workers were born in this country, mostly of foreign parentage at least on one side. They hardly spoke the native languages of their parents and cared little about their old countries. During an entire year I never witnessed a nationalistic dispute among these people. There was something humorous about our racial differences in this American shop. We cracked jokes at one another and imitated the various foreign accents in our English speech. There was an Italian who never took offense when called "Spaghetti." A pro-Hitler German laughed every time we grotesqued the Nazi salute and yelled "Heil Hitler!" at him. "Hey, you! You took our country!" shouted a Hungarian at me from his machine one day, referring to Yugoslavia's annexation of southern Hungarian provinces after the World War. "Sure!" I retorted, swinging my hammer; "you had us for a thousand years, and it's our turn now!" We both laughed. And yet I knew that in Europe, or even in their native-quarter saloons, these same fellows would fight bitterly on less provocation.

Fifth theme. Supported with illustrations.

The stories of some of the immigrant workers were tragic. There was an emaciated Scotchman with a finely chiseled face and trembling hands, who collapsed nearly every week and had to be sent home, his eyes glassy. Years before he had contracted tropical malaria working for a British company in India. A Swede, with all the symptoms of stomach ulcers, lips tightened, skin earthen, drilled and hammered doggedly. From time to time he crouched down behind his machine to endure silently an intolerable pain. A poor Italian, his wife long dead, had to leave his children without supervision while he worked at night in the shop. Almost every year his eldest daughter brought him an illegitimate child. She had been only sixteen when she had the first one.

A Croat with an ambassador's face had been worth fifty thousand dollars before the depression. Left without a cent, he was prevented by his children from committing suicide, and went to work in the shop. Another Croat was picked up in 1903 at the age of nineteen in a desolate mountain region of Croatia by the agents of an American railroad company, who took him away from his sheep and shipped him off to America. On his arrival in Pennsylvania he was lined up with many others in an open field. The foremen stripped off their coats and examined their muscles as if they had been cattle or African slaves. Still another countryman of mine told me that he came here at the age of thirteen to fell trees with the Negroes in the forests of Virginia. He is a fine machinist now and speaks good English. He made a very significant statement to me: "Nobody knows how many dramas are buried in American shops. Most of our people do not take the trouble to learn English. And they never will as long as they live in racial colonies."

Sixth theme. Supported with an illustration.

Yet most of the immigrants loved America with a peculiar sense of pride. "We are told to go back where we came from," exclaimed a Serbian worker from California. "No, sir! This is our country. And our affection for it is all the more deep for having watered it with the sweat of our labor. We made this country what it is today."

Seventh theme. Supported with illustrations.

I was amazed by the tenderness which the workers showed toward the inanimate objects of their labor. "Oh, she'll be all right again," said a youngster of a machine he was repairing, and patted it as though it were a sick person. After "tapping"—cutting screw threads in—a big turret one night, I left it dripping with oil on the bench and turned to my next job. Immediately a bushy-haired fellow ran up to me and shouted angrily: "You can't leave her like that! Are you a machinist?" And he neatly wiped it off with his rag. "See?" he said and looked fondly at the shining metal.

Eighth theme. Supported with details and an illustration.

I took such rude reprimands without resentment, learning that these men did work of fine quality and that infinite care was the first requirement. Helping to take complicated parts out of the machine "heads" and to replace them, I always had the vivid impression of assisting at an operation on a human body. Even their tools—wrenches, pincers, scrapers, pliers, drills—were similar to a surgeon's or dentist's instruments. A mechanic's work is surgery on metal. In spite of scale and micrometer, the human eye and hand have the final control. No mechanical device can supplant the craftsman's sensitive fingers in fitting a bar to a hole, in feeling the evenness of a slide, or in the finishing touch of smoothing and polishing.

Whenever I got stuck and called for help, unable to find the cause of trouble, my neighbor would shout over the noise: "Find out! Think!" Then he would come closer, look the machine over, and adjust something at the far opposite end which had made my bar in front fit badly. It was this power of quick mechanical diagnosis that my legally, abstractly trained mind could not grasp. But no worker or instructor ever troubled to give me a theoretical explanation of a job. They would say: "Watch me!" then pull a lever, push a button, turn a wheel, and stand back for me to repeat their movements. They would tell me how, but never why.

Ninth theme. Supported with illustrations and details.

The invisible control of the worker's activities through bookkeeping and job cards was so ubiquitous and inexorable that the office could at any time find out which worker had put which screw on which part, and on what day. Once I broke a small handle. "You can't get away with that; they'll find it out," said a man who saw me do the damage. "You'd better go to the foreman and report." Every operation, no matter how small, had to be accomplished within the prescribed standard time, marked on special cards. On my first day in the shop I was warned by fellow-workers not to "ring out" my cards before the allotted time was up, or the office would cut down the standard norm for everybody. This had been tacitly agreed by them all to prevent the management from speeding us up. Whoever "rang" less than one hundred per cent time was a scab. Intelligently, the management took no steps against this. But the collective work of a shift could sometimes be speeded up imperceptibly. One week we were told we were to work six days and be paid time and a half for overtime. When Friday came the foreman said he had changed his mind. Asked why, he answered: "The department has caught up." In other words, under his continual gentle urging during that week we had all worked slightly faster, with the result that the shift accomplished six days' work in five days for five days' pay.

Tenth theme. Supported with illustrations.

Most men disliked the time-card system. "I like to do a good job but I hate to have a time limit for it," said a German scraper to me. It was easy to keep to time norms either in very simple or in very mechanized jobs; but when the quality of each piece depended on the skill of the worker's hands, the uniform time rules became meaningless bureaucratic measures. Once I took three hours and a half to scrape the slides properly and ream the holes on eight parts. Another time I took nine hours. In spite of the time cards the foremen had to give us individual allowances on all quality jobs.

Eleventh theme. Supported with details and illustrations.

The workers work hard all their lives and get enough for a living, sometimes a comfortable living, but never enough to stop working. "Once in a shop, always in a shop," was the gloomy refrain in every department. Sitting on wooden boxes or machine levers at lunch or dinner time, we often exchanged confidences and talked about our intimate ambitions. The old workers would shake their heads telling of twenty, thirty years spent in shops. The young ones would dreamingly speak of their hopes for the future. A fine machine operator said bitterly: "I get sick looking at this machine. Shall I run it when I am fifty? What a life!" Another hoped to get an office job some day. Still another dreamed of becoming a school teacher. He had finished high school; then he had got married, had had two children, and had gone into the shop instead of to college. Most wanted to go into "business for themselves" some day. Not one wished to remain a shop worker.

Twelfth theme. Supported by details and illustration.

At work a curious mental trance would occasionally take possession of me. I came to like monotonous jobs which left my mind free. Sometimes I would gradually lose control over my thoughts. Memories would begin to play before my eyes, and the factory would seem a fantastic vision where I saw workers and machines only through a mist. At such moments my fingers worked with relentless, mechanical speed. Once I turned threads in 270 holes and made altogether more than 6,000 identical arm movements. My mind sank into a complete oblivion of the world, and all night I swam in hallucinations and reveries like a drug addict.

In the fall I was transferred to the Machining Department, a huge white room where countless machines were lined up in impeccably straight rows, and the noise was so hellish that one had to shout into one's neighbor's ear. There I had the thrill of my life starting and stopping the motor, putting my turret lathe into high or low speed, throwing it into reverse, pulling the levers and handles, turning the wheels, and watching the indicators. The docile monster responded sensitively to every touch of my hand and turned out identical finished pieces at equal intervals. It was easy physically, but exhausting mentally. No more dreaming at work. The slightest mistake in the synchronization of movements resulted in a damage to the machine, the product, or my hands. Every day there came a moment when the attention suddenly gave out from overstrain, and an attack of dizziness made things swim before the eyes. I was advised by older workers to stop working for a while at such moments. I have often read that, generally, the two or three first hours of work are the most productive. That is not always true. In the Machining Department we regularly took one or two hours to "warm up." Then, after several hours of efficient work, a short period of mental weakness and distraction would set in. Renewed concentration would follow, and during the last one or two hours we worked at our best and fastest—because subconsciously we strove to get home.

Thirteenth theme. Supported by details.

There was a symphony of strange noises in the Machining Department. Some machines beat like the tom-toms of the jungle. Some puffed like locomotives. Some whistled, hissed, or howled. Some hummed or purred gently like cats. The steel under the cutter screamed like a human being, and when the huge machine drill pierced a one-foot iron bar the room resounded with the angry roaring of a lion. The men, grimly earnest, worked in tense concentration. Suddenly somebody would shout: "Hey!" A chorus of men would answer him, yelling at the top of their voices. Then they would fall back into silence for hours. Again a laugh would ring out from a corner. For a moment all the men would stop their work, and the entire place would echo with nerve-racking laughter. At first I felt uneasy every time I saw the men lift their heads from the machines. But later I too was carried away and howled with them. It was fun. But underneath it I recognized the need of relaxation from the mental tyranny of the machine.

The end. A general summary. Here is indicated the author's general purpose to evaluate his year in the factory. His judgments form the series of themes that make up the essay.

After a full year spent in the factory I returned to New York. Looking back upon my year-long experience in this American shop, I am fully aware that it does not give a general picture of the American industrial life. One can arrive at a just evaluation of it only by comparing it with industrial conditions elsewhere, here and abroad. We were paid at an average rate of 84 cents an hour. We worked 40 hours a week, in clean, healthy surroundings. We were given time and a half for overtime. We had time for rest, amusements, and cultural activities. We had a two weeks' vacation with pay. We were treated fairly as men and as workers. The foremen were willing to make exceptions in emergencies and to help out in trouble. Not seldom they would give us time-saving jobs (the so-called "good jobs") when we were behind on our time cards.

But the people whose character left the deepest impression on me were the workers. Humaneness and sympathy were concealed under their brusque ways and manners. On their faces, which sometimes reminded me of those of the peasants in my old country, lines of dishonesty or wickedness were rarely to be found. Many of them came from distant, forlorn corners of the United States, or from far-off, backward countries; they grew into the soil of a new community, excelled at work, and managed to give their children better care than they had enjoyed. When I think how tremendously handicapped they were by lack of means as well as of background and education, I wonder if perhaps they are not more able fellows than I. They were men of simple taste and reasonable, sane attitude toward life. No fanaticism colored their discontent. And their ambitions were undistorted by megalomaniac wishes to make "a career" or do "great things." Their objectives in life were within the limits of the possible.[21]

Exercises

A. Prepare a class discussion of the following essays: "School 'Life,'" page 289, "The Nation's No. 1 Publisher," page 297, and "Scholarship in College," page 304. Find the themes. Discuss the types of data used to support the themes. If you have any criticism of the way the author treated his data, be ready to explain what you think is wrong and to make suggestions for corrections.

B. Write an essay about a job or vocation you know well, presenting in a series several of your own judgments, each with adequate support. Underline the judgments.

C. Investigate what goes on in your department in school, or in any other campus activity, and write an essay in which you present and support three or four judgments drawn from your investigation. Underline the judgments.

D. Write an essay in which you make and support three or four judgments about a place you know well or about an experience you have had. Underline the judgments.

[21] "In An American Factory," by Stoyan Pribichevich. *Harper's Magazine*, September 1938. Reprinted by permission of the author and *Harper's Magazine*.

Third Pattern

The next pattern is exciting and dangerous. The excitement lies in new possibilities for expressing our opinions, and the danger in the traps that must be avoided. By now we are all aware of the relationship between judgment and the data from which judgment springs. We know that sound judgments have a good foundation of data—details, illustrations, etc. Our thematic writing up to this stage has been careful to present the judgment *and* the data. Now we are going to abandon, but only in so far as the writing is concerned, much of the data. This may seem like a declaration of freedom, but there is a catch to it. The catch is in the parenthetical remark, *but only in so far as the writing is concerned*. The thinking which precedes the writing still must consider the data; and even in the writing, as will soon appear, some data are used. If we gave up data as a basis for thinking, our judgments would be wild; if we gave up data entirely in our writing, we would run the risk of being unconvincing or of getting lost in the difficult air of high-level abstraction.

The following student paper shows at once the pattern and its dangers. The author failed to reflect on data before he drew his conclusions. Challenged on them, he replied that everyone has a right to his own beliefs. Again he was challenged, for a classmate told him the right has to be earned by working through the data that support one's conclusions. The student author wanted to establish a central theme and to support the theme with a series of judgments, themselves unsupported. He got into trouble. Here is his paper:

I believe that the New York *Times* is the best paper, not only in the Metropolitan area, but in the country as well. Of this I am firmly convinced. I think the paper best sums up its own attributes when its motto states "All the news that's fit to print." For total over-all coverage this paper cannot be matched. Its news articles, foreign and domestic; the men who write them; the features and various sections are all done with more detail than can be found in any other paper.

In these days of strife and conflict I think it is necessary to have an available source of information about what is happening from day to day. What we get in some of the tabloids and in many of the so called good out of town papers cannot compare with the selection and detail of the articles appearing in the New York *Times*. Since it is printed after nightfall, it has a detailed account of what has just happened during the day in all parts of the world. To the seeker of important news, he cannot do better than secure a copy of the *Times* and get a full account of the day's doings in London, Vichy, Washington, and as much as is passed by the censors from Berlin, Rome, Moscow and Tokyo.

In the matter of general news for the country and for the city, the *Times* prints things that are of interest and yet are not sensational. It does not have to go into the gutter for some of the trash that the *News* and *Mirror* so blaringly set forth on their second and third pages.

The *Times* makes a student conscious of good grammar. It is not full of slang terms and shortcuts in describing something. It does this in the best terms, with the proper punctuation, and with a natural choice of words.

The most important trouble with this little essay is that the author made judgments where he had neither the general experience nor the data to guide him. He says that the New York *Times* is the best paper, "not only in the Metropolitan area, but in the country as well." He says that the paper "cannot be matched"; that the detail of all the departments in the *Times* exceeds the detail which "can be found in any other paper"; and, to skip some similarly bold assertions, that all of this is done "in the best terms, with the proper punctuation, and with a natural choice of words." The student was promptly asked if he knew the papers published in Washington, D. C., San Francisco, Seattle, Denver, St. Louis, Chicago, New Orleans, and Philadelphia. He confessed he had never seen papers from those cities nor had ever read any accounts of them. He was asked if William Allen White, then alive and editor of the Emporia *Gazette,* was not considered one of the leading American journalists, equal to the best in New York. He confessed to having overlooked White and admitted the man's great value. He was asked if the grammar and diction of the New York *Sun* and of the New York *Herald Tribune* were inferior to the grammar and diction of the *Times*. Again he confessed that he was not certain. Before the discussion was over, the student was aware of his errors. He asked for permission to write an essay comparing the types of domestic stories in the *Times* with the domestic stories printed in one of the tabloids. He agreed to use enough illustrations from the papers to support whatever judgments he made, as he was not yet ready for reflective freedom in matters journalistic.

To be successful in writing that is made up primarily of judgment, the author must use subjects he knows well. He must have considered "long and long," as the old phrase put it, the evidence for his conclusions. Only then will he have the authority that permits the use of unsupported assertions. To be successful he must also have readers who can see the truth of his assertions, that is, he must have readers who themselves can see what his supporting data are. This requirement forces the author to consider his audience most carefully. A series of assertions about international economics, for example, needs much more support if the audience is popular than will the same assertions made before a body of economists. The inexperienced audience has to be shown. The experienced audience needs only the judgments.

A great many editorials are written as a series of judgments without supporting evidence. Editors have the benefit of their position and of long experience with evidence. They have mulled their conclusions over and over, because they have watched the data as they came in for days and, sometimes, years. In addition, the successful editor uses for topics, if he is writing with this pattern, only those which have a high degree of familiarity to his readers.

The following editorial is an example of the pattern. Every remark is a judgment. None gets any support *except from the reader*. The editor counts on that support.

This is Victory Fleet Day, set aside to celebrate the building of America's incredible merchant fleet, without which we could not now be standing on the soil of the Third Reich or pressing the Japanese ever more closely into their home waters. The statistics of our fleet created since Pearl Harbor are staggering. Expressed in tons produced, in man-hours worked, in material furnished and fabricated and, above all, in speed of accomplishment, the creation of this fleet represents an industrial marvel of the first order. And if we have been able to produce the ships, we have been also able to find men of steel to man them. They have taken them and their precious cargoes to the farthest corners of the seven seas. They have sailed them into port despite the long harrying of the submarine wolf-packs and under terror of bombs from the air, while the Luftwaffe still was able to exert opposition in force. They have braved every obstacle that two ruthless enemies have thrown into the war against them.[22]

Writing which does not present any of the concrete data that support the assertions of the author has the disadvantage of being abstract. Abstractions come from the mind, not from the senses. Their chief appeal is to the intellect. When the author is content with abstract material only, he depends, as we have seen, heavily upon his audience. If the author has an original mind, if he is making judgments of importance to his readers, and if his readers can follow him without getting lost in doubts, the author will succeed. For most of us it is wise to keep our pages of abstraction buttressed with *some* data. The data make an immediate appeal. They give foundation. They hold us on the ground even while we are exploring the heavens. In the essay that follows most of the material is a series of judgments, but some of it is composed of data. The first two paragraphs, for instance, are exactly like the editorial we just read. The next three paragraphs contain illustrations of the judgments found in the first two.

Nevada's Dead Towns

The beginning: a series of judgments introducing the general subject. No theme or series of themes for development is indicated; but the tone of "ruin" is established.

Nevada is one of the very youngest and wildest of the States; nevertheless it is already strewn with ruins that seem as gray and silent and timeworn as if the civilization to which they belonged had perished centuries ago. Yet, strange to say, all these ruins are results of mining efforts made within the last few years. Wander where you may throughout the length and breadth of this mountain-barred wilderness, you everywhere come upon these dead mining towns, with their tall chimney-stacks, standing forlorn amid broken walls and furnaces, and machinery half buried in sand, the very names of many of them already forgotten amid the excitements of later discoveries, and now known only through tradition—tradition ten years old.

[22] Editorial. From The New York *Times,* September 27, 1944. By permission of The New York *Times.*

A paragraph of judgments.

While exploring the mountain-ranges of the State during a considerable portion of three summers, I think that I have seen at least five of these deserted towns and villages for every one in ordinary life. Some of them were probably only camps built by bands of prospectors, and inhabited for a few months or years, while some specially interesting cañon was being explored, and then carelessly abandoned for more promising fields. But many were real towns, regularly laid out and incorporated, containing well-built hotels, churches, school-houses, post-offices, and jails, as well as the mills on which they all depended; and whose well-graded streets were filled with lawyers, doctors, brokers, hangmen, real-estate agents, etc., the whole population numbering several thousand.

Specific illustrations of ruined towns.

A few years ago the population of Hamilton is said to have been nearly eight thousand; that of Treasure Hill, six thousand; of Shermantown, seven thousand; of Swansea, three thousand. All of these were incorporated towns with mayors, councils, fire departments, and daily newspapers. Hamilton has now about one hundred inhabitants, most of whom are merely waiting in dreary inaction for something to turn up. Treasure Hill has about half as many, Shermantown one family, and Swansea none, while on the other hand the graveyards are far too full.

More specific illustration.

In one cañon of the Toyabe range, near Austin, I found no less than five dead towns without a single inhabitant. The streets and blocks of "real estate" graded on the hillsides are rapidly falling back into the wilderness. Sagebrushes are growing up around the forges of the blacksmith shops, and lizards bask on the crumbling walls.

More specific illustration.

While traveling southward from Austin down Big Smoky Valley, I noticed a remarkably tall and imposing column, rising like a lone pine out of the sage-brush on the edge of a dry gulch. This proved to be a smokestack of solid masonry. It seemed strangely out of place in the desert, as if it had been transported entire from the heart of some noisy manufacturing town and left here by mistake. I learned afterwards that it belonged to a set of furnaces that were built by a New York company to smelt ore that never was found. The tools of the workmen are still lying in place beside the furnaces, as if dropped in some sudden Indian or earthquake panic and never afterwards handled. These imposing ruins, together with the desolate town, lying a quarter of a mile to the northward, present a most vivid picture of wasted effort. Coyotes now wander unmolested through the brushy streets, and of all the busy throng that so lavishly spent their time and money here only one man remains—a lone bachelor with one suspender.

All judgment, with the exception of the brief illustrations in the last sentence.

Mining discoveries and progress, retrogression and decay, seem to have been crowded more closely against each other here than on any other portion of the globe. Some one of the band of adventurous prospectors who came from the exhausted placers of California would discover some rich ore—how much or little mattered not at first. These specimens fell among excited seekers after wealth like sparks in gunpowder, and in a few days the wilderness was disturbed with the noisy clang of miners and builders. A little town would then spring up, and before anything like a careful survey of any particular lode would be made, a company would be formed, and expensive mills built. Then, after all the machinery was ready for the ore, perhaps little, or none at all, was to be found. Meanwhile another discovery was reported, and the young town was abandoned as completely as a camp made for a single night; and so on, until some really valuable lode was found, such as those of Eureka, Austin, Virginia, etc., which formed the substantial groundwork for a thousand other excitements.

Illustrative material.

Passing through the dead town of Schellbourne last month, I asked one of the few lingering inhabitants why the town was built. "For the mines," he replied. "And where are the mines?" "On the mountains back here." "And why were they abandoned?" I asked. "Are they exhausted?" "Oh, no," he replied, "they are not exhausted; on the contrary, they have never been worked at all, for unfortunately, just as we were about ready to open them, the Cherry Creek mines were discovered across the valley in the Egan range, and everybody rushed off there, taking what they could with them—houses, machinery, and all. But we are hoping that somebody with money and speculation will come and revive us yet."

More judgments.

The dead mining excitements of Nevada were far more intense and destructive in their action than those of California, because the prizes at stake were greater, while more skill was required to gain them. The long trains of gold-seekers making their way to California had ample time and means to recover from their first attacks of mining fever while crawling laboriously across the plains, and on their arrival on any portion of the Sierra gold belt, they at once began to make money. No matter in what gulch or cañon they worked, some measure of success was sure, however unskillful they might be. And though while making ten dollars a day they might be agitated by hopes of making twenty, or of striking their picks against hundred- or thousand-dollar nuggets, men of ordinary nerve could still work on with comparative steadiness, and remain rational.

More judgments. To test the fact that these are judgments ask yourself how Muir knows the truth of his remarks. The answer is that he knows of miners and mines that illustrate the truth.

But in the case of the Nevada miner, he too often spent himself in years of weary search without gaining a dollar, traveling hundreds of miles from mountain to mountain, burdened with wasting hopes of discovering some hidden vein worth millions, enduring hardships of the most destructive kind, driving innumerable tunnels into the hillsides, while his assayed specimens again and again proved worthless. Perhaps one in a hundred of these brave prospectors would "strike it rich," while ninety-nine died alone in the mountains or sank out of sight in the corners of saloons.

More judgments.

The healthful ministry of wealth is blessed; and surely it is a fine thing that so many are eager to find the gold and silver that lie hid in the veins of the mountains. But in the search the seekers too often become insane, and strike about blindly in the dark like raving madmen.

Illustration.

Seven hundred and fifty tons of ore from the original Eberhardt mine on Treasure Hill yielded a million and a half dollars, the whole of this immense sum having been obtained within two hundred and fifty feet of the surface, the greater portion within one hundred and forty feet.

Judgments.

Other ore-masses were scarcely less marvelously rich, giving rise to one of the most violent excitements that ever occurred in the history of mining. All kinds of people—

shoemakers, tailors, farmers, etc., as well as miners—left their own right work and fell in a perfect storm of energy upon the White Pine Hills, covering the ground like grasshoppers, and seeming determined by the very violence of their efforts to turn every stone to silver. But with few exceptions, these mining storms pass away about as suddenly as they rise, leaving only ruins to tell of the tremendous energy expended, as heaps of giant boulders in the valley tell of the spent power of the mountain floods.

Illustration. In marked contrast with this destructive unrest is the orderly deliberation into which miners settle in developing a truly valuable mine. At Eureka we were kindly led through the treasure chambers of the Richmond and Eureka Consolidated, our guides leisurely leading the way from level to level, calling attention to the precious ore-masses which the workmen were slowly breaking to pieces with their picks, like navvies wearing away the day in a railroad cutting; while down at the smelting works the bars of bullion were handled with less eager haste than the farmer shows in gathering his sheaves.

Judgments. The wealth Nevada has already given to the world is indeed wonderful, but the only grand marvel is the energy expended in its development. The amount of prospecting done in the face of so many dangers and sacrifices, the innumerable tunnels and shafts bored into the mountains, the mills that have been built—these would seem to require a race of giants. But, in full view of the substantial results achieved, the pure waste manifest in the ruins one meets never fails to produce a saddening effect.

Judgments. The dim old ruins of Europe, so eagerly sought after by travelers, have something pleasing about them, whatever their historical associations; for they at least lend some beauty to the landscape. Their picturesque towers and arches seem to be kindly adopted by nature, and planted with wild flowers and wreathed with ivy; while their rugged angles are soothed and freshened and embossed with green mosses, fresh life and decay mingling in pleasing measures, and the whole vanishing softly like a ripe, tranquil day fading into night. So, also, among the older ruins of the East there is a fitness felt. They have served their time, and like the weather-beaten mountains are wasting harmoniously. The same is in some degree true of the dead mining towns of California.

Judgments.

But those lying to the eastward of the Sierra throughout the ranges of the Great Basin waste in the dry wilderness like the bones of cattle that have died of thirst. Many of them do not represent any good accomplishment, and have no right to be. They are monuments of fraud and ignorance—sins against science. The drifts and tunnels in the rocks may perhaps be regarded as the prayers of the prospector, offered for the wealth he so earnestly craves; but, like prayers of any kind not in harmony with nature, they are unanswered. But, after all, effort, however misapplied, is better than stagnation. Better toil blindly, beating every stone in turn for grains of gold, whether they contain any or not, than lie down in apathetic decay.

The ending: a judgment supported only by other judgments, none of which is supported.

The fever period is fortunately passing away. The prospector is no longer the raving, wandering ghoul of ten years ago, rushing in random lawlessness among the hills, hungry and footsore; but cool and skillful, well supplied with every necessary, and clad in his right mind. Capitalists, too, and the public in general, have become wiser, and do not take fire so readily from mining sparks; while at the same time a vast amount of real work is being done, and the ratio between growth and decay is constantly becoming better.[23]

Muir's concern is with a great many judgments; therefore a good sentence outline of the essay is impossible. This does not mean that the essay is disorganized, or is "bad." A careful reading shows that Muir is interested in three leading topics and that through each of them runs an impression of loss and ruin. The topics are the following:

I. The dead mining towns of Nevada
II. Mining discoveries, retrogression and decay
III. The human cost of the search for mineral wealth
  A. Cost in men and material
  B. Cost in moral values

[23] From *Steep Trails,* by John Muir. New York: Houghton Mifflin Company, 1918.

Muir's technique is to divide his subject into parts and to put down his conclusions about each part. Any subject can be treated this way if the author knows the facts thoroughly. The factual knowledge is necessary if the conclusions are to be of any value.

Muir's transition-points between the major topics are easy to find. They are the first lines in the sixth and eighth paragraphs. But if a reader should try to find a theme for each topic, that is, a judgment supported throughout the development of the topic, he would be puzzled by many statements that would seem out of place and by others that would seem as important as the themes selected, yet not at all useful in developing the themes. Because there are no serious violations of unity in the essay, we need to ask how such apparent disunity is actually not disunity at all. The unifying principle is in the word *ruins,* found in the first sentence. The impression of ruin is built up, not so much by concrete data—we have seen there are some—as by a series of judgments we know Muir has the right to make because he was there, because he did see the data, and because he did ponder over them. Though he put in three rather bulky masses of data, his chief method was to add his judgments, under the three topics, one by one, each an accrual to the impression of ruin, unfolding the whole in somewhat the same manner as a bud unfolds to a full blossom. The whole flower is in the bud, and the whole essay is in the word *ruins*. Each judgment, directly or by the implication carried in Muir's contrasts and comparisons, contributes to the sense of ruin. The author could easily have found data to support one central theme, or to support a series of themes; but he was, however, a philosophical naturalist more than an objective scientist; and as a result he was concerned with the many abstractions he drew from his observation. His writing technique requires a man who has worked through much data to the conclusions he wants to communicate. The contrast between Muir and the student writing about newspapers is chiefly the contrast between an undeveloped mind and a fully matured one.

One other unifying device that Muir uses is *emotional tone*. He selects words and phrases that carry the saddening effect of ruins. This is a good device. Writers use it where the audience and the subject make it appropriate. Technical subjects and their audiences generally need objective directness, and tonal appeal is avoided. Popular audiences can be held to closer attention by it. Some of the tonal words and phrases Muir uses are the following: *strewn, mountain-barred wilderness, forlorn, broken, dreary, graveyards, crumbling walls, desolate, wasted effort, prayers of the prospector,* and *stagnation.* These words carry associations that make the reader feel ruin. Emotional tone is much enjoyed by writers who are stirred by life. They feel as well as think. Control of emotional tone requires correct identification of the emotion to be built up and selection of the words that carry associations which pluck the right reader-response.

Muir wrote much of the time in the glow of a romantic tradition; and as is known by anyone who has studied the ghost towns of the West, he comes close to falsifying his picture by making his saddening effect too pleasurable. Self-control and near-perfect observation are required of the writer who uses emotional tone with his judgments. When we first try it, perhaps we should do it coldly and deliberately, and not in some mood, mawkish or genuine; and when we have finished, perhaps it would be wise to put our work aside for a few days, so that when we pick it up for final revision we get a fresh look at it and can separate the false in tone from the true.

The essay made up in this pattern is found everywhere these days. It is especially popular in "studies," because the judgments are useful as summaries of the factual data that make up a study. Any subject can serve: Salmon conservation, a gang of juvenile criminals, the history of the term *O.K.* The one requirement is that the author be familiar with the subject. He must be something of an authority. We need not be alarmed, for becoming an authority does not always mean a life spent in study. It means that we have searched for and recorded all the facts that can be found, that we have arranged them in appropriate groups, and then have whipped them into control by summarizing them in a series of judgments.

Exercises

A. Prepare for class discussion analyses of the following essays: "Portrait of My Mother," page 313, "Practical Farming for Beginners," page 323, and "The Great Salmon Experiment," page 330. Make a topical outline of each essay. Be ready to point out some of the judgments and to estimate what data the author must have had in mind as he wrote. Show where he has used data to support his judgments.

B. Write an essay using "third pattern" technique. Select for your subject one with which you are already familiar so that you need not get all of your materials from your reading. Perhaps a novel you have recently read will be a good subject for you. A person you know intimately might serve as a subject. (See "Portrait of My Mother," page 313.)

Beginnings

Because there are no fixed rules for beginning an essay and no standard models, any beginning that captures the reader's interest and starts him on his way without confusion is a good one. Often the beginning is a clearly marked section. A reader can reach a certain point knowing that he has come to the end of the beginning and is entering a developmental section of the essay. At other times there is no place where the reader can say he has come to the dividing line, for beginning and development occur together. Something more helpful than this needs to be said, however; for an essay does "begin." Perhaps if we try to isolate some of the qualities found in the first lines or paragraphs, we can get some hints for our own practice. The isolation of the qualities should not be taken to mean that they are characteristic only of the first few lines of an essay.

A good beginning is interesting. It need not interest every person who comes upon it, but it should catch at those for whom it is written. Interest is at least partly an emotional experience, and it is linked with the personal problems and desires of the reader and with the trait called curiosity. If a reader is getting or is being denied what he wants, or is threatened with losing what he wishes to keep, he is interested up to the point of satisfaction or defeat. The author appealing to reader desire needs to phrase his topic statement in such a way that the reader feels he has come upon a solution to a problem or has been threatened. When the reader finishes the first few lines of the essay, he should see, and feel, significance to himself in the topic. If he does not see significance, or if his curiosity is not engaged, he will be disinterested. Most of us have a lot of curiosity in our make-up. We want to know things because we want to know and not because we have any use for the knowledge, or because we feel insecure without it. Curiosity may be semi-conscious, or it may be a highly developed, inquiring alertness. Good appeals to curiosity are found in beginnings that contain narrative or contain statements of unusual, and concrete, detail, just to name two types.

A good beginning is clear. Though interest depends in large part on clarity, clarity is important for the sake of efficient reading. The sooner we know what is happening and where we are going, the sooner we get into the essay topic with attention to its purpose. Of all forms of obscurity, the vague circumlocution is about the most irritating. We have read too often the student report that begins as follows: "Before I can discuss the problem of our present need for Federal support for rural schools, I must give a résumé of the history of public school education in this country." The reader is killed off at once. There may be a connection between the past and the present that needs to be shown, but no one will climb over that sentence with anything but a feeling of resentment that he must wait for the discussion to get down to the real problem. A better start might be an anecdote about a rural student or teacher; or it might be some such sentence as this: "In September of this year, 18,000 rural school buildings will be kept locked because there is no money to hire teachers"; or it might be a statement of the author's theme: "Federal aid is the only method by which thousands of rural schools can be opened this fall to tens of thousands of rural youngsters who need education." These beginnings at least have the virtue of showing that the author knows what he is up to. They are clear and purposeful. They make a promise of efficient progress through the essay by starting the reader on the way without bewilderment.

Sometimes a direct statement of intentions is not enough; limits have to be set, or terms defined so as to provide common ground for reader and author. Other forms of clarification may be useful, such as a statement of the author's point of view or a break-down of the topic into its parts. Whatever is required to orient the reader is part of the problem of clarity and goes into the beginning.

The following illustrative beginnings and the analyses that accompany them will show some of the possibilities open to an author.

From "Scholarship in College," page 304:

The first object of education is to make one a better consumer, to increase one's capacity to enjoy, to live broadly and deeply, to appreciate philosophy, science, history, art, literature, and music, to understand things and events, to see their interrelation, their significance. Compare the reactions of an educated man with trained powers of appreciation and those of an uneducated, untrained man on visiting for the first time the Acropolis at Athens, on looking at Michael Angelo's Last Judgment, or on witnessing the rendition of a great opera like *Parsifal*. What one really sees depends much more upon what is back of his eyes than upon what is in front of them. It was Aristotle who said: "Education is an ornament in prosperity and a refuge in adversity." This development of one's powers to enjoy, to appreciate, to be a good consumer, is sufficient justification in itself for seeking an education.

The second object of an education is to make one a better producer. In this connection the fundamental ideas are of service, power, wealth. Here the important word is not enjoyment but achievement. It is in this narrower sense of the term that the word success is most often used, and in this sense I am using it this evening.

What I have to say this evening will be an attempt to throw some light on the answers to two questions: first, does a college education contribute to success in life? Second, what type of man in college is most likely to succeed? [24]

The first two paragraphs of this excerpt are used to define the term *education* and to imply a definition of the term *success*. Limits are set on the meanings of these words. The last paragraph states directly what the author's purpose is. Only a very careless reader could miss the direct statement of intention to answer two questions.

From "Don't Work Your Way," page 248:

"Don't Work Your Way Through College" is not meant as a message to raise your eyebrows. It is a message that has never been fully brought home to parents, college students and potential college students. Yet it bears the almost unanimous stamp of approval of college administrators and of college graduates who did work their way. The quicker parents

[24] From "Scholarship in College," a lecture at Wesleyan University by Edwin W. Kemmerer. Published in *Vital Speeches of the Day*, Vol. III, No. 19, July 15, 1937. Reprinted by permission of the author and the City News Publishing Co.

and students realize it is generally harmful for a young man to work his *entire* way through college, the better off both will be.

This is to be no brief against courage and perseverance. The warning need not apply to the genius, nor even to the superior type of young man. Nor does it apply to the many happily-situated *part-time* college workers. But the large group of students who must, of necessity, earn every cent of their college expenses should beware. The difficulties that confront them are formidable indeed.[25]

The beginning of "Scholarship in College" asks questions. No themes are stated. They are indicated as coming, of course, in the answers to the questions. The author of "Don't Work Your Way" states his theme at once, in the title and in the first paragraph. The second paragraph sets limits on his theme by pointing out to whom it applies. Those of us who worked our way through college, who plan to, or who are now doing it find the essay interesting because we are directly affected by its message. Others, unless they happen to be administrators or parents concerned with working students, are attracted by curiosity.

From "The Nation's No. 1 Publisher," page 297:

A single publisher, last year, sold over 13,000,000 books and other publications without benefit of a line of advertising, a salesman on the road, or a cocktail party for reviewers. The list of over 65,000 titles contains no mystery stories, no novels, no volumes of poetry—only authoritative information about cooking, farming, health, industry, law, military and naval matters, mining or statistical reports. And nobody cashes in on this Gargantuan output—except the reader—for the publisher is the United States Government.[26]

This beginning contains no statement of purpose or of theme. It launches itself with a scattering of impressive facts. The title and the subject matter of the beginning tell the reader all he needs to know of the writer's intentions. The appeal is to curiosity, though there is a tinge of practicality about the author's remarks: we do need the

[25] From "Don't Work Your Way," by Roy A. Benjamin. *Current History and Forum*, September, 1940. Reprinted by permission of *Current History*.

[26] From "The Nation's No. 1 Publisher," by Edith M. Stern. *The Saturday Review of Literature*, January 15, 1941. Reprinted by permission of *The Saturday Review of Literature*.

information published by the government and one way or another we do pay for it. The first sentence, however, shocks us into alert curiosity by the facts it contains. We go on from there to find out more about this phenomenal publishing activity.

From "The Cat: Vicious Predator *or* Harmless Pet?", page 273:

Last winter at the annual dinner of a large sportsman's club the toastmaster read a report of the number of predators that clubs members had shot or trapped during the year. It made an impressive showing; so many foxes, so many owls, a considerable number of hawks, weasels—even a shrike or two. There was considerable applause, but the man who sat next to me, a widely known sportsman and conservationist, did not join in. Instead he snorted, and turned to me.

"Not a word about house cats," he commented. "There's no telling how many beneficial hawks and owls were killed by these well-meaning but uninformed men. Foxes, coyotes, hawks, owls, and all the rest are blamed for killing off our game birds and song birds. But the house cat does more harm than any or all of them!"

I probably looked surprised.

"Don't tell me *you* don't know that is true? You get around. Don't you know what's going on?"

"Frankly I haven't given the matter much thought," I parried. "But if it's so, why don't these hunters here come right out and say so? Why don't they do something beside killing hawks and owls?"

"Half of these men here are farmers. If anybody started a campaign against cats, you'd see some of them walk out, never to return. They feel that cats are a necessity on the farm to keep down rats and mice. The other half are men who value the privilege of hunting on farms. They will do nothing to forfeit that privilege. Besides, like you, they probably 'haven't given it thought.'"

Obviously, if what this man said were true, the facts should be brought out and laid before the sportsmen of the country. But where could such facts be obtained? While the standing of the sportsman was such as to warrant respect for his opinion, it was still only opinion—and that may be based on incomplete observation or on unconscious prejudice.

So I set out as a reporter to get facts, and I went to men in key positions throughout the country—heads of state conservation commissions, ornithologists, naturalists, and other scientists. Of each I asked this question:

"What is the truth about the house cat? Is it an economically useful pet, or is it a pernicious predator among song birds, game birds, and small game?"[27]

Here we are pretty close to narrative. The subject grows from the situation. It is developed by the dialogue, and dialogue is inherently interesting. With the phrasing of the questions the author asked of the scientists, the reader is launched and ready to go ahead. He wants to know the answers, for he can see that his attitude toward cats will be affected by the answers and that his attitude is important.

From "Comparisons of Secondary School Magazines . . ."

For seven years it has been the duty of the writer to supervise the publication of a school magazine, at least six or eight times throughout the year. Not only does such a project involve the expenditure of hundreds of dollars, but it also necessitates the skillful motivation of supervisors and the willing devotion of innumerable hours of labor on the part of the children.

It has been the hope of the investigator to present a study which will indicate, in some measure, the necessary standards to be borne in mind in the arrangement of the content into departmental sections and in assembling and writing of advertisements. This is not a critical survey of the quality of material published in a school magazine. . . . This survey is intended to give a view of the best make-up of school magazines as disclosed by a comparison of certain elements of eighty school magazines with the score sheets of four scholastic press associations. It is also intended to be a picture of the different ways advisors have of initiating and running a magazine and an abridgment of values and problems of such a publication, as secured from a summary of the data compiled from questionnaires sent to all parts of the United States.

The specific aims of this study are:

1. To compare the general make-up of eighty school magazines with the criteria shown on score sheets and manuals issued by scholastic press associations
2. To indicate the different methods
   a. Of initiating the magazine
   b. Of getting the staff cooperation
   c. Of financing the magazine

[27] From "The Cat: Vicious Predator *or* Harmless Pet?" by Allen Parsons. ***Outdoor Life,*** November, 1941. Reprinted by permission of *Outdoor Life*.

3. To summarize the values of the magazine
4. To show the interest in the magazine once it is established
5. To state some of the problems that confront advisors [28]

Because the writing situation faced by the author of this beginning is formal, we get here a break-down of the topic into its parts. There is some indication of what the problem does *not* include. Then come generalized statements of what is included. This is followed by a formalized repetition that puts the writer's aims specifically, and visibly, before the reader. The reader appeal is chiefly in the problem itself. Though school magazines may be an object of curiosity to some persons, the approach here shunts curiosity aside.

We need in conclusion only remind ourselves that beginnings offer a wide range of possibilities to an author. His own imagination sets the limits of what he can do. But always he seeks to be interesting and clear. To be interesting he tries to find in his topic the elements that appeal to reader desire or need; or he tries to make his material catch at reader curiosity. He can do both at the same time. To be clear he avoids obscurity by stating his theme or purpose directly or indirectly; by setting limits to his topic; by defining his terms; by explaining his point of view; by analyzing his topic; by showing, when it is not clear, the connection between parts of his topic. The author's aim in seeking interest and clarity is to take his reader into a co-operative partnership in the development of the essay.

Arranging the Data

To keep the partnership of author and reader from languishing, the author sees to it that his material is so arranged that his reader can follow it without unnecessary trouble. Though much of our study of thematic patterns has dealt with arrangement, the following additional observations will help fix our knowledge of some of the principles.

The statement of a theme may precede the supporting data or it may come after them. Perhaps ninety per cent of the time the theme precedes the data.

[28] From "Comparisons of Secondary School Magazines . . ." by Thelma J. Weidman. Unpublished M.A. dissertation, New York University. Reprinted by permission of the author.

If the essay develops a series of themes, the series may be arranged in the order of ascending importance—that is, beginning with the least important and working toward the most important. If there is no difference in importance, the series of themes may be put down in the order the author thinks of the items or comes upon them in his notes.

The data used to support a theme may be put down as the author thinks of them. It is often effective, however, when using data of unequal weight to put an impressive item in the end position. The order of logical development may sometimes control the placing of data. Some data are progressive, one item leading logically to the next through a system of expanding relationships. A formal instance of logical development is the proof of a geometry proposition. Though some of the supporting items of the proof may be shifted, the problem usually unfolds step by step, not chronologically, but by the system in which one thing leads to the next.

Formal arrangements such as the logical proof are not often come upon in ordinary essay writing. A more common illustration of logical development is the kind revealed in the outline below.

Outline: Don't Work Your Way

Beginning
- A. Thesis stated: don't work your way through college
- B. Thesis limited to full-time workers

Presentation of data
- A. Anecdote: George Withers comes to college
  - 1. Advised to go back home
  - 2. Declines to take advice
- B. Argument that work interferes harmfully with study
- C. Authoritative opinions on the problem
- D. More argument
- E. Anecdote: back to Withers, who is hurting himself in many ways, misled by parents, friends, and college

Concluding remarks
- A. Suggested solutions of the problem of going to college without enough money
- B. Thesis restated

The author began his essay by stating and limiting his theme. He began his support of the theme with a hypothetical illustration that set his stage; then he went into data, grouped by types and the groups arranged as he came upon them; then he went back to the hypothetical illustration; and finally he offered a solution to his problem and restated his theme. Any other placing of his hypothetical illustration and of his solution would have been unnatural. He would have been setting his stage long after his action was under way, and solving his problem before he had fully described it. In such essays as "Don't Work Your Way" the author must discover the natural progression of the material and use it.

Transitions

After the writer has the parts of his essay in an appropriate sequence, his responsibility is to see that the shifts from part to part are clear enough so that the reader can easily make them. The marks of each shift do for the reader what signposts do for a traveler: they tell him his changes in direction and his progress toward his goal. Without the marks, the reader, like a stranger on an unposted highway, has to carry the whole burden of keeping himself oriented. Much of the burden belongs to the writer, not to the reader.

In some of the other chapters of this book transition has been mentioned in relation to a specific situation. Since thematic writing requires a wider variety of transition devices than those already discussed, our purpose now is to sum up the familiar and add the new. The conventional devices are the following. The order in which these appear is that of convenience, for all are important.

Transitional Paragraph. When an essay is divided into two or more large sections, a transitional paragraph may be used to carry the reader from one to the next. Usually the paragraph is short. Its function is to announce the end of one large section and the start of the following one. The announcement is made directly. The following examples may be taken as good models of the transitional paragraph:

Since to show the effects of repeal it has been necessary to dwell at some length on the drinking habits of Sigourney's population, it would seem well at this point to strike a balance with a report of the community's less frivolous activities.[29]

In order to understand the extent of the problem that confronts American cities, one must pause for a moment to appraise their earlier development. We must understand how impossible it would be, even if we wished it, to carry their typical methods and aims into the future.[30]

Headings. A formal essay or chapter composed of several sections may use headings to label the changes. Headings are typical of textbooks and of scientific or industrial reports. By labeling each section, the author informs the reader of his progress. The headings need a consistent position and typographical set-up to indicate the relative value of the sections. Main divisions, for instance, might be labeled with boldface, entered on the page between sections. The divisions within a main section might use headings in italics at the left side of the page and between the sections. The divisions within this could be in capital letters, placed at the left side of the first line of text in that division. Turn the pages of this chapter and note the arrangement of headings.

Nearly any textbook or formal report will provide models of headings in use. *Facts and Judgments* is replete with them.

Transitional Sentences. Transition from one paragraph to another is often made by a sentence which looks ahead to the succeeding paragraph or looks back at the preceding paragraph. Skilfully used, this device is excellent.

What talk do we commonly hear about the contrast between college education and the education which business or technical or professional schools confer? The college education is called higher because it is supposed to be so general and so disinterested. At the "schools" you get a relatively narrow practical skill, you are told, whereas the "colleges" give you the more liberal culture, the broader outlook, the historical perspective, the philosophic atmosphere, or something which phrases of that sort try to express. You are made into an efficient instrument for doing a definite

[29] From "Main Street in 1940: Sigourney, Iowa," by Dale Kramer. *Forum,* April, 1940.

[30] From "The Future of the American City," by Louis Mumford. St. Louis *Post-Dispatch,* December 11, 1938.

thing, you hear, at the schools; but, apart from that, you may remain a crude and smoky kind of petroleum, incapable of spreading light. The universities and colleges, on the other hand, although they may leave you less efficient for this or that practical task, suffuse your whole mentality with something more important than skill. They redeem you, make you well-bred; they make "good company" of you mentally. If they find you with a naturally boorish or caddish mind, they cannot leave you so, as a technical school may leave you. This, at least, is pretended; this is what we hear among college-trained people when they compare their education with every other sort. *Now, exactly how much does this signify?*

It is certain, *to begin with,* that the narrowest trade or professional training does something more for a man than to make a skilful practical tool of him—it makes him also a judge of other men's skill. Whether his trade be pleading at the bar or surgery or plastering or plumbing, it develops a critical sense in him for that sort of occupation. He understands the difference between second-rate and first-rate work in his whole branch of industry; he gets to know a good job in his own line as soon as he sees it; and getting to know this in his own line, he gets a faint sense of what good work may mean anyhow, that may, if circumstances favor, spread into his judgments elsewhere. Sound work, clean work, finished work; feeble work, slack work, sham work—these words express an identical contrast in many different departments of activity. In so far forth, then, even the humblest manual trade may beget in one a certain small degree of power to judge of good work generally.[31]

Parallel Construction. When an essay contains sections each of a similar nature, transition is often made by starting each section with sentences exactly parallel in structure. For instance, an essay by Edward A. Ross on modern sin begins the separate discussions of the qualities of modern sin as follows:

> Modern sin is not superficially repulsive . . .
> Modern sin lacks the familiar tokens of guilt . . .
> Modern sins are impersonal . . .

Each statement is followed by considerable development; thus the repetition is not monotonous. The parallelism serves as a signal that the reader easily accepts. To illustrate further, an essay by Calvin

[31] From "The Social Value of the College-Bred," by William James. Reprinted by permission of Longmans, Green and Company, Inc.

Kinney describing what he missed by not going to college begins each section as follows:

> I missed the opportunity of association and friendship with men of wide culture and high ideals in an atmosphere of quiet and detachment . . .
> I missed a training in systematic and orderly thought . . .
> I missed the best part of my youth . . .
> I missed making friends of my own age . . .
> I missed the sense of equality with better educated men . . .

Parallel structure as a transition device is useful when the sections themselves are parallel. Each section has to be a similar part of a whole in the same way that quarters of an apple are similar. When the sections are not similar, for instance in the way that the core, pulp, and skin are dissimilar parts of an apple, the parallel beginnings are unsuitable. They would mislead the reader by indicating in the divisions a parallel rank that does not exist.

Enumeration. Somewhat similar to headings is the device of enumeration. The parts of the essay are numbered: First, Second, Third; (1), (2), (3); (a), (b), (c). Enumeration is useful for labeling either major divisions or the divisions within a paragraph. Its use for a major division and for a section within the major division is likely to be confusing.

> The special stresses to which the miliary pilot is subjected, particularly when the country is at war, fall chiefly into three categories: (1) air neurosis, which is a breakdown of co-ordination, caused by flying in exciting and dangerous circumstances; (2) lack of oxygen at high altitude, a physiological condition in which, however, the chief danger is its subtle attack on the judgment of the pilot; (3) the "blackout," a simpler phenomenon caused by the effect of centrifugal force on the blood stream during the turnout from a high dive.[32]

> But we have outgrown the town meeting. *In the first place,* we vote through representatives. And representative government is widely misunderstood. We are mistaken when we suppose that the number of letters and telegrams that reach our Congressmen before action on an important

[32] From "Selection of Military Pilots." *Fortune,* September, 1940. Reprinted by permission of *Fortune.*

bill is the measure of the working of democracy. This bill hurts agriculture; the farmer writes his Congressman to oppose it. Another bill limits business profits; the business man wires his Senator to defeat it. But who are we to ask our representative to care for our particular interests? He is your representative not in the sense that he is your mouthpiece, but rather in the sense that you elect him as a man wise enough to care for the welfare of the entire electorate. Write your Congressman? Yes, if you as a specialist can offer sound advice. But never command him.

Secondly, the problems we face are larger than were those in town meeting. We are asked to vote on foreign policy . . .[33]

Words of Time. Changes in time may be noted by direct reference to the hour, day, season; or they may be indirectly noted by association with details that belong only to a certain hour or period. Sequence of time may also be noted by such words or phrases as *next, at last, now, immediately, at length, finally.*

Words of Place. Changes in place are made by direct reference. The reader's attention is shifted by such words and phrases as *beyond this, beside, next in line, at the rear of, outside, inside, to the right of,* used in conjunction with the place last under examination.

Transitional Phrases. Transition from idea to idea within a paragraph or sentence is usually made by words and phrases which show the relationship of idea to idea and reveals the *turn* the thought is taking. Examples of such words and phrases are the following:

Moreover, further, in addition
But, yet, however, on the other hand, on the contrary
Meanwhile, at the same time
For example, for instance, to illustrate
Indeed, in fact, too, also
Likewise, hence, thus, accordingly

Endings

The end of an essay does not offer complex psychological difficulties to any such degree as does the beginning. The reader, if the essay began well and progressed easily and clearly through its development, is prepared to stop. He has advanced with the author through the

[33] From "Citizenship," by Roger W. Holmes. *The Atlantic Monthly,* November, 1940. Reprinted by permission of *The Atlantic Monthly.*

material and has recognized that it is running out. If the treatment of the subject has fulfilled the promise made at the start, the reader wants to quit; and all that remains for the writer is to break off cleanly.

If the essay is formal, a summary may serve for the ending. A suggestion of what can be done next, or of the importance of the author's ideas, might be enough; or these might be added to the summary. An informal essay can be efficiently ended by a phrase or sentence that by hinting at a summary ties up the whole and marks it finished. A repetition, in different phraseology, of the ideas that began the essay is often a sufficient ending. Formal or informal, the ending is part of the material developed in the essay. It leaves the reader thinking directly about the essay subject or about something closely related.

The illustrative endings that follow are from some of the essays whose beginnings we have already seen.

From "Portrait of My Mother," page 313:

To give—was not that what life was? That was the easy summary: twenty years or so given to younger sisters and the like; two-thirds of a century and a little more given to her own family. She had given.

But what she had achieved within herself seemed more. In a world where life was always hard and often cruel, she met the requirements without ever flinching, without ever thinking of running away to some remote place in pursuit of an evasive happiness. Just to have remained steadfast in itself would have been much. But she persisted until she made a greater usefulness of the hard conditions. She persisted until she saw herself in relation to things, to all things, and, right where she stayed, came to know the deeps of a serenity from which she could look out on whatsoever and be undismayed.[34]

From "The Polkadot Gang," page 354:

The roundup of the other members of the Gang followed. It had taken not quite twenty years of life at Aberdeen and Erie, in the heart of Chicago's slum, to prepare the boys for their career as members of the Polkadot Gang. The corporate life, if it may be so described, of the gang had lasted barely four weeks. The total take of the gang had come to about $10,000, which, among twelve people, meant $833 apiece. In addition to the sen-

[34] From "Portrait of My Mother," by Rollo Walter Brown. *The Atlantic Monthly*, October, 1944. Reprinted by permission of the author and *The Atlantic Monthly*.

tences for armed robbery and grand larceny already listed, Sharleen got twenty years and Leo Piscopo thirty-five years and Tony Moskal fourteen years and Nick Gianos fourteen years, all for murder. Joe Piscopo got from one to ten years for grand larceny in two stickups. Gene Guzy's entry on the blotter was closed out forever. His life and Officer Storm's canceled out.[35]

From "The Cat: Vicious Predator *or* Harmless Pet?", page 273:

At first blush, then, it would seem that conservationists and cat lovers are as far apart as the poles. But a few thoughtful sportsmen aren't convinced of that. They feel that if they could get together with farmers and cat lovers, and discuss the matter sanely and without passion, perhaps much could be done to find a common, sensible viewpoint, and an ultimate solution.

Maybe you could in your town.[36]

From "Don't Work Your Way," page 248:

But working part time to pay part of one's expenses is a very different thing from working full time to pay all of them. It is the latter type of student work to which Edward S. Jones, Director of Personnel Research at the University of Buffalo, refers when he says: "Not more than one in a thousand students should attempt to work his way." [37]

Among these examples we can find summary, hint of summary, suggested action, suggestion of importance, and repetition of the theme. From each example, especially when it is read in its full context, we get the intellectual sense of completion and the emotional satisfaction that go with a well-conceived and well-executed act. We are through: *we know it; we feel it.*

Exercises

A. Prepare for class discussion an analysis of the essay "The Woman M.D.," page 369. Your concern will be with technical qualities: pattern, types of data, arrangement, transitional devices, beginning and ending, appeals to

[35] From "The Polkadot Gang," by John Bartlow Martin. *Harper's Magazine*, September, 1942. Reprinted by permission of the author and *Harper's Magazine.*

[36] From "The Cat: Vicious Predator *or* Harmless Pet?" by Allen Parsons. *Outdoor Life,* November, 1941. Reprinted by permission of *Outdoor Life.*

[37] From "Don't Work Your Way," by Roy A. Benjamin. *Current History and Forum,* September, 1940. Reprinted by permission of *Current History.*

your interest—everything you can think of or discover. Make any criticism you think applies for or against the author's writing skill.

B. Procure a copy of any magazine. Bring it to class prepared to analyze the beginnings and endings of the most important essays you find in it. In addition, select one of the essays for a topical analysis of its subject matter. Show the logic of the author's arrangement. Point out his use of transitional devices.

Part Three
Illustrative Readings

A NOTE ON THE READINGS

Discussion of subject matter with one's fellows is an important part of the training of a writer, and it is hoped that the following readings will be fruitful of good talk. The talk, however, should go further than subject matter and include writing techniques. So important is talk about "how writing is written," to use Gertrude Stein's phrase, that it needs to be a planned part of a training program. Classrooms provide opportunity for free discussion. So do study rooms, where friends can get their heads together over a piece of work. The reading section of this book is therefore designed to invite relaxed talk as well as formal study.

To help the talk about expository prose fall into its proper place, the pattern of the readings follows exactly the pattern of the chapters on techniques. The section on informative techniques is paralleled by a section of informative readings, using the same classification in the same order. The section on thematic techniques, also, is paralleled by appropriate readings. Furthermore, the exercises that follow each division of the text are tied to the readings by suitable references. A program that uses the text of any technical division and the exercises that accompany it will thus include the proper readings and the discussion questions that go with each. Tied in this manner, text and readings provide easily managed units of work.

1. INFORMATIVE READINGS

Directions

Fruit Molded in Jelly

5 tablespoons granulated gelatine
1 cup cold water
2 cups boiling water
1⅓ cups sugar
1⅓ cups peach sirup
1 cup sherry
⅔ cup orange juice
⅓ cup lemon juice
Few grains salt
½ can peaches
1 quart box strawberries
1 banana
⅔ cup seeded raisins

Soak gelatine in cold water, dissolve in boiling water, and add sugar, fruit juices, sherry, and salt. Brush over inside of a large fancy mold with olive oil, then wipe out with a piece of tissue paper. Put mold in pan of ice water and pour in just enough of mixture to cover top ornamentations. When firm, put in each ornament a strawberry, blossom end down; add mixture to cover strawberries and let stand until set. Cut banana in slices, crosswise; shape with small round cutter; and arrange a row around strawberry which is in center of mold. Add more jelly mixture to keep banana in place and let set. To remaining jelly mixture add peaches cut in pieces and raisins (cooked until plump in small quantity of boiling water, drained, and cooled). Fill mold with mixture. Chill. Unmold and garnish with strawberries with hulls left on.

TECHNICAL DISCUSSION

1. Does this recipe have any entertainment value? Explain your answer.

2. Describe the style. Rewrite some of the sentences to make them complete. What kind of additions do you make? Do the changes make the recipe any clearer? Why does the author use "cookbook" style?

3. Is the beginning clear? Is the ending too abrupt?
4. Can you sense the personality of the writer?

Conversation with Passengers

Attitude

1. Flight Attendants shall not make remarks to any passengers that could be considered "off color." A pleasant but impersonal attitude shall be maintained at all times—never flippant, never personal.
2. Avoid remarks to passengers regarding religion, racial topics, politics, or other controversial subjects.
3. Speak in pleasant, low-pitched tones. Profanity within hearing of passengers or public will not be tolerated. Slang is not desired.
4. Do not give one passenger all your attention.

Talking of Air Experiences

5. Occasionally passengers will ask the Flight Attendant about his air experiences. In response, use care to avoid the thrilling or exceptional. Emphasize the routine nature of air transportation. Direct the conversation along pleasant lines—scenery, comfort, etc. —and away from sickness, danger, etc.

Weather Diplomacy

6. In your reference to weather conditions concerning flying, we request that you use the term *"flying conditions."* The customary idea of the words "bad weather" for most people is "rainy weather," etc., whereas prevailing flying conditions during rain may be excellent. It is not entirely sensible to say that the weather is fine when it is raining. It is frequently sensible to say that the flying conditions are fine when it is raining. Similarly, when weather or other conditions make a landing advisable at some point other than the scheduled destination, rather than using the term "emergency landing" or "forced landing," use the preferable term "precautionary landing."

"Conversation with Passengers." From *Flight Attendants' Manual,* 1944. Reprinted by permission of Eastern Air Lines, Inc.

7. Some people are seriously perturbed by thunder and lightning, whether on the ground or aloft. Therefore, it appears obvious that normal diplomacy will cause you to avoid using such terms as "thunder," "lightning," "thunderstorm," "storm," etc. when discussing *flying conditions* with passengers, either at the station or aloft. If the seat belt sign goes on, and the passengers ask for an explanation, use such terms as "a little rain," "some turbulence," "a mild front," or similar casual term in describing flight conditions ahead. You must, of course, insist on the necessity of fastening seat belts. However, the passengers' unnecessary concern will be reduced if you use casual terms and a casual unexcited manner in discussing actual or expected flight conditions, even though it may be rough and wet. For further details, refer to "Weather Information as Related to Aircraft," Section C, Paragraphs 13-23.

Inquiries from Passengers

8. Keep well informed on our operations details both aloft and on the ground in order to reply intelligently to a maximum number of passenger questions. When delays occur either at stations or aloft, many passengers may feel the delay is occasioned by mechanical trouble, and are inclined to worry. It is, therefore, of greatest importance that you keep passengers pleasantly and completely informed regarding the reasons for any schedule irregularities, such as unexpectedly returning to a station, or passing over a scheduled stop. Whenever you are obliged to answer a passenger's inquiry with, "I don't know, Sir," always follow with, "but I will find out for you, Sir." Be familiar with EAL [Eastern Air Lines] route maps, timetables, and airline connections (Universal Guide). Acquaint yourself in a general way with the type of plane, its speed and engine horsepower, radio airway facilities, etc. However, do not try to be technical. It is not expected of you. Make no statement that can be considered "official." Refer all such inquiries to the Captain, Field Manager, or nearest EAL official. Whenever any passenger indicates special interest in technical details, ask the Captain or Pilot to talk with the passenger.

9. Study route maps, and be able to identify from aloft cities and points of scenic interest on the route. If passengers inquire, and you do not know the answer, ask the Captain.
10. The Flight Attendant shall make a special effort to call the passengers by name as indicated on the Manifest. Try to add the passenger's name to all short replies, "Yes, Mr. Jones," or "No, Mr. Jones." In the absence of the name, always say, "Yes, Sir," or "Yes, Madam." *Never* merely say "Yes" or "No," except to children under fifteen years of age. In addressing service men and women, always use their ranks: i.e., Major, Lieutenant, Sergeant, Private, etc.

TECHNICAL DISCUSSION

1. Why do you think the paragraphs in this set of directions are numbered?
2. Are the topical headings clear?
3. Can you imagine conversational situations between the Flight attendants and passengers on these topics that are not covered by the directions?
4. Are these directions more interesting to you than those for the fruit molded in jelly? If so, why? Does the author intend any purpose except a practical one? Who are his readers?
5. Can you sense the personality of the writer? If so, explain how it happens you can.

Corn Chowder

A prudent man hesitates to take issue with the book through which Noah Webster has some justifiable claim to fame. It is difficult to believe he takes no cognizance of corn chowder. To the countryman who rates corn chowder on the same high plane as baked beans, or fried salt pork and milk gravy, it is astonishing that Mr. Webster thus off-handedly defines chowder: "A dish made of fresh fish or clams, pork, crackers, onions, etc., stewed together, often in milk." The only solace for the corn chowder connoisseur is that we are told the word comes from the French word meaning kettle or pot.

That is important. Those whose education has been neglected do not realize that the only genuine, history-proved, traditionally accepted

"Corn Chowder." An editorial, January 13, 1945. From The New York *Times*. Reprinted by permission of The New York *Times*.

method of making real corn chowder is in an old iron kettle which sits in a hole ordinarily occupied by one of the stove covers. Such folks, unfortunately, wouldn't know that a good, big, wood-burning kitchen stove has three rows of two each. But if you're going to make corn chowder that's something more than a mess of potatoes, onions and corn in a quart or two of liquid, then these stove lids are important. Corn chowder, to reach the heights of which it is capable, must be started slowly and permitted to gather momentum in flavorful lusciousness as the hours tick by.

First, of course, one tries out two or three slices of salt pork which have a few streaks of lean marbling the white goodness. Then the nut-brown, crisp slices are cut into small cubes and, together with the tried-out fat, placed in the bottom of the kettle sitting in one of the middle-row holes. Two or three onions are cut up and fused with the pork scraps for a period. Next add some half-boiled potatoes and mix the three in friendly confusion. After a half hour or so, add a couple of quarts of whole milk and a can or two of cream-style corn. Little by little, the chowder warms. When all is blended, move the kettle to a front hole over the crackling fire. It should be stirred constantly and with frequent tasting. Never let corn chowder boil. When piping hot, place kettle in one of the rear holes to keep warm. Then, and only then, add salt and pepper to suit.

Unlike beef stew, corn chowder should not entirely cool before the final reheating. A chowder made right after dinner is in its prime for supper. Served with plenty of crackers to crumble into the savory bowlful, a good pat of butter floating on top, plus a few dill pickles, biscuits, deep-dish apple pie and creamy milk, it's a supper dish that the countryman looks forward to as he comes through the ell after the day's chores are done.

TECHNICAL DISCUSSION

1. What are the two purposes of this set of directions? Does the author succeed with both?

2. What is the specific purpose of each paragraph?

3. Describe the tone of the article and point out words and whole sentences that build up the tone.

4. Point out the places where the shift is made from one step in the directions to the next. How is it done?

5. Does the author allow his personality to get into the directions? Explain your answer.

Buoyant Hollow Aquaplane

Few thrills compare with a ride on an aquaplane behind a fast runabout. Of course, the aquaplane must be a good one, easy to manipulate, but stable. It must have the right hitch, the riding angle must be correct, and there must not be too great a drag for the power available. To meet these conditions at minimum expense for materials, a hollow board like that illustrated will be found satisfactory and at the same time comparatively easy to build. The materials cost less than $2.50.

The board has a natural buoyancy of about 60 lb., due to its hollow construction, and this greatly reduces the initial drag at starting. It consists of a frame, made of 1 by 2-in. strips of spruce, cedar, or white pine, shaped around cross ribs to a conventional boat shape. The frame strips are rabbeted on upper and lower inner edges to take a 1/4-in. waterproof (that is, casein-glued) three-ply fir covering, top and bottom. The edge strips and rear rib are of uniform depth, 2 in. The three intermediate ribs are flat on top and flush with the lower surface of the rabbet in the frame. This results in a flat top or deck on the finished aquaplane. The lower surface of the intermediate ribs, however, is dropped to make the board deeper in the center, and deepest at a point 18 in. back from the nose.

As the drawings show, the aquaplane is 2 in. thick around the edges, but 2 3/4 in. thick at the center of the forward rib, 18 in. from the nose. The other two intermediate ribs are 2 1/2 and 2 1/4 in. deep respectively. Since the board will leak to some extent, each of the ribs is notched so that the water may be drained from a corked hole in the rear rib.

After the frame is assembled, the deck is fitted to the rabbet and set up in marine glue or white lead with 1-in. No. 6 brass screws, spaced 2 1/2 in. apart. The board should then be clamped, top down, to a flat surface to prevent warping or twist while the bottom is applied over the curved ribs. The inner surfaces of the entire board should be

"Buoyant Hollow Aquaplane." From *Amateur Craftsman's Cyclopedia,* published by Grosset & Dunlap. Reprinted by permission of Popular Science Publishing Company.

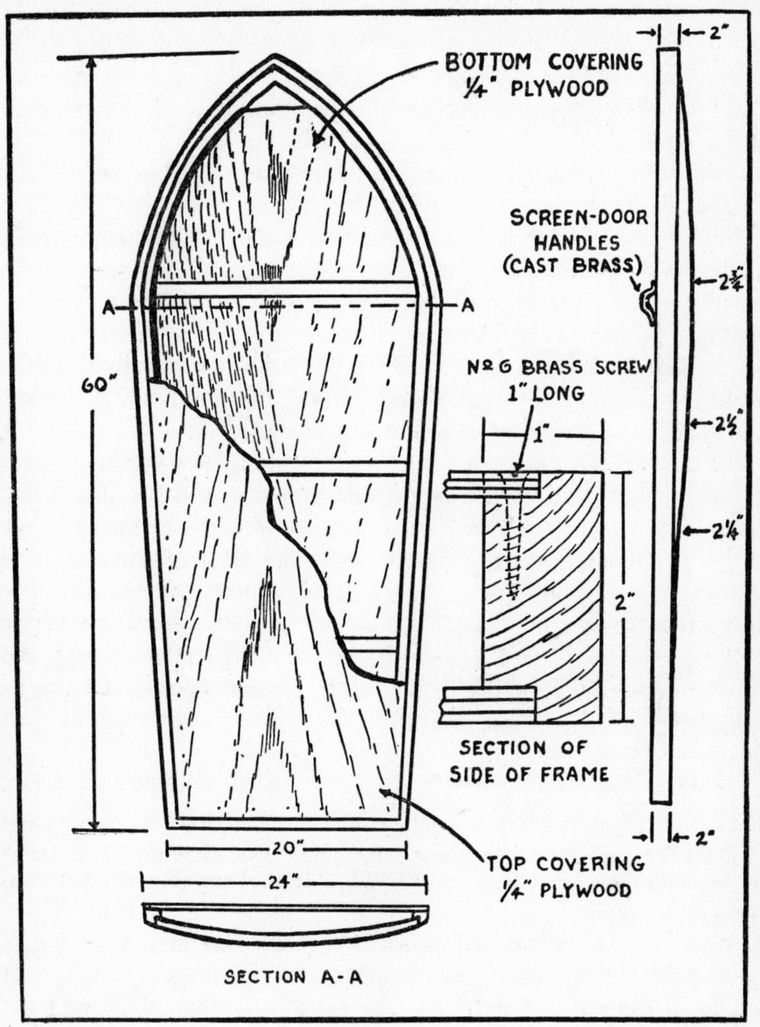
BOTTOM COVERING
1/4" PLYWOOD
60"
A
A
SCREEN-DOOR
HANDLES
(CAST BRASS)
Nº 6 BRASS SCREW
1" LONG
1"
2"
SECTION OF
SIDE OF FRAME
2"
2 3/4"
2 1/2"
2 1/4"
2"
20"
24"
TOP COVERING
1/4" PLYWOOD
SECTION A-A

primed with white lead just prior to assembly to prevent absorption of water. After assembly the entire board may be given a natural finish with spar varnish, or primed with white lead and finished with colored lacquer, the edges being painted a contrasting color.

Two cast-brass screen-door handles are fastened to the upper edge, at the ends of forward rib, for a ½- or ¾-in. hemp rope pull-off bridle, to which the tow rope is attached. A ¾-in. hemp rope handhold bridle of suitable length is also spliced to the handles.

The best planing angle is as flat to the surface of the water as can be maintained without cutting into the waves. A standing position about 18 in. forward from the tail, between the two rear intermediate ribs, seems to be correct. By inclining the board to right or left, it may be skidded completely across the wake of the towing vessel; by inclining acutely—"kicking" the board—and pulling up on the bridle sharply, the board can be jumped clear out of the water.

This board has been used successfully behind a 16-h.p. twin outboard motor with a 14-ft. boat at 16 or 18 m.p.h., and has also shown its stability and its responsiveness to control when being towed in the wake of a homemade 16-ft. sport boat. The latter is powered by a 32-h.p. inboard motor with a 12 by 18 wheel, and pulls the board at better than 20 m.p.h.

Because of its shape, the board has a natural rise at the start and a greater degree of flexibility in the water, especially for stunts, than a solid board of equal proportions.

TECHNICAL DISCUSSION

1. Do these directions have any entertainment value? Explain.
2. Does the reader need to know something about carpentry in order to understand these directions easily? What is the meaning of the word *rabbeted?*
3. Would these directions be clear without the drawing?
4. Point out the transitions between steps in the directions.
5. Are there directions here for something else than making the aquaplane?
6. Does the author end his article appropriately? Explain.

Early American End Table

The simple lines of early American design are best displayed in the many small tables, stools and benches which originated during this

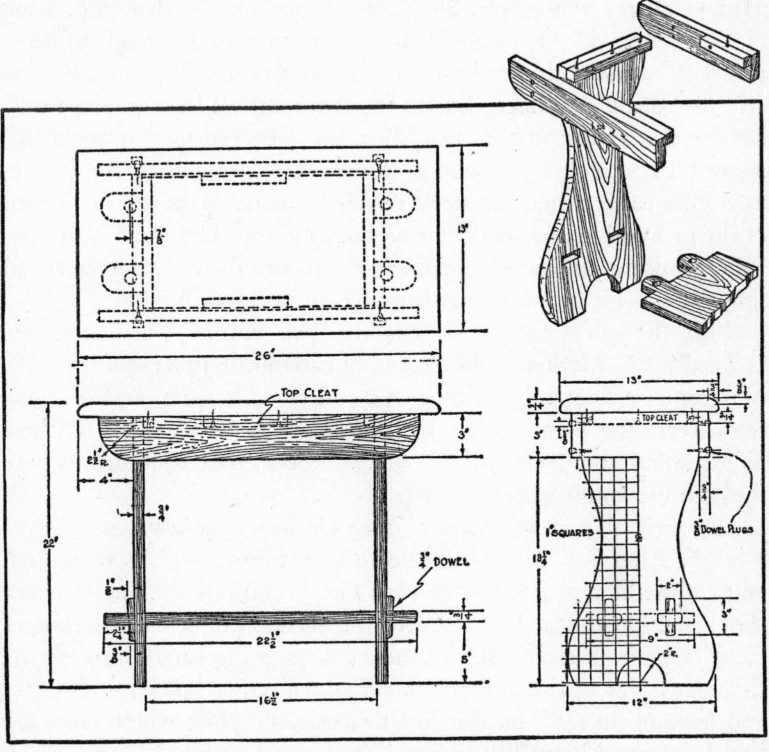

DETAIL DRAWINGS OF THE EARLY AMERICAN END TABLE

era. Such pieces were solid in construction because they were built for hard service; yet their essential proportions and restrained scroll work contributed to make them distinctive and even worthy of copying for homes of today.

The table illustrated here possesses all the attributes of solid con-

"Early American End Table." From *The Home Craftsman Magazine,* January-February 1941. Courtesy *The Home Craftsman Magazine.*

struction, good proportion and simple design. Moreover, it is a type of table which the home craftsman can make with little difficulty. It is just the right size for use beside your favorite chair, or you may decide to make a pair for both ends of the sofa.

The table should be made of any of the typical colonial woods such as pine, cherry and maple. Start construction on the two ends. Each end measures ¾" x 12" x 21¼". If you are fortunate enough to get a board 12" wide (this should be easy if you choose white pine) the job will be greatly simplified. Locate the two mortises in each end member for the tenons on the shelf, then cut these mortises, using a ¾" auger bit and a sharp chisel. Do this work before cutting the design, as it goes easier when the stock remains square. Make a half pattern of the end design and mark this on both surfaces. Cut the design carefully, working just outside the line, and smooth the edges to the actual line, using a file or a sanding drum set up in the drill press.

With the ends completed, cut the two aprons which measure ¾" x 3" x 23". Mark and cut the end of each apron to a radius of 2½". Mark square lines 2⅞" in from the end of each apron and on these lines locate the points where the screws are to be inserted. At these points counterbore with a ⅜" bit, ¼" deep, and continue to bore through the apron with a ¼" bit.

The shelf should be made of a single board, measuring ¾" x 9" x 22½". After squaring this piece to size, measure 3" in from each end and make a square line on each face to indicate the line of tenon shoulders. Do this at both ends of the shelf. Complete the layout of the 2" tenons on each end. Cut these tenons, being careful to keep the shoulder edges square and accurate. Make a center line on each tenon and measure in 2⅛" on this line to locate the place where holes are bored for tenon keys. The boring is performed with a ¾" bit.

The ¾" table top is squared to size, 13" wide and 26" long. A line is marked around the top ¾" in from the edge to limit the area that is to be rounded with plane, file and sandpaper.

Before assembling the table, sand the parts thoroughly and round all corners slightly. Start the assembly by connecting the shelf and end pieces. Dowels, ¾" thick and 3" long, are used to key the tenons. These dowels should be planed flat and slightly tapered on the edge that will adjoin the table ends.

With the shelf in place, proceed to attach the two aprons, using 1½" No. 10 flat head screws. As indicated in the drawings the screws are concealed with ⅜" dowel plugs the ends of which are slightly rounded and protrude ⅛" beyond the surface. During assembly of the table it is important to check the squareness of joined units. The top is attached to the under structure with ¾" cleats which are fastened inside the ends and the aprons with screws located as indicated in the sketch.

Before applying the finish be sure that all parts are thoroughly sanded. If the end table if made of pine an excellent pine stain may be provided by mixing one part burnt umber, three parts raw sienna, and one-half part burnt sienna. These colors are obtainable compounded in oil. They are mixed in turpentine with a small amount of linseed oil added. The resulting stain should be sufficiently heavy to be worked after being applied to the wood. This is important because thin, penetrating stains are absorbed more quickly by porous portions of the wood and the final appearance is uneven and blotchy. The heavier stain, however, may be applied and rubbed with a cloth in such manner as to compensate for the peculiarities of grain and texture of the wood.

After the stain has been applied and allowed to dry, the table is given three coats of very thin shellac. Each coat of shellac is permitted to dry and is then rubbed thoroughly with fine steel wool before the next coat is applied. Several coats of paste wax are applied to form a protective surface.

TECHNICAL DISCUSSION

1. What is the function of the first two paragraphs?
2. Do these directions require a knowledge of carpentry if they are to be easily followed? Explain.
3. Explain (or ask a student in shop to do it) the following terms: *mortise, tenon, counterbore, dowel.*
4. In what way do the drawings aid an understanding of the directions?
5. Point out the places in the text where the author refers to the drawings Do you think he should have made more references?
6. How does the author end?

How to Cast a Fly

BREEMS FORREST

I remember back in the days when I was a youngster that I stood still as a mouse on the banks of a famous English trout stream one warm spring afternoon watching "some feller" casting a wet fly. His rod must have been all of 16 feet long!

But he handled it easily, gracefully. His pick-up was smooth as a ballet dancer's exit and his delivery delicate and amazingly accurate. The long, clumsy rod flexed backwards and forwards in a perfect arc and he took three trout from the same pool before he went on down-stream. I ran most of the way home, goggle-eyed with excitement, to tell the family what I had seen and to announce that I wanted a fly rod more than anything else in the world.

Now, whenever I think about fly casting, I remember that performance and wonder what that old-timer would have been able to do with one of our lighter, modern, more delicate fly rods. Without question he would have found his fishing less fatiguing to the wrist and forearm, but I doubt if he would have enjoyed it more than he seemed to be doing.

What I was watching that afternoon, although I did not realize it at the time, was a finished demonstration of the basic principle of good fly rod handling. The angler was allowing the rod to do the work, and this is as much the basic principle today, with our slim slivers of tempered bamboo which may weigh no more than three or four ounces, as it was then when rods were made of greenheart of lancewood and weighed a pound or more.

Fly casting with present-day rods is really quite easy and takes but little practice for even the most awkward beginner to acquire sufficient skill to catch fish. The important thing is to start correctly, to learn the proper way to hold the rod and line during the act of casting. Studying the illustrations accompanying this article will be found very helpful not only to the beginner but to those who, by reason of a faulty style, may not be getting all the enjoyment there is in fly casting.

Remember that it is the *line* which carries out the leader and fly—

"How to Cast a Fly." From *Hunting & Fishing*, March, 1941. Reprinted by permission of *Hunting & Fishing*.

not the fly or leader which carries out the line. Cut off leader and fly, and rod and line will cast perfectly without them.

It is the *weight* in the fly line which makes fly casting possible. After you have made a few casts by following instructions pictured in the accompanying casting charts and have discovered for yourself that putting out line is simple, read over the following hints on good fly casting.

Pick up line from the water only after first raising the rod tip and being sure that none of the line is under the water.

Keep both elbows close to the side whenever possible. (The casting arm should always be kept with the elbow at the side if you want to develop good form.)

Try to keep your back-cast *above* the level of your head. A high back cast means an easy, graceful forward cast.

When "stripping in" line with the left hand, keep the coils of even length.

On the back cast, be sure your rod goes no more than a few inches beyond the perpendicular.

Before any casts are attempted, fix your mind's-eye on an imaginary bull's-eye—a mark about 20 inches above the spot where the fly is to be placed. Always cast at this imaginary spot—20 inches above the water—not directly at the surface of the water. The allowance is necessary to prevent the line landing forcibly on the water. This will soon become an automatic action. Now let's try a cast.

Pull a few feet of line, in addition to the leader, through the tip of the rod (Fig. A) and let it rest on the water. The hand holding the rod also presses the line against the cork grip above the reel, preventing more line being pulled from the reel.

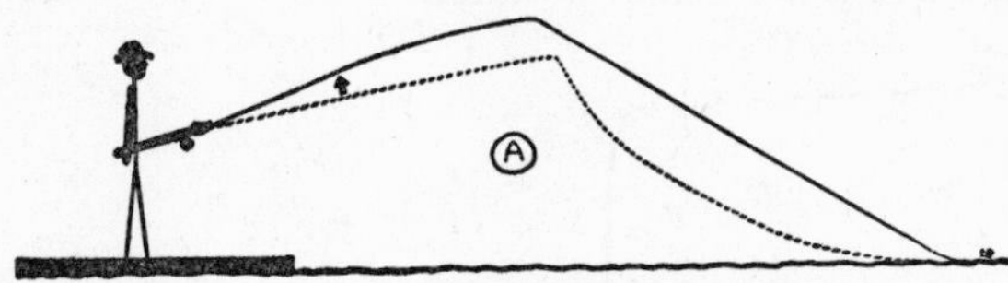

Raise the rod until only the leader and six or eight feet of line rest on the water—the rod tip should not be higher than shown in the diagram. This is to eliminate slack and place a slight drag on the rod tip.

Without allowing this slight tension to be lost, snap the rod into the position shown in Fig. B, propelling the line high and backward. Stop the rod at the vertical position shown and *wait.*

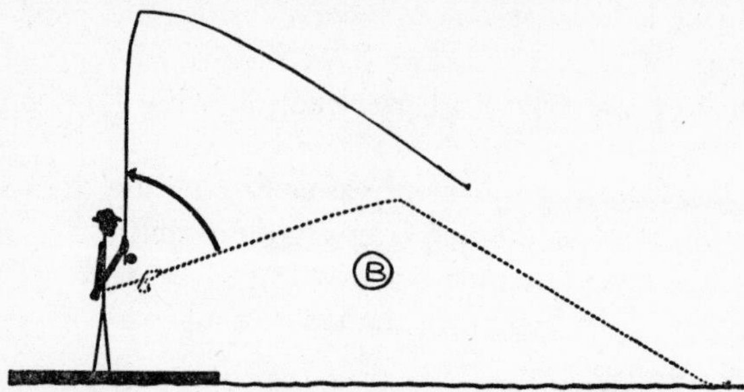

This pause (Fig. C) is necessary to allow the line to straighten out behind the caster. With very little practice, the slight backward "pull" of the line as it reaches the end of the back cast will soon be recognized. *Wait* for it, as it marks the point to commence the forward stroke.

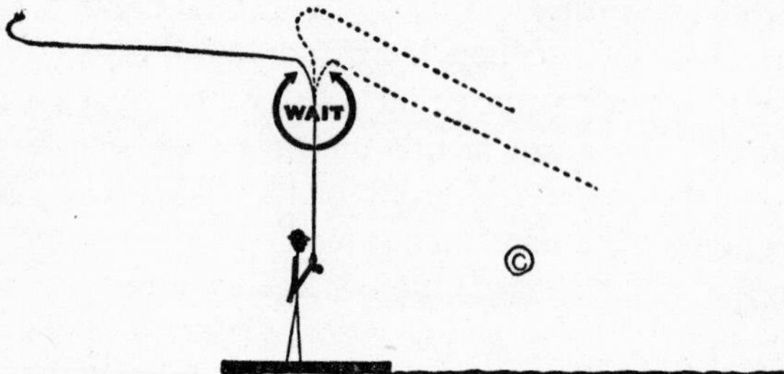

At the instant of maximum "pull" start the forward cast (Fig. D)—a clean, unhesitating tack-hammer-like stroke that follows through until the rod is in a horizontal position.

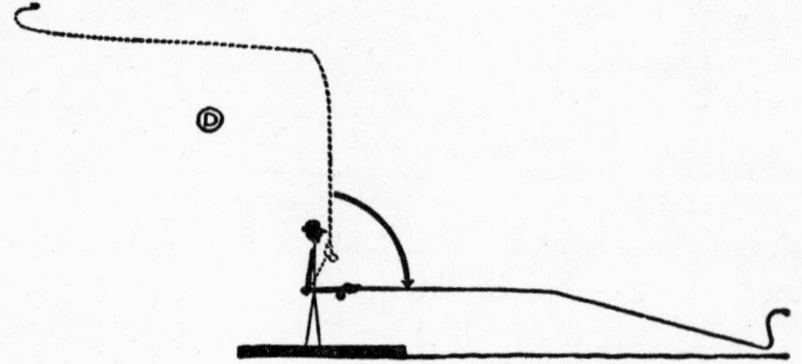

To cause the fly to drop to the water before leader and line do so (Fig. E), raise the forearm, sharply elevating the rod tip as the cast reaches the stage shown in Fig. D.

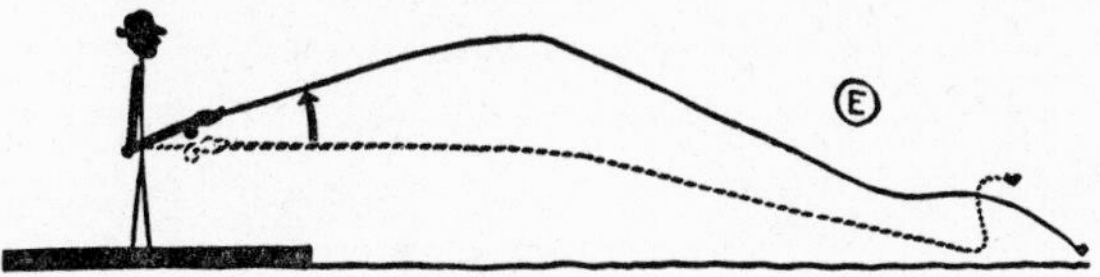

TECHNICAL DISCUSSION

1. Why is the author of this article so long in getting to the directions?

2. Does the preliminary material contribute to understanding the art of fly casting? Explain.

3. What help to understanding is provided by the drawings?

4. Point out the places in the text where the author refers to the drawings. Explain his method of keeping the textual material and the drawings in clear relation to each other.

5. How does the author end his article?

Scientific Description

The First Robot Bomber

GAITHER LITTRELL

Experimental work on radio-controlled bomber planes is being carried on by technical experts of every major nation in the world today. But self-propelled, pilotless, automatically-disintegrating planes were developed and flown in the United States 28 years ago!

To Robert Modisette, technical expert and chief of the contract termination group at Consolidated Vultee Aircraft Corporation, Vultee Field Division, Downey, Calif., there is nothing new in the theory of airplanes of the self-flying type, except radio. For it was Modisette who, back in 1916, built and flew what is believed to be the first plane of that kind.

"The First Robot Bomber." From *Flying,* November, 1944. Reprinted by permission of *Flying.*

Modisette developed the self-flying plane when he was vice president of the Mullin Manufacturing Company of Salem, O. The Mullin concern, which is still on the New York Stock Exchange and currently engaged in building parts for truck bodies, was producing boats, automobile bodies and airplane parts before World War I.

"It was my belief at that time that airplanes had an extremely important future in military usage, so we started designing them," Modisette relates. "We were especially interested in producing training planes for would-be pilots—at that time there was nothing but the finished combat plane."

Mullin's first venture in this new field was a training aid that resembles the present day Link Trainer. Next came an advanced "semi-flying" trainer that could rise only six feet off the ground. Finally they developed a full-sized, twin-engined biplane that really could get up in the air and cruise for miles.

It was from this plane that the self-flying bomber was developed.

Four such pilotless planes were loaded with practice bombs, flown to their targets, and disintegrated by release of the bomb load in an exhibition staged for United States Navy officers in July, August and September of 1917. Success of the demonstrations resulted in preliminary negotiations of the Mullin company with the Navy for mass production. The Armistice put a stop to the project, however.

Modisette, whose inventive talent has currently been put to use by Consolidated Vultee in following up suggestions made by employees for a speed-up in producing *Liberator* bombers and other projects, became a Navy flyer at the time his self-flying plane was first developed and demonstrated for the Navy.

He called his bomber creation the "Hot Shot." The "Hot Shot" was built of scrap spruce, rejected airplane cloth and dope at a total cost of $452. Its prototype, the orthodox trainer regularly sold by the Mullins firm to pilots and flying schools, had cost $2,450 to build nearly two years earlier.

The "Hot Shot" had a wingspread of 46 feet and measured 19 ft. 8 in. from nose to tail. Unloaded, it weighed 1,790 pounds and carried three bombs weighing 65 pounds each. It was powered with two Ford automobile engines that mechanics had "hopped up." It had a maximum speed of 72 m.p.h. at a ceiling of 1,500 feet. Cruising range was 160 miles.

When the plane released its bombs, it fell apart in mid-air and hurtled in pieces down upon what would be enemy troops. This disintegration was planned so that the enemy could not reload it and send bombs back to the owners.

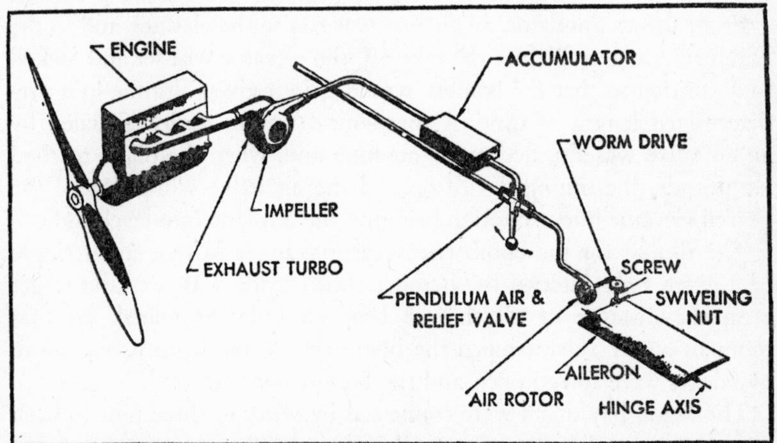

DIAGRAM SHOWING SIMPLE OPERATION OF THE FORCED AIR SYSTEM WHICH CONTROLLED AILERONS, KEEPING BOMBER IN LEVEL FLIGHT. TIMING GEAR CAUSED ELEVATORS TO LEVEL PLANE OFF AT DESIRED ALTITUDE

The principle of the plane is explained by Modisette as follows:

An exhaust turbo and air impeller were connected to the exhaust ports of the engines on the same shaft. The turbo was turned by the force of the exhaust. From the impeller, the air was forced into an accumulator and through this to a pendulum air and relief valve and, when the air line was open, through this pendulum air valve to an air rotor.

A worm was cut directly into the end of the air rotor shaft. The worm gear meshing with the worm reduced the speed of the actuating screw. A thread was cut on the worm gear shaft which went through a swiveling unit attached to the end of each aileron; thus the function of the pendulum air valve in opening or shutting off the air line acted upon the aileron; under all conditions the pendulum air valve remained in a position perpendicular to the surface of the earth—despite the airplane's banking to port or starboard.

When the "Hot Shot" banked, the air valve opened and, through the air rotor, the action of the worm drive automatically forced the ailerons into a position which brought the ship back into level flight.

The take-off, climb and leveling-off processes were equally simple.

From the accumulator, an air line was run to the elevator and to the bomb release gear. Before the take-off, the elevator was set and locked in a position so that the bomber would gain a given altitude in a predetermined length of time. A mechanical timing device actuated by an air valve was attached to the air lines and, when the plane reached its altitude, the timing device opened the air valve which forced the geared elevator into a position bringing the airplane into level flight.

The timing for the bomb release gear was set so that upon elapse of a given time interval the bomber theoretically was over the target area, the distance of which had been carefully estimated. At that moment an air valve tripped the bomb release mechanism, the bomb bay doors were forced open and the bombs were released.

The bomb bay doors were connected by wires to three pins in each wing, upper and lower, port and starboard. These pins were placed in joints which joined the center sections and outer wings together. The opening of the bomb bay doors pulled the pins out of their fittings, the wings folded upward, and the airplane hurtled earthward like a disjointed goose, following its bombs down upon a startled enemy—a theoretical enemy, that is.

On one of the four tests for the Navy, Modisette said the timing mechanism—which he described as "nothing more than an accurate clock with a few improvisations"—was set for a 90-mile flight. The target was not hit squarely because of an unexpected change in wind, but bombs—and the plane—fell in "the general area," the designer declared.

The other three demonstrations were more successful because of the shorter distances and "were almost right on the bull's eye," he claims.

Today, scientists are expending tens of thousands of dollars to perfect remote-controlled bombing planes. Modisette firmly, but modestly, believes that some consideration might be given to the theory he and the Mullin company put in practice 28 years ago, now that scientific developments are advanced to make his principle even more simple and inexpensive.

Since the jet bomb, most unorthodox of Nazi war weapons, is little more than a winged, long-range artillery shell, Modisette's argument seems to have point. Inaccuracy of the jet bomb might well be circumvented through radio control of a pilotless bomber.

TECHNICAL DISCUSSION

1. Where does the description of the robot bomber actually begin?
2. Which of the preliminary details are helpful in describing the robot bomber?
3. What value do the other preliminary details have?
4. Is the bomber described so completely that a builder could use the description for technical purposes? For what type of reader do you think the article is written? Explain.
5. How does the author explain the mechanics of level flight?
6. Does the ending seem appropriate?

Classification

The A B C's of Hats

HELENE GARNELL

"H" is for hat—so much for that.

Before we go further in our millinery primer, we must learn the basic hat silhouettes—otherwise we may not know what we are doing.

It would be sad, indeed, to start out to make an angelfood cake and wind up with a devil's food. It would be just as bad to plan a sailor and make a turban.

Basic hat silhouettes have remained much the same through the years, in successive fashion eras and in many lands. Every country, for instance, has its native turban, just as it has its native pancake and its native stew.

The first and most versatile of our basic hats is the *sailor*. This is a

"The A B C's of Hats." From *It's Fun to Make a Hat,* by Helene Garnell. Reprinted by permission of Liveright Publishing Corporation.

hat with a crown and a straight brim—flat, straight, uncompromising. But tilt the brim on one side, and you have something frivolous and gay; turn up both sides and you have a *padre* sailor; turn down the brim and take a tuck in the back, and it's a *cloche;* bend the brim up on three sides, and it's a *tricorne*—on two sides, it's a *bicorne;* turn the brim up in front, and you have an *off-the-face* hat; use a crownless

THE SAILOR—
MOST VERSATILE

THE TURBAN—
IT'S ALL IN THE TWIST

brim, tilted and crimped, and you have a *Watteau*. The variations are endless, depending only on the limits of your own imagination—but the basic shape is still the sailor.

The next basic hat is the *turban*. This is simply a piece of fabric, twisted and manipulated to suit your fancy. It has very little foundation, depends entirely on drape for its character. You may make turbans high or low, flamboyant or discreet, frivolous or practical. It is all in the twist of the fabric, having no rules—therefore we shall not go into lengthy details.

Then comes the *calot,* another basic hat from which you may make innumerable variations. The calot proper is simply a beanie, or skull cap, fitted exactly to the crown of your head. Make it of felt or fabric, straw or cellophane. If you like, trim it with anything under the sun. Let your fancy be your guide.

From the calot we derive the many varieties of the *pompadour hat,* the *half-hat,* the *coronet,* the *curvette,* the *templet* and many others.

THE PILLBOX AND THE CALOT

The calot crown may be used in combination with a sailor brim for endless shapes of hats.

You may make the calot in sections if it is of fabric, or block it on your "doll" if it is of felt. You start with a complete headcovering, then cut it out as you desire.

Cut a calot in two pieces, and you have two half-hats, which may be decorated in many ways. Take two calots, one for each side of the head, and you have a templet.

Cut a little sliver and add it to the front, and you have a coronet.

The calot is basic, like the sailor and changes little from year to year. It has been one of woman's favorites since the days of Romeo and Juliet, or even before.

Cover it with sequins or beads, and you have a little glittering dinner or cocktail hat. Add flowers or fantasies, and you have another type of dressy, frivolous hat. Wear it plain, and it's right for the most tailored suit.

"B" IS FOR BASIC BERET

You may add quills, plumes, veils or what-have-you. Next to the sailor, the calot is your most versatile basic hat.

Another classic in your list of basic hats is the *beret*. This is the flat, brimless, pancake type of hat worn by women of all ages and all nations. Best known is the Basque beret of France which has been adopted as a sort of uniform by American schoolgirls and borrowed by their mammas.

The beret is curved, and may be big or little, flat or puffy, dashing or discreet. It may be worn straight on the head, just on top of a pompadour, for a highly sophisticated effect. It may be plastered on the back of the head, schoolgirl fashion, or it may be pulled dashingly forward over one eye, in the General Montgomery style.

If made of fabric, it must be made in sections; if of felt, it must be carefully blocked.

To me, the beret has always looked a little like a sausage on the head, and just now I don't like it much. Next year, however, I may be wild about it. Our tastes change, along with the seasons.

Next on the basic hat list is the *breton*. This is a simple, tailored type of hat with a rounded brim turned up all the way around. The crown usually is rounded, too, and the whole depends for its effectiveness on careful blocking. This, too, is a favorite youthful style, worn by young girls a great deal, but also adaptable to more sophisticated styling. It varies only in size, material and trimming. But it is an important basic for the repertoire of the home milliner, and cannot be made from any of the other basic shapes.

Last in the basic hat parade is the *pillbox*. This is a small, brimless, shaped hat, differing from the calot in that it is not shaped to the head but perches on top. It may be round, oblong or square, can be stiff and crisp or soft and manipulated. It is basically the crown part of the classic sailor. It is highly important, because it is used in so many variations and combinations.

Like its sisters in the basic hat family it may be made of practically any material, from felt to straw and from satin to gingham. If it is of fabric, it must have a fairly firm foundation of crinoline or willow or one of the other foundation fabrics.

It may be used for any occasion, from sports to the dressiest restaurant dinner, depending on fabric and trimming.

You may make a high, narrow pillbox like a stovepipe, or a small flat one like the container for which it was named. You may make it of felt and decorate it with a flamboyant quill or a plume, or you make it of satin, sprinkle it with sequins, add a flower or two, and have a dressy dinner hat.

Of straw, it goes anywhere. Of felt, it may complement your tailored suit or your afternoon dress.

You use it as a crown for other brimmed hats. It is one of the most useful hat shapes to know.

These, then, are the basic hat shapes from which you can make all the other hats under the sun—all the hats of history, all the hats that beckon to you so beguilingly from the milliner's show window and frighten you with their fat price tags.

TECHNICAL DISCUSSION

1. Comment on the style of this article. Is it aimed at professional milliners? Explain.
2. Indicate the places where the description of each basic hat begins. How are the places marked so that you can find them?
3. Show where the author divides any of the basic types into secondary types and point out how the secondary division is indicated so that the reader is not confused.
4. The *breton* hat is not illustrated by a drawing. Can you draw one by using the written details as a guide? If not, can you add the necessary written details?
5. Does the author make any references to the drawings?

Types of Forest Fires

H. R. KYLIE, G. H. HIERONYMUS, and A. G. HALL

Three types of forest fires are recognized by foresters: (1) Ground fires, (2) surface fires, (3) crown fires. A fourth kind may occur in the forest when a tree is fired by lightning and is extinguished before it spreads to the forest. Such fires are known as "tree fires."

Ground Fires. Fires which burn in the thick duff and leaf mold and leaves on the ground or in peat lands are known as ground fires. Often they burn along under the surface, giving off little or no smoke. For this reason they are difficult to locate until they burst out in the

"Types of Forest Fires." From *CCC Forestry,* by H. R. Kylie, G. H. Hieronymus, and A. G. Hall. Department of Agriculture, Washington, D. C.

dry leaves on top. They may burn for days or weeks unnoticed, killing roots and underground organisms essential to tree growth, and on a dry day come to the surface to start a large surface fire. These fires often occur where campfires have been built on thick mats of duff. It is not uncommon to find a foot or more of duff in dense pine, hemlock, or spruce stands, as coniferous needles decay very slowly, particularly in the North. Often when a forest fire is thought to be out ground fires will smolder for weeks. Trenching of fire lines down to mineral soil is necessary to overcome outbreaks.

Surface fires spread over the ground, consuming dry leaves, sticks, low brush, and small trees. Small reproduction is killed, and although large standing timber is not burned up, the heat retards root growth, sours sap, and burns the bark from the bases of trees. Large, basal fire scars form a port of entry for insects and diseases when the protective bark has been burned away. In a few years the butt log becomes riddled with insect tunnels, and decay starts working upward to make the tree worthless.

Crown fires are of two classes. The "running crown fire" spreads through the tops, leaping from tree to tree ahead of the slower-burning surface fire. As flaming branches drop to the ground, showers of sparks spray the leaf litter, advancing the destruction along the surface. The "dependent crown fire" travels with the surface fire when the condition of the overstory is such that it must be dried before ignition. Heat waves, rolling up, evaporate all leaf and twig moisture, and tongues of flames lick upward from the burning brush to transform the crowns into fiery torches.

When the three types of fire sweep over a forest, an area of complete desolation remains, the ground fire penetrating deeper and deeper until only powdery ashes cover a baked mineral soil. The desolation is intensified when rains follow, washing the ashes into streams where their alkaline properties kill fish and make the water unfit for drinking; and erosion leaves a heap of rocks—sun-bleached and sterile—in place of a wooded hillside.

TECHNICAL DISCUSSION

1. Is this classification meant for professional foresters, foresters-in-training, or laymen? Explain.

2. Point out the variation in the way each type of forest fire is introduced. Do you approve?
3. Which of the three types is divided into secondary types. Are the secondary types clearly indicated? Explain.
4. What is the value of the last paragraph?

Factual Narration

THE GENERAL PROCESS

AM 23-3: NK to GX

An hour after she had arrived from Los Angeles they washed the dust of a continent from the ship, and when they had her shining as brightly as a platinum ornament in a jeweler's tray a rubber-tired baby tractor hooked onto her tail and dragged her into American Airlines' hangar at Newark Airport. There two crews of mechanics—a dozen men in all—at once started giving her an inspection, for there was a chance that she might be scheduled to fly back to the Coast on Trip 7—the Southerner—that night. They put tall ladders up by her nose and stripped the aluminum cowling from her 1,100-horsepower Cyclones preparatory to the engine check. They peered at her hydraulic landing-gear apparatus and examined her tires. They went into her cockpit and tested her controls, inspecting the hundred odd knobs and dials and buttons and switches and levers and gauges surrounding the pilots' seats, from the simple chronometers and altimeters to devices with cabalistic titles like Artificial Horizon, Turn and Bank, and Gyropilot. They wiggled her rudder and flapped her wing and stabilizer ailerons. They turned on her landing, navigation, cabin, and cockpit lights and replaced a couple of dimming bulbs. They pumped air in and out of the rubber de-icer boots on the leading edges of her wings, and checked the supply of wood alcohol and glycerin mixture that would prevent icing of her propellers. They went over every square foot of her glistening aluminum "skin," and every square inch of her three-bladed alloy propellers. They gave her two newly charged storage batteries for the ones she had flown from Los Angeles.

Presently they were joined by men from the commissary department, who entered the ship's cabin and took up the carpet for cleaning, stripped the berths and remade them with fresh linen, ran a vacuum over the seats, and washed the windows, walls, and ceiling. They checked the reading lights and the ventilators, installed fresh antimacassars on every seat, and in every seat pocket made sure there were American Airlines timetables, packages of post cards in glassine wrappers, maps of the route, cards stating that the seat was occupied, and printed messages from Mr. C. R. Smith, the President of the company, beginning with "How Did You Like Your Trip?" and ending with a request for suggestions on improving the service. Under every seat they placed a large cardboard carton for the accommodation of passengers who might become airsick. They tried the twelve-volt electric shaver in the tiny men's room at the rear of the cabin. They tallied the linen, the silver, and the plates and cups in the stewardess's serving pantry. They put copies of the latest issues of the *New York Times, Life,* and the *Sportsman Pilot* into binders and stowed them under the serving table along with the other magazines.

By evening the inspection had been completed. By evening, too, the ship—a Douglas DST fourteen-passenger sleeper with "Flagship *Arizona*" painted on her nose—had been scheduled not on Trip 7, but on next afternoon's American Mercury, Trip 3. By evening the New York reservations office had sold three of her berths clear through from Newark to Los Angeles, and one from Newark to Tucson. Nashville, her first scheduled stop, sold another to Los Angeles, and Dallas a fifth. New York reservations informed the publicity department in the same offices at 25 Vanderbilt Avenue that one of the passengers was to be Miss Gloria Goldilocks, coming in on the *Queen Mary* at 3:00 P.M. and going out on the Mercury at 5:10 P.M., en route between a six-month contract with Gaumont-British and a three-year contract with Metro-Goldwyn-Mayer. It went without saying that Miss Goldilocks would be assigned the plane's "Skyroom." The Skyroom was aft of the cockpit in the noisiest and shakiest part of the ship, but it was semiprivate and it was generally reserved for eminent travelers.

By morning New York reservations had sold three more spaces to Los Angeles and one tentatively to Nashville. The weather reports coming in almost continuously from the governmental meteorological service, from the airport ground observatories, and from dozens of pilots in the air suggested that by sundown Nashville's 1,000-foot ceiling might be closed in below the 400-foot minimum permitted by American Airlines and the Civil Aeronautics Authority for letdowns. Reservations pointed this out to the Nashville passenger, but told him that if the Mercury had to take Atlanta or Memphis as an alternate airport he would be given train transportation to his destination. Nashville meanwhile made a similar proposition to its Los Angeles passenger and persuaded him to go out on the Southerner from Memphis if the Mercury was unable to get into Nashville.

Toward midafternoon the *Arizona* was towed out of the hangar and parked near the terminal. A little cart containing a storage battery was rolled up under her nose. Wires from the cart were plugged into the ship's electrical circuit in order to spare her own batteries the heavy starting load; the chief mechanic climbed into the cockpit and turned up her motors. At four o'clock the co-pilot assigned to the flight—"first officer" in the naval terminology of American Airlines—came out of the hangar and joined the mechanic. At five after four the flight pilot, or "captain," arrived from the Newark hotel in which the company maintains a suite of rooms for the use of its male personnel, and at four-ten the stewardess arrived from another Newark hotel designated by the company for its female personnel. The pilot, whose name might have been King, was an ex-army flier who had covered a million miles during his nine years with American Airlines. He was tall enough and handsome enough and rugged enough to have stepped into the hero's role in any movie epic of the airways without plastic surgery, dentistry, or an ounce of padding in his dark blue uniform. He was a union man, holding a card from the Air Line Pilots' Association, an A. F. of L. affiliate, but a very de luxe union man with very de luxe wages. Last year he had earned $3,000 base pay for merely belonging to American Airlines. In addition he had been paid on a sliding hourly scale for flying the maximum of eighty-five hours per month per pilot allowed by the Civil Aeronautics Authority —from a low of $4.20 per daytime hour with slower equipment to a high of $7.50 per night hour with Douglas Sleepers doing 195 miles per hour or better. With certain bonuses for the months in which he had flown more than 10,000 miles this had given him a total annual income of over $8,500; this night's flight alone—he would take the ship only as far as Nashville where a new crew would board her and fly her to Dallas—would net him $62.80.

The stewardess—Miss Jones, for convenience—was a registered nurse, an inch shorter than the five-feet-five maximum prescribed by American Airlines and five pounds under the 120-pound weight ceiling. She had been hired when she was twenty-six, the last year in which stewardesses are ever hired, and she was now twenty-seven, earning $125 per month. In three more years she would be forced to retire on account of her age, but the chances were that long before then she would quit the service and get married—probably to a passenger rather than to Captain King or any of the other 233 pilots and co-pilots in the company. Miss Jones was neither beautiful nor glamorous. Plenty of girls with better features and more figure had applied for her job and been rejected, it being against company policy to take on conspicuously attractive young women. But if she was somewhat usual in appearance, Miss Jones was undeniably a "clean-cut, clear-thinking young woman, adept in dealing with people, not too retiring nor too forward," as the stewardess's manual bade her to be. Furthermore, Miss Jones knew a great deal. She knew, for example, the right moment at which to present aromatic spirits of ammonia to a queasy passenger gagging in rough air. To curious travelers who were forever asking "What keeps an airplane up?" she could patiently explain that it was a combination of planing surface and speed, and that the vacuum created by air rushing over the top surface of a wing exerted twice the lifting force of air pressure on the lower surface. She knew how to describe the intricacies of instrument flying and the simplicities of contact flying. She knew the genuine art of escaping the attentions of occasionally amorous passengers while leaving them with the delightful impression that she was reluctant to escape. She knew that she should never use the word "trouble" in conversation with a passenger. An American Airlines ship might land "to make an adjustment" but not on account of "trouble."

These basic things and a great many others like them Miss Jones had learned during her training course at the school for stewardesses in Chicago. They were all down in her manual, and in case she should ever grow confused about any situation she had only to consult her copy of "The *Best* Way," a little mimeographed book that applies a Dale Carnegie brand of psychology to her dealings with passengers. Altogether Miss Jones was an engaging young woman, and in spite of a certain sexlessness resulting from thick stockings and an overtight girdle beneath her severely cut uniform, she would have little difficulty acquiring a husband. The prospect of so doing had been her chief reason for becoming a stewardess in the first place, and the same was probably true of most of the 117 girls in the service. Their success in this pursuit largely accounts for the 33 per cent annual turnover in American Airlines stewardesses and occasionally worries Mr. Newton Wilson, the Supervisor of Passenger Service, who has charge of them. Someone in the company is supposed to have suggested that if American Airlines hired girls that were just a wee bit less attractive than the incumbents both the marriage rate and the turnover would drop and over $10,000 a year might be saved in the operation of the training school, where it costs about $425 to prepare each candidate in a six-week course before she can be assigned to a run. But Mr. C. R. Smith would certainly veto any attempt to lower the quality of stewardesses. No one in the company has ever tried to calculate their goodwill value, but it is conceded that they are the most effective salesmen in the organization, and that as far as the predominantly masculine traffic is concerned they represent by themselves a good reason for traveling in airplanes.

Captain King and Miss Jones went at once to the flight-control office in a small annex to the hangar. In this close and smoky place, full of the mingled noises of telephones and radiotelephones, radiotelegraphs, typewriters, and teletypewriters, King studied the Flight Release for Trip 3, containing a digest of the day's weather reports. In the Newark area conditions were "Genrly CAVU," meaning ceiling and visibility unlimited, with light west-southwesterly winds, the dew point at 34 and temperature at 39° Fahrenheit, and the barometric pressure 30.11 inches. Washington reported rain and some icing at 4,000 feet, and southwest of Washington there were fifty-mile head winds and a heavy overcast. Nashville still remained open but might close up at any time, and King would receive definite landing instructions by radio during the flight. Attached to the release was a pink slip titled "Pilot's Warning," which informed him that "KM [Camden]: SRN BORDER SOFT. STAY ON RUNWAYS. 100 FT. PILE DRIVER ESE OF FLD MARKER. WA [Washington]: CONSTR. E OF INTER OF BOTH RNWYS. NEW RNGE IN OPERATION WITH QUADRANTS REVERSED FROM OLD RNGE. NA [Nashville]: CNSTR ON FLD MARKED." After studying the weather data and the other entries on the release, and noting that the ship was departing with 200 quarts of oil and 800 gallons of gasoline—enough to take her to Nashville, from Nashville to Memphis, her alternate airport, and to fly her for at least three-quarters of an hour beyond Memphis—King made out his Flight Plan, giving his magnetic courses, his wind-drift corrections, the horsepower he expected to use, the altitudes he expected to fly, and the times at which he expected to pass over the radio check points along the route.

Miss Jones meanwhile went over the passenger manifest. There was only one other woman passenger besides Miss Goldilocks, but she was a mother with a nonrevenue infant—under the age of two—and Miss Jones made a note to have a lower berth made up so that the child could be retired immediately, and to take aboard enough New York milk and New York water to last to the Coast. Of the men, the reservations office had noted that two were first fliers who would require special attention and probably some reassurance when the ship hit the rough air beyond Washington. Another was a coast-to-coast commuter with whom Miss Jones was acquainted—he had confided several times that he was a "big Hollywood producer." Another was an Admiral of the Flagship Fleet—a sales-department title conferred on notables and on particular friends of American Airlines—with a card in his pocket and a thirty-five-cent piece of imitation parchment hanging on his office wall to prove it. The next two were neither Admirals nor first fliers nor commuters but ordinary businessmen traveling on scrip tickets at a 15 per cent discount from the regular $149.95 one-way fare. The last was an American Airlines publicity man taking a winter vacation and using some of the free air mileage that everyone in the company receives as a perquisite. If his space were sold anywhere the ship landed he would be deplaned and made to wait over. For that matter, even company executives traveling on business almost never take advantage of their privilege when there is a chance of selling an extra seat to a cash customer. C. R. Smith himself often rides the *Cen-*

tury from Chicago to New York rather than discourage a passenger who might be going up for the first time.

Toward half past four all the preliminaries to Trip 3 began to converge on the actual take-off. Having run up her motors and tested her communications system by talking to American Airlines flight control and to WREE, the Newark Airport traffic-control tower, the co-pilot accepted the ship from the chief mechanic. A few minutes later Captain King himself tried her controls, and, finding them satisfactory, signed the Flight Release, which stated: "I hereby acknowledge receipt of the foregoing clearance, including weather report, and consider all conditions including my own physical condition suitable for the scheduled flight." Had he not found weather conditions suitable he would have refused to sign and thus effectively canceled the trip, for it is against company policy to permit another pilot to volunteer to fly after one has turned down his assignment.

At four-forty the ship was pulled up in front of the terminal building. Miss Jones went aboard, slipped her metal name plate into a slot on the door leading to the cockpit, and made a rapid check of the cabin equipment. At four-forty-five a delivery truck rolled up and unloaded big Thermos jugs and aluminum cases containing food that had been prepared by a caterer in Newark earlier in the afternoon. At four-fifty-five an American Airlines air-conditioning truck came alongside and pumped warm air into the cabin to take off the chill until the motors and the steam heater were started. At four-fifty-seven the bus from New York—a black Cadillac limousine seating ten persons—drew up at the terminal and the passengers got out and handed dollar bills to the driver, one or two of them muttering that it was a "damned outrage" that the fare wasn't included in the price of the ticket. Inside the terminal they queued up at a counter and had their names checked off on the passenger manifest. One man, somewhat tipsy, gazed at a photograph of C. R. Smith on one wall and at a photograph of Vice President Ralph Damon on the opposite wall and remarked to no one in particular that they were fine-looking fellows, fine-looking fellows. Another man bought a ham sandwich at the Union News lunch counter. Others purchased cigarettes, newspapers, and chocolate bars at the newsstand. The two first fliers lined up in the broad window in the waiting room and stared dubiously at ships landing and taking off on the field. The woman with the nonrevenue infant sat down in a corner and bundled the little one in the folds of her mink coat. The tipsy gentleman passed in front of her and tripped over her feet, apologizing with a sweeping bow that nearly knocked him down. A ticket clerk watched him narrowly, trying to decide whether he was drunk enough to deserve having his passage canceled.

At five o'clock some 330 pounds of mail and air express were loaded aboard the ship. It appeared that Miss Goldilocks and a Mr. Edward Belcher had not yet arrived at the terminal, for over the public-address system a plaintive voice kept repeating: "Miss Gloria Goldilocks and Mr. Edward Belcher, passengers on Trip 3, kindly step to the ticket counter." Still no Miss Goldilocks, and at five-seven the voice boomed: "American Airlines Trip 3 for Nashville, Dallas, Tucson, and Los Angeles, now loading at Gate 5. Passengers will please go aboard. Please give your name to the stewardess, Miss Jones, as you board the plane." The men promptly threw on their overcoats and marched out in a sort of platoon to the ship, where they were greeted by Miss Jones, standing "in the men's dressing room with the binder resting on the wash basin," as regulations instructed.

At five-nine a Rolls-Royce escorted by two lesser vehicles raced up to the terminal and disgorged the luscious Miss Goldilocks in the midst of an incredible number of press agents, photographers, reporters, friends, and porters. Miss Goldilocks had seven suitcases and a Siamese cat on a leash. The suitcases weighed 200 pounds, and the press agents fought for the privilege of paying $108.75 for the excess over the fifty-five pounds allowed to trans-oceanic passengers; ordinary passengers are allowed only forty pounds. The clerk announced that the cat would have to travel in the baggage compartment, and Miss Goldilocks looked as though she might make a scene, but there wasn't time. At five-ten and one-half she ran through Gate 5 so fast that an orchid dropped out of her corsage. The ticket counter had given up Mr. Belcher, and as soon as Miss Goldilocks disappeared into the *Arizona* the cabin door was slammed and locked from the outside, and blocks were yanked out from the front of the wheels. Captain King touched a button on the dashboard of the cockpit and started the motors. The co-pilot talked to the Newark traffic-control tower through his radiotelephone and asked if it was all right for Trip 3 to take off.

At five-eleven the ship turned and taxied toward the runway. Just before reaching it she stopped, and with his brakes on Captain King gunned each motor so hard that the plane strained and quivered along her whole length. Then she started rolling again and halfway along the runway left the ground so smoothly that none of the first fliers in the cabin realized what had happened until they saw the whole field rushing away behind them and the factory lights winking through the Jersey murk ahead. Up in the cockpit the co-pilot stretched an arm out of the window and took down the little blue pennant that always flies above the cockpits of flagships on the ground because passengers never heard of a flagship that didn't have a flag. Then he switched his radio over from the frequency of the Newark Airport traffic-control tower to American Airlines flight control and announced that the Mercury was in the air.

With the thin whine of the on-course signal coming through his headphones Captain King flew the ship out on the southwest leg of the Newark range and passed over New Brunswick at five-twenty-three. The co-pilot reported the position to flight control, and on his Flight Log entered the time, the altitude, wind, temperature, horse-power, air speed, and magnetic course. He would make similar notations at every check point on the route, so that the position would never be in doubt, and in case of a radio failure the ship could be flown back to her point of origin merely by following the data in reverse order. Over Camden at five-forty-five he picked up American Airlines' flight control at the Washington airport and was told that two army planes en route between Mitchel Field and the Edgewood Arsenal in Maryland were almost directly above him at 10,000 feet and that a northbound Eastern Air Lines ship at 5,000 would be off Washington airport at six-five; the Mercury was then flying at 8,000, and the co-pilot transmitted back his weather observations, remarking that visibility was good except for smoke over urban areas. He made a note of this on one of a sheaf of forms in the cockpit, for in addition to keeping the Flight Log he was expected to compare actual weather conditions aloft with the ground station predictions and grade the meteorologist accordingly.

By the time the Mercury passed over Roanoke most of the passengers had finished their dinners of soup, lamb chops, vegetables, salad, ice cream, and coffee, served with the compliments of American Airlines at a cost of ninety cents per compliment. Over Bristol, Virginia, at eight-five, flight control announced that the landing at Nashville was now definite, but that the approach and letdown would have to be made entirely on instruments. Captain King proceeded to Knoxville where the co-pilot made contact with Nashville flight control. Another contact was made at Smithville, Tennessee, and then Captain King rode straight down the Nashville beam, occasionally getting a dash-dot in his headphones as the drift of strong lateral winds pushed the ship into the N twilight of the range. The signal volume steadily increased as the Mercury drew closer to the beacon; then it suddenly faded out altogether for a few seconds as they passed over the cone of silence directly above the ground radio transmitter. They were on top of the overcast at 3,000 feet, and as the co-pilot reported the position to flight control and prepared to switch over to the frequency of the Nashville traffic tower Captain King dropped the landing gear, adjusted his propeller pitch, and throttled down to an air speed of 120 miles per hour. He flew out the northwest beam for three minutes, made a procedure turn, and came back over the cone at 1,200 feet, losing altitude at the rate of 400 feet per minute. There were holes in the overcast now, and he could see the fuzzy, candy-pink glow of neon signs along a street; in a few more seconds he picked up the characteristic pattern of flashing beacons and boundary lights ahead and dropped down on Nashville as smoothly as he had taken off from Newark.

At Nashville it took fifteen minutes to give the ship a quick visual inspection on the field; to refuel, change crews, discharge mail and a passenger and take aboard more mail and a new passenger, and to install in the stewardess's pantry Thermos bottles of coffee, Ovaltine, and hot water for tea. By ten o'clock Central time the Mercury was in the air again, heading southwest down the Memphis beam on the way to Dallas. It took a little over four hours to fly this leg of the trip, and a few miles east of the Dallas airport the westbound Mercury at 2,000 feet passed the eastbound Mercury at 3,000. West of Dallas visibility was limited only by the far horizons of the curving earth, and the pilot flew on contact with the miles of beacon lights that stretched in a great beeline across the plains. Beyond El Paso the sun came up behind the ship, and at Tucson a little before seven there were shadows. There was a wall of sharp-edged mountains ahead, and the ship flew across and between them for most of the next two hours. At ten minutes of nine Pacific time the Mercury landed at Glendale Airport on schedule, and after the passengers had been deplaned the ground crew washed the ship and then turned her over to the mechanics for inspection.

TECHNICAL DISCUSSION

1. Comment on the beginning of this essay and on the ending. Are there any flourishes? The essay begins and ends with the airship in the hands of mechanics. Is this appropriate? Explain.
2. Mark all the major shifts of subject matter. Do you have trouble finding them?
3. Underline the passages that indicate changes in time and progression in the flow of the narrative.
4. Are the descriptions of Captain King and Miss Jones part of the story of an air flight? Discuss.
5. Are the technical details and terms clear to the average reader—for instance, the instrument landing at Nashville?
6. This essay is notable for its details. Do they become a burden to the reader? Discuss.
7. Why are the descriptions of the tipsy passenger and the glamorous Miss Goldilocks put in the story?

Rescue by Radio

OLIVER READ and ERNEST BARCELLA

On Christmas Eve, 1940, a lost Douglas DC-3 unwittingly proved to be a most benevolent Santa Claus. Its aimless wanderings were destined to bring to this nation and its armed forces a direction-finding service that has since shepherded hundreds of lost planes to safety.

This service was to play an extremely vital role a year later, immediately following Pearl Harbor. It was then that the aircraft direction-finding service of the Federal Communications Commission's Radio

"Rescue by Radio." From *Flying,* November, 1944. Reprinted by permission of *Flying.*

Intelligence Division (RID) was to make its most timely contribution to the national defense.

For sometime RID's long-range direction finding had done a valiant job in another important way—policing the air waves in search of illegal and espionage stations. But not until the night of December 24, 1940, did there develop the idea of utilizing these direction finders in another role—locating lost or distressed aircraft equipped with two-way radio.

That was the night that the DC-3 with full crew and passenger complement, was lost in the vicinity of Tucson, Ariz. For three hours the big airliner flew in circles trying to find a landing place. Finally it came down.

That episode gave the airlines an idea. Soon afterwards they contacted RID and asked if it would be possible for that agency to use its long-range direction finders as an aid to lost planes.

How quickly that idea was realized is attested by the following memorandum, dated March 27, 1941, from the RID monitoring unit at Tucson.

". . . Yesterday about sundown CAA Tucson called and reported an itinerant ship lost.

"The pilot was positive that he was northeast of El Paso. Although we were forced to take bearings with the Adcock on five- and ten-second transmission, we were able to report a bearing in a few minutes. This bearing was so far from the ship's estimated position that it was completely discounted. The ship finally reported that he was landing in a small clearing—position unknown—out of gas.

"At 6 A.M. today, the pilot finally reached a telephone and reported that he was in Sonora, Mexico, near a small town.

"Plotting this position on the map indicated that we had given a bearing good to better than two degrees, that the ship was south of Douglas, Ariz., and that if the pilot had followed the information given by this office he would have been able to land at Douglas or Tucson before running out of gas. It is believed that this situation is being made a part of the Civil Aeronautics Administration's official report, since they seemed to be much impressed with the possibilities of the system."

CAA was duly impressed, especially after it received a detailed report of the above incident from H. T. Bean, Superintendent of Airways at Santa Monica, Calif., who recommended that CAA consider using the service.

By midsummer of 1941, after meetings and correspondence between RID and CAA, a procedure was worked out whereby FCC would furnish emergency bearings on lost aircraft. All CAA regional managers were notified of the availability of this radio direction-finding service and were given a list of addresses of RID primary and secondary units.

From these incidental beginnings, RID developed an elaborate system of locating lost or distressed aircraft by Adcock radio bearings, a system which:

1. Greatly aided the United States in its war against Japan.
2. Guided safely home more than 500 bombers and other warplanes.
3. Came to the aid of the nation's anti-submarine defenses in the ominous days of 1942.
4. Saved scores of shipwrecked merchant seamen.
5. Saved millions in expensive planes which otherwise might have been lost and achieved a saving of many hundreds of human lives.
6. Will add another great measure of safety to post-war flying.

How does the RID system work when a plane is lost?

The telephone rings at the RID Eastern Intelligence Center at Washington. The call is coming in from the CAA Airway Traffic Controller at the Washington National Airport. The time is 10:28 P.M. EWT. "Another bunny is lost," the voice reports. This information is followed by the call letters, frequency and the time of emission (phone, code, etc.) of the plane's radio transmission. Immediately the RID officer on watch types out "LOP" on his teletypewriter. The message appears simultaneously on the TLT (teletypes) of other primary monitoring stations—in this particular case, on the east coast. The cryptic word "LOP" is the emergency alert signal which indicates that a plane is lost and is seeking a bearing.

Operators on duty at the monitoring stations in that area immediately tune their receivers to the exact frequency supplied and listen for signals from the lost plane. In most cases, the plane is instructed to send a series of MO's comprised entirely of dashes. This coding lends itself to easy reception. The operators on duty at the Adcock long-range direction finders are alerted over an intercom system connecting to the cruising room in the main building of the station. The operator tunes immediately to the frequency supplied over the intercom and by the exchange of information back and forth makes sure that he is listening to the signals which are the subject of observation. He proceeds to take a long-range bearing which is sent to the Eastern Intelligence Center over the teletype network. Other DF operators take similar bearings at the same moment and their findings are likewise transmitted to Washington where they are evaluated and plotted in order that a "fix" may be established. It is imperative that several bearings be taken simultaneously, since the aircraft is flying at a high speed and changing position continuously.

When the fix has been established, it is given to the CAA controller, in this case, and the correct bearing is transmitted by radio to the lost plane. Knowing his position, the pilot brings his ship home.

The most important piece of equipment in the entire RID setup is the Adcock direction finder, a sort of radio searchlight. It consists of an elaborate rotatable beam antenna looking very much like the capital letter "H" stood on its side. This "H" revolves above a small hut mounted some 20 feet above the ground. Within the hut is a Hallicrafters SX-28 communications receiver, a frequency standard used to check the calibration of the receiver, and a large wheel above which is mounted a calibrated scale graduated in degrees with respect to true north. The operator rotates the antenna while listening to the signal under observation until it can no longer be heard. This is known as the "null." By reading the scale before him, he can tell within one or two degrees the exact direction of the arriving signal. So exact is the direction finder that a spiderweb across its transmission line will upset the calibration. It is obvious that in order to take accurate long-range bearings the calibration of each direction finder be known at all times. To insure proper performance, the operator takes "check bearings" on known stations at known distances at certain intervals.

At least four radio bearings are required for an accurate fix. They must be taken from widely separated locations. Accompanying illustrations point out the necessity for taking multiple bearings. The more bearings, the more accuracy will be had.

There are certain instances, for example, when a plane may be forced down with its radio still in operating condition and where short-range bearings would be desirable in order to determine the exact location of the grounded plane. The RID has 50 special mobile units equipped with compact direction-finding equipment and take bearings in similar manner to the Adcocks, except that they operate

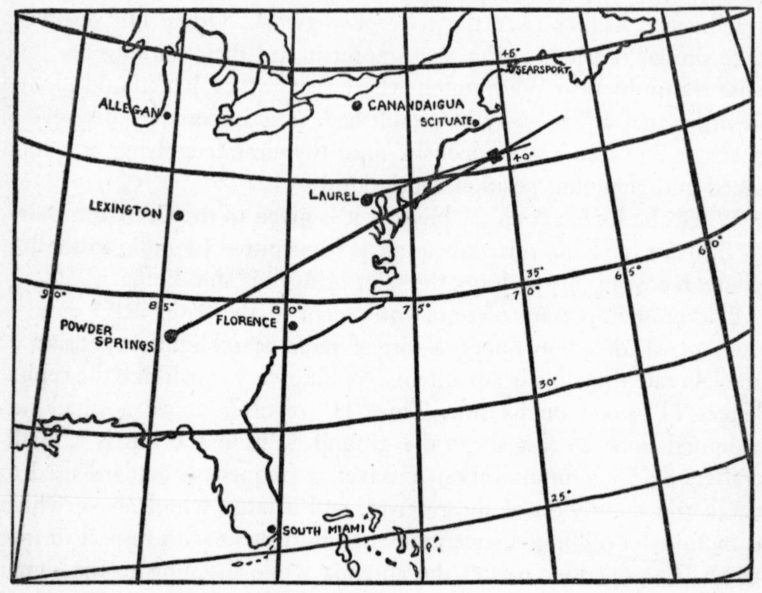

A plane is roughly located east of Cape Cod by two stations which, because of their position, have left a very wide margin for error.

"close-in" within small areas. Equipment includes a Hallicrafters SX-28 receiver and a Telecord wax cylinder machine. The latter is used when a permanent record of any transmission is desired, such as in locating a clandestine radio station. When mobile units are necessary, several may converge on the area under observation.

Adcock direction finders are found at all of the 12 primary stations located throughout the United States, its territories and possessions. In addition, there are 32 secondary monitoring stations. These satellites operate in conjunction with primary stations within their area. All primary and secondary stations are linked together for instantaneous communications by private tieline or by radio links. Each primary station, for example, is equipped with several radio transmitters which may be used to communicate with other stations or Intelligence Centers should the teletypewriter tieline fail. These are ready for duty at a moment's notice.

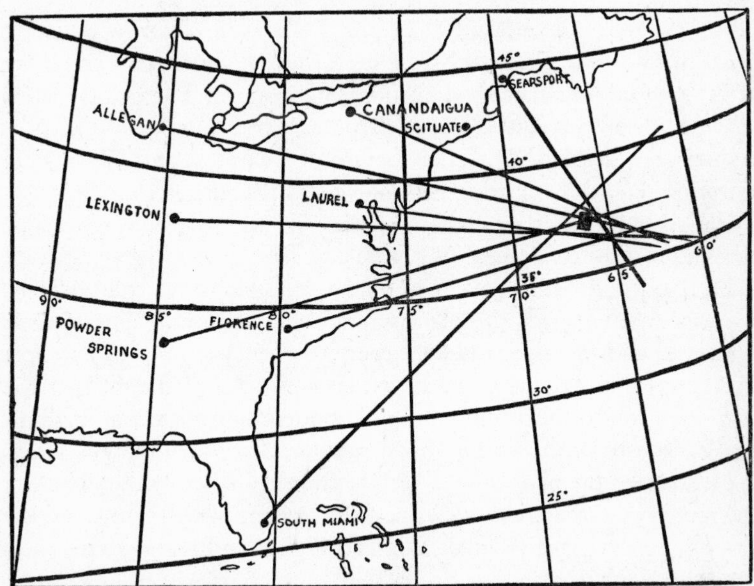

The reason for taking numerous bearings is illustrated here. Location of plane is accurately known, while that at left is quite uncertain.

Too much credit cannot be given the operating personnel of the RID. Seventy per cent are, or have been, licensed radio amateurs or "Hams." Operators patrol the ether 24 hours daily year after year. They copy signals which the ordinary person could not even hear. Their receivers are never turned off and they work in regular shifts. They scan the ether on all frequencies as a daily routine. They know every licensed station throughout the world and are able to spot a "hot one" in a hurry. The very existence of the RID is due to the efforts of George Sterling, chief of FCC's Radio Intelligence Division and himself a prominent radio amateur holding the call letters W3DF.

In the first few days after the Pearl Harbor attack, RID participated in the rescue of at least 12 planes. The service was especially valuable in the case of Army bombers on patrol flights. Lost Navy amphibian bombers, in contrast, could sit down on the ocean when they ran out of gas, call for help, and wait in comparative safety for relief.

Here is an actual case which speaks for the efficacy of the system:

At 9:23 P.M., October 23, 1942, the FCC radio security center at Honolulu was advised by the Seventh Army Air Force that a bomber en route to the mainland had encountered a storm. The plane headed back for the islands but its gyro instruments had failed and one of its engines was disabled. The pilot reported he was lost and asked what course he should fly to bring his crippled craft home safely.

The six RID direction-finders on the islands took bearings which were supplemented by bearings from the west coast primary stations at Portland and Santa Ana. The plane was told what course to fly. But shortly afterwards the plane's radio "blacked out.'" The stations in Hawaii and the mainland kept every frequency covered in an effort to pick up the disabled craft. It wasn't until after midnight that the plane came on the air again—and was spotted immediately and almost simultaneously by the six Hawaiian stations. They took more bearings and instructed the pilot to fly a certain course. Gradually the meter on the receiver at the FCC radio security center, which measures the strength of the plane's signals, climbed higher and higher. This indicated the plane was getting closer.

We quote the pilot's conversation as he approached the islands:

"I believe I see the searchlights . . . Yes, I see a large cluster of lights directly ahead of me . . . It looks like a small village . . . We are at 12,000 feet and beginning to let down . . . It is perfectly clear ahead of us . . . I see the lights on Diamond Head . . . I see the city of Honolulu . . . !"

Five minutes later the plane landed safely.

The system was so successful in the Hawaiian-West Coast area that within a few months it was adopted in other areas.

A system incorporating procedures similar to those used in Hawaii was adopted and placed in effect immediately on the east coast. So well did it work that in October, 1942, the First Bomber Command advised that the private tieline circuit between its offices and the RID was so "helpful to them in their work" that they "would not under any condition consent to its removal."

The following month headquarters of the Army Air Forces requested that steps be taken with a view to making the direction-finding services available in all of the various commands of the Army Air Forces throughout the United States. This was done immediately. The FCC pamphlet incorporating the uniform procedure was distributed widely in the Army Air Forces pursuant to an Army directive. The various Air Force Commands subsequently circulated further directives to their units, listing locations and telephone numbers of the nearest FCC stations and summarizing procedures to be followed.

One case involving a Navy plane occurred April 9, 1943, while RID monitors cruised the spectrum seeking illegal transmissions. Suddenly, they picked up this urgent call:

"S O S, S O S, S O S . . . Landing at sea southwest of island. Wind 25 from west. Sea moderate."

The Anti-submarine Command was notified immediately on the private tieline. It replied:

"We have checked with our controllers and they are unable to identify the call on that. However, if you are able to get a fix we would like to have it."

Three minutes later the Anti-submarine Command was advised that the plane in distress "is very possibly Navy aircraft."

Ten FCC stations took bearings. They gave a fix 250 miles east by north of Bermuda—the island referred to in the S O S—rather than "southwest of the island" as the distressed plane had thought its position to be. The Anti-submarine Command later reported:

"The fix you gave us on the plane in distress was a very good fix. It was a PBY plane [*Catalina*] out of Bermuda."

The plane was refueled and reached its base safely.

No less important than its plane-saving role is the life-saving function of the RID.

On February 6, 1943, the agency's secondary station at Searsport, Me., notified the Eastern Intelligence Center that it had received from the Army at Presque Isle, Me., a telephone call stating that an Army plane had made a forced landing at an unknown location. Search planes were sent out. RID was requested to track the course of their flight continuously. The instructions were that if one of the search planes located the lost plane it was to circle over it and transmit so RID could obtain an accurate fix. That was precisely the way it worked out. The lost plane was found on a frozen lake. All hands were rescued, and the searching party even succeeded in reclaiming the disabled aircraft.

In the field of saving human lives, no function performed by RID has been more important than the aid it has provided in rescuing shipwrecked merchant seamen.

One of a number of such actual cases of RID assistance occurred on January 3, 1943. An Army lieutenant was returning to his base from a routine patrol. Some distance off the coast he spotted a lifeboat carrying 31 survivors from a sunken freighter. His fuel supply running low and his plane not suited for rescue, the lieutenant circled the lifeboat and advised the First Bomber Command of the situation by radio.

It was necessary that the exact position of the lifeboat be established so another plane could locate it and make the rescue. Accordingly, the Bomber Command asked RID to furnish a bearing as the plane transmitted "MO" signals. A fix was obtained in this manner. Another plane was sent out and subsequently located a freighter which was directed to the scene and rescued the 31 men.

The RID system is destined to play an important role in peacetime commercial flying. Procedures for co-operation between the FCC and the Civil Aeronautics Administration in locating commercial and private air craft already have been formalized, in much the same manner as with the military.

From its humble and incidental beginnings, RID's direction-finding system for locating lost aircraft has become a vital part of military and commercial aviation. This $8,000,000 system has paid for itself many times over in planes brought home safely—more than 600. And in terms of human lives saved its value can never be measured.

TECHNICAL DISCUSSION

1. Why do the authors begin with material about a lost Douglas DC-3 transport plane and the itinerant airship?

2. Does the "alphabet" title RID bother you? Would the full title be awkward if it were used constantly?

3. Does the early history of RID serve any particular function? Would you be fully oriented to the authors' purpose without it?

4. Where do the authors state their purpose to tell how RID works?

5. Do you find any place where the authors use scientific description in connection with the story of how RID works? If so, where?

6. Do the authors make any reference to the drawings with which they explain how a plane is located?

7. Are the stories of airplanes and personnel saved that the authors use to conclude the essay necessary or helpful in describing RID?

SPECIFIC NARRATION

The Barge Folk

MEYER BERGER

The canal barges were tied up for the winter off Coenties Slip on the South Street water front. They would ride the bay tide now, until the ice broke up in the Hudson and in the Lakes. Canal barge women would get in their winter knitting and crocheting. They had packed their unwilling moppets off to city schools and they would spend most of their days and nights in their tiny barge cabins, gently rocking with the tide and with the wash of passing tugs and ferries. There would be visits from one barge to another, long nights of listening to the battery radio or hugging the "Mascot" wood stoves in the galley with their numerous pets about their feet. The men would loll in their chairs and swap fresh-water yarns about high adventure on the 525-mile stretch from South Street to Buffalo.

A latent envy for the barge folk, dating back to my first reading of *Huckleberry Finn,* urged me to South Street. In the subway rumbling southward from the Village I plagued myself with dreamy memories stored from that reading. I recalled Huck's heart-warming story; how he and Jim sprawled on their backs on the raft as it moved on the current; how the skies were speckled with stars, or streaked with

"The Barge Folk." From *The Eight Million,* Journal of a New York Correspondent, by Meyer Berger. Reprinted by permission of Simon & Schuster, Inc.

shooting stars; how they would watch the candles in shore cabins wink out, one by one; how the towns slipped by in the dark, and how the Mississippi steamboats, all the way off to one side, would shower the night with sparks. Barge life, I figured, must be something like that.

It was coming on dusk; clear, crisp New York October twilight. The wind was sharp off the Bay. Shabby wretches, mostly in browning blue dungarees and threadbare jackets, scrounged in ancient rope-shop and chandlery doorways facing the water. Thinning sun diffused a kindly reddish gold on the little old buildings, filled with deep, ponderous shadow the clifflike rise of the Wall Street buildings massed beyond them. Brooklyn shore vanished slowly in crepuscular haze, with land lights dimly showing through the shimmer. On either side of the low concrete pier by the New York State Canal Terminal shed, the barges rose and fell, shoulder to shoulder, on the tide.

I climbed from the splintered stringpiece to the lifting deck of the nearest barge. A middle-aged man, huddled in a pea jacket with peaked cap down on his eyes, surveyed my approach through pipe smoke. Two dogs, a half-sized collie and a very soiled poodle, peered through an equally tangled hair screen and sniffed shyly at my pants. The barge man silently motioned to another chair against the low cabin wall and as silently heard my mission.

He didn't know Huck Finn but, from my eager sketch of the raft trip down to Cairo as Huck told it, he guessed barge life was "something like." I stared through the cabin window. A woman moved about inside in the weak yellow glow of a kerosene lamp. The smell of wood smoke and of cooking meat came downwind from the little tin chimney lashed to the cabin wall.

"About all them lights, and all," the barge man said, "we get all that. There's fifty-seven locks, and God knows how many towns, along the canals. We see them go dark like you said, and we see the towns by day."

He named the towns and the villages: Yonkers, Newburgh, Kingston, Albany, Troy. He mentioned Cohoes, Waterford, Crescent, Amsterdam, Fultonville, St. Johnsville, Little Falls, Herkimer. Four days, in tow, from South Street to Troy, always in fleets of six, with a tug to pull the tow. All kinds of cargoes: grain, mostly, but sand, too, and iron, soda ash, coal. Take up to 2,800 tons. The skipper is the only man aboard. He sees to loading and unloading.

"There's more to loading than you'd think," the skipper said. "Get it stored wrong and a barge can buckle, even break in half."

He admitted, though, that he'd never seen one actually break in half; only heard of it.

Tows come at any time. If the woman and the kids happen to be away when a tow call comes, they come back to the slip and find their home is gone. They go to the barge owner, then, and find the tow's destination. Usually they can borrow train fare and catch the tow at Kingston or at Troy, where the Hudson connects with the Erie system. This happens fairly often. The barge owner, incidentally, furnishes kerosene for the cabin lamps, oilcloth for the cabin floor, and all cooking utensils.

"Oilcloth has to be worn through though," the skipper said, "before they'll honor a requisition."

Tugs pushed noisily by, off the far end of the dock, as the skipper talked. Gulls spiraled and dived with the fading sunlight warm on their breasts. The barges strained heavily at their ropes and groaned, when they rubbed together, like old men with rheumatism.

Barge folk, the skipper said, eat well; great ones for meat. A skipper gets from $115 to $125 a month, depending on his worth and his record. Keep a wife and two or three kids on it, but never save a penny. The women shop on shore, Fourteenth Street, mostly, but sometimes in the uptown stores. They are just as fussy in their dress as city women are. Go to beauty parlors, sometimes, too.

It was dark now. Ferry blasts shattered and broke on the Wall Street skyscraper fronts. The harbor put on its diamonds. Brooklyn Bridge wore a string of pearls.

I went down three steps to the cabin. It was orderly and filled with the sweet scent of freshly baked chocolate cake. The whole room was no more than ten feet by ten feet. A row of three bunks was neatly made up. Cots, for the children, were ranged against one wall. A canary hopped in a battered cage and sang as if its throat might burst. The barge woman half curtsied when I was introduced. A towheaded boy, fussing with a damaged scooter, stared at me, round-eyed, from the floor.

The skipper explained about Huck Finn. The woman seemed puzzled at first, but finally caught on. January, the collie, sat at her feet and looked wistfully at the bubbling pot. The soiled poodle sank into a corner and drowsed with its head between its paws. The woman talked about parties on the different barges, about dancing in the crowded cabins or on deck, to the music of guitars and harmonicas. And she talked about the mountains and the woods and the country scenes along the Hudson and along the locks.

"People says," she shyly told me, "that you can't find no better scenery in the whole world, but after you've been going up and down with the tows for eleven years, like we have, it gets to be ordinary, sort of beautiful ordinary."

The woman looked very tired.

"If you seen her with rouge and jool'ry and lip stuff," the skipper assured me, "you'd swear by heck she was a city woman."

The woman shrugged but seemed pleased. She showed her barge garden ivy, curly-leaf begonia, and geraniums in window boxes.

"You see, everything shipshape," she said, "but there's nights on Oneida Lake when you can't keep a pot on the stove or a cup on the table." Barge life is healthy for children, though, she told me. "My tykes is all fleshed up," she said.

It was full dark when I stumbled onto the pier. Lamps burned in all the barge windows. The air was sharp with October wind and rank brine. I took one last, sentimental look at the swaying craft. I headed uptown.

TECHNICAL DISCUSSION

1. Why does the author use the first paragraph for general description of barge life?

2. Why did the author visit the barges? Point out the place that indicates the reason?

3. Does the author have any purpose other than to tell the story of his trip? See if you can find another purpose and demonstrate that you are right.

4. Find good examples of description of setting.

5. Are the people made to seem real? Explain.
6. Does the author romanticize the details of barge life? Would he like to? What is his tone? Point out how he builds up the tone.
7. Prepare a list of the best verbs in the story.
8. Prepare a list of the best nouns and their modifiers.

Smoke Clouds Blowing

WALTER HAVIGHURST

Frontier towns burned like tinder. The board streets and sidewalks, the open frame buildings, the lack of water pressure and of fire-fighting apparatus made them terribly vulnerable. Nearly every American city has had a great fire in its brief history. Often the lumber towns had a series of them. The very ground they rested on, built up of sawdust, slabs and refuse from the mills, was inflammable. The drying yards, with lumber stacked and open to the air, could quickly roar into acres of flame. There were always sparks from the big consumers and the straining boilers of the steam engines to start the disaster. Sawdust towns lived violently, with the rumble of logging, the snarl and scream of the buzz saw, and the tumult of the loading wharfs. And mostly they died violently. A sawmill town could not expect a peaceful end.

In that strange, remembered autumn of 1871 there were many dramas on the lakes. One of them is the story of Menominee, the busy lumber port on the pine-dark shores of Green Bay.

From Green Bay and Bay de Noc the woods stretched north over a wild country, marked only by tote-roads, a few scattered logging lines and an occasional sawmill settlement beside the rivers that run down to Lake Michigan. The summer of 1871 was a hot, hazy season, with brush fires burning in the cut-over sections and miles of slash smoldering beside the newly completed railroad lines. An occasional shower kept them from spreading, though there was not enough rain to put them out. As autumn came on, the ground baked dry and the fires

"Smoke Clouds Blowing." From *The Long Ships Passing,* by Walter Havighurst. By permission of The Macmillan Company, publishers.

grew larger. Still it was not alarming. Forest fires were no novelty, in that country. People got used to hazy sunsets and a sharp smell in the air. But when September passed with a succession of hot, windless days and not a drop of moisture, the weatherwise old settlers began to look puzzled. There had never been a season like this before.

During the first week of October Menominee's narrow harbor was glassy still, under slow-drifting curtains of smoke. Schooners groped in to anchorage, and before they became visible there was the sound of sailors coughing on their decks. At midday the sun was a dull coin that men could stare at steadily; there were no stars at night. Rumors came down the river—of inland camps wiped out in a sudden spread of fire, of people standing all night in the streams, of farmers walking over their blackened fields and eating potatoes that had baked in the ground.

There was nothing to do about it. Work went on in Menominee. The logs came snarling through the mills, the smoke from the consumers thickened the haze that hung around, and people scanned the sky thinking of a long, deep autumn rain.

Young Charlie Ingalls, son of a Menominee lumberman, was getting out cedar posts on his father's Hay Creek farm a few miles up river from the town. He had a schooner in the river and a crew of fifteen men working in the woods. On Sunday morning, the seventh of October, most of his crew had gone to town to chat with sailors on the docks. But Charlie, feeling uneasy about the thick gray air, had stayed at the farm instead of going to his mother's house in Menominee for a good Sunday dinner. He was thinking of the dry woods, the miles of pine needles like a floor of tinder, and acres of slash piled up along the railroad where the swampers had gone through. All through the country wells and cisterns were empty and the rivers ran low in their banks. A fitful west wind brought a hot smell and waves of heated air from Oconto and Peshtigo, where the swamps were burning. At times he heard a low and distant sound, softer than thunder. In the quiet Sunday, under the heavy sky, there was a kind of premonition. Even the hens in the barnyard wandered abstractedly, forgetting to scratch for grain.

In mid-afternoon people appeared on the road to Menominee, carrying baskets and bundles. The woods along Birch Creek were burning, they said, and the village was doomed. At that Charlie Ingalls looked grim. There was fire on two sides of them now. He got his few remaining men to work with spades and shovels, digging a trench around the farm buildings.

That evening a color like sunset edged the woods, but it was in the wrong direction. Soon half the horizon was tinged with light and waves of smoke passed over. The mutter rose to a roaring.

There was no darkness that night. There was a fierce sky and a land terribly illumined. At Hay Creek farm the fire struck suddenly, not with a wave of flame but with a rain of sparks and embers. The dried fields took fire like scattered haycocks, flowering up in many places and spreading quickly. When the barnyard was smoking Charlie turned out the cattle and horses, except one team that he hitched to a light wagon, quieting them with his voice as he hooked the traces to the double-trees. He called to his men, but they had crowded into the dry cistern and would not come out. He had to leave them there. Before the night was over squirrels, rats and rabbits were huddled with them in that pit.

Charlie turned his team toward Menominee and the harbor. The horses needed no urging. Their hooves pounded the dust, the buckboard rocked like a rowboat. On the road ahead were cattle and horses, running wildly, sometimes plunging into the woods or racing over fire-patched fields to escape the blowing smoke. Deer and wolves fled together across the dried swamps. Ahead, under the lighted sky, Charlie Ingalls saw that Menominee still stood. His team plunged on through the town and into the harbor. They did not stop till the wagon bed was floating.

Charlie waded ashore and met Ed Byers and Nate Nickerson on their way to the docks. They looked at the water running out of his clothes.

"Where you been, Charlie?" Nate asked.

"Tying my horses." Charlie grinned as the puddle collected under him. It was the first time he had smiled that day and it was gone quickly. "Any fires in town?'"

"Yes, a couple on the west side. Come on over to Jones Dock with us. The *Northern City* is coming in. We'll get the captain to take the women and children aboard."

Out at the harbor entrance a big passenger steamer was swinging. She came up cautiously, with men stamping out sparks that fell on her decks. In the river mouth two schooners began to blaze. Small boats jerked away from them over the polished water. Slowly the steamer crept in.

Before his lines were ashore the captain heard men calling him from the dock. He leaned over the bridge rail.

"The town may go before morning, Captain. Can you stand by?"

"Yes. I'll stand by till it gets too hot to hang around."

"Will you take the women and children aboard?"

"All I got room for."

"Thank you, Captain. How are you fixed for fuel?"

"Got plenty." He breathed the acrid air. "It don't take much to get up steam in this weather.'"

Soon women were streaming up the gangplank, women with babies in their arms and wide-eyed children around them, grim-faced women lugging baskets of food and bundles of clothing, trembling old women with bright distracted eyes, carrying a gilt clock, a big black Bible with a metal clasp, or a porcelain lamp with a shattered chimney.

While the steamer stood by there was a way out of Menominee. But that could not help the neighboring settlements. Stragglers came in, smoke-blackened and exhausted, from Birch Creek and Peshtigo. A few had left those burning towns before the fire closed them in. The women went aboard the steamer; the men threw themselves down on the harborside and when they got their strength back they went to join the citizens throwing water on Menominee's smoking buildings. Even the streets were taking fire. Sawdust streets, they flared up in sudden bright patches that went on smoking after the blaze was trampled out. The whole town was ready to burst into flame.

In the lighted fitful night people brought out their treasures, carrying them to the water's edge or burying them in the ground. George Horvath, the dry goods dealer, hurried through the streets with a big gilt mirror that gave back the lurid color of the sky. Old Frenchy Theriault, who fiddled for all the dances in Menominee, trotted down to the beach with a box of his fine cigars. He clawed a hole in the sand and covered it so smoothly that he never found the cigars again. The rest of the night he spent marching up and down Main Street with his fiddle under his arm. A distracted old man was found feverishly burying a hammer and a lighted lantern in his garden.

Back on the steamer at Jones Dock under the mate's watchful eye a consignment of fine furniture was going ashore. A team of restless horses pawed the wooden wharf while it was loaded in Charlie Fairchild's dray. At last he drove through town toward E. L. Parmenter's big new house on State Street. That house was the show place of Menominee in 1871.

It was two A.M. and the bright sky gleamed on the polished mahogany.

"Where you taking the furniture, Charlie?"

"Taking it to Parmenter's. It just came in on the steamer."

The big house stood untouched and impressive, but no house in Menominee was a good bet that night. A little shift of wind and E. L. Parmenter's mansion could burn like any mill shed.

"Better take it back to the boat. The hills are all on fire up Kirby Creek."

"Nope," said Charlie Fairchild. "It's got to be delivered to Parmenter's. They'll get th' insurance if it's in the house, but not if it's in the boat."

The fire reached its height three hours after midnight when a strong west wind blew up. All at once the dry swamp along Kirby Creek was blazing. It threatened the whole town. There was but one good road across the swamp, Pengilly Street, which led to a row of mills on the creekside. Over this road Charlie Ingalls hurried a troop of weary townsmen. Their only hope was to make a firebreak of the road. Working without words, the breath grunting in their throats, they threw up a trench. The wind was scorching in their faces and it was like breathing pain to inhale that fiery air. But the town depended on them. Sparks streamed across the road, lighting up the brittle reeds and grasses beyond. Men beat out the fire with their own shirts and raced with pails of water from the sinking well on Oscar Saxon's place. They worked till their legs buckled. Then they lay flat, scooping out holes for their faces and gulping the air. They got to their feet and fought the fire again. They plunged their shirts into pails of water, they pounded and trampled the spreading flames. Fire scorched their arms and feet and faces and the smoke was tightening in their throats. But those were things they would remember later; now it was only the fierce struggle, fighting the foe that licked hungrily toward their homes and their people.

When daylight came, a dull, ash-colored light, the men of Menominee stood in a smoking grassland with blistered hands and blackened faces. But behind them their town was saved.

Charlie Ingalls went to his mother's house on Menominee Bay. Inside the house children were stretched out everywhere; he counted eight babies sleeping in one bed. He found the back yard filled with refugees from Frenchtown, up the river. His mother was in the kitchen making two big kettles of coffee. They had a breakfast of bread and coffee for forty people. Suddenly a lake breeze blew in, cool and clean and reassuring. They put their coffee down and breathed the air like a perfume.

Down at Jones Dock the refugees began to come ashore from the steamer. Women stood on the wharf blinded with tears when they saw their homes still there. Children raced ahead through the empty streets. Then down the gangway came a few awkward women with their faces hidden and their feet stumbling on their long skirts. As they crossed the wharf Oscar Saxon, the town's official teamster, eyed them sharply. He spat into the bay, scowled, and clumped over beside them. All at once he let go a volley of oaths. His foot swung and the toe of his boot landed hard. The women tried to run but they got tangled in their skirts. Oscar kicked and pounded them and the oaths kept pouring out. Finally the skirts dropped off and a half-dozen Menominee cowards, who had hidden all night with the women, took to their heels. Oscar's voice followed them down the street.

All through Menominee there was rejoicing over the spared town. But when news came from the shore below them, the faces were startled. The whole town of Peshtigo had gone up in the night, with seven hundred dead in her burning streets and drowned in her river. Then came word of a more fearful disaster. During the hours when Menominee was fighting for its life a great city had burned at the foot of Lake Michigan. Now six hundred city blocks lay in ruin and the ashes of Chicago were strewn over Lake Michigan for fifty miles.

At noon the captain of the *Northern City* prepared to cast off lines and make his scheduled run to Mackinac. The lines came aboard and the engines turned over. But the ship didn't budge from the dock. The captain scowled down from the bridge.

"The guldam ship is aground!" he said in a hollow voice.

The mate stared at him and they had a slow realization. The wind and heat of the night had lowered the water and hung them in the mud. If Menominee had caught fire the rescue ship would have burned like a haystack at her moorings.

For miles around Menominee the woods lay blackened. The peat bogs along Little Cedar River were burned so deeply that fire smouldered underground for many months. That winter smoke came through the snow.

TECHNICAL DISCUSSION

1. What does the first paragraph in this story lead the reader to expect?
2. Find details that show the conditions leading up to the night of the fire. Are these details useful in building suspense?
3. Find the major turning points in the narrative. How does the author indicate them?
4. Find words and phrases that indicate time and its flowing. Not all of them make direct statements of dates or hours. See if you can find some indirect statements of time.
5. Does the use of a specific man (Charlie Ingalls) add interest to the story? Explain.
6. Make a list of a dozen of the best verbs you find in this story.
7. Make a list of the best modifiers you find (include modifying phrases).
8. Find examples of grim humor in the story.
9. How does the author end his story?

Life in Montana

MARY ELLEN CHASE

When I look back on my second and last year at Mrs. Moffat's, I am never able to divide its weeks and months into separate and vivid periods of time. I am sure that things went on in their same ordered, yet frenzied way. I know that we kept up our assiduous correspond-

"Life in Montana." From *A Goodly Fellowship,* by Mary Ellen Chase. By permission of The Macmillan Company, publishers.

ence and that I listened to Mrs. Moffat's midnight thoughts and schemes. I know that I taught my German far better because of Fräulein Franke's Prussianism and the warm reality of Fräulein Elster's kindness. I gave up my graduate study at Chicago because of the lack both of time and of sufficient energy.

I was, in fact, ill most of the time during my second year at Mrs. Moffat's, although neither she nor I recognized this fact. Mrs. Moffat hated illness. She said that the sight of impaired physical or mental powers was not only painful to her but in an odd sense distasteful. She was visibly annoyed by the cough which I had in some unknown way contracted in Germany and which all her advice and concoctions could not cure. Neither she nor I could understand why I grew so thin with all the good food she so amply provided for us all.

My father died in February of 1914 after a long and terrible illness. I was in Maine for a fortnight before he died, a fortnight of almost constant northeast snowstorms, which banked our great old house and made sickness and death seem even more inexorable. When I returned to Chicago and waited for the long, slow spring, I realized that for the first time in my relatively short life I could be so completely exhausted that even my problematical future held no interest for me.

After two months at home in the summer, months spent chiefly in coughing, I was sent in August upon the insistence of certain good, if annoying, doctors to the Rocky Mountains. There had been hurried conferences as to just where I should go, and the decision had at last fallen to a town in Montana called Bozeman. This town meant little to me although a college friend of mine lived there, her husband being a member of the faculty of the Montana State College. Her presence there meant that I should not be entirely among strangers; the altitude of Bozeman possessed the seemingly requisite thousands of feet; and, above all else, the specialist who had sealed my fate knew an excellent doctor in that town who would look out for me.

I shall always remember my arrival in Bozeman. I reached there in the late afternoon of August twenty-second and in a driving snowstorm. I had been journeying for hours through brown, sun-baked country with spurs of mountains lying here and there, as though in some long-past upheaval of nature they had been hurled from the higher ranges in the distance to fall upon the barren land. Now and then this barren land had given place to acres upon acres of harvested ground, some set about with shocks of grain, some bare, and so wide in extent that the houses and barns beyond them looked diminutive and insignificant by very contrast. There were miles, too, of rolling, tumbling foot-hills, brown, and shaven close by innumerable herds of cattle. The warm, summer sunlight lay over all, so that to come suddenly into gray obscurity and driving snow held something of terror in its suddenness.

2

Bozeman in 1914 was a small city of some seven thousand people, set in the fertile valley of the Gallatin River with mountains towering on every side. I had never before seen a mountain higher than the Harz or the Mt. Desert hills, and for some days I was at a loss to know whether I should be awed or comforted by them. Long before I had lived three years among them I discovered either emotion, or even a combination of the two, quite insufficient.

In 1914 the State of Montana still had its open ranges. Here it was easy to picture the scriptural cattle upon a thousand hills and quite as easy to assume their belonging to God since there was no other visible owner about. In 1914 there was also land still open for homesteading; and I have never quite recovered from the urge I had then to live in a shack at the corner of some great piece of land which would ultimately become my own. Automobiles were rare in Bozeman in those days. Ranchers drove in from their homes throughout the valley in cumbersome rigs and through clouds of summer dust to do their trading. Cowboys in chaps were a common sight as was their uproar on Saturday nights a common sound.

I never grew either accustomed to or tired of the weather in the Gallatin Valley. Hazlitt says somewhere that an interest in weather is the final resource of the end of a life spent in study. Life was still strong within me, ill as I was; far from its end, I hoped and believed; and yet Montana weather became a resource in itself and remained so during my three years there. Reared as I had been by the sea and weatherwise as all coast people are, I was constantly baffled by mountain weather. Fair days followed fair days, sometimes for a month at a time, motionless days of high, clear sunshine, nights of innumerable stars. It would never rain again, I thought. Then, with seemingly no warning, a warm wind blew from the Pacific over the mountain ranges to the west, and long streamers of rain came in its wake.

I never grew used to the winter cold. It held a terror there as in no other place I have ever known. Sometimes for days at a stretch we were smitten by bitter cold, cold twenty degrees and more below zero, wrapped and hooded in it, almost suffocated by it. There was something terrifying in the way this sharp, dry cold seemed to descend from the mountains, fall in icy streams from the winter sky, to lie upon the submissive earth. When one went to bed at night, one saw the cold from one's windows, ruthless, engulfing, cruel. I have never forgotten the sense of helplessness before it.

Then on a bitter, brilliant February day, when we had been held for weeks in an icy vise, when our nerves were taut with a strange fear, the temperature would suddenly start to rise. It leapt up by quick degrees, fifty sometimes in a few hours, and by nightfall the air would be soft with a false promise of spring and a warm rain would begin to fall. A "chinook" they called this wind. It was a blessing to one's mind as well as to one's shivering, nervous body.

3

Before I had been a week in Bozeman, my doctor, whom I liked as I have liked few persons and to whose care and common sense I owe blessings incalculable, suggested that I go out into the country upon a cattle ranch which he knew for a stay of some weeks. This ranch, known as the Wilson ranch, was high in the foothills of the Rockies, some ten miles from town and three miles from any neighbors. The ranch house, which lay in a depression among the hills, was small and inconsiderable although comfortable enough. Numberless corrals for cattle shelters at branding-time or in bad weather stretched beyond it. A barn or tool-shed stood near at hand across the small dooryard.

I always had the odd and sometimes uneasy feeling on the Wilson ranch that others besides Mrs. Wilson, her daughter of my age, and some migratory cattle-hands were with us; in fact, I could have sworn to any number of invisible presences about the place. Perhaps this conviction of mine arose from the personality of Mrs. Wilson herself. She was a silent woman with large staring dark eyes which were always gazing into some unfamiliar distance. She literally never spoke unless occasion demanded it. She gave me numberless fresh eggs and gallons of milk while I sojourned with her; but those completed her offerings. Her daughter rode the range most of the day on some mysterious business with the cattle, and when she was within the house paid as little attention to me as did her mother.

I was rarely within the house myself. The September days succeeded one another, clear, flawless, with no hint of rain. I have never seen such steady, golden light over any land as over our wide sweep of hills and mountains. Beyond the corrals and through a narrow gulch I could easily reach the side of a hill on the open range where a small enclosure of iron fence-posts marked the grave of some "old-timer" buried there years before. This burial-place was seemingly made for my purposes. It held the sun from ten until four o'clock; it was securely fenced from roaming cattle; and its raised grave and slanting tomb-stone formed a comfortable couch and a rest at just the proper angle for my back.

I spent most of my days on the Wilson ranch on this grave. I read most of the morning, swallowed two eggs at noon, drank my milk from a small stone jar, and ate several chicken sandwiches provided by Mrs. Wilson. After my lunch I took a nap lying with my head in the short grass and with the sun warm upon my back. The coloring of the hills and mountains about and above enchanted me as the day wore on. It was impossible to discover the source of the shadows which stalked over them since there were almost never clouds in the sky. In the hollows and depressions among them yellow quaking-aspens and brilliant red service-berry bushes flamed by hidden streams. Sounds of distant cattle broke the still air now and then, and, if one listened carefully, the running of water in numerous mountain creeks.

I did not like the short evenings at the Wilson ranch, but I loved the nights. I slept out-of-doors on an army cot in the corral that surrounded the house. When I was once settled there, deep below my blankets, I wanted for nothing. The air was cold and clear; the stars were numberless. The silence did not so much lie over the earth or surround it as it enfolded and enveloped it. It seemed to come steadily down from the mountains above like an engulfing stream until it had covered everything and become one with sleep.

On these nights before I slept I thought of Gabriel Oak on Norcombe Hill. The sky, its September constellations, the Great Bear, Cassiopeia, and the Northern Cross, seemed timed by one common pulse, and, as I lay still, I could feel the roll of the world eastward and watch my steady progress through the stars.

4

Had I known when I went to the Rocky Mountains how long my stay would be among them, I should doubtless have felt vastly sorry for myself. But, as a matter of fact, even after I had begun to realize that it might be a long time before I could again turn my steps eastward, I was having a very good time of it. In the first place, I had never before been thrown upon my own mental resources with no pressure from without, never before, as Mrs. Abbie Moffat would have piously said, been "master of my own fate." Here in Montana for the first time in my life people began to assume positions of relatively little importance in my existence. By the very fact of being ill I was naturally set more or less apart from them and from their multifarious activities. This resulted, rather to my surprise, not in a sense of deprivation but rather in an exciting sense of freedom. My long days were mine as they had never been mine before, and I set about enjoying them to the full.

I could always read even in a cold room with open windows; and as the winter in town came on and I found myself with pleasant people who left me very much alone, I began to read for long, uninterrupted hours. I kept on with my German, renewed my Latin and Greek, read poetry, drama, philosophy, and fiction. In those long, quiet days and evenings I lived in a world far more real than I had ever known it to be, a vast, immeasurable world, whose height, breadth, and depth had been created by others greater than I for people like me. Before, I had read largely for incident, situation, and sentiment; now, hardly knowing it, I read for thought and meaning, vision and wisdom. I became in that winter literally intoxicated with books and with thoughts, half grasped, perhaps, but leading on and on into mazes of speculation. I divided my months into weeks, a week of Hardy, a week of Shakespeare, a week of Pater. I read *Marius the Epicurean* that winter, holding it in my mittened hands, reading it aloud in my still room, excited beyond all excitement by its music. I discovered Dante in Montana, the metaphysical poets, the dialogues of Plato. These books, many of which I had seemingly read before, now became mine forevermore by the very miracle of undistracted time.

Fiction took on new light in that long winter of reading. It ceased to be a chronicle of events and situations, of characters interesting or dull as the case might be. It came to be a many-faceted outlook on life, created and propelled by thoughts and ideas rather than by incidents and action. I read *The Brothers Karamazov* for the first time, *Anna Karenina,* and *The Way of All Flesh; Diana of the Crossways, The Mayor of Casterbridge,* and *Madame Bovary.* "We begin to live," says Yeats, "when we have conceived life as a tragedy." I do not know that I had ever heard it said at that time, or even if it had been said in those words; but I could then have understood its meaning as never before: not as a dark thought, but rather as a bright one, touched with humanity, filled with pity and understanding, embracing the world with wisdom.

I had other pastimes that winter besides my reading. On a long square table in the corner of my room I had a large map of Europe tacked securely to its edges. I had colored pins for opposing forces, which I moved day by day or week by week as I consumed the latest despatches of the War. This exercise, rueful as it was, took on the excitement of a game. I was much distressed in late autumn by a letter from Fräulein Elster in which she begged me to understand her distress and to be as kind as I could toward accusations against her country. No letter ever came to me from Fräulein Franke.

I began to write that winter, sometimes imitating styles and diction which I liked, sometimes striking out for myself in simpler fields. I had dreams of writing a novel based on one of a dozen new ideas which I had gained from my reading; but the consciousness of my own immaturity held me back. In 1915 twenty-eight was a far younger age than it is today; and I at twenty-eight was far younger than most of that age. I began, therefore, to write a story for girls of fourteen or thereabouts and continued with it for two hours daily throughout the winter. When in April it was accepted for publication by a Boston firm and I received a check for one hundred and fifty dollars, I sincerely believed that the world of literary achievement and success lay at my feet!

I remember how, when I had found the letter with the check in my post-office box, I stood on the street longing for some acquaintance to pass by so that I might electrify him with my good tidings. The few persons whom I knew being elsewhere, I sent a telegram to my mother and then proceeded to consume great quantities of chocolate ice-cream all by myself in an ugly restaurant. This delicious fare has always been my indulgence, whenever procurable, in all hours of triumph!

5

I had not been a month in Montana before strength began to return to me. At first it came like the hardly perceptible motion of the tide creeping over brown flats. Then, as October gave place to November, it came hurrying on like the racing waters on a full spring moon. I could feel it flooding my body, driving away weakness and pain. I recognized it in the new ease with which I held my book, in the new spring in my legs upon my daily walk, in new comfort and security at night. Milk and eggs, beef and butter, fruit and cream began to cover up my bones. One hundred and eighty fresh eggs a month, I thought, even at a cost of four dollars and fifty cents, were proving to be worth the ghastly swallowing of them. The vulgar, according to Pope, imitating Horace, boil eggs; the learned roast them; but I had the compensation of neither the vulgar nor the learned!

By the time the slow spring had loosened the streams in the canyons, I felt strong and peculiarly new in body and in mind. I had discovered like Hazlitt and Mrs. Blodgett that I was never less alone than when alone. Like Hazlitt, too, in *On Going a Journey* I wanted to run, leap, and sing for joy. My doctor, although he did not encourage the running, said I might ride if I wished; and for ten dollars a month I procured the companionship and labor of an Indian "cayuse" called Siwash. Siwash, like Rozinante, was thin and angular in spite of good feeding. He was likewise of a contemplative nature, peaceable upon most occasions, and quite unremarkable for speed. He seemed framed for my purposes, and I rode him for miles over mountain trails and through canyons.

The mountain flowers proved a source of great delight to me: the forget-me-nots by the streams, the lupines covering sandy slopes, the white columbines, penstemon, and hare-bells, the Indian paint brush, half flame, half feather. I loved the hot June sun on miles of silver-gray sagebrush, the clear outlines of the mountains, thin and sharp in the bright distance, as though one could sit astride them and touch the sky.

I spent the summer months in a mountain camp called Cold Spring, on the West Gallatin, miles from anywhere at all. I made friends with prospectors and cattle men, their faces filled with weather, their hands marked by work, and with the few other sojourners at Cold Spring, who had come up to the West Gallatin to fish. The days were long and often pleasantly hot, clear with the transparency of still, sunshot water; the nights were clear and cold. Sudden snow flurries came over us more often than rain.

That summer in my screened cabin on the west fork of the Gallatin with the sound of swift water always in my ears I read certain of the English essayists. I thought I had read many of their essays before, but I now discovered that I had never really done so. A friend had sent them to me in small volumes which I could carry, one or two at a time, in my pocket. I read Lamb with new pleasure, Hazlitt with admiration and sympathy, De Quincey with a passion of excitement and wonder. Pater again delighted my ears and satisfied me with other good things. I memorized certain sentences, which I liked because of their rhythm and diction, and said them over to myself on my walks or after I had gone to bed at night.

She was tumbled early by accident or design into a spacious closet of good old English reading and browsed at will upon that fair and wholesome pasturage.

No dignity is perfect which does not at some point ally itself with the mysterious.

And those simple gifts, like other objects as trivial, bread, oil, wine, milk—had regained for him, by their use in such religious service, that poetic and as it were moral significance, which surely belongs to all the means of daily life, could we but break through the veil of familiarity with things by no means vulgar in themselves.

It was on the tenth of April, 1798, that I sat down to a volume of the New Eloise at the inn at Llangollen, over a bottle of sherry and a cold chicken.

I knew by the time I had finished and re-read many of them that prose was more to me than poetry. One expected beauty in poetry; the very name assured one of it; but when an equal beauty was discovered in prose, the discovery was that much more exciting and satisfying. I was intrigued by the thought, doubtless old to many but new to me, that ordinary words, carelessly used in every-day speech, could, with no help of meter or of rhyme, with no form already set for them, be endowed with such distinction and meaning that they became both music and poetry.

Words began to fascinate me, their choice and combination, their sound and color, their height and depth, the possibilities within them of rhythm and movement. Like Stevenson I began to imitate: to try to write in honest yet vivid monosyllables like Hazlitt; to use participles like Pater's; to frame my sentences so that they would make one conscious of a great height like De Quincey's. My attempts were poor enough in all truth; but they served to prove to me that in the study and teaching of English prose, rather than of philosophy or history, I wanted to spend my days.

Yet I knew the time for that was years away. A long apprenticeship was first in order. I was poorly trained in English literature at best, and my very desire to specialize in my new discovery meant graduate study before the least of colleges would see fit to take a chance on me. Moreover, I had no money. All the little I had earned on my book had been converted into eggs and milk and duly swallowed. Much more had been borrowed. I must teach again as soon as I was able and in any position I could secure.

I am sure that the English essayists had themselves added to my new health and strength both by their words and sentences and by the vision of my future which they had given me. Now I knew the truth of Socrates' advice to the young Charmides when he remarks that headaches are cured easily by the cure of the soul, and that the soul is cured by the charm of "fair words."

6

My doctor was insistent upon my not returning east for another year at least; pleading made not the slightest impression upon him; and in late August I returned to Bozeman to begin to seek another fortune. I found it in early September in the office of the superintendent of public schools.

Mr. Cunningham, the superintendent, was an angular, completely bald man, a Methodist, and a Christian. He was frankly sceptical of my fitness for public school teaching, and he said so in the kindest possible manner. Had my entrance into his office not coincided with the sudden and unexpected withdrawal of one of his teachers of English, had he not, as he told me, been a believer in Destiny, I am sure he would not have considered me for a moment. But since circumstances seemed to have placed me in his hands, he was disposed to take me for better or for worse. The position which he offered me was in the seventh and eighth grades of what was then known as departmental teaching; and, poor as I was, I accepted it as unwillingly as he offered it.

I fear that I did not enter upon my new position in September with any extra grace of spirit. I had never taught in a public school system and, with my new ambition warm and glowing within me, I did not wish to do so. But whatever grace I lacked on my first day in the Irving School was provided for me, pressed down and running over, by its principal.

Leora Hapner was a woman in her late thirties, perhaps, a Montana product and a native of Bozeman. She was not only one of the best teachers I have ever known, but she was also a genius at school management. She was, moreover, a woman of fine cultivation and finer spirit. She knew precisely of what stuff most of her three hundred children were made, and, accepting them for what they were, she began to pull her school into order and action after the inroads upon her charges of a summer vacation. She was a fine-looking woman, tall and thin, with an olive skin and arresting dark-gray eyes.

She looked, and was, honest and fair, just and kind, energetic and resourceful. She was a genius, too, at discipline. She knew how to speak the language and get inside the minds of tall, strapping youths from the ranges and ranches. She could wield a wide leather strap across the knees of unruly boys, who sat calmly in a chair without the least outcry and liked her while she was doing it. Punishment of this sort, still not only allowed but encouraged in Montana, at least, seemed not to flurry her at all. She did not like it, but she took it, as she took everything else, in her stride.

There was every reason why she might not have relished my entrance into her well-run school. I had had neither training nor experience in public school teaching. I knew neither western children nor the social environment from which they came. I was obviously using the school as a stop-gap and interim before I should go into other fields. I had been ill and conceivably might be ill again. I was completely unknown to her and, for all she knew, might have none of those qualities which she required in her teachers.

If any of these deficiencies rendered my presence in the Irving School problematical to her, I was never for a moment conscious of the fact. From the day I walked into her office and was introduced by her to the other teachers, I had the odd, yet comfortable, feeling that I was exactly where I belonged. All the nonsense which had been in my mind, that to teach perhaps inferior youngsters of twelve and thirteen was a definite step-down from what I had been doing and from what I wanted to do, vanished in her presence as the most unworthy of notions. I began at once to love my teaching, and I continued to do so as long as I remained in the Irving School.

I liked my associates also. They were mostly from the west; no one but me was from New England; but whatever suspicion they may have had of me was lost in the common friendliness engendered in the principal's office and disseminated throughout the school. Most of them were better teachers than I, for they were on their home ground, had had generous experience in public school teaching, and knew what was expected of them as I did not.

I afforded them amusement both by my ignorance and by my handwriting, which could never fulfill Montana standards. We were all required to write according to the Palmer Method of Penmanship;

in fact, until we had satisfied the chirographic ideas and ideals of Messrs. Palmer and Company of Chicago, we each sacrificed every month five dollars of our salaries. Since my monthly pay check was only eighty dollars, I felt a righteous resentment at the five dollars docked each pay day because I could not write in a manner which I secretly despised; yet try as I would, I could never master the inditing of a certain sentence which proved conclusively to the Palmers whether or not we were possessors of their art. This sentence, which I practised daily under the tutelage of some good-natured teacher, already arrived at excellence, read

I am pining for a pin to use in pinning.

Since in the course of a year and a half I never learned to write it to the satisfaction of the Palmers, to whom I hopefully sent my efforts weekly, my salary remained at seventy-five dollars during my stay in the Irving School.

7

The work at the Irving was hard and from Monday to Friday never-ending. The school was organized to the last degree. From eight-thirty until four, we marched on, in time with bells and schedules. I taught six periods a day to classes of forty or fifty, English grammar in three periods, reading in three. When I was not teaching, I was in charge of a room of sixty boys and girls from thirteen to sixteen years of age, to most of whom school was merely to be tolerated and none too graciously tolerated at best.

I learned at once that the children of a mountain state were different in most respects from those of New England. Surely they resembled in nothing the boys and girls of Hillside and my affable, well-to-do little girls in Chicago. Montana in 1915 was still young. Its first settlers had come only fifty years before in the wake of gold suddenly discovered at Alder Gulch. There are few more potent magnets than gold to draw undesirables from one place to another; and in her early days Montana had her soldiers of fortune, adventurers, and ne'er-do-wells. The permanent settlers who followed the miners were of far better stock; they came for the most part from middle and southwestern states in search of farms and ranches and of whatever else a new land might offer; and yet the very fact that the new territory was in a state of actual blockade for several months under the control of its lawless elements proves something of the rigor of an existence which still boiled and bubbled in the active memory of hundreds of families.

The children, many of whom were of the first generation and none beyond the second, partook of the enterprise of their parents. They partook also of their energy and restlessness. Except for the few children of professional families, most of those whom I taught or strove to discipline in my crowded room cared little for books and nothing for study. Both seemed unrelated to cattle ranges and wheat ranches or even to many of their homes in town. They were lazy in certain ways, and yet resourceful, crude in certain ways, and yet instinctively decent. Some of them were lawless in the extreme. They loved courage and scorned weakness; they knew horses, cattle, and wheat, rattlesnakes, rifles, and round-ups. They were, like their parents, new people in a new state; and they had about them all the fearlessness and activity, all the strength and elasticity of a new and lively portion of the earth six thousand feet in the air. They were, in short, the most intensely physical, the most vitally alive, of any youngsters I had ever known; and high-pressure methods of dealing with them were the order of the day.

Needless to say, they thought English grammar the most senseless of subjects; and few of them saw any relation between it and their speech. Reading was acceptable if it had sufficient punch in it, but poems like "The Chambered Nautilus" were so much bunk that had to be learned and then were forgotten as quickly as possible. The rude bridge that arched the flood meant nothing to them; and the Pilgrim fathers on their stern and rockbound coast were pale and paltry enough when compared with Lewis and Clark and with Custer's Last Stand. My chief resource in their minds, my one possession which they envied, was my knowledge of the sea which few of them had ever seen. My tales of shipwreck and pirates, which I told them as a reward for decent behavior, lent to me my chief value as their teacher.

There were, of course, notable exceptions among them. Not all the sixty in my room were ignorant of the so-called amenities of life.

Wealth and substance had brought to several families advantages which they were quick to seize upon for their children. Among the hundred or so from other rooms were boys and girls of college professors, of doctors, lawyers, and ministers. One of my girls now writes detective stories in New York. Several of my boys are intelligent and well-educated ranchers with books in their homes. Only last winter in San Francisco I met a young woman, once in my room in the Irving School, now in an educational position of trust and responsibility.

But in my presentation of young Montana in 1915 I speak of the rank and file, for it was they who made my teaching there distinctive and adventurous. They somehow gave me an abiding respect for life quite outside of books, for physical resourcefulness and vitality, for courage and rough humor, and raucous abounding health. Some of them rode into school from farms and ranches on bitter mornings, stamping into my room with such animation and spirit that I felt strong on the instant. What they lacked in tradition and background they made up for in a quite unconscious love of life and a basic kindliness characteristic of people in a wide, new land.

They little understood what they gave to me. The world in a curious way seemed new while I was among them. And although I could never have been satisfied to stay with them or with others like them, I carried away with me to the graduate school because of them, quite as much as the memory of illimitable country, the sense of basic, untutored natural excellence—in other words, a sense of those virtues and values which in the early ages of the world, when other lands were new, marked out gods and heroes and made them immortal in art and song.

8

I taught a year and a term in the Irving School without a dull moment. I grew strong like my youngsters and even physically resourceful to a certain degree. I rode hundreds of miles through Montana and Wyoming; I learned the ways of mountain camping; I became a fairly good shot with a rifle. Saturday and Sunday in fall and spring and all vacations found me in the canyons with or without others like-minded. I learned a great deal about birds and flowers, a little about geology, much about weather.

I had, or at least took, little time to read during my last two years in Bozeman. The memory of my long year spent with books was still warm within me, ready to be built upon again when the time should come. But my days were too filled with a life outside individual study for me to accomplish much therein. In odd hours during the two years I wrote another book, as lacking in distinction as the first.

In December of my last year I moved from the Irving School to the Gallatin County High School where a teacher of history and English was suddenly needed. The work was more advanced; the problem of discipline less vigorous; and the experience all to the good. My students there were of basically the same type as in the Irving School although the forcibly fed had largely eliminated themselves. I grew to know well certain of my boys and girls, visited several of them on their ranches, and enjoyed them to the full.

I left Bozeman in the spring of 1917 to enter the University of Minnesota in the autumn as a graduate student. I have never been back, but I shall go some day to render tribute where tribute is due. From time to time I see certain of my friends who taught there with me and laugh with them about pining for pins. Occasionally one of my former students appears in one or another corner of the country. The principal of the Irving School, to whom I owe more than I can ever repay, is now on the faculty of Montana State College as a teacher of economics. I feel sure she understands with me that in the liveliness, rigor, and fun of the Irving School we gained resources incalculable for graduate study and for college teaching.

TECHNICAL DISCUSSION

1. Some of the details in the opening paragraphs in this narrative depend for full clarity on events told in earlier chapters. Point them out.

2. At what point does the reader begin to feel oriented and well started on the story?

3. Point out the paragraph that contains the cause of the trip to Montana. Is this a necessary part of the beginning?

4. Point out the places where the general setting gets its first description: land and climate.

5. Point out places where the social setting is described.
6. Point out effective description of specific places.
7. Point out effective description of people.
8. Are the numbers between sections necessary if the reader is to notice the divisions, or does the author provide additional indications.
9. Do the first five sections seem more factual than sections 6 and 7? Give the evidence on which you base your answer.
10. Describe the kind of person you think the author is and point out the details that lead you to think so.

Atomic Age

In World War I, when the British did not dragoon their scientists as sternly as in this one, somebody asked gruff Sir Ernest Rutherford (later Lord Rutherford) if he would please stop puttering with the atom and work full time on anti-submarine devices. Rutherford answered, in effect: Gentlemen, I am trying to split the atom. If I succeed, it will be more important than the war.

He did succeed, in 1919, and he was right about its importance.

Some of the dazed publicity that followed the unveiling of the atomic bomb gave the impression that it was created from scratch, under the terrible urgency of war.

Nothing could have been farther from the fact. The urgency of war had indeed hastened the achievement. But the explosive release of atomic energy was clearly foreshadowed by the ferment of atomic physics in 1940, before the security blackout was clamped down. The experiments popping all over the world (including Japan) were based on a number of fundamental discoveries in the past half-century.

In 1896 Henri Becquerel discovered radioactivity, which is the spontaneous release of atomic energy by certain heavy metals. Becquerel had some photographic plates lying in a dark drawer near a bit of uranium; he found the plates light-struck. His researches led to the discovery of radium by Pierre and Marie Curie, and it was by using radium for cancer therapy that man first harnessed atomic energy to his own ends.

In 1905 Albert Einstein, no experimenter, launched the idea that mass and energy are the same thing, in different states. The matter in the nucleus or core of the atom (which is practically all the matter there is) was conceived as a packet of energy in highly concentrated form.

For the conversion of mass into energy, Einstein wrote what is probably the most important equation ever devised by man: $E = mc^2$. This means simply that energy is equal to mass multiplied by the square of the velocity of light. Light's speed is so enormous (186,000 miles a second), and its square (self-multiplication) so much more enormous still, that one pound of matter is equal to more than ten billion kilowatt-hours of energy.

To those who then believed Einstein, his equation explained how radioactive metals could keep on shooting out particles and radiation for millions of years, and how the sun could continue shining for even longer ages. It also aroused Sunday-supplement dreams of driving an ocean liner around the world by releasing the atomic energy locked in a cupful of water.

Nitrogen's atomic nucleus was the first to succumb to human attack. Bombarding with radioactive particles, Rutherford succeeded in changing a few nitrogen atoms into oxygen.

In 1932 James Chadwick of England discovered the neutron, a particle which has no electric charge and therefore slips straight through the powerful electric shields outside and inside of heavy atoms. Soon Italy's brilliant Enrico Fermi (who has lived in the U. S. since 1939), was attacking all sorts of heavy atoms, including uranium, with neutrons. The neutron became the trigger of the atomic bomb.

In 1934 Jean-Frederic and Irene Joliot-Curie succeeded in making boron, magnesium and aluminum artificially radioactive. The atoms of these normally stable substances continued to shoot out particles for some minutes after the preliminary bombardment stopped. Artificial radioactivity is the key mechanism of the atomic bomb.

Late in 1938 a distinguished German chemist named Otto Hahn, of Berlin's Kaiser Wilhelm-Institute, was bombarding uranium with "slow" neutrons of low energy. As one of the end products, he identified barium. This puzzled him, but he published a diffident note on it in *Naturwissenschaften*.

Hahn had been repeating experiments performed by a onetime

colleague, Lise Meitner, a Jewish woman scientist who had fled from Hitler's Reich to Copenhagen. Meitner's own experiments had puzzled her—but when she saw Hahn's report she guessed that the huge uranium atom had been broken into two nearly equal fragments.

She passed this idea on to Denmark's great atomist, Niels Bohr, who was just about to leave for Princeton. Bohr told U. S. experimenters about it. They sprang to their atom-smashing machines and quickly confirmed it. They also stood gallantly back while Dr. Meitner published the first notes on uranium splitting. She called it "fission," a familiar word in biology but a new term for physics.

Fission was revolutionary, sensational—not only because the heaviest of all elements had been cracked wide open, but because of the tremendous energy profit. Up to then, scientists had always had to put more energy into their projectiles than was released in the break-up. Now, an explosion of about 200,000,000 electron-volts was touched off by idling neutrons of less than one electron-volt. Matter equal to about one-fifth of a neutron's mass was converted into energy according to the Einstein formula.

The first uranium explosions produced secondary neutrons, which in turn seemed capable of touching off uranium atoms, which would yield more neutrons, and so on. This "chain reaction" looked like the clue to a large-scale release of atomic energy. France's Joliot-Curie did in fact produce a chain reaction, but it died out after a few cycles. The problem was to start one which would not dwindle but multiply.

The prospect was difficult—but hopeful. Soberly summarizing nearly 100 reports which appeared during 1939, Dr. Louis A. Turner of Princeton concluded in the *Reviews of Modern Physics:* "For the first time it seems that there is some reasonable possibility of utilizing the enormous nuclear energy of heavy atoms. . . . The practical difficulties can undoubtedly be overcome in time."

Shortly thereafter atomic researchers ducked behind a veil of secrecy. There the "practical difficulties" were overcome.

Behind the blackout curtains, physicists got their work orders. A few, horrified by what was planned, refused the summons. But most went to work, knowing that discovery could not be stopped, that the U. S. and its scientific allies must make it first. Many hoped that they would fail and that their failure would prove forever irrevocable.

Recently the War Department told the story of their success. Professor H. D. Smyth, chairman of Princeton's physics department, who wrote the report, could not tell it all. But what he could tell, even in the prim language of the scientific laboratory, made the most fantastic and meaningful story to come out of the war.

The U. S. entered the atom race in the fall of 1939 when Franklin Roosevelt appointed an informal "Advisory Committee on Uranium." It was a small project until the Nazi panzers roared over France. Then the world was struck by a terrible urgency. On Oct. 11, 1941, nearly two months before Pearl Harbor, President Roosevelt wrote to Winston Churchill, offering British nuclear physicists a plan to work in the U. S.; Churchill accepted. The U. S. and Britain were partners.

All through the perilous spring of 1942, the scientists worked. In numerous guarded laboratories, their strange apparatus glowed and hummed. By June they had made progress. The program mushroomed, was transferred to the War Department.

"The Manhattan Engineer District" was the purposely deceptive name given the project. Its centers were full of G-men. Its couriers were Army officers, brief cases chained to their wrists. It rated highest priorities for men and materials. From dozens of universities and industrial plants physicists, chemists and mathematicians vanished into thin air; the Manhattan District had snatched them.

Before the war it was discovered that slow-moving neutrons could split the atoms of the uranium isotope, U-235, giving a mighty gush of energy. Besides energy, their "fission" produced more flying neutrons. If enough of these in turn split uranium atoms, the reaction would maintain itself, gain momentum. It would flash through all the uranium, like the flame of a match through excelsior.

This "chain reaction," which the Manhattan District now had to develop, did not happen naturally, chiefly because only one part in 140 of ordinary uranium is U-235. Most of the rest is another isotope, U-238—which, instead of splitting like U-235, absorbs the new-born neutrons with the result that the atomic flame goes out like a match in wet excelsior.

Obviously, the remedy was to separate the active U-235 from natural uranium, getting rid of the U-238. It was simple in principle, like drying the water content out of a sodden fuel. But the physicists shuddered when they finished their calculations. No chain reaction, they found, could take place in a small bit of U-235, but a large enough chunk would surely explode.

The problem, once they had the big chunk, might be to keep it from exploding whenever it was struck by any wandering neutron. The explosion, they calculated, would certainly be more violent than anything yet seen on earth.

There was one more possibility. When natural uranium (one part U-235, 140 parts U-238) is bombarded with slow neutrons, more happens than the cracking of the U-235 particles. Some of the neutrons produced by these fissions are absorbed by the more phlegmatic U-238. This forms a new, unstable element, neptunium, which soon turns into plutonium.[1]

Plutonium is a fairly stable element. Like the rare U-235, it is also "fissionable"; it can be made to explode in a violent chain reaction. Furthermore, it is not an isotope of uranium, but an entirely different chemical element. Therefore it can be separated from uranium comparatively easily by chemical means while U-235 clings to U-238 with tenacious obstinacy.

The atomic reaction producing plutonium did not take place in nature as a chain reaction. Many of the neutrons from the splitting U-235 flashed right out of the material. Others were wasted on impurities. Only a very few changed U-238 into plutonium.

The scientists went to work to change that. One measure: increasing the size of the active material to keep the neutrons from escaping so soon. Another: eliminating impurities. Another: slowing down the neutrons to keep them near the uranium until they could be absorbed.

This last could be done by imbedding small bits of uranium in a "moderator"—a substance which would slow the speed of the neutrons but not absorb them. The Germans may have tried heavy water for this job. The Manhattan District men decided on graphite, which was easier to get. If they could produce plutonium at an orderly controlled rate, they would have a charge for the bomb that would change the world.

1 Named for the planet Pluto, which is beyond Uranus and Neptune in the solar system. Pluto was also the god of the underworld.

So far nearly all the work had been on the level of theory. No chain reaction had been achieved; no appreciable quantity of U-235 had been isolated; no plutonium had been produced. But on June 17, 1942, the various committees concerned sent their report to the President: let's make plutonium as well as U-235.

Full-scale plants, the committees urged, should be built at once. It was not known which processes were the best, so all the more promising ones should be started immediately. There was no time for failures, or even for pilot plants. The Nazis might be ahead in the race for Doomsday.

The President agreed, made money available. Theory had felt out the road to the goal. Now production would bulldoze it wide.

Like an ever-growing snowball the Manhattan District rolled around the nation, picking up men (125,000), money ($2,000,000,000), mountains of materials, trainloads of equipment. It enlisted famed corporations—Eastman, Dupont, Stone & Webster, Union Carbide and Carbon, and others.

Professors, including many Nobel Prize winners, deserted their campuses to live in dusty deserts. Workers trekked in their trailers—careful New England craftsmen, burly Southern Negroes, all the races and types of the great U. S. In general terms they were told the shouting urgency of the mighty thing they were doing, but few of them knew its extraordinary character.

Under the cover name of "The Metallurgical Laboratory," some of the most important discoveries were made at the University of Chicago directed by famed Dr. Arthur Holly Compton. His leading associate: Italian-born Dr. Enrico Fermi, whom many consider the world's foremost nuclear physicist. But there were also scores of other laboratories where the work went on: Columbia, University of California, Iowa State, industrial research centers.

There were many possible ways of separating U-235 from natural uranium. Two processes at least were found to work well. In the first (mass spectrograph), uranium particles were electrically charged, fired through a huge electromagnet, sent into a curving course. The lighter U-235 swung more widely on the curve. Traps were set at the end of the turn, and U-235 was caught there, while U-238 was discarded.

In the second, as incredibly delicate as the first, a gaseous uranium compound was pumped through the finest of sub-microscopic filters. The faintly more volatile U-235 passed through more easily. Result: a higher percentage of U-235 beyond the filters.

The experimental work of the electromagnetic method was done at the University of California under blond, boyish Dr. E. O. Lawrence; on diffusion, at Columbia under Dr. H. C. Urey. By 1943, before the experiments were completed, vast plants to carry out both processes were being constructed at Oak Ridge, a sparsely inhabited region near Knoxville, Tenn.

Into that brand-new city (called Dogpatch) flooded weird equipment: thousands of powerful, new-type pumps, gigantic electromagnets, innumerable other machines and instruments. Amid oceans of mud and battlefront confusion, they finally found their places. Both plants were successful, produced effective quantities of precious U-235.

Production of plutonium was probably no more important, but vastly more dramatic. On a squash court under the stands of University of Chicago's football field, a strange apparatus took form. It was an oblate spheroid (doorknob shape), built up of graphite bricks with lumps of uranium or uranium oxide imbedded in their corners. This was the world's first chain reaction "pile"—a uranium "lattice" and a graphite "moderator." If it worked according to Dr. Fermi's theories, it would produce the first chain reaction ever set up on earth.

With care, and great trepidation, the physicists laid the bricks. They knew they were deep in unknown territory; anything might happen. Around them hummed southside Chicago. Nearby, students passed on their way to classes.

By theory, the chain reaction should start spontaneously when nearly all the bricks were laid. Then it could be stopped short of a disastrous explosion by inserting strips of cadmium to break the chain.

But far below the "critical size" of the theory, instruments gave the alarm. The reaction was starting to cook. Luckily, the cadmium strips had been inserted at "retard" position. Slowed down by their influence, the reaction was easily stopped. "This," commented Dr. Smyth dryly, "was fortunate."

This momentous experiment—the very first chain reaction—marked the beginning of the Atomic Age. The pile was successful. Long before the queasy process had been reduced to an orderly procedure, a gigantic, full-sized plutonium plant had been started at Hanford on the desert near Yakima, Wash. Advantages of the unattractive site: isolation, a good supply of Grand Coulee power and the Columbia River which would carry away the enormous heat generated in the piles.

The original pile at Chicago had been a ticklish business, but the giant piles at Hanford were studies in unexplored dangers. Theory warned that as soon as they started working, they would generate floods of deadly radiation and produce unknown radioactive elements, most of them fiendishly poisonous. These effects could conceivably be so powerful and so long-lasting that no living thing could approach a pile which had once been in operation.

Accordingly, elaborate devices were developed for operating the piles by remote control from behind thick protective shields. Even so, the deadly unknowns escaped. The cooling water was radioactive. It had to be impounded and exhausted of radioactivity before going back to the river. The wind blowing over the chemical plant picked up another load of peril, for the stacks gave off a radioactive gas. The City of Pluto was a place of grim possibilities.

Rigid precautions guarded the health of the workers. They all carried small electroscopes or bits of photographic film for nightly tests to show the amount of radiation to which each had been exposed. A gadget called "Sneezy" measured radioactive dust in the air; "Pluto" watched lab desks and instruments. Clothing was carefully checked. Devices rang an alarm when a radioactive worker came near.

Besides plutonium, the Hanford plant produced two frightening by-product effects. The water which cooled the piles carried off enough energy, derived from the chain reaction, to heat the Columbia River appreciably. No definite figures have been released, but the hints in Dr. Smyth's report are portentous. Some relative of the uranium pile may still prove a power source great enough to run all the world's machines.

The second by-product was pure horror. In the ordinary operation of a large-scale pile, calculated Dr. Smyth, enough radioactive poisons could be produced every day to make "large areas uninhabitable."

While the mighty plants were being built and the processes studied to make them run, another team of physicists was colonizing still another desert. In March, 1943, a group led by Professor J. R. Oppenheimer of the University of California, gathered at Los Alamos, New Mexico. Their job was to design, assemble and test the atomic bomb itself. The pile constructors had struggled to keep their brain child from blowing up. The bomb men had the more deadly mission of finally blowing up theirs at the time and place that war demanded.

For obvious reasons, Dr. Smyth's description of the bomb is incomplete. But he gives some hints. U-235 and plutonium do not have to be exploded by a detonator like TNT. They explode automatically whenever gathered together in large quantities. Therefore a main problem in an atomic bomb is to design a mechanism which will bring small masses to the explodable "critical size." Until the explosion is well started, they should be held together by a heavy-material "tamper." A possible source of heavy material: the hoarded gold of Fort Knox.

Dr. Smyth's War Department report breaks off at the end of June, 1945, shortly before the fearful test on the desert which proved the bomb a smash-hit. Dr. Smyth was sure of success before the test was made, but he was not completely happy about it: "Initially, many scientists could and did hope that some principle would emerge which would prove that atomic bombs were inherently impossible. This hope has faded gradually. . . ."

For the future, rapid improvement in the technique of atom fission is foreseeable. For science this will be progress but, says Dr. Smyth: "Should a scheme be devised for converting to energy even as much as a few per cent of the matter of some common material, civilization would have a means to commit suicide at will."

TECHNICAL DISCUSSION

1. This essay tells the story of the development of atomic energy. It also attempts some explanation of the principles of atomic energy. Point out the sections that contain explanation.

2. Why did the author begin with an anecdote?

3. Find the places where the story of atomic energy turns from one phase to another. How does the author indicate that he is making a turn?

4. What class of readers does the author expect to reach—general or scientific? How can you tell? Do you think the author gives sufficient explana-

tion of the technical principles? Is it possible for a general audience to understand the principles fully?

5. Make a list of the scientific terms used in the essay. Are their meanings clear to you? Look up textbook and encyclopedia definitions of such words as *fission, neutron,* and *chain reaction* and be ready to define them in class, using all the means of illustration you can find or devise.

6. Does the author's emphasis on danger help carry the reader's interest? Point out places where the danger was emphasized.

7. Find peculiarities of style commonly associated with *Time:* short sentences, incomplete sentences, items in summary, etc. Discuss the value of these devices.

2. THEMATIC READINGS

First Pattern

Plenty of Grass in Parks: A Letter to the Times

TO THE EDITOR OF THE NEW YORK "TIMES":

For many years The *Times* has been a great and good friend of the city park system, whose support no park man can fail to acknowledge.

Even Homer, however, nods occasionally. You devoted Wednesday's "Topics of the Times" to a discourse on grass and concrete in city parks. Your writer said that at the new Corlears Hook Park asphalt, concrete and granite are ousting grass and trees. He asks what today is the proportion of grass and concrete or asphalt in the renovated, modernized parks, and comes to the mournful conclusions that only active youth is considered in our present recreation system, that the grass-and-bench motive has been declining and that in spite of the relative increase in the number of old people, less and less is being done for them.

When a writer is in a nostalgic fireside mood and is rambling along pleasantly to his own satisfaction, it seems a pity to interrupt with a few cold statistics.

First, as to Corlears Hook Park and East River Park, which is part of it: the fact is that by acquiring some land, pushing the new bulkhead out into the East River and filling back of it, we have created a 52-acre park in anticipation of the rebuilding of the whole of the lower East Side, so that the old Corlears Hook Park is now only one-fifth of this new park area. The so-called greensward, which has been a mass of mud and weeds, and an informal playground and baseball diamond as far back as I can remember, now has genuine landscaping and even a flower garden which we believe can be maintained.

"Plenty of Grass in Parks: A Letter to the *Times*." From The New York *Times*, September 18, 1941. Reprinted by permission of the author and The New York *Times*.

The total "lawn" area in the old Corlears Hook Park contained a little more than 5,000 square yards, while in the new park we have more than 77,000 square yards, exclusive of the baseball diamonds. Where the old park had 2,300 square yards devoted to shrub area, the new park has more than 16,000 square yards. The old park had about 11,000 square yards of paved walks, while the new park has 60,000 square yards. The old walks were lined with about 840 linear feet of portable benches, while in the new area we have 11,335 linear feet of benches. The old park had 93 trees in it, and there are about 1,200 in the new area. The old promenade along South Street was about 600 feet long, but today we have a promenade a mile and a quarter long, which is bound to attract those who want to sit quietly and look out over the water. At the same time, youth has been provided with active play facilities, and the temptation has been removed to destroy what the older people can now enjoy.

Precisely the same logic has prevailed throughout the entire city park system. With very few exceptions, additional playgrounds have been placed on entirely new plots not hitherto part of the park system at all. Old parks have, of course, been reconstructed so as to provide more active play facilities, but at the same time landscaping is protected. Everywhere more benches have been installed. Actually, there are today three times as many benches for older people, mothers and children, as there were before the present administration took office.

In Central Park, where we have provided a number of marginal and other playgrounds, the total active play area is less than half the new lawn and passive recreation area provided on the site of the old reservoir.

We now have five times as many benches in Central Park as there were in 1934, and in this one park alone we have planted approximately 3,000 trees and 50,000 shrubs.

Manhattan is not the whole of New York City. A large amount of entirely new park space has been acquired and developed in neighborhoods previously neglected, much of it consisting of natural woodland which was about to be denuded and subdivided for real estate purposes.

Moreover, many miles of landscaping, walks, benches, and other park facilities for people of all ages, including particularly passive recreation areas, have been provided along the Belt Parkway and other parts of the parkway system, in the nature of shoestring parks where no green vistas existed before. When in the history of this city, or any other large city, have there been so many miles of new walks opened to pedestrians and older people in so short a time? On the Belt Parkway alone we have provided 26½ miles of pedestrian walks, 78 acres of lawn, exclusive of recreation areas, and 10,000 linear feet of benches. A large percentage of these promenades are along waterfront which up to the present time was never accessible to old or young.

A quick glance at some of our new areas might indicate failure to plant trees and shrubs. Unfortunately, we can't afford to transplant large, old trees, so we must plant small ones and wait for them to grow. Every year shows a marked improvement of landscaping in the new parks. Prior to 1934 very little was done in the way of replacing old trees which died and had to be removed. Not only have we made progress in replacing the annual loss of 6,000 trees but we have started a tree nursery on Riker's Island which should eventually solve the problem.

No doubt, in the course of the changes necessitated by the growth of the city, by movements of its population, by increased demands for active recreation, and by our honest efforts to give every age group its due, some leisurely traditions and landmarks have disappeared which were precious in their time and evoke pleasant memories today in those whose attention is focused on the past. If I remember my classics, the Romans had a phrase for the fellow whose mind is turned backward and who is always bemoaning the past. They called him "laudator temporis acti." Your writer is one of these fellows, and he is entitled to a good comfortable seat by the fireside. His pleasant discourse, on the other hand, will lose nothing if he sticks to the facts.

Robert Moses,
COMMISSIONER OF PARKS.

New York, Sept. 18, 1941.

TECHNICAL DISCUSSION

1. Why does the author make the friendly remark in his opening paragraph?

2. Why does he summarize "Wednesday's 'Topics of the Times'"?

3. What is the purpose of the third paragraph?

4. What is the author's theme? How does he tell his reader what the theme is?

5. What kinds of data does the author use? Illustrate.

6. Point out the major divisions of the essay and the transitional devices used between each division.

7. Why does the author end with a repetition of the ideas that he expressed in his third paragraph?

TOPICS FOR PAPERS

1. Make a study of the college landscaping problems, such as maintenance, future plans, tree repair, building up-keep, seasonal plantings, student depredations on the flower beds.

2. Come to a conclusion about the landscaping or the buildings of the college campus and write a paper that fully supports the conclusion.

3. Investigate and describe the activities of some department of college up-keep, such as the greenhouse, the heating plant, the janitorial service in one of the buildings. Use one conclusion for a central theme and support it with data gathered during the investigation.

Don't Work Your Way

ROY A. BENJAMIN, JR.

"Don't Work Your Way Through College" is not meant as a message to raise your eyebrows. It is a message that has never been fully brought home to parents, college students and potential college students. Yet it bears the almost unanimous stamp of approval of college administrators and of college graduates who did work their way. The quicker parents and students realize it is generally harmful for a young man to work his *entire* way through college, the better off both will be.

This is to be no brief against courage and perseverance. The warning need not apply to the genius, nor even to the superior type of young man. Nor does it apply to the many happily-situated *part-time* college workers. But that large group of students who must, of neces-

"Don't Work Your Way." From *Current History and Forum*, September, 1940. Reprinted by permission of *Current History*.

sity, earn every cent of their college expenses should beware. The difficulties that confront them are formidable indeed.

Let us picture the average American high school graduate. Take George Withers, eighteen-year-old favorite of Little River Junction. George was a football player at high school, a class leader, a young man who bolstered family finances with returns from his newspaper route. He is keen and confident. He knows that he wants to go to the state university nearby. There can be no assistance from home—the family simply cannot afford it. But, endowed with youth's energy and optimism, George has no fear. Others, less conscientious than he, have made it. He can make it too. Listen in on George's interview with the University's Dean of Students.

"How much money do you have?" the Dean asks him.

"Fifty dollars, sir."

"Do you expect to go through college here on those fifty dollars and what you can earn?"

"Yes, sir. I know what I'm up against and I'm not afraid. I want a college education more than anything else. I've worked for what I've wanted all my life and I'm willing to do anything for the chance to work my way through four years at State."

"Withers," the Dean tells him, "I like your record and I like your spirit. But, listen to me. A college education can and should be the greatest thing in your life. You must not try to make it on a shoe string. A boy of your type is capable of getting the most out of everything we can offer. But you won't do it, Withers, if your college benefits come between afternoons of washing dishes and nights of theater ushering. Go home. Work a year, or even two. Come back then with enough reserve so that you won't remember college as a nightmare of making financial ends meet."

For George's sake, let us hope he takes the Dean's advice. Let us hope he goes back to Little River Junction, works for two years at "Pop" Thornton's soda fountain, saves a few hundred dollars, and then returns to State. Many a youthful George Withers, however, has politely thanked the Dean for his counsel, carted his belongings to an attic room rented in a house six blocks from the campus, put in his order for a freshman cap and officially become a "State man." Later he thought he was getting a college education when one-third of all his time was taken in struggling to feed and clothe himself and yet get enough sleep.

There is a widespread notion that one must suffer and sacrifice to realize the benefits of college. How absurd! Educators have long been aware of the handicaps that a too heavy burden of work imposes on college men, though they have failed to make students and parents fully aware of these handicaps. There have been scattered efforts to spread enlightenment on the subject. Some years ago the Cornell bulletin said: "Some parents or guardians have the notion that it does a young man good to earn his board or his room at college. The notion is as false as it is queer. Self-support handicaps a student. It is honorable if it is necessary, but it takes time and energy that any student might much better be employing otherwise."

Harvard gave this warning: "Students who must rely on earning part of their expenses should keep in mind the fact that too much time devoted to this problem may defeat the very purpose for which they come to Harvard—the acquirement of a well-rounded education. Excessive efforts toward self-support often result in lowered grades and in the curtailment of desirable extra-curricular activities. Ordinarily, it is not wise for the average student to spend more than twenty hours a week in part-time work."

Are sentiments like these undemocratic? Not at all. They are good, common sense. They reveal, in advance, what too many young men learn when it is too late.

In the 1920's, you will remember, the man who worked his way through college was one of America's idols. He was a junior partner of the "self-made man." His handicaps were envied; his difficulties were revered; his ability to overcome obstacles was the theme of innumerable success stories.

Things changed during the subsequent depression. People were too busy worrying about themselves to give much thought to struggling college men. Still, countless students gave their all, staggering through four years of college so that they might flash sheep-skins which they hoped would give them an advantage in the business world over non-college competitors. And many students plan to do exactly the same thing in the college year which will get under way in the next few weeks. They will do so, however, against the advice of college officials.

In recent months, I have interviewed deans and employment directors at more than a hundred colleges and universities throughout the country. I asked them for complete information about working students—the effect on their studies, health, campus life, post-college viewpoint. The replies did not contain tributes to brave youths who wallow in economic depths in order to achieve academic heights. Dramatic stories of serious young men who nibble on bread crumbs and write history-making theses are missing. Instead, there is a unanimous warning that students and parents should give careful consideration to the handicaps and disadvantages that face the man who, while at college, must give a large part of his time to earning his expenses.

Here are typical opinions I received from college officials:

"Only a few determined souls should try working their way through college"—Dean C. H. Pettee, University of New Hampshire.

"Working while attending college has distinct handicaps which often overshadow the advantages obtained"—William J. Buntain, Bureau of Placement and Vocational Guidance, Northwestern University.

"It is commendable for a man to work his way through college only if he is able to do it without injuring his academic course"—Clarence E. Clewell, Chairman, University of Pennsylvania Placement Service.

"If he has to work to earn a part of his expenses, it would be best in most cases to extend the college period over five or more years"—Annie B. Gary, Assistant Registrar, Southwestern, Tennessee.

"It depends upon the man. Some men work their way out of instead of through"—Lonzo Jones, Assistant Dean, Iowa State.

What has brought about this new attitude? Perhaps it is changing times. In the stepped-up twenties, colleges were too much engaged in turning out assembly line products to worry if certain units were put together badly. When the depression started it was no longer a question of mass production. The question was whether the factory would be able to stay open. The plant hobbled along at reduced capacity, thankful that there was still a slight market for its product and not too concerned whether the raw material it took in was solid enough to withstand factory treatment.

Today, the picture has altered. Colleges are aware of it. Record graduating class totals are not so important as well-equipped graduating classes. It is now realized that a student who must give much of his time to working for his living loses out in much that makes a college training valuable. He must miss extra research into favorite subjects, participation in campus activities, even the social and sporting phases of college life which often go unappreciated in an outside world.

Remember that we are concerned, in most cases, with the full-time college worker. Fifty per cent of the 750,000 men attending college today earn some part of their expenses. College officials and students alike say that most of this work is beneficial. When it bears directly upon the interests of the student, such as laboratory work for science majors, or affords him a practical outlet for classroom theories, such as campus newspaper correspondence for journalism students, and when it demands only reasonable time and energy, it is a phase of college life to be sought.

But 75,000 students—ten per cent of the entire group—earn all their expenses. The fact that they make few complaints about their plight does not lessen the damage being done to them. Naturally, they are sincere and courageous, else they would never have set out on such a difficult road. But most of them are so engrossed in struggling for immediate pennies that they are forced to overlook the very phases of college life which in future years would prove most valuable to them.

Let us pick up young Withers in his two-by-four attic room and see how he is managing. He is at a state university where tuition is free and so he has only his living expenses to consider. Being thrifty and willing to sacrifice many normal comforts, he sets forty dollars a month as his budget. He divides it this way: twenty dollars for food, ten dollars for rent, ten dollars for books, clothes, laundry, and other expenses.

Withers works at the accepted student pay-rate of thirty cents an hour. Thus thirty-five hours of each week must be used in the support of his budget. He makes one-fourth of his expenses as a soliciting agent for a dry cleaning concern. Another quarter comes for long

Saturdays as clerk in a downtown grocery store. The remainder is the result of about three hours daily waiting on tables.

George also goes to classes twenty hours a week. Each hour of class work requires an hour of outside preparation. Add forty study hours to thirty-five work hours and his week is already nearly twice as long as a good labor leader would allow.

To healthy, conscientious George, it's worth it. He doesn't mind the blood-shot eyes and the hazy class hours that often follow a sleep-slashed night. He doesn't mind missing the fraternity activities of his classmates. He cheerfully overlooks Saturday night dances when he knows the grocery store money goes a long way toward keeping him at State. He's getting a "college education" and the sacrifices are all part of the game.

Still, if only he had the time, there is nothing he would like better than to finish and submit to the University Players the one-act comedy he had partially completed the summer before. George is popular. Several of his fellow-classmates would like him to run for a freshman office in campus elections. He begs off; he hasn't time for politics. But secretly he wishes he had.

That was chiefly what the Dean had meant when he spoke of the benefits that George would miss if his time were taken up with too much outside work. Too many people underestimate their importance —the campus yearbook, the glee club, fraternities and societies, the symphony orchestra, student executive positions, and the scores of other features that are listed in college bulletins as "extra-curricular activities."

George may revel in the independence that washing dishes affords him. He may pity the men who depend upon weekly checks from home. But he should not overlook the fact that the latter have the time, if not the inclination, to try out for the college debating team, edit the newspaper, or act as chairman of the junior prom. And George should know that these activities arouse interests, yield experiences and develop personalities that make for success when college is over.

But worst of all is the fact that George's work interferes with his studies. There is no time in his crowded days for the supplementary reading, research, and investigation which make for real mastery of a subject.

Some educators, in fact, insist that the only way to learn is by the single-hearted pursuit of learning. This is their thesis: "The man who works and studies at the same time may be better able to appreciate what opportunities he has, he may make the most of the time at his disposal, but he cannot serve two masters at once and do a good job for both."

Meanwhile, George's health is not improving, though he may not realize it until the facts become apparent in flunked examinations. Working night and day and getting little sleep is bound to have its effect. The rush of George's double life allows little time for exercise or relaxation.

Missing college social life is another distinct disadvantage in George's schedule. Some colleges may place too much emphasis on prom-trotting, but it would be idle to deny the value of dances and other forms of collegiate social life in fitting a student for the modern world.

Who is responsible for leading George—and the thousands of others like him—into this unsatisfactory college existence? The three groups closest to the problem—colleges, parents, and students themselves—have done most to spread misinformation. Until recently, colleges and universities often gauged their success in proportion to total enrollment. College publicity directors outdid themselves in describing Old Union as the place where young America could spend the most beneficial, enjoyable, unforgettable four years of its life. Finances need be the least of its worries. Easy jobs were plentiful.

Many parents contributed to the error and confusion. Some assumed that their child was a superior sort of person who could topple all obstacles with ease. Others thought that plenty of work would be the best possible thing for their youngsters. Still others realized the truth but were financially powerless to help.

As for the students, their actions were youthful, brave and dramatic. Hardy boys, like young Withers, set their sails for a college cruise and never dreamed that a dearth of time and money could upset them. Most of them, even after finding the campus ocean so rough, were content with their diplomas. They worried only slightly that a dash of political science and a deluge of dish washing were the two things they could remember for the best four years of their lives.

Today, college deans and employment experts are doing their best to aid the ambitious and industrious, but fundless, college hopeful. Three solutions are suggested. He can postpone his entrance into college and in the interim build up a reserve from which he can draw. He can stretch his curriculum from four to five or six years. Then his academic load is lessened and he has time for study, work, and the "extras." Or, if he can make certain of a steady helping hand, he can rely on income from part-time work to balance the books.

Energetic youths should not mind putting college off for a year or two. Patience will find its reward in a fuller and happier college life. Indeed, a breathing spell between high school and college usually makes for a better freshman, for in it the student often gains a more adult outlook.

The second proposal, that of stretching college life over five or six years, also makes good sense. Some colleges permit students to alternate six months at school with six months at work in their chosen field. Manufacturing and business firms are offering practical, job-paying positions as part of this work-study course.

The third proposal, that of part-time work, is usually satisfactory to everyone. Colleges like it because it means active and enthusiastic students. Parents approve it because it permits students to lead healthy, happy lives. The students themselves find that it leaves time for many of the things that are impossible when work and study are the sole diet.

Part-time supporters are pressing the issue. Campus employment bureaus and service agencies are making intensive studies of students' work problems and are emphasizing jobs that coincide with the interests and talents of the men who take them. Class schedules are being arranged so as to provide the most convenient work hours for scholar-employees.

Cooperatives are doing their part. There is scarcely an institution in the country that does not have some type of student cooperative movement. Sharing work and expenses in dining rooms, laundry and dry cleaning agencies, book stores and soda fountains help to save money and at the same time provides jobs for fellow students.

But working part time to pay part of one's expenses is a very different thing from working full time to pay all of them. It is the latter type of student work to which Edward S. Jones, Director of Personnel Research at the University of Buffalo, refers when he says: "Not more than one in a thousand students should attempt to work his way."

TECHNICAL DISCUSSION

1. What is the author's method of stating his theme?
2. What kinds of data does the author use to support his theme? Illustrate.
3. Does the fact that "Withers" is obviously invented harm the value of the story about him as data?
4. Find several examples of transitions.
5. Can you improve the style the author used to present the typical opinions from college officials? Try it. If you wish, look at the way a similar problem was treated in the essay "The Cat: Vicious Predator *or* Harmless Pet?", page 273.

TOPICS FOR PAPERS

1. By interviewing students who are working, teachers, and other college officers who will co-operate, find out campus opinions about working one's entire way through college. Arrange the opinions into an essay that presents the pro and con of the problem.
2. Write an informative paper on how students on your campus are working to earn their way through school. Get the facts as to the kinds of work, wages, hours. Use specific cases for illustrations of what is being done. Inquire of the Dean of Men or of the employment bureau if possible. Keep your judgments out of the paper or limit them to casual remarks.
3. Write a thematic paper on this subject. Perhaps one of these themes will interest you: (a) My experience leads me to believe Roy A. Benjamin, Jr., is wrong (or right); (b) Student co-operatives and college assistance help to solve the problem of the student who has too little money; (c) The State ought to provide more scholarships and long-term loans for students who belong in college but cannot afford it; (d) I am missing (gaining) a lot because I must work my way through college.

Grizzlies Are Bad Actors

J. B. HOOKER

What will a grizzly do if he suddenly meets up with a man on his own stamping grounds? You can get plenty of opinions on that, most of them different, from men who have had some experience hunting the big beast. Some years ago I read a magazine article in which the writer claimed he could chase all the animals in North America with a buggy whip and a tin whistle.

I have reason to doubt that statement—not because it may be difficult, in this automobile age, to obtain a good buggy whip—but because I've spent practically 365 days a year in grizzly country for the last twenty-seven years. And I know of several occasions when the best buggy whips would have been a poor line of defense.

Take the case of Tom Meanie. In the late winter of 1925 Tom was working his trapline about twenty miles north of my place in British Columbia. He shot a moose for meat, and then left it for a week. Later he and a helper returned to spring the traps, and Tom sent his friend down a side line to pick up traps while he went over to the carcass to get meat. Never expecting a bear to be out that early, he took only an ax to chop off the frozen flesh.

From what we could reconstruct from his tracks later, he got within thirty-five yards of the moose carcass when a large grizzly ran out to meet him. That's the place where Tom's body was found. The bear had struck him and driven him down through the snowshoe trail to his knees; then he had fallen backward. The first blow seemed to have taken off half his skull and practically all his face; the second savage swipe removed the rest of the scalp.

The bear ran away and never returned directly to the body, although it came back and circled it several times before the police came in a week later.

I and my son Edward have had meet-ups with grizzlies, when tin whistles would have been pretty poor weapons. Back in 1933 Edward, also working a trapline, was on his way home for Christmas, when

"Grizzlies Are Bad Actors." From *Outdoor Life,* November, 1941. Reprinted by permission of *Outdoor Life*.

about a mile and a half from the house he saw an animal moving in the twilight. At first he thought it was a wolverine, but when he came within 150 yards he discovered it was a young grizzly. He started to whistle to scare it away, but the whistle had no terrors for the bear. Getting his scent, it started for him on the jump. Ed hollered and banged on a tree with a stick he carried to knock snow from his snowshoes, but the little battler came on with increased speed.

Ed decided it was time to clear the decks for action, so he unslung his .30/30 and when the bear was twelve feet away, he fired. The bullet struck the grizzly in the chest, passed through its heart, and killed it instantly.

From these incidents you might come to the conclusion that grizzlies will invariably charge a man. That wouldn't be correct either. The truth is, or so I've found it, you never can tell just *what* the big bears will do. They seem to be very temperamental, to act on the spur of the moment. If they decide to run, then the whistle gets credit; but if one makes up his mind to charge, you'd better be ready with a rifle.

Years ago I was trapping beaver and had just finished springing traps before setting out for home. Loading my boat I heard some walruses howl south of the cabin, so I paddled quickly across the river and started out to see if I could get a shot. Just entering the timber I got a whiff of decayed flesh; I turned to face the wind, and there about thirty feet away I saw the head of a large bear over the alders and small spruce. I swung my .300 and fired, then moved out into the open. I soon found the bear, down and bleeding from the ears—finished. The bullet had struck him squarely in the mouth and blown up in the base of the brain. What might have happened, had I missed, no one knows, but from the look I got as he towered over the low growth I suspect it wouldn't have been pleasant.

I took Herb Rondall, of Minot, N. D., out for bear in the spring of 1925. Well on the way, our boat got into trouble, and filled. Most of the duffel was lost or ruined, so I had to go back afoot for replacements. Since Herb was going to use my gun in shooting, we only had that one along—and I left it with him for protection. Well, about two miles downriver I came on a large silvertip feeding on the remains of a cow moose and two calves which had been walrus-killed some time during the preceding winter.

The bodies were in a little clump of spruce, so I didn't see the bear until I was less than twenty yards away from him. He was chewing on a strip of skin that he'd torn from a moose leg. All I had was a hunting knife—no buggy whip or whistle—so I stood still and watched Mr. Grizzly. He chewed away on his moose skin, came out about five yards to look me over, walked off to the side for ten yards for a second once-over, and then ambled away, never looking back.

I beat it on downriver, deciding that I'd been born to be hanged.

In the fall of 1931 James Butler and Charles Husler of Saskatoon, Sask., went out with me for their fourth consecutive hunt. Each of them carried a rifle, while I toted a fishing pole and a pack sack with grub. I was in the lead, following a game trail back a little way from the river, when we came into a little meadow. There I saw a large pile of earth and grass, a grizzly cache, and beside it the grizzly himself. He sniffed, got our scent, and raised up on his hind legs.

Something warned me he was going to charge and I told the boys to get ready, dropping to the ground as I did so as to give them a fair shot. Without a pause the silvertip started for us, like a big silver ball bouncing down the slope. Visions of Tom Meanie flashed through my mind; then one of the hunters fired. Not so good—a hit in the left front leg. But the grizzly turned and went for a clump of spruce. The other rifle blasted out and I got up and ran out to see the result. The bear was heading for the timber and not wasting time. Later on we discovered that he came back every night after that to finish his moose carcass.

Later I took out a party made up of Dr. E. M. Stanton, of Schenectady, N. Y., and his son Don. Don and my son Ed went up to the mountains for caribou, and after they'd gone the doctor got a moose about half a mile above the cabin. When we went back, the day after, we found that the carcass had been covered up by a grizzly, so we fixed up a seat and waited.

About 6 P.M. the old boy came down for his feed, and the doctor got him, first shot. We straightened the bear out for skinning and returned to the cabin. Next morning we went back to do the skinning. Here's what happened, quoting from the doctor's diary:

"We reached the carcass about 8 A.M. A casual glance showed that two bears, a large grizzly and a smaller one, had left the moose carcass only a few minutes before—their tracks still held muddy water. We proceeded to take several photos, the last one being of me seated on a log beside the bear. Just as it was snapped I became aware that at the other end of the log—perhaps seventy-five feet away in the alders—there was live bear.

"We paid little attention and got busy with the skinning. But in about twenty minutes we were startled by the crack of a branch in the woods above us, and on looking up, saw two grizzlies—a large female and a cub about three quarters her size—coming down a moose trail not fifty yards away.

"Hooker told me if I'd stand guard he'd take their pictures. Now, wild bears seem to pay no attention to the human voice, although they are greatly interested in other noises—breaking twigs, footfalls, etc. These two now came within thirty yards of us, stood up side by side, sniffed a bit, and then retired into the undergrowth.

"Until 12:30 P.M., when I started to boil up our tea, those bears kept revisiting us, at intervals of about half an hour. First they'd arrive from one angle, then from another. At one time, the old she-bear came within thirteen yards of where I stood—I paced it off afterward.

"Unfortunately there were only two unexposed negatives left in the camera when the bears came on the scene. When Hooker finally got a chance to photograph them, as I stood on the alert with my rifle, he *seemed* calm, but he hopelessly underexposed the shots."

So I say—you can't tell what a grizzly will do.

The next year I went out with Dr. G. Scott Towne, of Saratoga Springs, N. Y. The doctor, having killed a grizzly and two caribou, was waiting for a shot at another caribou, while I cut some dry poles and ran them up river to the spot where the caribou carcasses were lying, intending to build a crow's nest in a tree.

At a spot about 150 yards from the caribou I beached the boat and started inland. Passing the carcasses I noticed they'd been covered up by a grizzly, so I turned around to go back for the doctor. There, ninety yards in front of me, was a nice big grizzly, just emerging from a bunch of alders.

Without any reason that I can discover, the bear rose up on his hind legs, let out a snort, and came for me—making about fifteen feet to the jump. I stood my ground until he was about twenty-five yards away, then decided it was time for action, so I cut loose and hit him in the chest. He let out a bellow and fell on his right side, but he got up again and headed away. I thought he was hard hit and I might as well finish him, so I fired again as he went through an opening. Down, with another bellow you could have heard for miles, then up and away.

I got Dr. Towne and we followed the blood trail for half a mile. The grizzly was bleeding badly—the doctor thought it was a lung shot and that he could not go far. But after he'd lain in a stream of cold water for a while, the bear's bleeding apparently stopped, and we had to give up the chase as it was getting dark.

Wounded badly? The very next night he came back and had a feed! Personally, I think he's alive and well today. Sometimes, thinking over my meetings with grizzlies, I wonder that I am too.

TECHNICAL DISCUSSION

1. What is the author's theme? Find the places where he states the theme.
2. What kind of data does the author depend upon? Is he convincing? Could a similar array of data be lined up on the other side of the argument?
3. Point out places where the author made transitions. Is he effective in keeping the essay moving forward?
4. Does the style of the essay interest you in any way? Explain your interest if you have any. Do you find any words that are not used in your locality, such as *meet-ups* and *walrus-killed?*

TOPICS FOR PAPERS

1. Do some research on one of the following themes and write a paper that presents both sides of the argument: (a) Bears are predators and should be exterminated; (b) Our wildlife is vanishing; (c) It is not always beneficial to drain swamps and turn them into farms.
2. Tell the story of a hunting or fishing trip, choosing between an informative approach and a thematic approach.

3. Write a review of a book dealing with wildlife conservation or with hunting. You will probably find titles in your library catalogue listed under "wildlife," "conservation," "big-game hunting," etc.

The Blind Do It Better

ENID GRIFFIS

In the face of the growing shortage of manpower for essential war industries we are just beginning to become aware of a tight little reservoir of competent, dependable labor that has been waiting for years to be tapped—the blind workers of this country.

The moment the word "blind" is mentioned there leaps to the mind of most of us the picture of a white-haired man laboriously caning chairs or binding corn straw for brooms; a woman with patient, resigned face, bent over a loom; a boy shuffling through the streets with sightless eyes, playing old tunes on a wheezy accordion; or merely a figure in dark glasses standing at a street corner with a bundle of pencils and a tin cup. Few of us realize that outside and beyond these familiar types are thousands of men and women trained and skilled for work in professional fields, business, industry, or agriculture, and that all of them are eager for an opportunity to prove their worth. Not only can they perform certain tasks just as well as the seeing, despite their obvious and burdensome handicap; actually they can and do perform many of them *better*. This is clear from the reports of foremen, supervisors, and factory heads in all parts of the country where blind men and women are now being employed in war work.

There is, for example, the case of a blind inspector of shells in a large arms factory in Connecticut. Since he was placed on regular production last May this man has maintained a perfect record. In all that time not one bad shell has slipped through his sensitive fingers, and his foreman has said he would like to use this blind employee as a model for the instruction of new operators.

Some months ago a large motors corporation in Texas employed a blind man to work on the "burr bench" detecting and removing "burrs" or rough spots left on metal parts by swift-boring mechanical

"The Blind Do It *Better*." From *Harper's Magazine,* April, 1943. Reprinted by permission of the author and *Harper's Magazine*.

drills. Today that man, because of his unerring accuracy, has been appointed supervisor of his department to check the deburring work of a long line of fully sighted workers.

Last June an aviation corporation in New York hired a blind girl as an inspector in the rotor and stator department of its factory. The work consisted of running the fingers over the edges of small steel disk laminations to detect bends, rough spots, cuts, dents, or buckles. By November both the superintendent and the foreman of the plant had no hesitation in stating that her work was definitely superior to that of the thirty-seven sighted girls working at the same task.

Last August a manufacturing plant in New Jersey ran into a serious bottleneck. It could obtain no steel precision gages for measuring the mica spacers used in electrical condensers which, in turn, are needed in every plane, tank, ship, and jeep that rolls off the assembly lines. At the suggestion of the New Jersey Commission for the Blind they were persuaded to try out a young blind girl on the job. To their amazement they discovered that she could quickly gage the thickness of the inch-square separators with a tolerance of only .0005 of an inch; that her performance was more accurate even than the mechanical gages devised to do this type of work; and that within a week her production record was 25 per cent above that of any other girl on the job. Already more than one hundred blind men and women are employed at gaging and sorting mica in shops and factories throughout the country.

A blind man hired last August 11th to weld speakers in one of the nation's biggest radio factories achieved by October 8th a production record of 2,000 speakers welded in a single day—a figure 600 above the average for the plant.

The list of jobs in industry in which blind workers are excelling is surprisingly long. It includes such work as packing, assembling, shell loading, flush-pin gaging, shell inspection, rivet sorting, quartz grinding, wire stripping and retinning, burr detection and removal, drill-press operating, power-press operating (where it is not necessary to place the hand under the die), kick-press operating, lathing (when worked to definite stops), and welding. And the range of possibilities is even wider than this.

For example, a car and foundry company on the West Coast employs a blind man to put bolts into wooden rails which then go into the main assembly line in the production of refrigeration cars. A radio corporation employs a blind man to assemble one of the most intricate dial assemblies which the company produces. He is one of the few men in the department to whom this particular work can be assigned because of the exceptional demands its special nature makes on the sense of touch. An air depot in New York is using several blind persons to load film magazines for use on aircraft cameras. And one aircraft corporation in Kansas City has four blind workers on its payroll—two men and two women. One of the girls operates a stakon power machine which fastens terminals on the ends of wire, while the other works a one-shot riveter on subassembly. One of the men operates a tube-flaring machine; the other is employed on a precision job assembling bomb releases.

And there are still further possibilities which as yet are unexplored. For example, at present there is no record of a blind man in this country ever having been employed to fit instruments into the instrument boards of airplanes; but in England a young airman, blinded in the war, is fitting 20 airplane boards per day, as compared with a maximum of 17 achieved by his sighted co-workers.

Obviously the blind workers' greatest asset in such work is their highly developed sense of touch. But there are many other factors which combine to make them particularly desirable employees. For one thing, they have greater powers of concentration. This is due partly to the absence of temptation in the form of visual distractions, and partly to their need for focusing full attention on the operation in hand when the sense of touch must be substituted for the sense of sight.

Then too, because of the limitation which blindness automatically imposes on freedom of physical movement, blind men and women early learn care and precision in their movements and orderliness in their working habits. You will seldom find a sightless worker indulging in waste motion or misplacing his tools or working equipment. This means time saved, greater economy of movement and effort, and a higher rate of production.

Again, the average blind person actually possesses a greater store of physical energy to put into his work. Dammed in other directions, this energy is channeled directly and fully into his job and results in a steady, consistent, and efficient day-after-day performance.

One of the main objections to the employment of blind people in the past has been that they might have accidents. Actually the record shows that they are the safest workers in the world. So far not one case of compensable accident involving a blind worker has been reported from any of the many plants and factories in which they are employed! The reason is that they exercise greater care in their movements, evidence a quicker recoil from obstacles, and possess a keener sense of potential danger than do people with sight.

Employers in all fields have long agreed that one of the greatest factors in determining the desirability or undesirability of an employee is his attitude toward his job. Is his only interest in his weekly pay check, or does he regard work as a privilege, and his own particular job as an opportunity to perform a useful service?

If it is ever safe to generalize, then certainly it is safe to say that this latter is the attitude of *all* blind workers. The explanation is simple. Ask any blind person to name the greatest hardship which his handicap imposes, and he will reply without hesitation: "Idleness, inactivity, the inability to obtain employment." To him, this, and not the lack of sight in itself, is the black curse of blindness. A job is to him more than a means of livelihood: it is a godsend.

Make no mistake on this count. Give a blind man a job and you can know that he will give that job the best that is in him. And his presence, far from depressing the workers about him, will actually strengthen their morale. The evidence is that there is something about the mere presence among them of a person working industriously, painstakingly, and cheerfully despite a severe handicap, which shames normal men and women out of petty grumbling and complaining, makes them more conscious of their own blessings, and inspires them to greater effort. So marked has been this effect that many employers have expressed the opinion that, if for no other reason than this, every department where a suitable job can possibly be found should employ at least one blind worker.

If there is a single completely encouraging result of our grave manpower shortage, it is the way in which it has brought to fruition the long labors of State commissions and other workers for the blind, who have been training these people, trying to persuade factory and office heads to employ them, and keeping a supervisory eye on them once they were employed. This has always been an uphill job, for employers were very skeptical. Now, at last, the opportunities are opening up and the blind are coming into their own.

TECHNICAL DISCUSSION

1. Does the author state her theme in any place other than the title?
2. What is the chief function of the second paragraph?
3. What types of data does the author use to support the theme?
4. Do the remarks in the second section of the essay support the theme? Explain your answer by pointing out appropriate sentences or paragraphs.
5. Point out transitional phrases.
6. Does the last paragraph of the essay repeat anything found in the first paragraph?

TOPICS FOR PAPERS

1. Select one of the following topics and write an informative essay: (a) Rehabilitation of wounded soldiers; (b) Braille; (c) Glasses that slip on the eyeball; (d) The story of spectacles; (e) Seeing-eye dogs: their training; their uses; (f) Problems of adjustment that the blind must solve.
2. Write a paper on Helen Keller or on some other handicapped person who interests you. Make several judgments about the person and his contribution to society. Support each judgment fully.

Who Owns Your Letters?

MELVILLE CANE

No matter how unsentimental we may think we are, or how interested in worldly good, almost every one of us treasures and preserves through the years a few precious articles with a personal meaning, a near-silver medal won at school, a tin-type of one's first sweetheart, a keepsake from a parent. And, most highly prized of all, letters.

Perhaps some of these letters are from persons of importance or

"Who Owns Your Letters?" From *The Saturday Review of Literature*, December 25, 1943. Reprinted by permission of *The Saturday Review of Literature*.

prominence, possibly dating the pre-fame of the senders. Let us suppose you have decided, for one reason or another, to dispose of these letters. The big question, however, is: What have you got that's salable?

Take the case of Reginald Roe, who with ardor exceeding prudence, takes pen in hand and sets down in language warm and/or daffy his devotion to Pansy Doe. It's the popular belief that Pansy, if it suits her mood, can sell Reginald's letters to a yellow journal and cash in on their publication. In fact the threat of exposing a former suitor's emotional imbecilities is an old, common, and lucrative source of blackmail.

But if Reggie is well advised, he'll call the bluff, hire a lawyer, and get an injunction against the threatened circulation of his love letters.

Not only in the sordid case of Reggie versus Pansy, but in most instances of correspondence, the courts have held for over two hundred years that ownership of letters consists of two separate rights, the right to the physical manuscript and the right of publication. The former belongs to the recipient or addressee, the latter is reserved to the writer.

The same rules apply, regardless of whether the communication be weighty or trivial, artistic or news of the family, confidential or repeatable. The many attempts to modify the basic rules by making distinctions along the foregoing lines have been rejected by judges.

Strange as it may seem, even publishers and their attorneys have been known to suffer through ignorance of the well-established legal doctrine. A striking instance of such unawareness is reported by Mr. George H. Doran in his colorful memoirs, published a few years ago under the title, "Chronicles of Barabbas." With candor unusual in a person guilty of a howler the publisher tells the story on himself. It concerns his purchase of an intimate series of letters written by Woodrow Wilson to a friend, Mrs. Peck.

I was convinced, Mr. Doran reports in his "Chronicles of Barabbas," of the authenticity and real quality of these letters and was eager to publish them, just as I would eagerly publish the letters of any great man. I submitted the manuscript to my legal counsel and was told that I was quite within legal rights in concluding a contract and proceeding with publication. The contract was drawn. The sum involved was quite a substantial amount and I agreed to pay $10,000 on the signing of the agreement. We were to have custody of the original letters for a period of two years following the publication of the book. Everything seemed to be in order, the money was paid, and we had in our possession the working manuscript and the letters themselves.

Then fell the blow. One morning very early my attorney called on the telephone at my home and said he must see me at the earliest possible moment. We met at his office at nine that morning. There he showed me a citation from an old English law dating back to the seventeen-hundreds but which by usage and practice had become, as so many other laws had become, an integral part of American jurisprudence. Briefly, the citation was to the effect that, while the actual piece of paper containing a message was the property of the recipient, the thought contained in the message remained for ever the property of its writer or his heirs. Consequently we had no moral right to print these letters without the consent of their writer and obviously such consent was impossible. Here was a serious predicament, for we were under contract to publish. However, after much negotiation the contract was cancelled by our forfeiting the $10,000 paid on account of the contract. A sad and expensive lesson in law, for it did appear most strange to me that the possessor of letters had no property rights in their contents. Probably I should have known this years before, but the question had never arisen in my experience and my legal counsel, an eminent attorney, had no greater knowledge than I.

Curious, indeed, that this was the first time the question had arisen, since, on a smaller scale, any submitted manuscript which includes even a single letter should be notice of possible trouble to a publisher, unless he first receives leave to print from the writer of the letter.

Perhaps the earliest case of this sort involved Alexander Pope, the poet, who sued to prevent one Curl, a bookseller, from circulating a volume containing some of his letters. It was argued, in the year 1741, in the English Court of Chancery. Curl contended that when a man writes a letter it is in the nature of a gift to the receiver. But Hardwicke, the Lord Chancellor, disagreed, laying down the groundwork for the law as it exists to this day not only in England but in the United States.

"I am of the opinion," he announced, "that it is only a special property in the receiver, possibly the property of the paper may belong to him; but this does not give a license to any person whatsoever to publish them to the world, for at most the receiver has only a joint property with the writer."

Curl further urged that since the letters were "on familiar subjects and inquiries after the health of friends," they could not properly be called a learned work.

This contention stirred Hardwicke to a piece of literary criticism: "It is certain that no works have done more service to mankind than those which have appeared on familiar subjects, and which perhaps were never intended to be published; and it is this that makes them so valuable; for I must confess, for my own part, that letters which are very elaborately written, and originally intended for the press, are generally the most insignificant and very little worth any person's reading."

A generation later came the celebrated case of Sir Charles Thompson, executor of Lord Chesterfield, against the widow of Chesterfield's son. It dealt with the famous correspondence from father to son, especially on the subjects of education and proper personal behavior. In preventing their use the court extended the ruling of Lord Hardwicke by holding that publishing rights belonged not only to the original writer, but on his death, to his estate.

In 1804 the children of the poet Burns were equally successful.

A new theory on which to escape the decisions was presented to the English Chancery Court in 1818. A Mrs. Gee had written many letters of affection to William Pritchard, the bastard son of her late husband. It seems that later Mrs. Gee, finding that Pritchard had been unworthy of her sentiments, publicly repudiated him—and them. Pritchard then set out to publish these early letters, claiming the right and need to vindicate his reputation. But the court held against him and in favor of Mrs. Gee.

The same plea, but with a different twist, and with the same result, was advanced in 1884 in another noteworthy litigation. Bulwer-Lytton, the elder, during a marriage terminating in divorce back in 1836, had corresponded happily with his then wife. After his death, his son wrote his biography, in the course of which he dealt with the marriage. A Miss Devey, as executrix of Lady Lytton's estate, claiming that the biography ascribed to her friend harsh and unfeminine conduct, attempted to publish the early letters from husband to wife in order to correct the son's picture. While the court conceived of a situation where the need of making such defense might let down the bars, it declared there was no reason for the exception in the case presented. So the younger Lytton prevailed in keeping his father's letters from the public eye.

Another literary case centered around the painter Whistler, whose estate brought an equity suit against Joseph and Elizabeth Robins Pennell. Although creating great public furor, it ended in something of an anti-climax. The Pennells had been authorized by Whistler, it appeared, to write his life. In the course of their labors they naturally had had access to Whistler's correspondence with various persons. It was this correspondence that Whistler's executor wished to keep out of the biography. The Pennells disclaimed any intention of printing it. They insisted, however, and the court was inclined to agree, that they had the right to consider the material and to make fair use of it, incidental to the portrayal of their subject.

The courts of this country have been fairly consistent in following the English doctrine of divided ownership. The earliest American case seems to have been decided by a Louisiana Court in 1811, where a single unimportant letter was involved. The great Justice Story, in the historic case of Folsom against Marsh, adhered to the English precedents. That case dealt with a mass of letters by George Washington which had appeared in Jared Sparks's "Life," and which a rival publication sought to utilize. It was Story who termed the use of letters by the recipient:

> One of the most odious breaches of private confidence, of social duty, and of honorable feelings which can well be imagined. It strikes at the root of that free interchange of advice, opinions, and sentiments, which seems essential to the well-being of society, and may involve whole families in great distress from the public display of facts and circumstances which were reposed in the bosom of others, in the fullest and most affecting confidence that they should forever remain inviolable secrets.

Few cases of prominence have appeared in the courts of this country. In fact, it was not until 1912 that the question arose in Massachusetts.

The case, which was brought by the executors of the estate of Mary Baker G. Eddy, caused Chief Justice Rugg to hand down an opinion covering the history of the doctrine from the earliest days, restating it, and reconciling possible conflicts in exceptional decisions. The opinion of Justice Rugg is comprehensive and probably represents more completely than any other the present state of American law on the subject. The suit was for an injunction against the use of a number of letters, written by Mrs. Eddy to a female cousin just after the first publication of "Science and Health" in 1875. The defendants, a firm of auctioneers, were advertising these letters and other manuscripts in their catalogue, in which some of the letters had already appeared. They claimed that the letters, dealing merely with business and family affairs, were free for anyone to publish, since they had no literary quality. The court, however, unanimously granted the injunction, at the same time adverting to the nature of the rights involved and the reasons for the historic judicial view. In protecting the privacy of the writer, the court quoted Lord Campbell, who had said in a similar case:

> That is a recognition of property in the writer, although he has parted with the manuscript; since he wrote to enable his correspondent to know his sentiments, not to give them to the world.

The Massachusetts court further approved of the statements by a New York court and by Justice Story that it mattered not whether the letters were literary compositions, familiar letters, or those dealing with business; that it wasn't for the court to assume the role of literary critic and pass on the worth of a letter as a piece of art.

Justice Rugg continued:

> The same conclusion is reached on principle and apart from authority. It is generally recognized that one has a right to the fruits of his labor. This is equally true, whether the work be muscular or mental or both combined. . . . The labor of composing letters for private and familiar correspondence may be trifling, or it may be severe, but it is none the less the result of an expenditure of thought and time. The market-value of such an effort may be measured by the opinions of others, but the fact of property is not created thereby. A canvas upon which an obscure or

unskilful painter has toiled does not cease to be property because by conventional standards it is valueless as a work of art. Few products of the intellectual reveal individual characteristics more surely than familiar correspondence, entries in diaries, or other unambitious writings.

The conclusions thus reached are not based primarily on copyright statutes but on common-law rights of literary property. The net result of the various decisions may be summarized as follows:

The recipient of a letter owns the material paper; this he may sell, as any other article, or he may destroy it or keep it. The right of publication, however, remains in the sender and on his death passes to his estate or heirs. To the foregoing rules there are a few minor exceptions which need not concern us here. It is enough for us to understand in general the curious two-fold aspect of epistolary ownership.

TECHNICAL DISCUSSION

1. Why does the author begin with a personal note?
2. Why does the author use the invented case of Reginald Roe?
3. What is the value of the excerpt from Doran's book?
4. Point out the first place where the author makes a formal answer to the question posed by the title. Point out the last place.
5. What types of data does the author use?
6. Does the author cite the complete source of his data—that is, could you use his citations to find the books he used?

TOPICS FOR PAPERS

1. The legal background of compulsory education.
2. What is property?
3. What is literature?
4. A criticism of Jared Sparks as a biographer.
5. A review of *Chronicles of Barabbas,* by George H. Doran.

The Cat: Vicious Predator or *Harmless Pet?*

ALLEN PARSONS

Last winter at the annual dinner of a large sportsman's club the toastmaster read a report of the number of predators that club members had shot or trapped during the year. It made an impressive showing; so many foxes, so many owls, a considerable number of hawks, weasels—even a shrike or two. There was considerable applause, but the man who sat next to me, a widely known sportsman and conservationist, did not join in. Instead he snorted and turned to me.

"Not a word about house cats," he commented. "There's no telling how many beneficial hawks and owls were killed by these well-meaning but uninformed men. Foxes, coyotes, hawks, owls, and all the rest are blamed for killing off our game birds and song birds. But the house cat does more harm than any or all of them!"

I probably looked surprised.

"Don't tell me *you* don't know that is true? You get around. Don't you know what's going on?"

"Frankly I haven't given the matter much thought," I parried. "But if it's so, why don't these hunters here come right out in meeting and say so? Why don't they do something beside killing hawks and owls?"

"Half of these men here are farmers. If anybody started a campaign against cats, you'd see some of them walk out, never to return. They feel that cats are a necessity on the farm to keep down rats and mice. The other half are men who value the privilege of hunting on farms. They will do nothing to forfeit that privilege. Besides, like you, they probably 'haven't given it thought.'"

Obviously, if what this man said were true, the facts should be brought out and laid before the sportsmen of the country. But where could such facts be obtained? While the standing of the sportsman was such as to warrant respect for his opinion, it was still only opinion —and that may be based on incomplete observation or on unconscious prejudice.

So I set out as a reporter to get facts, and I went to men in key

"The Cat: Vicious Predator *or* Harmless Pet?" From *Outdoor Life,* November, 1941. Reprinted by permission of *Outdoor Life.*

positions throughout the country—heads of state conservation commissions, ornithologists, naturalists, and other scientists. Of each I asked this question:

"What is the truth about the house cat? Is it an economically useful pet, or is it a pernicious predator among song birds, game birds, and small game?"

Almost instantly I discovered that I'd opened up a subject that is as explosive as a shipful of T.N.T. If the common cat numbers its enemies by the millions it also can count on other millions of stanch friends. Farmers believe that cats are absolutely necessary to keep down rats and mice, and usually keep two or three—even more. Many women love cats as pets and, like the farmers, can believe no evil of them. Various attempts have been made to reduce the number of surplus and useless cats by some form of licensing, such as is required of dogs. Then there is inevitably an uproar, and the question may assume some minor political importance.

This hot, blazing difference of opinion is well illustrated by the reception given to a single book. That study—still the foremost on the cat as a predator—was "The Domestic Cat, Bird Killer, Mouser, and Destroyer of Wildlife," by E. H. Forbush, noted ornithologist. Originally the study was backed by T. Gilbert Pearson, then president of the National Audubon Society, who wrote a bulletin about it. The study, of course, was intended as a scientific one, its ultimate aim being to aid in the protection of bird life. But even at that there was such a storm of protest, accompanied by resignations from the society, about "the cruel crusade against cats," that it was found advisable to have Forbush's work published under state auspices, although the society paid the entire cost of publication, as well as the postage bill for distributing it.

That was twenty-five years ago, and Forbush estimated then that about 700,000 birds were being killed annually in Massachusetts by farm cats. In a later letter to the state Division of Fisheries and Game, he stated that stray cats in the state killed approximately two million birds a year—among them quail, ruffed grouse, pheasants, woodcock, and many other game birds!

Max Hart, for many years Executive Secretary of the Virginia Commission of Game and Inland Fisheries, on three separate occasions has tried to have his State Assembly pass a bill making the abandonment of any living house cat or kitten a misdemeanor, and providing that any such cat, running at large anywhere in the state outside of the limits of an incorporated town or city, shall be deemed a public nuisance. Hart's bills were just laughed down. The same has been true of similar control bills in Oregon, Utah, and Missouri.

Hart, a close observer of wildlife, told me that on his many hunting trips he has seen more cat tracks than the tracks of any other animal—even far away from any human habitation. Just before I consulted him, while he was trout fishing in the Shenandoah National Park, he saw a house cat as wild as any bobcat. Hart says that the common habit of abandoning unwanted cats along highways and in the woods is a curse to wildlife. He is a strong advocate of a licensing law.

Guy D. Josserand, Director of the Forestry, Fish, and Game Commission of Kansas, last winter attempted to reduce the number of vagrant cats and predatory crows in his state by initiating a contest to encourage sportsmen to kill them. The newspapers of the state played up the story. The contest was withdrawn under heavy fire. Yet Josserand and his men estimate that there are ten surplus house cats to every section of land in the state, with a total vagrant cat population of somewhere between 750,000 and 1,000,000. Touch a Kansas cat, wild or semiwild, and the fur flies, but it's not cat fur.

Significantly, not one scientist of those consulted defends the cat. Frank M. Chapman, ornithological authority and author, Curator of Ornithology, the American Museum of Natural History, spoke of the large proportion of cats that are essentially wild, and said that it is obvious that they must destroy a great number of birds, "a form of life which is particularly attractive to them." He also called the cat an introduced enemy of birds and not a native one, and stated that there is no provision in the economy of bird life for loss due to cats. Dr. C. E. Cummings, Director of the Buffalo, N. Y., Museum of Science, told me there is no possible doubt that the predatory cat is a definite menace to bird life; and that it is pretty well established that the only way to cure them of this depredation is "to cut off their tails right behind the ears." Cornelius Denslow, Science Curator, Brooklyn Children's Museum, Institute of Arts and Sciences, Brooklyn, N. Y., advocates reduction of the number of cats by licensing, saying it would make a great difference in our song and game-bird population. He regards the house cat as one of the worst enemies of our song birds, and said: "It is not necessarily lack of food which causes cats to hunt birds, but a deep-seated instinct which cannot be trained out of them. If people would keep their cats confined to the house during the nesting season, it would undoubtedly help a great deal."

Clifford C. Gregg, Director, Field Museum of Natural History, Chicago, quoted the Curator of Birds of that museum to the effect that a large majority of cats on farms and in suburban areas are allowed to roam at will. From this, and the practice of abandoning unwanted kittens, the "wild" house cat develops.

"These animals," he pointed out, "many of which are as wild as any true wild animal, take a large toll of nesting birds. Any hunter, finding a house cat in the woods or fields, far from any habitation, should dispatch it as quickly and as painlessly as possible."

Lee S. Crandall, Curator of Birds, N. Y. Zoölogical Society, believes that from the point of view of total birds killed by predators, the proportion chargeable to cats would be large.

T. Gilbert Pearson, Chairman of the Pan American section, International Committee for Bird Preservation, and president emeritus, National Audubon Society, told me that domestic cats are great destroyers of bird life, and that many persons do not realize the destruction inflicted upon the bird population because the killing is done largely during the hours of darkness and in the early morning. He advocates control over the cat population, and "arrangements for humanely destroying vagrant and unwanted cats, the numbers of which are exceedingly great."

Lieut. Col. Walter B. Jones, Director of the Alabama Museum of Natural History, gave it as his opinion that any cat which leaves its owner's home should be destroyed, for "it most certainly is looking for something and that something is apt to be a song or game bird. If we are to perpetuate bird life—and we must—the house cat must be kept indoors or close to the house. Few of us realize that our occupation of the land has introduced many circumstances quite detrimental to natural biological combinations. The house cat stands high on the list. It has no fear of man, yet all the cunning of its wild brethren."

A few years ago Col. Jones was quail hunting with a friend on a fine preserve in Barbour County, Alabama. The dogs came to a point in a clover patch. A single quail flushed. The gunners held their fire, waiting for the rest of the covey. Theirs was the first hunt of the season, and all the coveys had been large ones. No more birds came out, but they did flush a large house cat, stalking the last bird in the covey. The nearest house was at least a mile away. They killed the cat, and were convinced that this cat had destroyed the whole covey with the exception of that one bird. Similar observations were reported by others interviewed.

Of the forty-eight directors of state conservation commissions, twenty-eight unqualifiedly damned the cat as a pest of the worst type; seven conceded its destructiveness but blamed largely cats which are "escapes," and live in a state of nature; four were unwilling to give an opinion, and nine were not interviewed. Obviously, in order to get all the facts, a nationwide study, involving hundreds of investigators and examination of millions of cat stomachs, would have to be made. No such study has been or perhaps could be conducted. But here is informed opinion, based upon the observations of hundreds of wardens and conservation agents, and covering every section of the United States. As in the case of the scientists it is significant that not one of these state officials came out in defense of the cat. The best that was said of the cat was that it has some value *around farm buildings*.

What Harold N. Gibbs, Administrator, Dept. of Fish and Game, Rhode Island, told me was typical of many statements which, because of space limitations, cannot be quoted here. He said: "The house cat, as a predator, should be brought to the attention of everyone interested in conservation—the farmer, the sportsman, and the nature lover. We hear enough of the depredations of foxes, hawks, and owls, and crows, but mention of cats as destroyers of small game and song birds seems to be taboo. For the last two years all pheasants and quail released in Rhode Island have been banded, and the sex, date, and locality where liberated were carefully recorded. Each year over 500 quail have been stocked in pairs, expensive birds, all locally raised from certified stock. The areas where they were released were carefully chosen. The results have been rather discouraging and, in my opinion, the common house cat is responsible.

"For the first week or so quail are easy prey to cats. Our records show this to be a fact. Bands are returned to us with the explanation that they were taken from quail 'brought home by kitty'! How many birds are killed and left in the field will never be known and the destruction of young rabbits must be appalling. The destruction of young song birds is common knowledge. I believe there is a definite place for foxes, hawks, and owls—I don't go so far as to include crows—and I am equally convinced that there is absolutely no place for cats; the only good cat is a dead one."

F. B. Wire, Supervisor, Oregon State Game Commission, told me that he personally knew of one case where a cat followed a hen pheasant with a brood of young birds, and killed them, one at a time, until seven had been destroyed. The seven birds were found by back tracking the cat from its last kill. This cat was not killing to eat, but from love of the chase. Wire also spoke of large cats killing full-grown pheasants. In one instance he could have prevented the killing, but thought, since the pheasant was a large cock, that it could take care of itself. The pheasant, too, was prepared to give battle. But the cat knew its job, made a leap, bit the pheasant in the neck, and killed it. Wire pointed out the difficulty of instituting control over the cat because of ranchers who keep cats as rodent catchers, and so oppose any definite measures of restriction.

The manager of a pheasant refuge in Ohio told George A. Montgomery, associate editor of "Capper's Farmer," that he was losing a large number of young pheasants to predators. He was uncertain as to what animal was doing the damage. He obtained a number of steel traps and set them at all holes that might be used by foxes, raccoons, skunks, weasels, and other wild predators. He caught only cats, the first night getting five. The position of the foot in the trap showed that four cats had been caught coming out of the hole, and one while going in. One hollow tree where he had expected to catch a raccoon yielded four or five cats. Montgomery, who is much interested in conservation, told me about farmers and ranchers near Matador, Tex., who have organized a cooperative association to increase the amount of wild game on their farms. They found that the cat was one of the worst enemies of quail.

They set aside a day for killing stray cats, advertised that a drive was to be made on that day, and asked all persons who had cats which they prized to pen them up for the day. During the day more than twenty cats were killed on the ranch of Elbert Reeves, secretary of the association, alone. A mother cat and litter of kittens were found in a raven's nest in a mesquite tree, six miles from the nearest habitation. The mother cat was as wild as any wildcat.

J. W. Cluett, Director, Department of Game and Fish of South Dakota, reported an instance where a group of sportsmen in that state put on a campaign against stray cats along a twelve-mile stretch of one of their highways. In the game-bird nesting season fifty cats were killed in that one stretch, and the increase of pheasants that followed was very noticeable. Cluett believes that there should be a widespread educational campaign against the stray cat, starting with farmers, because it is from farms that the large majority of wild and semiwild house cats originally come.

Gardiner Bump, Superintendent of Game, New York, quoted to me the report of one state-game-farm foreman, who spoke of cats as predators that have to be battled with the year around. In the spring they prey upon the chickens, in summer upon the young pheasants, and in winter upon the breeding pheasants. The foreman estimated the farm's summer loss of young pheasants as at least 250 birds. Another foreman reported losing in December four or five birds. Snow was on the ground and he tracked the cat, which was dragging a pheasant, to a fence which it had climbed. The trail then continued down a road for a quarter of a mile, disappearing under an old barn. There the foreman found the bird, a mature hen pheasant, intact. Traps were placed by the dead bird and the cat caught. Weighing 10½ pounds, it had carried a 2½-pound pheasant over a fence eight feet high. This same foreman reported that on two nights there had been kills of birds in breeding pens. The dead birds were lying on the hover, and it appeared that cats, working through the wire, had killed and partially eaten them, which was proved later, when the night watchman shot a cat on the outside of the pen, with paws through the wire, holding and eating a pheasant. Four adult birds had been killed in that manner.

Bump also spoke of the recent experience of Clarence Eddy, of Messenger Bay, on Oneida Lake, N. Y. Driving home at night along a dirt road the lights of his car showed a fawn being closely pursued by another animal resembling a bobcat. The car struck this latter animal and killed it. Examination by the district wildlife manager showed that the creature was a wild house cat, with part of its tail missing. The cat was judged to have been wild for years and, though lean, weighed 10½ pounds.

Elliott S. Barker, State Game Warden of New Mexico, told about a trapper employed by the game department to trap predators in an area where attempts were being made to reintroduce the masked quail. Visiting this trapper, Barker noticed that he had a very large cat at his place, and suggested to him that this cat might be wandering out into the game area and doing damage. The employee assured him that the cat never got away from the house. But later the trapper was surprised to find this same cat in one of his traps, nearly two miles away!

E. Lee LeCompte, State Game Warden of Maryland, is convinced that the cat is one of the worst enemies of wildlife, hunting 365 days and nights throughout the year, stealing up on game unheard, and with keen instinct for killing. He personally has seen cats carrying half-grown rabbits which they have killed, climbing trees and killing mother birds and their young in the nest. It was because of many such observations by him and his men that the Maryland game code authorizes game wardens and other state officers to kill hunting cats, and protects them from any action for damages as the result of such killing.

Nils H. Nilsson, a biologist now with the Texas Game, Fish, and Oyster Commission, made a study of the hunting house cat in Oregon. He tells me that as a result of this study he is convinced that the cat's hunting ability and instinct are as highly developed today as when the animal was first domesticated ages ago. "'Within a few minutes' time a tame cat may be both a highly prized pet and a vicious predator of small mammals and birds," he said. "The cat, urban or rural, is—through no fault of its own—actually a Dr. Jekyll and Mr. Hyde."

W. F. Dearman, Director, Mississippi Game and Fish Commission, summed up the opinion of most men holding similar office when he told me: "I would say that except for the person who turns cats loose in the woods to shift for themselves, the house cat can easily be classed as Enemy No. 1."

Thus the opinions of men who have spent years in the work of conservation. While wide factual surveys of the cat problem are not, as I've said, easy to make, the personal observations of men in the field—thousands of them—are accurately reflected in the considered judgment of their superiors. Of course, it must be conceded that conservationists are primarily interested in the preservation of wildlife, and that, ipso facto, any enemy of wildlife is their enemy too. Conversely, lovers of cats will consider any foe of the cat as their foe, and thus we have two great groups (each of unimpeachable integrity) at daggers' points.

In any event, summing up the opinions of the conservationists, this is what we find:

The house cat does a vast amount of damage to useful bird life as well as small game. That depredation is particularly great in nesting months, but it continues throughout the year. Thoughtless and inhumane people swell the tide of slaughter by releasing in the woods or along roads cats they no longer want. Less culpable are the cat owners who permit their pets to wander in nesting season—often putting them out each night to continue their reign of terror. Farmers are likely to harbor more mousers than they need, and even when such cats are well fed, they are likely to become predators.

Conservationists further maintain that the public is apathetic to the cat killer simply because most people seldom see a stalking cat, and perhaps never come upon the remains of a slaughtered bird or rabbit. But field men of the commissions *do* see these things. Thus, they and their superiors, as well as most naturalists in general, come inevitably to one conclusion: That the roaming cat is a wholly destructive nuisance.

As for the feline's vaunted ability with rats, it is interesting to note Forbush's claim that this useful trait appears only in a minority, say, one third—with perhaps one fifth really efficient. With mice, a greater efficiency exists, but even at that, Forbush wrote, one fifth of the country cats, selected for ability, could kill just as many rats and mice as *all* cats now do.

Between the two extremes of "Kill all cats!" and "Don't touch a single one!" what measures are being considered to control this great menace to our valuable wildlife?

Licensing, it is generally felt by conservationists, would be reasonably effective in getting rid of the strays. And some states—Louisiana, Pennsylvania, California, New York, New Jersey, and Maryland—have laws to provide cat control. The National Association of Audubon Societies has urged for years the enactment of state laws and municipal ordinances to reduce surplus cat population. As a matter of fact, some cities and towns have passed such laws, among them Harrison, Larchmont, and Roslyn Harbor, N. Y., Millburn, Montclair, and Pompton Lakes, N. J.; Seattle, Wash.; Grand Rapids, Mich.; Massillon, Ohio; and Maywood, Ill. But that has settled little, as far as conservationists are concerned—in most, if not all, of these places the laws are not observed.

At first blush, then, it would seem that conservationists and cat lovers are as far apart as the poles. But a few thoughtful sportsmen aren't convinced of that. They feel that if they could get together with farmers and cat lovers, and discuss the matter sanely and without passion, perhaps much could be done to find a common, sensible viewpoint, and an ultimate solution.

Maybe you could in your town.

TECHNICAL DISCUSSION

1. What is the author's theme? Where does he state it?
2. What kinds of data does the author use? Point out good examples of the kinds.
3. How does the author give the sources of his data? Point out places in the text where the sources are shown. Compare his method of revealing sources with the footnote method. Is one method more effective than the other?
4. Point out several transitional phrases or sentences and show what is being linked, or bridged.
5. Show how the author keeps the reader aware of the sources of quoted material by mentioning the speaker or author of the material.
6. Find the summary used by the author at the end of his essay.

TOPICS FOR PAPERS

1. My cat is innocent (guilty)! Illustrate fully.
2. Sportsmen kill pheasants, too.
3. I talk with a farmer and a housewife about cats.
4. I spend a day in the fields.
5. I investigate game conservation in my community.

Pro and Con—Abolish Intercollegiate Football?

In the following debate Mr. Pro and Mr. Con thresh out this issue with no holds barred. All attitudes treated are derived from acknowledged experts and all facts have been gathered by a skilled investigator.

So, when the smoke has cleared away, what do you think?

YES, SAYS MR. PRO:

"American football is a splendid game. That is why some of us would like to see the game given back to the boys before the over-enthusiastic public squeezes it to death. Here is evidence of the impending suffocation:

"Thanksgiving Day used to end the season. Now, the big intersectional post-season games are played on New Year's Day. Spring practice begins in another four months. Many college players spend their summers at manual labor conditioning for the September opening of the season. That adds up to seven or eight months a year. College football isn't a game any longer—it's a job.

"The University of Texas recently hired a first-flight football coach on a 10-year contract at $15,000 a year. How many college presidents receive as much?

"Radio advertisers paid college athletic associations some $400,000 this season for exclusive rights to broadcast their football games.

"The ultimate comment on football's present absurdities was made when Elbert Hubbard wrote that 'Football bears the same relation to education that bull-fighting does to agriculture.'

"Francis Wallace, realistic and intelligent friend of the game, summarizes the situation:

" 'The colleges enter the open market and bid against one another for the year's crop of athletes. They pay these boys and masquerade the payments. They present these athletes in great outdoor stadia and charge all that the traffic will bear. Football, as now conducted by most of our great universities, is, at best, semi-professional—as much show-business as Broadway.'

"Colleges do not need football profits to pay for the rest of their athletic programs. Stevens Institute of Technology abolished intercollegiate football in 1924. Since then it has maintained intercollegiate competition in full schedules of all other standard sports and provided an intramural program which takes in all undergraduates. Exclusive of maintenance on buildings and grounds, the annual cost to the college is around $10 per undergraduate.

"On that basis, the salaries of a high-powered football coaching staff (say $30,000) plus graduate manager and press agent (say $10,000) would pay for such a program for a male student body of 4,000.

"Massachusetts Institute of Technology, rid of intercollegiate football these 30 years, finances an extensive athletic program at much the same figure as Stevens from a student tax ($5.80 a year) and general college funds. This includes crew, the most expensive of college sports. Neither alumni nor students ever agitate for the return of intercollegiate football.

"Football victories are not necessary for keeping alumni and public in a financially generous frame of mind. An expert survey of representative colleges between 1921 and 1930 showed that those conspicuous for football success had increased their asset values by 117 per cent, their endowments by 125 per cent. Those going light on football did just a trifle better: assets were up 125 per cent, endowments 126 per cent.

"The publicity values of football have little to do with stimulating enrollment. The curve of increasing enrollment of male undergraduates at Columbia forged steadily upward in both the period when football was abolished (1905-15) and since it has been restored. The curve dropped after the depression, in spite of the college's developing football success.

"The enrollment of Reed College, without intercollegiate football, has grown steadily since the war. Its proportion of male students has increased and the student body compares favorably in height and weight with Pacific Coast students in general.

"Subsidizing of football players handicaps intelligent boys lacking conspicuous athletic ability, and loads colleges with a dead weight of the less intelligent. When athletes of Pennsylvania colleges, large and small, were given tests measuring intelligence and information, football players rated lowest. Football-playing Phi Beta Kappas are always rare enough to get publicity. The rank and file of paid football letter men are crammed and bullied into passing grades, or passed by professors who know better than to hold them to usual standards.

"Most of the scholarships that disguise subsidizing were really intended to help intelligent boys without money to get an education useful to society. A fast-running but slow-thinking halfback may be keeping out of college a bright lad who isn't so good at snagging passes.

"Many college jobs, usually the easiest ones, are reserved for athletes. The non-athletic poor boy gets what is left. Athletes are often paid far more than non-athletes for certain jobs.

"Francis Wallace wrote that he stopped scouting talent for big-time football colleges because too many of the football boys he had wangled into college graduated only to be too good for hard work and not quite good enough for the easy jobs they had expected.

"The days when a star end could count on a soft berth in a broker's office died with 1929. Professional football will pay a player only some $1,200 a season for the few years he lasts—provided he measures up to professional standards, which are terrific. Radio stations were mobbed this season by bewildered gridiron heroes hoping for soft work as football announcers. Most of them would have been better off if they'd never had the financial chance to die for alma mater.

"Guesses on how much went into football pools in 1937 range between $50,000,000 and $75,000,000. Nobody knows exactly. But everybody knows that the whole huge total, along with other large sums bet on individual games, is handled by the lowest type of racketeers.

"A boy who is living a lie learns a lot about cutting corners. Now put these facts together: big money staked every week—chiseling gangsters—players made cynical by a dishonest system. Those are the makings of what might be the nastiest athletic scandal since the Black Sox.

"Many admirers of football deny heatedly that the college game could be fixed. According to highly responsible authority, it is already being fixed right along in at least one football-crazy section of the country. When some such scandal does break wide open, the public will have finished its job of wrecking.

"The colleges will do much better to beat fate to the draw by performing the indicated surgery while there is yet time. All the college color in the country could hardly make up for the disillusioning spectacle of alma mater's young heroes pulling the kind of fast ones that class them with crooked jockeys.

"Football would still survive as a lusty game played, as at Emory University, for fun among intramural teams.

"Or, for the athletic connoisseur, it would survive in the professional leagues which are drawing more money and attention every season.

"But it would no longer pervert the atmosphere of higher education, warp the athletic programs of colleges and set a flagrant example of chicanery for American youth."

No, says Mr. Con:

"This agitation is old stuff. Way back in the day of bone-crushing mass plays, several important colleges bowed to public opinion and dropped football. Most of them have since restored it, as the game, opened and speeded up, became far less brutal.

"The public has responded to the change by filling huge stadia at high prices. The same public is discovering—and not minding much—the fact that one way or another colleges subsidize many of their players. It is learning to take them cordially for what they are—husky kids, using athletic skill to pay for education—and to honor them for their grit, skill, and perseverance.

"It also knows that, since dumb beef long since went out of football, the modern college player must be as quick on the uptake as he is on the charge.

"There is no way to repeal this popular enthusiasm for the spectacle of game youngsters fighting a wholesome, thrilling, mimic warfare because they enjoy it and because it helps some of them to an education.

"If intercollegiate football were abolished, the public would seek spontaneous color and drama in some other intercollegiate sport—and find it. The net effect would be merely the elimination of the most colorful and characteristic American spectacle.

"Professional croakers charge that 'College football has turned into big business.' So it has. And a darn good thing too for the American college and the American student.

"For receipts from football buy equipment, pay transportation, hire coaches and build facilities for basketball, baseball, track, hockey, swimming, lacrosse, tennis, squash, boxing, wrestling, fencing, rowing, and everything else.

"Every football player who is subsidized is only getting back a fraction of what he contributes in cash and inspiration to the physical good of the whole college community.

"Without football, college athletic associations owing large debts on new stadia would have to default on their bonds, which would outrage the sports-minded alumni who bought those bonds out of devotion to alma mater.

"Conversely, each football victory ties the alumnus closer to alma mater, and makes things far simpler for the college president when he needs funds for new dormitories. Where colleges are dependent on state funds, it works the same way on state legislators.

"College presidents know that live youngsters, recognizing successful football teams as signs of energy and enterprise and of that electric comradeship known as college spirit, are attracted to big-time football colleges.

"Football is the keystone of college sport. Its glories foster a vigorous athletic psychology inspiring every youth, dub or not, to play some game as best he can, building up a healthy habit of strenuous play that will pay him dividends the rest of his life.

"Since football demands a maximum of courage, discipline and perseverance, it is a superlative training for later life. Many a famous college tackle, now a success in his chosen career, testifies that the moral training he got from Coach So-and-So was more valuable to him than all the rest of his college education put together.

"Now that the cuss-and-bully type of coach is passing out of the picture, that factor is still more important. The modern coach is usually intelligent, smart with boys, soft-spoken, shrewd—perfect for leading and training youth.

"The healthiest thing that ever happened to intercollegiate football is the present tendency to admit subsidization and ask, with all the logic on one side: 'Why shouldn't needy boys be paid for their grueling battles in the interests of the whole college?'

"In a few years most colleges will have candidly brought things into the open. Already the members of one large conference have an agreement defining and limiting the amounts and number of athletic scholarships. All over the country various mutual agreements on talent-scouting and maximum rates of pay are gradually building up a code of ethics that will eventually either correct the worst abuses of intercollegiate football or put colleges that refuse to observe the code off the schedules of institutions that play fair in scouting and paying players.

"Stringent financial pressure on college athletic associations that are still paying off on boomtime stadia and other buildings is already lessening as the bonds are retired.

"By applying honest and realistic regulation to the present situation, the game can still be saved for the old grad, the student and the public, with all its pageantry and excitement and its nation-wide fostering of a healthy attitude toward physical courage and hard knocks. To abolish the game on account of its present minor extravagances would be to burn the house down to roast the pig."

TECHNICAL DISCUSSION

1. What is Mr. Pro's theme? What is Mr. Con's theme?
2. Write a brief outline of Mr. Pro's argument with the theme stated at the head and with the supporting reasons—those in italics—stated as reasons.
3. Why does the editor of this essay put all of the remarks in quotation marks?
4. Does the editor use authority apart from his main reasons? Examine the beginning of Mr. Pro's argument. Compare the beginning of Mr. Con's argument.
5. Which side of the argument has the better supporting data? Do you think the editor was biased? Do you think that there is no good material

for the weak side? How does Mr. Pro support his position? How does Mr. Con support his position?

TOPICS FOR PAPERS

1. Interview as many students as possible on the problem of intercollegiate football and write an essay in which you present all opinions, coming in the essay to *your* final conclusion.

2. Write a description of the campus and the stadium before and during a game. Select the day of the "big game" if possible. Come to conclusions about the setting and the event. Support your conclusions with details and anecdotes, comments of friends and visitors, and personal observations of your own. Select a tone for the whole paper and build it up consistently throughout.

Second Pattern

School "Life"

ROBERT S. LYND and HELEN MERRELL LYND

Accompanying the formal training afforded by courses of study is another and informal kind of training, particularly during the high school years. The high school, with its athletics, clubs, sororities and fraternities, dances and parties, and other "extracurricular activities," is a fairly complete social cosmos in itself, and about this city within a city the social life of the intermediate generation centers. Here the social sifting devices of their elders—money, clothes, personal attractiveness, male physical prowess, exclusive clubs, election to positions of leadership—are all for the first time set going with a population as yet largely undifferentiated save as regards their business class and working class parents. This informal training is not a preparation for a vague future that must be taken on trust, as is the case with so much of the academic work; to many of the boys and girls in high school this is "the life," the thing they personally like best about going to school.

The school is taking over more and more of the child's waking life.

Both high school and grades have departed from the attitude of fifty years ago, when the Board directed:

> Pupils shall not be permitted to remain on the school grounds after dismissal. The teachers shall often remind the pupils that the first duty when dismissed is to proceed quietly and directly home to render all needed assistance to their parents.

Today the school is becoming not a place to which children go from their homes for a few hours daily but a place from which they go home to eat and sleep.[1]

An index to this widening of the school's function appears in a comparison of the 1924 high school annual with the first annual, published thirty years before, though even this comparison does not reflect the full extent of the shift since 1890, for innovations had been so numerous in the years just preceding 1894 as to dwarf the extent of the 1890-1924 contrast. Next in importance to the pictures of the senior class and other class data in the earlier book, as measured by the percentage of space occupied, were the pages devoted to the faculty and the courses taught by them, while in the current book athletics shares the position of honor with the class data, and a faculty twelve times as large occupies relatively only half as much space. Interest in small selective group "activities" has increased at the expense of the earlier total class activities.[2] But such a numerical comparison can only faintly suggest the difference in tone of the two books. The description of academic work in the early annual beginning, "Among the various changes that have been effected in grade work are . . ." and ending, "regular monthly teachers' meetings have been inaugurated," seems as foreign to the present high school as does the early class motto "Deo

[1] This condition is deplored by some as indicative of the "break-up of the American home." Others welcome it as freeing the child earlier from the domination of parents and accustoming him to face adjustments upon the success of which adult behavior depends. In any event, the trend appears to be in the direction of an extension of the present tendency increasingly into the grades.

[2] The following shows the percentage of the pages of the annual occupied by the chief items in 1894 and 1924, the earlier year being in each case given first: Class data—39 per cent, 19 per cent; faculty—16 per cent, 8 per cent (brief biographies and pictures in 1894, list of names only and picture of principal in 1924); athletics—5 per cent, 19 per cent; courses of study—6 per cent, 0.0 per cent; class poems—13 per cent, 0.0 per cent; activities other than athletics—5 per cent (one literary society), 13 per cent (thirteen *kinds* of clubs); jokes—5 per cent, 17 per cent; advertisements and miscellaneous—11 per cent, 24 per cent.

Duce"; equally far from 1890 is the present dedication, "To the Bearcats."

This whole spontaneous life of the intermediate generation that clusters about the formal nucleus of school studies becomes focused, articulate, and even rendered important in the eyes of adults through the medium of the school athletic teams—the "Bearcats."[3] The business man may "lay down the law" to his adolescent son or daughter at home and patronize their friends, but in the basket-ball grandstand he is if anything a little less important than these youngsters of his who actually mingle daily with those five boys who wear the colors of "Magic Middletown." There were no high school teams in 1890. To-day, during the height of the basket-ball season when all the cities and towns of the state are fighting for the state championship amidst the delirious backing of the rival citizens, the dominance of this sport is as all-pervasive as football in a college like Dartmouth or Princeton the week of the "big game." At other times dances, dramatics, and other interests may bulk larger, but it is the "Bearcats," particularly the basket-ball team, that dominate the life of the school. Says the prologue to the high school annual:

> The Bearcat spirit has permeated our high school in the last few years and pushed it into the prominence that it now holds. The '24 *Magician* has endeavored to catch, reflect and record this spirit because it has been so evident this year. We hope that after you have glanced at this book for the first time, this spirit will be evident to you.
>
> However, most of all, we hope that in perhaps twenty years, if you become tired of this old world, you will pick up this book and it will restore to you the spirit, pep, and enthusiasm of the old "Bearcat Days" and will inspire in you better things.

Every issue of the high school weekly bears proudly the following "Platform":

> 1. To support live school organizations.
> 2. To recognize worth-while individual student achievements.
> 3. Above all to foster the real "Bearcat" spirit in all of Central High School.

[3] In the elementary grades athletics are still a minor interest, though a school baseball and basket-ball league have been formed of recent years and the pressure of interschool leagues and games is being felt increasingly.

Curricular and social interests tend to conform. Friday nights throughout the season are preëmpted for games; the Mothers' Council, recognizing that every Saturday night had its own social event, urged that other dances be held on Friday nights instead of school nights, but every request was met with the rejoinder that "Friday is basket-ball night."

This activity, so enthusiastically supported, is largely vicarious. The press complains that only about forty boys are prominent enough in athletics to win varsity sweaters. In the case of the girls it is almost 100 per cent vicarious. Girls play some informal basket-ball and there is a Girls' Athletic Club which has a monogram and social meetings. But the interest of the girls in athletics is an interest in the activities of the young males. "My daughter plans to go to the University of ——," said one mother, "because she says, 'Mother, I just *couldn't* go to a college whose athletics I couldn't be proud of!'" The highest honor a senior boy can have is captaincy of the football or basket-ball team, although, as one senior girl explained, "Every member is almost as much admired."

Less spectacular than athletics but bulking even larger in time demands is the network of organizations that serve to break the nearly two thousand individuals composing the high school microcosm into the more intimate groups human beings demand. These groups are mainly of three kinds: the purely social clubs, in the main a stepping down of the social system of adults; a long distance behind in point of prestige, clubs formed around curriculum activities; and, even farther behind, a few groups sponsored by the religious systems of the adults.

In 1894 the high school boasted one club, the "Turemethian Literary Society." According to the early school yearbook:

> The Turemethian Society makes every individual feel that practically he is free to choose between good and evil; that he is not a mere straw thrown upon the water to mark the direction of the current, but that he has within himself the power of a strong swimmer and is capable of striking out for himself, of buffeting the waves, and directing, to a certain extent, his own independent course. Socrates said, "Let him who would move the world move first himself." . . . A paper called The Zetetic is prepared and read at each meeting. . . . Debates have created . . . a friendly rivalry. . .

Another very interesting feature of the Turemethian Society is the lectures delivered to us. . . . All of these lectures help to make our High School one of the first of its kind in the land. The Turemethian Society has slowly progressed in the last year. What the future has in store for it we can not tell, but must say as Mary Riley Smith said, "God's plans, like lilies pure and white, unfold; we must not tear the close-shut leaves apart; time will reveal the calyxes of gold."

Six years later, at the turn of the century, clubs had increased to the point of arousing protest in a press editorial entitled "Barriers to Intellectual Progress." Today clubs and other extracurricular activities are more numerous than ever. Not only is the camel's head inside the tent but his hump as well; the first period of the school day, often running over into the next hour, has recently, at the request of the Mothers' Council, been set aside as a "convocation hour" dedicated to club and committee meetings.

The backbone of the purely social clubs is the series of unofficial branches of former high school fraternities and sororities; Middletown boasts four Alpha chapters. For a number of years a state law has banned these high school organizations, but the interest of active graduate chapters keeps them alive. The high school clubs have harmless names such as the Glendale Club; a boy is given a long, impressive initiation into his club but is not nominally a member of the fraternity of which his club is the undergraduate section until after he graduates, when it is said that by the uttering of a few hitherto unspoken words he comes into his heritage. Under this ambiguous status dances have been given with the club name on the front of the program and the fraternity name on the back. Two girls' clubs and two boys' clubs which everyone wants to make are the leaders. Trailing down from them is a long list of lesser clubs. Informal meetings are usually in homes of members but the formal fall, spring, and Christmas functions are always elaborate hotel affairs.

Extracurricular clubs have canons not dictated by academic standards of the world of teachers and textbooks. Since the adult world upon which the world of this intermediate generation is modeled tends to be dominated primarily by getting a living and "getting on" socially rather than by learning and "the things of the mind," the bifurcation of high school life is not surprising.

"When do you study?" someone asked a clever high school Senior who had just finished recounting her week of club meetings, committee meetings, and dances, ending with three parties the night before. "Oh, in civics I know more or less about politics, so it's easy to talk and I don't have to study that. In English we're reading plays and I can just look at the end of the play and know about that. Typewriting and chemistry I don't have to study outside anyway. Virgil is worst, but I've stuck out Latin four years for the Virgil banquet; I just sit next to —— and get it from her. Mother jumps on me for never studying, but I get A's all the time, so she can't say anything."

The relative status of academic excellence and other qualities is fairly revealed in the candid rejoinder of one of the keenest and most popular girls in the school to the question, "What makes a girl eligible for a leading high school club?"

"The chief thing is if the boys like you and you can get them for the dances," she replied. "Then, if your mother belongs to a graduate chapter that's pretty sure to get you in. Good looks and clothes don't necessarily get you in, and being good in your studies doesn't necesarily keep you out unless you're a 'grind.' Same way with the boys—the big thing there is being on the basket-ball or football team. A fellow who's just a good student rates pretty low. Being good-looking, a good dancer, and your family owning a car all help."

The clubs allied to curricular activities today include the Dramatic Club—plays by sophomore, junior, and senior classes in a single spring have replaced the "programs of recitations, selections, declamations, and essays" of the old days; the Daubers, meeting weekly in school hours to sketch and in evening meetings with graduate members for special talks on art; the Science Club with its weekly talks by members and occasional lectures by well-known scientists; the Pickwick Club, open to members of English classes, meeting weekly for book reviews and one-act plays, with occasional social meetings; the Penmanship Club; and the Virgil Club, carrying with it some social prestige. Interest in the work of these clubs is keen among some students. All have their "pledges," making their rituals conform roughly to those of the more popular fraternities and sororities.

On the periphery of this high school activity are the church and Y.M.C.A. and Y.W.C.A. clubs. All these organizations frankly admit that the fifteen to twenty-one-year person is their hardest problem. The Hi-Y club appears to be most successful. The Y.M.C.A. controls the extracurricular activities of the grade school boys more than any other single agency, but it maintains itself with only moderate success in the form of this Hi-Y Club among the older boys. A Hi-Y medal is awarded each commencement to the boy in the graduating class who shows the best all-round record, both in point of scholarship and of character. The Y.W.C.A. likewise maintains clubs in the grades but has rough sledding when it comes to the busy, popular, influential group in high school. According to one representative senior girl:

High School girls pay little attention to the Y.W. and the Girl Reserves. The boys go to the Y.M. and Hi-Y club because it has a supper meeting once a month, and that is one excuse for getting away from home evenings. There aren't any supper meetings for the girls at the Y.W. It's not much good to belong to a Y.W. club; *anyone* can belong to them.

All manner of other clubs, such as the Hiking Club and the Boys' and Girls' Booster Club and the Boys' and Girls' Pep Club hover at the fringes or even occasionally take the center of the stage. Says the school paper:

Pep Clubs are being organized in Central High School with a motive that wins recognition. Before, there has been a Pep Club in school, but this year we are more than fortunate in having two. Their business-like start this year predicts a good future. Let's support them!

Pep week during the basket-ball season, engineered by these Pep Clubs, included:

Monday: Speakers in each of the four assemblies. . . .
Tuesday: Poster Day.
Wednesday: Reverend Mr. —— in chapel. Booster pins and pep tags.
Thursday: Practice on yells and songs.
Friday: Final Chapel. Mr. —— speaks. Yells and songs.

Pep chapel [4] for all students will be held in the auditorium the ninth period. Professor —— and his noisy cohorts will furnish the music for the occasion. Immediately following the chapel the students will parade through the business district.

[4] The evolution of the chapel to anything from a "Pep chapel" to a class rally is an interesting example of the change of custom while the label persists.

With the growth of smaller competitive groups, class organization has also increased, reaching a crescendo of importance in the junior and senior years. In a community with such a strong political tradition it is not surprising that there should be an elaborate ritual in connection with the election of senior and other class officers. The senior officers are nominated early in the school year, after much wire-pulling by all parties. "The diplomatic agents of the candidates have been working for weeks on this election," commented the school paper. The election comes a week later so as to allow plenty of electioneering; the evening before election an "enthusiasm dinner" is held in the school cafeteria at which nominees and their "campaign managers" vie with each other in distributing attractive favors (menus, printed paper napkins, and so on), and each candidate states his platform.

Amid the round of athletics, clubs, committees, and class meetings there is always some contest or other to compete for the time of the pupils. Principals complain that hardly a week passes that they do not have to take time from class work in preparation for a contest, the special concern of some organization. In 1923-24 these included art and music memory contests, better speech and commercial department contests, a Latin contest, a contest on the constitution, essays on meat eating, tobacco, poster making, home lighting, and highways.

In this bustle of activity young Middletown swims along in a world as real and perhaps even more zestful than that in which its parents move. Small wonder that a local paper comments editorially, "It is a revelation to old-timers to learn that a genuine boy of the most boyish type nowadays likes to go to school." "Oh, yes, they have a much better time," rejoined the energetic father of a high school boy to a question asked informally of a tableful of men at a Kiwanis luncheon as to whether boys really have a better time in school than they did thirty-five years ago or whether they simply have more things. "No doubt about it!" added another. "When I graduated early in the nineties there weren't many boys—only two in our class, and a dozen girls. All our studies seemed very far away from real life, but today—they've got shop work and athletics, and it's all nearer what a boy's interested in."

TECHNICAL DISCUSSION

1. This essay develops a series of themes. Find them.
2. What kinds of data do the authors use? Illustrate.
3. Does the third paragraph develop its own theme, or does it contribute to the theme expressed at the beginning of the second paragraph? Explain.
4. Would you prefer to use the data in footnote 2 in the text, rather than in the footnote? Explain.
5. Find effective transitions.
6. Is the last paragraph effective as a conclusion to the essay?

TOPICS FOR PAPERS

1. A study of student values: college or high school. What does the student value in school?
2. The high-lights of a school year.
3. Types of club activity open to students on the campus.
4. Religious activities on the campus.
5. What it takes to be elected to a fraternity or sorority.
6. Honorary societies.

The Nation's No. 1 Publisher

EDITH M. STERN

A single publisher, last year, sold over 13,000,000 books and other publications without benefit of a line of advertising, a salesman on the road, or a cocktail party for reviewers. The list of over 65,000 titles contains no mystery stories, no novels, no volumes of poetry—only authoritative information about cooking, farming, health, industry, law, military and naval matters, mining or statistical reports. And nobody cashes in on this Gargantuan output—except the reader—for the publisher is the United States Government.

The Government's volume of sales is the triumph of meeting real needs over lack of merchandising. Take, for example, its unalluring retail outlet, the Government Bookstore. Housed obscurely in the vastness of the Government Printing Office, the shop breaks every rule of

"The Nation's No. 1 Publisher." From *The Saturday Review of Literature,* January 15, 1941. Reprinted by permission of *The Saturday Review of Literature.*

sales appeal. There is no direct entrance from the street; no show window; no indication, in the modest set-up, of the stock of 8,076,752 publications. The interior is drab—golden oak, and tiled floor. Three affable young men in shirtsleeves, who function from behind a solitary counter, comprise the sales force. No sign invites you to "Come in and browse"; the small collection of books on display is locked in glass cases, and only an assortment of price lists is available for thumbing. Poster displays consist of a couple of framed signs on the counter. "Books of interest for the city-bred man and the university graduate as well as the farmer and everyday man of affairs. We will be glad to help you find what you need," one of them reads. "Yes, they were here when I came, twenty years ago," one of the clerks said, when I commented on the signs' old-fashioned typography, the swastikas that embellished them.

Yet the bookstore does an enviable business. In the short time I was there a succession of lawyers' clerks and Western Union messengers carried off piles of Supreme Court decisions, Congressional Hearings, and pamphlets. A young man ordered a bulletin on fox farming to be sent to him in Attica, N. Y. A shabbily dressed old gentleman scanned the rack of price lists, tucked No. 51, "Health," and No. 69, "Pacific States," into a brown paper bag, and meditatively departed. A husky in overalls purchased two copies of "Safety Regulations for Motor Carriers." About 100-150 customers a day come in, I was told. In the fall, when schools open, there's some lift: national affairs bring about occasional booms like the current demand for C.A.A. regulations and Army Manuals, and the quondam rush for N.R.A. regulations; but, in general, business is pretty constant and such commercial phenomena as the Christmas rush are unknown.

Heaviest business of the U.S.A., bookseller, goes on upstairs, in the office of the Superintendent of Documents—familiarly known, in government publishing circles, as the Soup of Docks. There a staff of 450 fill an average of 5,000 mail orders every day. They come in from individuals, from hospitals and educational institutions, from scientific publications and foundations here and abroad, and from book dealers. On quantity lots there's a twenty-five per cent discount. Payment can be made in several ways: by check or money order (no stamps accepted!), C.O.D., by coupons purchased from the Superintendent of

Documents at twenty for one dollar, or through deposit accounts, which make it unnecessary to know the price when ordering. For the asking, you can be put on the mailing list for weekly notices of Government publications, or topical price lists.

The Superintendent of Documents disposes of stock under handicaps that would appall a commercial concern. Paid advertising is nil. Publicity is limited to post office displays of notices to the effect that ninety-six governmental units engage in fact finding with published results "valuable to you" or to an occasional chance newspaper item mentioning the existence of a Government bulletin on Veterans' Benefits or bedbug elimination or venereal disease. Few, if any, reviewers expatiate on the verbal lucidity of "Personal Hygiene" (price ten cents) or the beautiful illustrations of "The National Parks Portfolio" ($1.50).

Like other word merchants, however, the Superintendent of Documents has his best seller lists. In periodical subscriptions *Venereal Disease Information* at fifty cents a year, *School Life* at $1.50, and *Survey of Current Business,* a weekly at two dollars, are among the ten leaders. All the first dozen among individual best sellers in 1939, were about children or health. "Infant Care," that hardy perennial, as usual topped the list. "Healthy Happy Womanhood" and "You Can End This Sorrow," a pamphlet on syphilis, now total nearly 600,000 copies sold, respectively. Others among the fifty-six best sellers further hobbies, such as "Postage Stamps," "Basic Photographs," and "You Can Make It"; some are practical handbooks like "How to Judge a House," "Stain Removal," and "The Home Canning of Fruits and Vegetables"; still others, such non-utilitarian but educative booklets as "Fifty Common Birds of Field and Orchard" and "The Story of the Declaration of Independence." Even so esoteric a segment of human knowledge as "Determination of V factor in the urine and tissues of normal dogs and of dogs with black-tongue by the use of Hemiphilus para-influenzae" has its market, though, like other technical publications, it's unlikely to join the best sellers.

Original cost of the research, composition, typesetting, and printing of Government documents is borne by the issuing department, which has an appropriation for the purpose. When you buy a Government publication you pay only for cost of subsequent press work, paper, and binding. For this the Superintendent of Documents has no appropriation; he has to carry costs through sales. Consequently he shares the need of all booksellers to stock carefully. The various departments are encouraged to "write their jackets—" *i.e.,* to recommend which of their publications they think are likely to sell, on the basis of the demand for free copies. The Superintendent of Documents bases his guesses, also, on sales of similar type publications in the past. And, also like his commercial confrères, sometimes he guesses wrong. "Postage Stamps," for instance, was a surprise seller; "American Battlefields" was a flop; "Furniture, Its Selection and Use," though it made the best seller list, sold well below expectations.

No editorial decisions must be made by the Superintendent of Documents: what is published is decided by the issuing department, and decided under continual fire of "propaganda," "waste of taxpayers' money," and "not a function of government." Recently the same magazine which carried a diatribe against the imbecility of bulletins on care of canaries and on window curtains, a few months later lauded to the skies the government publications which have raised rural living standards and sweetened the lives of farmers' wives! As a matter of fact, popular departmental publications are nearly all issued in response to letters of inquiry on this or that subject: a marginal point is reached when demand makes it cheaper to print than to send out letters. So, for instance, "Reindeer Recipes," once excoriated by a Senator as an example of extravagant inutility, came into being. There were numerous inquiries on utilization of reindeer meat; cost of reply was twenty cents or more by individual letter, half a cent per printed bulletin. The booklets on lawn care are, too, the result of years of inquiries from home owners.

All free distribution comes from the departments, not from the Superintendent of Documents. So vast a part of the Government's activities as publisher is this donation of literature, that many a citizen doesn't even know that a federal publications sales office exists. The Department of Agriculture, for instance, annually fills 800,000 requests for its 50,000 titles. Some, like "Born in Irrigation Waters" and "Notes on the Habits of Certain Coprophagous Beetles and Methods of Rearing Them" come under the heading of technical bulletins, and, designed for specialists, are printed in lots of only 2,500-3,500. Others, like "Diets to Fit the Family Income," a best seller both purchased and gratis, are popular in writing, format, and illustrations; aimed at Mr. and Mrs. John Doe, their printings run from 10,000-100,000.

In addition to what the Department of Agriculture sends out direct on request, each Congressman, by law, gets 12,500 of its nontechnical Farmers Bulletins and Leaflets to bestow where and as he wishes. This reading matter takes the place of the old-time largesse of seeds, and sending out lists of what's available is an excellent way for politicos to keep memory green among their constituents. "Dear Senator," a letter read, "Thank you so much for thinking of me. Please send me your bulletin on shade trees."

In other departments, Congressmen must request publications like any other citizen. With certain exceptions, not more than one copy each of ten publications can be got free; beyond that, you have to purchase through the Superintendent of Documents. You must pay, too, if a department's free supply is exhausted, so it may happen that a publication available free the first Monday of this month must be paid for on its second Friday. Conversely, if copies for free distribution are on hand, you get for nothing the bulletin listed at ten cents . . . or for which your neighbor, who ordered through the Superintendent of Documents, has just paid ten cents . . . a state of affairs equally disconcerting for the citizen and for the clerks who have sometimes to return money, since the departments make no direct sales, pass it on to the Superintendent of Documents, or refer you to him.

There are, of course, abuses of the free publications privilege. Constituents who check every title on the list sent them by their Congressman are not unknown. One woman wrote to Agriculture for a long list of publications covering such diverse topics as gas engines, house cleaning, and caponizing "because I sure love to read." School children are a continual pest to overburdened officials in Agriculture, Interior, Commerce, and Public Health. "Please send me everything you can," they write. "Our teacher promised a prize to the one who collects the most bulletins . . ." or "the more you send the better mark I will get." "If only," one publication's official said to me, "all teachers would follow the practice of some—appointing one child to act as librarian for the class instead of encouraging forty to fifty pupils to fill scrapbooks—or wastebaskets!" What's more, most publications bearing the Government imprint aren't exactly slanted as juveniles. The Bureau of Standards' "Dress Patterns" isn't what it seems to the high school girls who request it, but a technical treatise, in the interest of manufacturers, on standardization of ready-to-wear sizes. "Homes for Birds," frequently asked for in childish script, begins "That the affection felt by many people for birds should manifest itself in the provision of homes for them is highly appropriate."

There are, also, attempts to get for-sales-only publications gratis. As one instance: the Department of Commerce issues a certain book at three dollars. (The corresponding English publication, product of a commercial concern, costs the equivalent of thirty dollars.) "Sometimes big companies who can well afford to buy the volume spend more trying to get it free than they would if they mailed their orders and checks direct to the Superintendent of Docks," one of the responsible issuing officials remarked grimly. "If we complied with all the requests for free copies, the cost of the book to the Government would be quintupled." While I was interviewing him, his telephone rang several times; each call came from someone trying to wangle free copies of "For sale" publications.

Scrutinize an average day's mail in any of the departments, however, and you'll find that the vast majority of requests for literature are legitimate. Householders, who assume that the Government can be more objective than manufacturers with something to sell, ask for information on insulation and plumbing and efficient kitchen arrangements. Engineers ask specifically for specific answers to specific problems. Literate, typewritten requests for the results of scientific experiments pour in from all over the world. To Public Health come pencilled, misspelled postcards from the backwoods of the deep South, asking for material on pellagra. Parents, many of them brought up on "Infant Care," ask the Children's Bureau for the latest edition; this handbook is the free, as well as purchased, best "seller" of all, among a clientele who would feel the expenditure of even a dime. "Please send me the following copies as I am a new farmer and would like to learn all about dairy cows and how to take care of them," read one letter to Agriculture. The name of a large city was crossed off on the letterhead; the name of a small town in the same state, substituted.

Often there is a real note of urgency in the requests. "If I don't receive these bulletins before the rainy season begins," wrote a California farmer, "it will be too late." "Please send me whatever you have on milk goats right away. My baby is dependent on my goat, and it's sick."

Very rarely, a correspondent has to be told that the Government has published nothing that meets his need. Such requests as "photographs of vitamins, so I know what to swallow and what to let alone," "directions for airing and dyeing of cows' tails," "information on cockroach production," and "something on witches" could not be filled. Nearly always, however, seek and you shall find it in a government bulletin.

But not always promptly. Letters that are addressed to the wrong department have to be shunted about Washington. Mistakes along this line are often natural: it would take second sight to know that "Health of the School Child" emanates from the Office of Education, "Good Food Habits" from Agriculture's Bureau of Home Economics, "Good Posture in the Small Child" from the Children's Bureau, and "Good Teeth"—with an attractive picture of an open-mouthed small boy on its cover—from Public Health; that you procure fish recipes from the Bureau of Fisheries, meat recipes from the Bureau of Home Economics.

The whole question of sales versus free distribution is a controversial one among publication's officials, and they present arguments on both sides. England gives nothing away—why should we? . . . Yes, and look at health conditions in England compared to ours. . . . Government publications are paid for through taxation; if you have to buy them, you're being taxed twice. . . . Why should all of us be charged for literature valuable only to special groups, like mining engineers or manufacturers? . . .

An interdepartmental committee on printing and publishing is working on a scheme to harmonize the present somewhat chaotic system of distribution. It recommends a certain amount of "official distribution" free to libraries; to meet special situations like localized plagues of insects, or epidemics; when necessary for national safety, as in the case of venereal disease or soil conservation. Beyond these special cases, it urges purchase only. But whether or not anything comes of the committee's efforts, in the meanwhile the happy fact remains that, one way or another, the U.S.A., publisher, makes a super-encyclopaedia available to the whole world.

TECHNICAL DISCUSSION

1. Why does the author begin with the item about 13,000,000 books?

2. Identify all of the themes used by the author.

3. Classify the types of data used by the author to support each of her themes.

4. Do you find a paragraph that does not develop a theme, but serves as a sort of catch-all for miscellaneous facts?

5. Does the author end her essay with a summarizing remark?

6. Explain the author's method of tying the paragraphs together so that there is no break or jar as the reader moves from one to another.

TOPICS FOR PAPERS

1. Study one of the following subjects until you have several judgments and their supporting data well determined. Write a paper as a series of themes, each supported in turn. If you have trouble getting judgments, ask several persons who know your subject for opinions; then look for data to support what the persons say: (a) the college farm; (b) the library; (c) the college advisement system; (d) summer school.

2. Read a book that you are interested in and write a discussion of it that presents your judgments in series, each judgment well supported with data taken from the book or from sources related to it, such as reviews of the book.

Scholarship in College

EDWIN W. KEMMERER

The first object of education is to make one a better consumer, to increase one's capacity to enjoy, to live broadly and deeply, to appreciate philosophy, science, history, art, literature, and music, to understand things and events, to see their interrelation, their significance. Compare the reactions of an educated man with trained powers of appreciation and those of an uneducated, untrained man on visiting for the first time the Acropolis at Athens, on looking at Michael

"Scholarship in College." From a lecture at Wesleyan University, published in *Vital Speeches of the Day,* Vol. III, No. 19, July 15, 1937. Reprinted by permission of the author and City News Publishing Co.

Angelo's Last Judgment, or on witnessing the rendition of a great opera like *Parsifal*. What one really sees depends much more upon what is back of his eyes than upon what is in front of them. It was Aristotle who said: "Education is an ornament in prosperity and a refuge in adversity." This development of one's powers to enjoy, to appreciate, to be a good consumer, is sufficient justification in itself for seeking an education.

The second object of an education is to make one a better producer. In this connection the fundamental ideas are service, power, wealth. Here the important word is not enjoyment but achievement. It is in this narrower sense of the term that the word success is most often used, and in this sense I am using it this evening.

What I have to say this evening will be an attempt to throw some light on the answers to two questions: first, does a college education contribute to success in life? Second, what type of man in college is most likely to succeed?

First, let us consider the college man's chances of success as compared with those of the non-college man. On this subject there have been a number of studies.

In 1893, Dr. Charles F. Thwing published the results of a study of this subject based upon the 15,142 names in Appleton's *Encyclopedia of American Biography*. Broadly speaking, his conclusion was, that one out of every 40 college graduates succeeded and one out of every 10,000 non-graduates. This gave a ratio of 250 to 1 in favor of the college man.

Of course this study refers to conditions as they existed some time ago. It may well be that the situation is different today. A larger percentage of the public receives a college education now than did a few generations ago, and it is possible that this may be resulting in important changes in the quality of the graduates that the colleges are turning out. In 1880, there were 687 male college graduates for every 100,000 males in the country over twenty years of age. By 1920 this figure had risen to 1,137. Some light on the present situation is given by studies recently made on the basis of the 1928-29 and the 1934-35 editions of *Who's Who in America*. For both these years approximately three-fourths of all the names mentioned were for college graduates, and approximately 85 per cent for collegians, graduates and non-graduates combined. Persons whose education was limited to the common and elementary schools represented only 6⅔ per cent of these names in the former edition and 7⅙ per cent in the latter. This is true despite the fact that the number of college graduates in the United States is a very small figure compared with the number of adults whose school education ended prior to the college grade. Furthermore, the figures show that, from 1900 to 1934-35, the percentage of names in *Who's Who in America* represented by collegians continually increased. At the present time, therefore, as in the past, the college man seems to have a very much better chance of succeeding than the non-college man.

This conclusion, moreover, seems to apply to the business world as well as to that of the professions. Taussig and Joslyn, in their book, *American Business Leaders,* say:

"The figures seem to indicate that the larger the scale on which business is conducted, the greater is the extent to which college graduates are employed in the important executive and managerial positions; and, correspondingly, the less is the extent to which grammar-school graduates are employed in a similar capacity. An unmistakable positive relation thus appears to exist between degree of schooling and degree of business achievement, when the latter is measured solely in terms of size of business. This relation seems to argue for a certain measure of superiority in college graduates as compared with men of less schooling . . . [The data] seem to indicate that, the more responsible is the position to be filled, the more largely do college graduates tend to be employed."

For statistical studies of the kind just cited there are many pitfalls, and conclusions drawn from them should be taken with great caution. It must, furthermore, be frankly admitted that, even if a much larger percentage of college graduates succeed than of non-college graduates, this fact does not prove that college education was the cause of the collegians' greater success.

By and large, the men who go to college are a select group. On the average they come from more prosperous homes and have had greater opportunities in other respects than men who do not go to college. In fact one of the advantages of a college training is the opportunity to associate with such a select group of men. Some men are doubtless harmed by attendance at college. All in all, however, such meager evidence as is available is strongly favorable to the conclusion that, as a general proposition, a college education greatly improves a man's chances of success in life.

Our next question is: What type of man in college is most likely to succeed? On this subject there have been a number of studies of limited scope. They are not conclusive, but since they nearly all substantially agree, their evidence is highly significant. I will cite merely a few of these studies.

A quarter of a century ago Professor Paul Van Dyke of Princeton summarized the results of such a study in an article on "College Life," published in *Scribner's Magazine*. His study covered from 13 to 20 classes at Harvard, Yale, Princeton, Amherst, and Brown. The criterion of success was inclusion in *Who's Who in America*. Deductions were made for those who had not reached a sufficient age for attaining fame. The figures showed that one-half of all high-honor men succeeded, and one-third of all second-honor men.

Professor George Davies, a few years later, found that of graduates taking first honors in college, 50 per cent were mentioned in *Who's Who in America,* and of those taking second honors, 33⅓ per cent were mentioned.

Ten years ago Professor Hugh A. Smith of the University of Wisconsin gave an account of some extensive studies made by a special committee about 1917 on the subject of "College Records and Success in Life." The study was limited to one college, covered a period of 45 years, and the records of 1,800 alumni. Only the records of persons who had been out of college fifteen years or over were included. Two different criteria of success were employed. The first was the judgment of a few selected persons acquainted with the alumni studies as to the success of these alumni. The second was the inclusion of the names in *Who's Who in America*. Both criteria gave essentially the same results.

Let us take first the criterion of the judgment of friends and acquaintances. Ten consecutive classes were taken from the middle of the period covered. These classes were represented by 550 graduates. Of these graduates two lists of names were made: one consisting of 93 men who had the highest grades in their classes; the other consisting of a list of 97 men who were considered the most worthy, successful, or eminent, according to the information compiled from various sources. "The point to note is that these two lists *contain 87 names in common*. This means that of the 93 with the highest marks only six failed to make good in later life; only 1 out of 15 has not in later life maintained the distinction shown by his marks during the four years of his college course. . . . The total number of those in the lower group is 467. Only one out of 46 of these has attained distinction in later life."

Referring to this study Mr. Smith says, "If a man was high in one list, he was almost invariably high in the other; and if low in one, low in the other. This situation was repeated with such monotony, in the 1,800 names, that the temptation became strong when one factor was known, to accept it as a certain indication of the other."

Let us now turn from the general situation, that is from broad averages, to success in the professions and in business specifically.

In the Harvard Law School there has long been a jocular saying among students that those with A grades become the professors of law, those with B grades the judges, and those with C grades make the money. As a matter of fact there is no evidence to support this idea—the evidence in reality is exactly to the contrary. Those with A grades are much more successful than those with B or C grades in attaining eminence as professors, judges, and lawyers and those with B grades are more successful than those with C grades. The competition of the country's leading law firms for the highest-stand men in our best law schools is usually very keen. These are the men who get the best professional opportunities at the beginning of their law practice and the ones who advance the fastest.

Furthermore it is the men with the high academic standing in college who become the high-stand men in the professional schools. The scholar in college is likely to be the scholar in law school, in medical school, and in schools of engineering, and the "dub" in college, if he is admitted to the graduate professional school at all, is likely to be the dub there. And this principle not only applies in the movement of students from the college to the professional school, but also in the movement from the preparatory school to the college.

In support of this conclusion there is much evidence. Permit me merely to cite the following. I quote first from an article by former President A. Lawrence Lowell of Harvard University on the subject "College Studies and Professional Training—A Statistical Study in Harvard University" published in 1911. This study covered bachelors of art of Harvard College who afterwards graduated from Harvard Law School and Harvard Medical School. The Law School figures refer to classes from 1891 to 1910 inclusive and the Medical School figures to classes from 1895 to 1900 inclusive. President Lowell's conclusion is that the higher the men rank in college, the better their chance of winning a *cum laude* in the Law School, and the chance increases rapidly with the excellence of the college rank. The chance of winning a *cum laude* in the Law School, he found, was more than three times as great for the man who left college with a *cum laude* as for the man with a plain degree; six times as great for the man who graduated at college with the *magna cum laude;* and nine times as great for the graduate with *summa cum laude.*

On this same subject [former] President William Trufant Foster of Reed College said in 1916: "So difficult it is for a student to change his habits of life after the crucial years of college that not one man in 20 years, who was satisfied in Harvard College with grades of C and lower, attained distinction in the studies of the Harvard Law School." Dividing 250 graduates of Yale who received their degrees in law at Harvard between 1900 and 1915 into nine groups according to undergraduate scholarship, beginning with those who won the highest senior appointments at Yale and ending with those who received no graduation honors at all, he found that the first group did the best work in their studies of law, the second group next, the third group next, and so on in the same order, with but a single exception to the bottom of the list. The performance at Harvard of each of the eight groups of Yale students, in other words, was in precise accord with the promise of these men as shown by their academic records at Yale.

This same principle runs all the way back to the preparatory school. For example, President Lowell shows in the article previously cited that of the Harvard Law School men who entered Harvard College without conditions, 26.4 per cent won a *cum laude* and of those who entered with conditions only 9 per cent won a *cum laude*. Here, as elsewhere, the famous aphorism of Pope still applies, "Just as the twig is bent, the tree's inclin'd."

There is a widespread belief that, while scholarship may be conducive to success in professional and literary lines, it does not count heavily in business. On this subject very little statistical evidence has been collected. Useful data are difficult to obtain. There are no satisfactory standards or yardsticks of business success. The amount of biographical information available for businessmen is meager. Success in business is not well recognized in our biographical dictionaries.

A few years ago a most suggestive study on this subject was made by Walter Gifford, President of the American Telephone and Telegraph Company. The results were summarized in an article by him, entitled "Does Business Want Scholars?" Mr. Gifford's study was based on the records of Bell employees who had been out of college over five years. His conclusion was:

> In general, men in the first third of their college classes are most likely to be found in the highest third of their group in salary; those in the middle third in scholarship to be in the middle third in salary, and those in the lowest third in scholarship to be in the lowest third in salary. . . . Of the 3,806 men studied, 498 had graduated in the first tenth of their respective classes. By about the fifth year of their employment this group began to earn more than the other college men. They continued to increase their advantage little by little until they were twenty-five years out of college. Then they began to go ahead still more rapidly. . . . The 784 men who graduated in the lowest third of their classes have earned the least, and the curve of the earnings of the median man in this group has exactly the opposite trend to that of the median man in the upper tenth of their classes; the longer the best students are in business, the more rapidly their earnings rise. The longer the poorer students are in business, the slower their earnings rise.

Broadly speaking, this study of Mr. Gifford's shows that men from the first tenth of their college classes have about four times the chance of those from the lowest third to stand in the highest salary group. It appears, therefore, that in at least one line of business, as well as in the professions, scholarship in undergraduate work makes for graduate achievement.

✦

There is a saying among golf "pros" that, while it is not true that only the dumb can play golf well, being dumb helps a lot. The evidence I have cited today seems to justify the conclusion that while it is not true that only men with high scholarship records in school and college succeed in afterlife, a good scholarship record helps a lot.

On the walls of many a college student's room is the motto: "Do not let your studies interfere with your college education." This is a humorous way of expressing the pleasant philosophy that the play of the side shows in college is more important than the work of the main tent. It is the philosophy of thoughtless, careless youth. Of this philosophy Ruskin said:

> When a man has done his work, and nothing can anyway be materially altered in his fate, let him forget his toil, and jest with his fate, if he will; but what excuse can you find for willfulness of thought at the very time when every crisis of future fortune hangs on your decision? A youth thoughtless! when all the happiness of his home for ever depends on the chances or the passions of an hour! A youth thoughtless! when the career of all his days depends on the opportunities of a moment. A youth thoughtless! when his every act is a foundation stone of future conduct, and every imagination a fountain of life or death! Be thoughtless in any after years, rather than now.

The biggest expense of a college course is four of the best years of a man's life. A college is, or should be, first and foremost an educational institution. The first task of any man in college should be to develop his brain. Education is the main tent: athletics, college publications, musical clubs, social clubs, and similar activities all have their place; but it should never be forgotten that they are the side shows.

The man who has the sense of proportions, the judgment, to realize this, and to concentrate his best efforts on that most important thing in college—the training of his mind—is the man of common sense. The false sense of values that often prevails among college students is astonishing. It is a pleasant philosophy, but a false one, that the things most worth while in college are the easy-going pleasures of college life and the activities that win for one the ephemeral praise of one's fellows. In college, as well as out, it is the vigorous discipline, the hard-won intellectual achievements, that make the strong man.

The man who does well in college the thing that is most worth while in college, namely, developing his brain, is the man who usually will do best the things that are most worth while in afterlife. He is the man who will achieve most.

TECHNICAL DISCUSSION

1. The author of this essay develops two themes. Point out his statement of them.

2. What is the function of the material that precedes the paragraph with the two questions?

3. How does the author support his first theme? Do you find a division of the first theme, for instance a division of the material between professional men and business men?

4. How does the author support his second theme? What divisions do you find in the material? What types of data do you find?

5. Is the author's array of data convincing?

6. Does the citation of sources help make the data seem more valid than they would be without the citation?

7. Write an outline in which you express the author's two themes. Put under the themes any secondary points that you find. Use complete, declarative sentences for your outline.

TOPICS FOR PAPERS

1. Write a paper in which you frankly discuss what you expect to get out of college and what you think college is actually giving you.

2. Write a set of directions on how to study.

3. Write a paper in which you defend or attack strict college-entrance requirements.

4. Defend the classroom and library against the encroaching appeal of campus activities.

5. Describe some of the interesting types of college students.

Third Pattern

Portrait of My Mother

ROLLO WALTER BROWN

Strangely I did not come to know the quality of my mother until I was a great overgrown boy larger than most men. She and my father were out of the same world—the world of vanishing forests—and he was austere, and I was "mother's boy"; yet early I knew him better. There was in him a pronounced trace of the poet that a child was sure to appreciate on sight. My mother was the battler of the two, the one who accepted life where she was and settled down to the unpoetic business of making ends meet. Anyone was in danger of assuming—as I did at first—that her endless concern with everyday matters indicated content with everyday satisfactions. And that was to misunderstand her entire life.

She spent her early childhood—at the very middle of the nineteenth century—in a clearing that overlooked a modest rapids in an Ohio hill river when the sight of people moving westward, always moving westward, was something to be expected every day. She was the eldest child in a family of an even dozen—every one of whom lived to be old.

All this army of brothers and sisters except one were born before my mother was married, and of the first nine only one was a boy. The mother of all these looked upon a household as something vital and florid right out of the magnificence of a stirring cosmos. There was something of freedom and expansiveness even in the names she gave them. When everybody round about was naming children Isaiah, Ebenezer, Rebecca, or Leah, she named hers Roselba (my mother), Sylvester, Byron, Lucinda, Elizabeth Alverta, Cora Ellen. Her family was a tribe pushing up into full life. It called for the ministrations of more than one mother, and the eldest daughter became a kind of associate mother entrusted with keeping track of as many as possible.

Something of this long childhood experience of being always en-

"Portrait of My Mother." From *The Atlantic Monthly,* October, 1944. Reprinted by permission of the author and *The Atlantic Monthly.*

trusted with life, of being always thoughtful about someone other than herself, was in everything she later did in her own household. She had three sons. Out of the depths of her dark eyes—that with her cheerful countenance made her a woman of unpretentious beauty—she expressed her constant preoccupation with giving these sons more of a push into the world than she herself had known.

It was not easy. For she had become a bride in the devastating years of President Grant's administration when the country seemed to be in the numbness of final death. Everybody needed the fruit jars, milk crocks, and butter jars that her husband turned in his bluebird potshop, but nobody possessed money.

And if the general atmosphere was dispiriting, the specific little world in which she put in her days could scarcely be regarded as a luxurious center of life. The log house in which she lived for many years had a great fireplace in which either coal or wood could be burned, a wide flagstone hearth, an oak floor of boards of enormous width covered with a rag carpet woven at a neighbor's house, side walls covered with flowered paper that went in and out in waves over the logs to the wide border of flowers of deeper color at the top, and a ceiling of neatly hewn whitewashed beams and whitewashed rough boards—the under side of the upstairs floor.

Beside a bright blue batten door that led to the kitchen was a shelf on which a Waterbury clock announced the hours with whirring bangs, and the seconds with ticktocks that could be heard upstairs through the cracks. And opposite the fireplace by a window where the sun shone in, there was a triangular flower stand that rose in terraced shelves to make a kind of half-pyramid four or five feet high of fuchsias and bleeding heart and geraniums and begonias and night-blooming cereus and ferns and other plants grown for their foliage alone.

In this world she moved energetically and always with an awareness that said, "Of course, we are hoping for something better." Her young life had been nourished on the stories of neighbor boys who had marched away and done great things on the battlefield, and she saw no reason why a woman might not proceed as if there were still important concerns to be occupied with. Occasionally she did one thing that gave her a look of importance in my eyes: she took her place in a sidesaddle decorated with red and tan needlepoint—or something of the sort—high on a somewhat angular horse, and with a long loose riding-skirt covering even the toe of her one foot that was in the stirrup, rode away to a meeting of some kind. My notions of great personages came from the Bible, or the pictures in the back of it, and when I saw her high on the tall horse I always thought of some beautiful queen on a camel.

2

Since her sons were going to be living where there would be persons of gentility, she thought they ought to be well grounded in essentials. If one of them slammed a door, or let it slam, he went immediately back and opened it and then closed it appropriately. When a son was ready to go to a neighbor's house to carry a message, he had to repeat to his mother what he was going to say when he got there. And when he returned he did not report approximately what the neighbor said, but gave it precisely, and in the neighbor's exact words—an experience that was almost more than the equivalent of a college education.

Where she got her understandings of how people in other and greater places surely must act, I was never able to learn. But she said she wanted her sons to have "behavior" that would stand them in good stead anywhere, and on the assumption that she knew something of what that would be, she proceeded. She had a backlog in etiquette that if we thought enough about other people, we'd probably do about the right thing ourselves.

We bounced up from our chairs when older people came into the room, and begged them to sit down. We spoke with respectfulness to every adult human being. And we were expected to appear in clean clothes and with what she called "becomingness" when we went where other people were assembled. When we were in our Sunday best and there had been heavy summer rains that had left the hill and hollow roads gutters and loblolly, she insisted that we pick our way along the roadside so that our shoes would not be all mud when we reached the church. Although I hit upon the less genteel way of carrying my shoes and socks and enjoying the elemental feel of the soft mud squashing up between my toes, and then washing my feet in the cool water below a spring within sight of the church, putting on my shoes, and appearing as mudless as if I had walked all the way on Fifth Avenue, I did accept her principle of making as decent an appearance as circumstances would allow.

Nor would she permit waste. When school might be had for the going, it was unpardonable to miss a day unnecessarily. Clothes were to be worn with care for their natural life. And food was to be eaten. If we did not eat all that was in our dinner buckets at school, we carried the scraps home for the dog or the chickens. It was a depravity not to be thought of to throw away the tiniest morsel of bread. And of course nobody had to be cautioned about throwing away cake.

We heard her admonitions, saw the reasonableness of them, and usually accepted them without so much as a question. But there was one that I could never accept even in the abstract. Since I was much younger than my two brothers, I required special cautioning. She told me not to fight. To pick trouble, she said, was very low-grade. But I could never see why these two were always mentioned together. I never picked trouble; but I had to fight. In the oncoming world of Coal in which I was obliged to operate, either a boy fought or he did not survive.

When a blustering ruffian of my own years hurried ahead to a level spot, turned to block my way, and said, "Here's where we find out whether I'm good, or you," there was such a healthy satisfaction in bloodying his nose, knocking him down, and sitting astride him and cuffing him with energy until he begged for mercy, that I always had to go through with it. "I hear you were in a fight again," she would say, looking at me with penetrable sternness out of her dark brown eyes; and I would answer, "But I didn't start it." And there the matter would rest.

From somewhere she had gained the sure belief, too, that people's lives should include music. A piano was out of the question, but an organ was not. She succeeded well enough with my two brothers. Eventually they played two or three different instruments in public, and one of them directed a stirring military band in college. For seventeen weeks the same teacher who had taught them struggled with me, and my mother daily released me from all other duties for a time in order that I might practice. Eventually she heard me floundering through the easy parts of "The Beautiful Blue Danube Waltzes" with long clumsy fingers—while the birds sang alluringly everywhere outside, or the Plymouth Rock and Brown Leghorn roosters met at their boundary line within full view of where I labored, and waged one of the decisive battles of the world. I worked conscientiously, but rebelliously.

I never knew where my mother learned of my true state of mind, for I was careful not to tell her. But one day when I had poison ivy on the back of my neck and she was bathing it in cool water and sugar of lead she said, "Son, you don't have to take the organ lessons if you don't want to." I was so overjoyed that I generously volunteered to take up the fife instead. With the money for three organ lessons, I could get a fife in rosewood.

3

The whole of her sense of entrustment was revealed when she sat in the crackling midwinter firelight. The light spread out and upward from the fireplace and made the beams and ceiling boards very white over her head, and touched the great semi-pyramid of blooming flowers behind her with brightness out of a spring dawn. While she sat erect and contemplative, everybody—including my father, who at other times seemed more or less her equal—shrank into subordination.

She could never remain inactive long, and while my father sat with his page twisted round to catch the light and read with great concentration, and the others of us cracked nuts or popped corn or hung apples from the enormous hewn log that supported the chimney above the fireplace so that they would come down just close enough to sizzle and roast without burning—or burning the string—she knitted away at a mitten or crocheted a shawl or did other "easy" work that she left for evenings. But there in the firelight, even while she worked, she was the custodian and guarantor of life—there in a room where most things were either her blood or her handiwork.

Just as sure, too, as her feeling of entrustment was her sense of practical adequacy. Her world was not a world of gadgets; there was little "to do with." But a part of the business of being intelligent, she supposed, was to make much of little. When she and her father-in-law philosophized together, she always approved his remark that the true pioneer could go into the woods with an axe, horse, and a plow shovel, and proceed to the growing of a crop and the establishment of a farm. She thought a woman likewise should be resourceful.

So she made any garment worn by a man or a woman—including a man's cap and a woman's hat. She knitted or crocheted mittens, mufflers, socks and stockings, shawls, wristlets, fascinators, ear-muffs, and lace of amazing beauty. She made, too, all kinds of woven or hooked or plaited rugs, quilts of the most complicated design and recurrences of color, crazy-quilts of ingenious variations in fancy stitching, stand covers, table covers. When a boy needed a suit of clothes, she carefully studied an old suit and then made the new one. Her aptitude seemed most startling, though, when she saw casually at church a new style of hood which she liked, and went home and proceeded to make one.

In addition to the everyday cooking done in a household, she made all sorts of jellies of the clearest colors and the most trembling consistency, grape marmalade, blackberry and raspberry jam, strawberry preserve, peach butter, the special Ohio kind of apple butter, melting yellow cakes with deep icing, mincemeat of her own proportioning that all the neighbors bought ravenously from her as long as she would sell, butter with such a distinct tastiness that an important industrialist who had known her when he was a boy had her—through some arrangement that he was able to make—provide him with a pound every week until she was eighty-five years old. But the dish which she herself professed greatest pride in was a strangely pungent pie made of green tomatoes and half-ripened grapes, and spices, including nutmeg.

Her day began at four-thirty in the morning, summer and winter, and ended whenever there was a stopping place in her work. Yet she never worked at anything as if it were the only thing she had in mind. She would pick up a volume from the table when she was tidying the living room, see something that interested her, drop into a chair, read the shortest possible section that would enable her to understand, and then go on with her work. But there was a cheeriness in her face which told that something out of the book had contributed to the encompassing enterprise of her life.

After she had taken a nap on a couch at noon—and there was no noise—she would sit up with startling suddenness and move off vivaciously into her work as if the nap had only given her a little clearer view of what she must always be about. She was quick-tempered, but always after the flash of hotness over the immediately vexing matter, she seemed more than ever a contemplative person occupied with inclusive concerns.

In her capacity to hurry and to think at the same time she equaled any commanding general. If a family came just at mealtime, she revealed a kind of magical dexterity in bringing a meal together for extra people in the twinkling of an eye. Nor was she flustered by people who were supposed to be important. A Governor of Ohio walked through the mud before daylight one morning to see her. He was a big boyish person who knew country life and country people, and was known to her somewhat through her sons. He went to the back door in the foggy half-light, and when she answered his knock he asked her if it would be possible for a hungry man to get a handout of some kind. "I guess it will," she replied; "so come on in." And then as he stood like a giant chuckling affectionately over her she added, "But for a half cent I'd box your ears for coming to the back door." Whereupon he became for the rest of his life a kind of fourth son in his devotion to her.

4

Since I was the youngest I was in time much in her immediate world after my brothers had more or less left it. It was then that I began to see the importance of the contemplative and less obvious side of her life. In solitude she considered the place that such a humble life as hers held in the world. The best she could do was to send emissaries out. That was what she had been busy doing. She said little, but sometimes she said enough to reveal her true intent. In a letter that through all the years escaped destruction she once wrote, "Now it affords me great pleasure to deny myself for my sons."

And once when we were alone and I had fallen full length and had struck my head with a terrific jolt and she thought I was at the end of my life, though I was only dazed, I heard her say, when she thought she spoke alone to the Infinite out of her heartbreak, what she thought of me, and of my brothers, and of the purpose of living.

But when the emissaries had gone, here she would be still—probably, for she as well as my father was of a tough breed. She would have to know how to live in solitude. And it was her adequacy in solitude that became more and more noticeable. It was in her manner while she worked; it was in her face when she reflected; it was in her eyes when she turned to you with a look that seemed to come from the experience of a thousand centuries.

I first noticed this depth from which she looked when we one morning picked berries together in the late dewiness down by the deep woods below the locust thicket where the sun scarcely entered. We had filled one large bucket and I took it to the house to empty it. When I returned, the birds were singing in every treetop, the crows scolded in the locusts, and two great turkey buzzards sat on the leaning steeple of a white oak so near that I could study their bare red vulture heads. My mother stood obliviously with one arm outstretched to a briar bending with berries, intent on reflection. Suddenly I was seized by a strange conviction that I had never seen her before; that she was a woman out of the Bible; that she was neither young nor old, but only representative and timeless. But when she saw me there in the edge of the walnut-tree shade, and asked me what time it was up at the house, we were both back where obviously we belonged.

There was nothing morbid in her solitude. It was only that she did not always feel sure of herself in the noisiness of big gatherings, and she did feel sure of herself when she could work things out alone. In consequence, she let her husband represent her more and more at gatherings, until in the end she quit going altogether. She had to write at least three letters every Sunday, anyhow. Thus it came logically that for twenty-one years in her late life she was never off the Ridge where she lived.

In these years she developed a great serenity. She was a part of something expressed everywhere about her. She would stop when she walked, look about in content at the clouds, and the wind in the trees, and the sun on the hillsides, and then stand contemplatively for minutes. She would put her hand against the stout trunk of a pushing young shellbark hickory, look at it as if she and the tree were on very good terms, and then walk on without a word.

She became, too, without any noticeable effort on her part, a special friend of creatures—a custodian of good relations between them and the representatives of mankind round about. Cows thrust their heads through the bars to have her—and no one else—soothingly rub their faces. When she started on one of her afternoon or Sunday morning walks out to the woods pasture, where there was a long vista through the hills, her hens would come running, sometimes half flying, until they were a great accompanying body. They were not hungry; they were expecting no feed; they only chose to go along. In winter she hung ears of yellow corn in an apple tree by the front porch and tacked strips of suet to the body of the tree and had several pairs of cardinals for company throughout the season.

And the environs of the house every spring and summer became a bustling wren sanctuary. If she hung her raincoat on the outkitchen porch and left it there for a few days, there was certain to be a wren's nest in one of the pockets. When she put a cracked old-style iron teakettle on a low shelf in the coal house, she discovered within a day or two that a wren was using the wide spout as an entrance and was building a nest. She could lift the lid later and exhibit the wren family.

Once when she was eighty she said a bit proudly to one of her sons, "Come out here to the milk bench and I'll show you something." She had turned a milk crock upside down and one edge of it extended an inch or two over the end of the bench. Within twenty-four hours a wren was building a nest under the crock. And now when she unhesitantly turned the crock up, seven lively-looking young wrens, about ready to fly, watched her intently, but did not move. She had been turning the crock up for a look at least once every day.

She knew, too, where to find every beautiful thing that existed in her world. She knew which redbuds in the thicket always bloomed a little ahead of the others, which dogwoods first began to lose their greenish cast and become pure white, where to find the prize patch of sweet williams, when to look for the black-haw bush in full bloom, when to expect the first odor of locust blossom, when in July to watch for an unfailing field lily on the hillside, where always to find the softest and greenest moss, where to look for the first maple branch that bespoke autumn, where to go for flint stones that had the most interesting spiral markings on them.

Whenever her friends from town came to see her—and they were always coming, as many as fifteen or twenty on one Sunday afternoon—she reverted to her more customary role of giver. They walked out to the locust trees, on out to the woods pasture, down to a romantic old orchard close in the hollow where one could still find fragments of Staffordshire blue tableware by the site of an early house, back up the hill to sit for a time in a clean pasture field and enjoy such quiet as they did not know existed. And when they were ready to go she placed something in their hands to be carried away—some fruit, some bitter-sweet, some slips of ruddier begonia, something out of the vegetable garden, some flowers from the profusion in which they grew from the first peonies to the last chrysanthemums.

To give—was not that what life was? That was the easy summary: twenty years or so given to younger sisters and the like; two-thirds of a century and a little more given to her own family. She had given.

But what she had achieved within herself seemed more. In a world where life was always hard and often cruel, she met the requirements without ever flinching, without ever thinking of running away to some remote place in pursuit of an evasive happiness. Just to have remained steadfast in itself would have been much. But she persisted until she made a greater usefulness of the hard conditions. She persisted until she saw herself in relation to things, to all things, and, right where she stayed, came to know the deeps of a serenity from which she could look out on whatsoever and be undismayed.

TECHNICAL DISCUSSION

1. This essay makes a mass of judgments, some well supported by data and some not. Be prepared to point out several judgments that are supported and several that are not.

2. Explain how it is possible for the author to make unsupported judgments. Do you question the validity of anything contained in this essay?

3. What is the chief concern of the first section? Point out the parts of this section that are the most concrete.

4. The second section is concerned with the lessons the mother taught her children. Are the lessons amply illustrated? Are the transitions between each discussion efficiently contrived?

5. Pick out the anecdotes. Do they illuminate the mother's traits, or are they put in chiefly for the sake of interest? Test your answer by looking for remarks that link the anecdote with a trait.

6. Though there is no central theme that gets all the support, the author does convey a dominant impression of his mother. What is it? Point out details or judgments that are slanted at the impression.

TOPICS FOR PAPERS

1. Write a character study of a person you know well. Before you begin the actual essay, select two or three of the person's main traits and jot down anecdotes or events that throw light on the traits. Get details of appearance and speech which also throw light on the traits.

2. Write a paper of reflective comment on literature classes as you have known and reacted to them. Be frank and sincere. Illustrate fully, but don't hesitate to use judgments that are not supported.

3. Recall the teacher you liked best (or disliked most) in your high school days and write an essay about him (her).

Practical Farming for Beginners

E. B. WHITE

My publishers have presented me with H. A. Highstone's book *Practical Farming for Beginners,* the sly inference being that I have much to learn. Publishers are on the whole well satisfied to have their writers disappear into rural circumstances, but they are genuinely concerned about how we put in our time. I am sure that, like parents whose children have left home, publishers are often visited with vague forebodings, sudden twinges of fear, the feeling that something is about to fall on writers—an eight-pound striking hammer perhaps, or a fit of loneliness.

There are ample grounds for this alarm. When a person who has been accustomed to making his living by writing attempts to combine this heavy work with the even heavier work of growing some of his own food the consequences may be grave. If recent book lists are any indication, the country must be overrun with writers who are whipping their environment into shape for publication. The strain is very great, on both nature and man, and I sometimes wonder which will crack first. There is something rather ominous about an impatient author, with a deadline to meet, keeping petulant vigil in a pumpkin patch so that he will be on time with his impressions of fall.

For me, always looking for an excuse to put off work, a farm is the perfect answer, good for twenty-four hours of the day. I find it extremely difficult to combine manual labor with intellectual, so I compromise and just do the manual. Since coming to the country I have devoted myself increasingly to the immediate structural and surgical problems which present themselves to any farmer, be he ever so comical in his methods and his designs. I have drifted farther and farther from my muse, and closer and closer to my post-hole digger.

The blurb which accompanies *Practical Farming for Beginners* states that the book will be welcomed by "an increasing number of American people who, fed up with the pressure of city living, are going back to the land for their livelihood." That shows that publishers do not understand the situation. Pressure of city living? No pressure which I ever knew in town compares with the pressure of country living. Never before in my life have I been so pressed as in the past two years. Forty acres can push a man hard even when he isn't in debt, provided he loves them and is an easy victim to the stuff he reads in the bulletins. Pressure! I've been on the trot now for a long time, and don't know whether I'll ever get slowed down. Today is our bean harvest, and even the beans in their screw-top jars are under pressure (ten pounds) in our new pressure canner, so hot are we to get them processed in one-third the time it might otherwise take. And when there is pressure up in the kitchen it transmits itself to the whole place, and the tension becomes noticeable in all departments.

One morning a few months ago, during a particularly busy time, when I awoke I didn't dare get dressed: I knew that my only hope of getting this column written was to stay in bed—which is where I did stay. I told my wife it was a slight sore throat, but it was a simple case of voluntary confinement. It was the first time I had ever taken to bed in the full blush of health simply because I didn't dare face the economic consequences of putting my pants on.

Mr. Highstone's book presents a formula for subsistence farming, that is, farming for consumption rather than for profit, farming to produce *all* one's wants. It is the best diagram of that scheme I have studied. It is hardboiled, sound, persuasive, and convincing. On that account I regard it as one of the most dangerous of books, capable of destroying whole families, wiping them out like flies; for it suggests that any city man of average ability can create, within a couple of years and with his own hands, a satisfactory and secure economy based on the land, independent of any other source. This I do not believe. I believe that relatively few city-bred men are capable of achieving self-sufficiency through farming, and that, on the whole, the ones that might be capable of it wouldn't be particularly interested in it. Mr. Highstone is obviously a man with a gift for organization. He possesses a dauntless spirit, a keen financial sense, and the sort of mechanical ability which makes him Jack-of-all-trades. He even writes well. He is informed, and he tells what he knows. His chapter called "The Chicken Trap" could only have been written by a man who had experienced the disappointments of an ill-planned poultry venture, and who had learned to hate the very guts of a hen. It should certainly be read and digested by any person who dreams of lightening his old age by collecting eggs at sundown.

Briefly Mr. Highstone's formula is this:

To sustain yourself on the land, you must first get straight in your head that there is to be no nonsense about "making a profit." There is to be no buying of chicken feed by the bag and marketing of eggs by the dozen cases. You must simply create a farm which will produce, directly, everything you need including a small regular cash income (not profit). Any deviation from this course will get you into hot water. Furthermore, you must have enough capital at the start so that you won't be mortgaging your future. Mr. Highstone tells you how many thousands of dollars you will need to get started, how many acres you must buy (how many in grass, how many in grain, how many in gardens), and he names the animals you will need, the number of tons of every grain you must produce, the extra amount of cream and eggs you must sell to provide the monthly check, and the equipment you will need in house and barn. He faces life with confidence, and by the time you have read the book you too will face life with confidence, and will believe that you can hitch a team and hold a plow.

To create a self-sustaining farm, he says, you must have the following set-up:

Three cows.

One hundred hens (no more, no less).

A team of horses (which you buy after reading *Farmer's Bulletin 779,* "How to Select a Sound Horse").

Three or four hogs. (Usually Mr. Highstone is much more specific than this, and says definitely three, or definitely four, but in this case there is a little leeway and you can decide between three hogs and four hogs.)

A hive of bees.

Enough land to grow all the feed for the above animals and for yourself and family, namely, ten tons of grain, fifteen tons of hay, and the usual vegetables and fruits. That's what you have to have. From these animals and this land you will receive all the food you and your family need, plus forty dollars a month—$25 from eggs, $15 from cream.

The principle on which this method of subsistence works is this:

The cow is the foundation on which the structure is built. The cow provides the means of producing, from the land, the indispensable commodities, milk, butter, and cheese. Furthermore the cow provides skim milk, the by-product which makes diversification possible. Skim milk contains the protein which makes chickens lay eggs and which makes hogs grow. This protein is ordinarily provided (on profit-and-loss farms) by expensive concentrates bought at a grain store—laying mash, hog ration, etc. Mr. Highstone will have you buy nothing, and he is very stern about that. It's forbidden, and if you start slipping and buy a bag of grain, your whole structure will topple. The cow also provides surplus cream, which is saleable and from which you get a monthly check, along with a check for the eggs which the hens laid because they were fed skim milk and which they wouldn't have laid if they had been on a straight grain diet.

The author admits that there is nothing new or original about this scheme; his contribution is in establishing the correct balance and in pointing out the fallacy of disturbing the balance by adding here or subtracting there. Thus the scheme falls, for instance, if the farmer reduces his hens to a flock of twelve or increases them to a flock of five hundred; twelve hens won't provide extra money from the sale of eggs, and five hundred hens will turn into a poultry farm and will take more time than a diversified farmer can give and will consume more food than he can raise on his property.

Mr. Highstone, being himself a practicing farmer, knows one important truth about country life: he knows that farming is about twenty per cent agriculture and eighty per cent mending something that has got busted. Farming is a sort of glorified repair job. This is a truth which takes some people years to discover, and many farmers go their whole lives without ever really grasping the idea. A good farmer is nothing more nor less than a handy man with a sense of humus. The repair aspect of farming looms so large that, on a place like my own, which is not really a farm at all but merely a private zoo, sometimes months go by when nothing but repair goes on. I can get so absorbed in the construction of a barn door that I can let the spring planting season go right by without ever opening the ground or planting a seed. If I were engaged in making myself self-sustaining I should perhaps be a little wider awake; but I know, from experience, that at any given moment of the year I should be found doing the wrong thing, and with a dull tool. I mention this because the weakness in Mr. Highstone's book is not in his plan for subsistence but in the people who are going to try to carry it out. In spite of all his warnings, there will be plenty of them who will get sidetracked, probably along the line of some special hobby, hitherto unindulged. I have been fooling around this place for a couple of years, but nobody calls my activity agriculture. I simply like to play with animals. Nobody knows this better than I do—although my neighbors know it well enough, and on the whole have been tolerant and sympathetic.

Mr. Highstone wisely insists that the man who intends to get a living from the land begin not by studying agronomy but by learning to hollow-grind an ax and file a saw. He insists that you equip yourself, immediately, with dozens of tools and implements including a pipe vise, a drill press, a forge, and a 2-horse stationary gasoline engine. "The fact," says Mr. Highstone, "that a man may be unfamiliar with some of them should never daunt him." I have a strong suspicion, although I know nothing about Mr. Highstone, that his years in the city were spent dreaming not so much about fields of ripening grain as about a shop equipped with a pipe vise. The ecstatic passages in his book are not the ones dealing with husbandry and tillage, but the ones dealing with edged tools. He demands that the subsistence farmer equip himself right at the start with four hundred dollars' worth of implements and tools, including a walking plow, a two-horse spike harrow, a one-horse row cultivator, a wire hayrake, a mowing machine, a buck rake, a stoneboat, a farm wagon, a roller, a disk harrow, and a long list of tools ending with an assortment of nuts and bolts, washers, and wood screws. (Incidentally, he forgot a crowbar, a clawbar, a block and tackle, and a pair of tinnersnips, without which my own life would be empty indeed.)

In all this, and in fact in his pattern for a self-contained farm, he seems to me essentially sound. It is only in his assumption that a city man of average intelligence, strength, and will power can operate a self-contained farm that he appears fanciful. Some of the bald statements in his book are open to question. He says: "Anyone with brains enough to pound sand can successfully raise chickens." I think that is a misleading pronouncement. Raising chickens (except in very small quantities) is partly luck, partly experience, and partly a sort of gift, or talent.

In another place Mr. Highstone actually suggests that the subsistence family harvest its own grain crop by mowing it with a mowing machine and making sheaves by hand. Remember that the grain harvest is ten tons, or 200 sacks of grain each weighing one hundred pounds. And remember also that the grain harvest comes at the same season as the canning—those 600 Mason jars that have to be filled. It would take a large family of stalwart sons and daughters to put through that program without cracking. Some of the jars are going to crack even if the children don't.

The life of self-sufficiency in this 20th century is the dream of persons with a nostalgic respect for early American vitality and ingenuity. It conflicts, temperamentally, with modern ways. If I were to attempt to put myself on a self-sustaining basis I know that for practical reasons I should have to throw the master switch in the cellar and send my regrets to the Power Company, not simply because I couldn't afford to buy power on forty dollars a month but because the possession of power in the households leads on into paths that are inimical to self-sufficiency. They lead direct to the profit (and loss) system. Mr. Highstone devotes a section to the septic tank and sewage-disposal system; but my first step in the direction of security on the land would be to abandon all flush toilets not because I don't approve of them but because they can destroy one's economy. People differ about plumbing. Mr. Highstone proposes to lick plumbing with a pipe vise. His is the manly approach. But I know my limitations. The practical way for me to lick plumbing is not to have any. I should also have to abandon my electric refrigerator, my electric water pump, my electric water heater, my electric lights, and I should have to sell my furnace and use the coal bin for storing root vegetables. There are days when I could take the leap with a glad cry; there are other days when I should hesitate.

The great service Mr. Highstone has rendered in his book is to clarify the scene. He tells what self-sufficiency means, tells where back-to-the-landers go wrong, and how they confuse the idea of being self-sustaining with the idea of running a country business for profit. Of course even the most realistic subsistence farmers are sometimes wanderers in the paths of evil. I can picture the day in the Highstone family when the news got round that Father was writing a book called *Practical Farming for Beginners*. He started secretly, but writers give themselves away eventually, and pretty soon the family knew that something was up.

"What's Pop doing, Mom?" one of the little Highstones asked.

"Sh-h, he's writing a book, dear," replied Mrs. Highstone.

"You can't eat a book, Mom."

"Well, no-o. But you see your father will receive money from the sale of the book, and with the money we can buy what we need."

"What about that sauerkraut he was going to put up today?"

"He will soon have money so we can *buy* some sauerkraut."

"Will we have sugar in our coffee instead of honey?"

"Maybe."

"That's cheating, isn't it, Mom?"

"I wouldn't know, darling. Ask your father."

And so, above the Highstone farm, the specter of Profit raised its ugly head.

TECHNICAL DISCUSSION

1. This essay is a book review written in a highly personal tone. Find judgments that apply to the book. Find judgments that seem to you strictly personal. Do the two elements clash? Explain.
2. Does the author identify the book he is reviewing?

3. Does the author summarize the contents and purpose of the book? Show evidence for your answer.

4. Which of the judgments about the book seem to you to be the most important?

5. Note that the author begins several of his paragraphs with Mr. Highstone's name. Explain why.

TOPICS FOR PAPERS

1. The College Experimental Farm and what it is doing for farm betterment.
2. The wood-lot (small, private forest) and its values in farm economy.
3. The work of 4-H clubs.
4. Soil conservation.
5. Vacation on a farm.

The Great Salmon Experiment

RICHARD L. NEUBERGER

The first white men to journey down the Columbia River were a pair of American Army officers named Meriwether Lewis and William Clark. They were amazed by what they saw. From shore to shore the vast river was clogged with fish. The arching backs of these fish flecked the water like waves as they surged upstream in hordes which took three weeks to pass a point where the river had trenched a gorge a mile wide. Twenty-foot falls they surmounted in mighty leaps, and they turned the shallow creeks of the headwaters into a seething mass of fins, tails, and silvery flanks.

Lewis and Clark knew they had seen the greatest fish resource in the land. "Never," they reported, "have so many fish been collected together in one place before." They told President Jefferson that there were enough Chinook salmon in the Columbia River to feed Americans for infinite generations to come.

But the frontiersmen were unaware that in the swift water inhabited by the salmon there lurked, too, a mysterious force capable of transforming the face of the continent which they had explored.

Lewis and Clark knew nothing of hydroelectricity. They did not know that the river they had followed through the mountains to the Pacific contained more latent water power than any other stream in North America. Nor could they possibly realize that full development of this unseen energy might bring about the unbelievable day when the last Chinook would flip its fins in the Columbia.

Two huge federal dams now span the Columbia River—Bonneville, at tidewater 152 miles from the sea, and Grand Coulee, 400 miles upstream from Bonneville. These dams make possible forty per cent of the aluminum production for America's military aircraft. In the top-priority postwar drawers of both the U. S. Army Engineers and the Department of the Interior are plans to construct eight more dams on the Columbia, notching the river into a giant staircase and generating five times the power produced in the whole TVA. If this proposal materializes—and many public works may be needed to cope with postwar unemployment—the U. S. Fish and Wildlife Service is ready with a corollary plan which calls for the most tremendous biological experiment in American history.

To save the principal fish runs in the nation, a commercial resource capitalized at $250,000,000, the Fish and Wildlife Service may have to transplant downstream to rivers near tidewater all the salmon and trout that now spawn in the tributaries of the Columbia between Bonneville and Grand Coulee.

What does this involve? Why is it so unprecedented in magnitude? Why does a committee of ichthyologists and fishermen recently appointed by Secretary of the Interior Ickes regard it as "a very difficult and extremely hazardous undertaking"? How good are the chances of success?

To understand the reasons for the experiment, it is necessary to understand the life cycle of the most remarkable creature of this hemisphere—the great Chinook or king salmon of the Pacific seaboard. No other beast, bird, or fish has so incredible an existence.

The baby salmon emerge four or five months after the adult fish have deposited millions of eggs far back in one of the mountain ranges which drain into the Columbia River. This is generally at the bottom of a foaming, gravel-strewn creek. After a year in what biologists call "the parent stream" the fry have developed into fingerlings five or six inches long. They drift down the creek, down innumerable other tributaries, and finally into the main stem of the Columbia. So at last they reach the sea, and there they remain for the bulk of their life. Exactly where they go no one is sure. They may range off the Alaskan coast. Possibly they swin to the Kamchatka. Perhaps they do not stray far from the Columbia's stormy mouth. After three years in the Pacific the salmon—a fingerling no longer but a strong, fighting fish powerful enough to conquer rapids and tear a hook from an angler's line—heeds the call of the river, just as once it responded to the urge of the sea.

The salmon fights its way upstream, stemming freshets and dodging nets and traps. Beside it swim all the other salmon which drifted down the Columbia more than three years before and have survived the perils of river and ocean. They thrash through rapids, over falls, up the ladders at Bonneville Dam, and deep into the uplands. Each fish hunts a particular creek or lake. This is what makes the Pacific salmon unique among wild creatures. The migrating Chinook does not seek *any* creek or lake, although the Columbia is ribbed with ten thousand tributaries, but rather the *one* creek or lake where half a decade earlier it emerged from the egg.

Sometimes a salmon will swim for miles up some canyon tributary only to discover that this is not the parent stream. In such a case, it retraces its course and pokes into another creek in search of its birthplace. Biologists have clipped the fins of fingerlings in the Kicking Horse River in the Canadian Rockies, the last glacial tributary of the Columbia. Five years later—in the British Columbia autumn—fish with these same markings have come back again, wanderers that found their home fifteen hundred weary miles from the ocean.

After it enters fresh water across the Columbia's bar a Chinook never feeds again. It will strike at a lure but will not take bait. The oily tissue beneath the salmon's scales must power it all the way to the parent stream. This oil is its fuel. Thus for countless epochs the strongest, stoutest-hearted, and biggest salmon specimens on earth have spawned in the final headwaters. Once the female fish has laid her eggs and the male has fertilized them, the life cycle of the Chinooks is completed. They drift downstream, tail foremost, and die within twenty-four hours.

Only one factor ever varies the pattern of this strange existence. If the salmon cannot reach the parent stream, it perishes without spawning.

If a series of dams is strung across the Columbia the Fish and Wildlife Service believes the one solution may be "to transplant the salmon runs inhabiting the upper tributaries to the rivers of the lower Columbia." Can this be done? Extraordinary though the experiment sounds, a similar one on a smaller scale has been going on for the past five years, and has met with remarkable success.

2

When Dr. Ira N. Gabrielson, director of the Fish and Wildlife Service, first saw Grand Coulee Dam looming above the Columbia like a great crenelated fortress, he knew that no Chinook ever would spawn again in the ultimate headwaters of the country's main salmon waterway. For as long as steel and concrete might endure, the 800 miles of river and the 100,000 square miles of watershed behind Grand Coulee were cut off as a spawning ground.

Bonneville Dam the fish could pass via wide, watery ladders. Bonneville, despite its 518,000-kilowatt capacity, is only 72 feet in height. Grand Coulee, largest edifice ever reared by man, towers 550 feet above the Columbia's granite bed. Water crashing over its parapet tumbles twice as far as Niagara Falls, with a roar heard for miles across the arid plateau of the Inland Empire. Not even the biggest salmon, which since time immemorial have spawned in the headwaters of the Columbia, could pass this battlement. In addition, the 151-mile lake formed back of the dam so raised the temperature of the river that most of the migrating salmon would be sure to die before they attained the spawning grounds. Chinooks en route to spawn are extremely susceptible to water variations.

Gabrielson and his associates answered this unique challenge with a unique solution. In 1939 they began trapping all the fish ascending the upper Columbia. The salmon were caught in specially designed cages at Rock Island Dam, a small structure a little below Grand Coulee built by the Puget Sound Power and Light Company. This dam was fitted with the best fish ladders ever constructed by a private utility corporation, and the traps were wedged into the ladders.

From the Rock Island traps the salmon were poured into long, 1,000-gallon tank trucks. Oxygen pumps and ice chambers kept the water in the trucks at the same temperature as the Columbia River. Aluminum paint warded off the glare of the sun. At a speed of 45 miles an hour, the fleet of eight silvery vehicles rolled up into the Cascade Mountains to the little town of Leavenworth, Washington, where the Fish and Wildlife Service had built the biggest fish hatchery in the world. Here the salmon were artificially propagated. Each female fish was hit on the head and split open for the precious eggs, approximately 10,000 to the female Chinook, considerably fewer to the smaller species. The sperm from the male salmon then was squirted onto the eggs. In fields of troughs and pools, the fingerlings thus were hatched and reared. To keep the water in Leavenworth's array of ponds at low temperature, the Forest Service drove a long rock tunnel tapping Ice Lake on the divide of the Cascades.

Finally the baby fish made their own excursion in the oxygenated tank trucks. They were driven to the sources of the Methow, Entiat, Okanogan, and Wenatchee Rivers and there dumped into the water. These streams join the Columbia *below* Grand Coulee Dam—the essential fact of the whole experiment. It manifestly is impossible for salmon ever to spawn again *above* Grand Coulee. The naturalists of the Fish and Wildlife Service were attempting to school the offspring of the salmon that spawned *above* Grand Coulee to take as their own parent streams tributaries which flow into the main river *below* Grand Coulee.

Frank A. Banks, the white-haired Bureau of Reclamation engineer who constructed Grand Coulee, once called this undertaking "Uncle Sam's Fish College."

Has Uncle Sam's Fish College trained its pupils? This past spring and fall told the tale. Up the Columbia forged the salmon which five years before had been the first class in the Fish College. They were the offspring of the fish originally trapped at Rock Island.

The weirs in the Rock Island traps were lifted for these voyagers. They were allowed to swim on through. The naturalists watched breathlessly. The critical question was whether the salmon would turn into the mouths of the Entiat, Okanogan, Methow, and Wenatchee Rivers or whether they would migrate on to Grand Coulee and perish in the man-made Niagara billowing over the crest of the dam.

Like well-drilled battalions, the fish swung off up the rivers in which they had been liberated as fingerlings four years before. No stragglers swam on to Coulee's impassable barrier, answering the upland call that had lured their ancestors. Chinooks marked for the Entiat and Methow swam unhesitatingly into those white-watered streams. Blueback salmon, a Columbia River version of the small but meaty Alaskan sockeye, spawn only in rivers with a lake at their source—rivers like the Okanogan and Wenatchee, into which the bluebacks turned as though they had been coached by a West Point drillmaster.

A few weeks ago Elmer Higgins, chief of the Division of Fishery Biology of the Wildlife Service, pronounced his verdict: "None of the salmon attempted to return to their ancestral spawning grounds above Grand Coulee Dam. The fish entered their appropriate streams, and it is expected that natural spawning now under way will be successful. We believe that the answer is conclusive—that the entire run of Columbia River salmon which formerly passed the site of Grand Coulee Dam has been transferred to the four major tributaries below the dam."

No longer will fish ascending the upper Columbia be trapped at Rock Island and artificially hatched at Leavenworth. The gates in the traps have been lifted permanently. The parent streams of these salmon are now rivers on the downstream side of Grand Coulee. After operation of Uncle Sam's Fish College from 1939 until 1944, five complete cycles of salmon have been put through the process. Yet Higgins interposes a few warnings:

> Present success does not mean, of course, that the races of salmon which through the ages have been adapted to conditions in the higher British Columbia tributaries of the Columbia River are equally adapted to conditions found in the streams to which they have been transplanted. It may well be that some of these races have suffered high mortality on being transplanted and may disappear from the Columbia River runs. We are hopeful, however, that most of the up-river fish have found conditions in their new parent streams sufficiently congenial to permit survival.

For the time being the experiment has succeeded—beyond their wildest dreams, some ichthyologists say. But this, after all, solves only part of the problem of saving the salmon runs.

In the past only about ten per cent of the Columbia's salmon have spawned back of Grand Coulee. They have been the largest fish in size but comparatively few in numbers. What about the others? Most of the salmon find their parent stream between Bonneville and Grand Coulee. These are the fish which must be transplanted if the other projected dams are built. Will artificial propagation and transplanting be successful when the number of salmon involved is multiplied many times? Hatchery fish seldom have the vitality and stamina of their wild brethren.

3

There are other obstacles to be overcome if the vast salmon industry is to be kept alive. The incursions of civilization on the miraculous life cycle of the salmon are not limited to cutting off the upland breeding grounds. Survival of the salmon depends on three conditions: (1) enough fish must escape the commercial nets at sea and near the mouth of the Columbia to get upstream to spawn; (2) the upstream spawning grounds must be protected from pollution and diversion, as well as blockade; and (3) the fingerlings must be able to migrate safely to the ocean.

These conditions have not been met for many years. They are not being met now.

In 1885, when the first trains of the Northern Pacific were swaying through the Columbia Gorge, canneries scooped out of the Columbia's wide waters 31,493,000 pounds of Chinook salmon. The canneries are still hauling fish out of the river—though by 1940 their output had been reduced by almost half. And the salmon are subject to peril from other sources too. Trollers take a deadly toll at sea. Cannery fishermen at Swiftsure Bank, off the entrance to Puget Sound, have caught nearly $10,000,000 worth of salmon every year for many decades. Swimming upstream, the fish must run another gauntlet of nets. Indian spearsmen at Celilo Falls have a treaty with the United States government, negotiated in 1855, which allows them to fish in the Columbia River for "as long as grass shall grow on the hills and the sun shall set in the sky."

Will the salmon last that long?

"Civilization and salmon don't mix," I was told by Grady Miller, hawk-nosed forest ranger at Wallowa Lake in Oregon, as he stood below a dam constructed across the lake's outlet, a dam built by a private utility company that completely destroyed one of the most valuable runs of blueback salmon in the region.

In recent years the settlement and exploitation of the Pacific Northwest have been greatly accelerated. Developments which might logically have required several decades have been compressed into a dozen months. The war has brought about an intensive demand for food, raw materials, and manufactured products of all sorts. Factories and shipyards have sprung up where not so long ago heron waded and deer foraged. Trees marked by forest rangers for protection and preservation have been sawed into beams, crates, and deck planks. Water which once a tired hiker could drink now bears the chemical residue of paper mills and metal plants and the sewage of new mushrooming war communities. Cattle and sheep have grazed off the bunch grass anchoring the silt on a thousand hillsides. War demands minerals, too, and the slag from mines helps to fill up creeks and choke rivers. Neither salmon nor the insect and crustacean life which sustains them as fingerlings can compete with this pollution and waste.

Not so long ago a large salmon run surged up the Willamette River each fall, leaping the nineteen-foot cataract at Oregon City in spectacular flips. Now no autumn Chinooks invade this major tributary of the Columbia. The offal, chemicals, and junk poured into the water at Portland have killed them off. One afternoon the Oregon State Game Commission released a batch of fingerlings in the Willamette below the interurban bridge. A few minutes later they floated bellies up. There had not been enough oxygen in the river to sustain them.

Even the fingerlings that do not have to cope with hazards of this sort must take their chances with man-made obstructions on their way down to the sea. At Bonneville Dam, where the fish ladders have proved successful and the returning salmon traverse them quickly and easily, the little fish on their way to the sea are at the mercy of the river. They cannot pick out the ladders. They must take the course of least resistance. Often they do not find the fingerling by-passes provided especially for them—concrete flumes which honeycomb the powerhouse. Most of the fingerlings are swept over the spillway. In the maelstrom at the base of the dam some of the baby fish die.

When Bonneville first was completed, the Oregon State Fish Commission released batches of fingerlings both above and below the dam. There were fifty thousand fingerlings in each batch. The fins of the fish were clipped in distinctive patterns so that the two groups could be distinguished. Awards were paid both commercial and sports fishermen for salmon with marked fins which they turned in. At the end of the fourth year they had turned in a considerably larger number of the salmon released *below* the dam than of those released above it. From this test biologists have come to the conclusion that perhaps 25 per cent of the fingerlings going down the Columbia are killed by the stunning impact of the Bonneville spillway. How great an effect will this have on the future of the salmon runs? Here again, the certainties are not yet known.

The fish ladders at Bonneville have made possible for the first time in history an accurate count of the salmon ascending the upper Columbia. These are wide watery staircases which cost $7,022,000 and were built by the Army Engineers with the constant advice of the Wildlife Service. Since the dam was completed in 1938, every salmon passing it on the way back upstream to the spawning grounds has been clocked by fish-counters who sit in doghouse-like structures, tapping a meter whenever a fish flips through the grating at the top of each ladder.

The fish count at Bonneville during the past seven years has just been released by the Bonneville Power Administration. This is it:

Year	*Chinook Salmon*	*Blueback Salmon*	*Silver Salmon*	*Steelhead Trout*
1938...	271,799	75,040	15,185	107,003
1939...	286,216	73,382	14,382	121,922
1940...	391,595	148,808	18,822	185,174
1941...	461,713	65,741	17,011	118,087
1942...	403,938	55,464	12,041	151,346
1943...	313,123	39,845	2,547	92,131
1944*..	238,191	15,071	4,073	93,047

* Up to and including October. (By this month the main run has gone up the river.)

What do these figures mean? What story do they tell a biologist? Inasmuch as the Bonneville Dam first barricaded the river in 1938, the progeny of the first fish passing through the ladders came back upstream five years later. That was 1943, a year the count of Chinooks went tolerably high. Why has the count been so low for 1944? Did Bonneville in any way cause these discouraging figures? Why was the count comparatively low in 1938, long before the dam could have had any effect at all? Why has the number of bluebacks dropped so sharply? Why have silver salmon almost completely disappeared from the Columbia? Why did the Bonneville count in Chinooks soar from a low total in 1938 to its highest point in 1941, and then gradually descend to an even lower level for 1944?

"I wish I could answer these questions," declared Elmer Higgins, "but we are in the dark too. This is the first time we ever had a salmon count on the Columbia. Considerable variations may be normal over a span of years. We have no previous standards to go by. But it is far more probable that the small 1944 count is due to the cumulative effect of uncontrolled commercial fishing for many seasons, as well as to the excessive exploitation of mineral, soil, and forest resources which guard the watershed."

But the naturalists do know several facts for a certainty so far as Bonneville Dam is concerned. First and foremost, the Bonneville fish ladders have been a success. Few fish on their way upstream collect in baffled schools at the base of the dam. Virtually all of them find the entrance to one of the big watery staircases. On a single September day in 1940 the ladders were spanned by 33,900 Chinooks, which turned the passages into a boiling melee of fins and backs. Even men who claimed the government was going "dam crazy" now concede that the Bonneville ladders are by far the best fishways ever built.

4

On the wall of Dr. Gabrielson's office hangs a map showing how man-made encroachments have gradually shrunk the spawning areas available to salmon in the Columbia Basin. An impassable dam here, unscreened irrigation ditches there, indiscriminate dumping of sewage and chemical wastes of a hundred towns, logged-off slopes, dredging for minerals—all this has blocked off nearly two thirds of the lakes and creeks where fish originally spawned. Today only a few major tributaries still offer sanctuary to the fish which come home from the sea with the autumn equinox.

In December the Fish and Wildlife Service reported, "The piecemeal destruction of the Columbia River spawning grounds has proceeded to such a point that no more tributary streams can be sacrificed if the largest salmon river in the United States is to continue to contribute materially to the nation's food supply."

To provide adequate spawning ground it may be necessary to move the entire salmon run downstream and to blow up the dams on the Clackamas, Sandy, and several other rivers near the tidewater. The plan contemplates trapping all migrating salmon in the Bonneville Dam ladders and propagating them in a series of immense hatcheries far larger than the facilities at Leavenworth. Then the resultant fingerlings would be released in the few available rivers near the sea.

The likelihood of successful transfer downstream is subject to many imponderables. Is there room in the lowland tributaries for the immense aquatic life of the Columbia? Will fish adapted to the high mountains spawn in rivers at tidewater? How many salmon will be lost in the elaborate transplanting process? Will the vitality of the species be irretrievably sapped by the intervening hatchery propagation? At what point does biology rebel against man's intrusion?

And at what point does the biologist rebel at the intrusion of the dam-builder? A vast new project imperils the salmon that survive. There exists the possibility that the construction of new dams is the wise course. The proposed structures would generate 5,894,300 kilowatts of power at the cheapest rates on earth. This hydroelectricity might rehabilitate countless other resources spent by the waste of war. It is claimed that the Grand Coulee Dam will turn arid sagebrush into 40,000 productive farms; that Umatilla Dam will cut down the cost of fuel shipped to the Inland Empire and reduce the price of the wheat, fruit, and beef that are transported out of that spacious region.

With these benefits in mind, the Fish and Wildlife Service has admitted that "the economic importance of water for purposes other than the propagation of fish is such that it cannot and should not be used solely for the sake of maintaining salmon runs. If conservation is wise use, it is the part of true conservation to choose the more valuable use of a resource whenever two or more uses conflict in such a way as to be mutually exclusive."

If the dam project is undertaken the vast salmon experiment will go on. Millions of eggs will be fertilized, millions of fingerlings sent on their way down to the sea, their fins clipped for identification. Each year, as one class of Uncle Sam's Fish College is graduated, alumni of a previous class will return for their quinquennial reunion on the tidewater tributaries of the Columbia. Each year the faculty will be that much wiser.

TECHNICAL DISCUSSION

1. Why does the author begin with the story about Lewis and Clark?
2. Why does the author ask so many questions in the sixth paragraph?
3. Write a topical outline of this essay, showing major topics.
4. Does the author use experimental data to support some of his conclusions?
5. One of the values of this essay is that it asks questions for which there are as yet no answers. What are some of the questions?
6. Find several effective transitions.
7. How do you think the author gathered his material?
8. Is the last paragraph a summary?

TOPICS FOR PAPERS

1. How salmon get over Bonneville Dam.
2. A report on TVA.
3. Fish hatcheries: how the fish are reared, economic values, getting ready for opening day of the trout season, etc.
4. The story of the accident that destroyed the Fraser River salmon run.
5. Life-cycle of the salmon: the complete tale.
6. Canning fish: a process.

The American Language

H. L. MENCKEN

The first Englishman to notice an Americanism sneered at it aloofly, thus setting a fashion that many of his countrymen have been following ever since. He was one Francis Moore, a ruffian who came out to Georgia with Oglethorpe in 1735, and the word that upset him was *bluff,* in the sense of "a cliff or headland with a broad precipitous face." He did not deign to argue against it; he simply dismissed it as "barbarous," apparently assuming that all Englishmen of decent instincts would agree with him. For nearly a century they seem to have done so, and *bluff* lingered sadly below the salt. When it was printed at all in Great Britain it was set off by sanitary quotation marks, or accompanied by other hints of deprecation, as *rubberneck, hot spot* and *nerts* are accompanied today. But then, in 1830, the eminent Sir Charles Lyell used it shamelessly in the first volume of his monumental "Principles of Geology," and from that day to this it has been a perfectly respectable if somewhat unfamiliar word in England, with a place in every dictionary.

Its history is the history of almost countless other Americanisms. They have been edging their way into English since early colonial times, and, for more than a century past, in constantly increasing volume, but I can't recall one that didn't have to run a gantlet of opposition in the motherland, at times verging upon the frantic. After the Revolution, that opposition took on the proportions of a holy war. Never an American book came out that the English reviewers did not belabor its vocabulary violently. The brunt of the attack, of course, had to be borne by the poetasters of the era—for example, Joel Barlow, whose "Columbiad" (1807) loosed a really terrifying geyser of abuse. But even the most serious writers got their share—among them, Jefferson, John Marshall, Noah Webster, and John Quincy Adams. Jefferson's crime was that he had invented the verb *to belittle.* It was, one may argue plausibly, a very logical, useful, and perhaps even nifty word, and seventy-five years later the prissy Anthony Trollope was employing it without apology. But when Jefferson ventured to use it in his "Notes on Virginia" (1787) "The London Review" tossed and raged in a manner befitting the discovery of a brace of duelling pistols beneath the cope of the Archbishop of Canterbury, and for several years following its dudgeon was supported virtuously by most of the other reviews. "What an expression!" roared the "London." "It may be an elegant one in Virginia, but for our part, all we can do is to *guess* at its meaning. For shame, Mr. Jefferson! Freely, good sir, will we forgive all your attacks, impotent as they are illiberal, upon our national character; but for the future spare—O spare, we beseech you, our mother-tongue!"

The underscoring of *guess* was a fling in passing at another foul Americanism. It was the belief of most Englishmen then, as it is today, that the use of the verb in the sense of *to suppose* or *assume* originated in this country. It is actually to be found, in that meaning precisely, in "Measure for Measure" and "Henry VI"; nay, in Chaucer, Wycliffe, and Gower. But such historical considerations have never daunted the more ardent preservers of the King's English. When a word acquires an American flavor it becomes anathema to them, even though it may go back to Boadicea. *To advocate* offers an instructive example. It appeared in English in the dark backward and abysm of time, but during the eighteenth century it seems to have dropped out of general use, though Burke used it. Towards the end of the century it came into vogue in this country, and soon it made its way back to the land of its birth. It was received with all the honors proper to an invasion of Asiatic cholera. The reviews denounced it as loutish, "Gothic," and against God, and lumped it with *to compromit* and *to happify* as proof that civilization was impossible in America, and would be so forevermore. Even Benjamin Franklin, returning from England in 1789, was alarmed into begging Noah Webster to "reprobate" it, along with *to notice, to progress,* and *to oppose*. There is no record of Noah's reply, but it is most unlikely that he did any reprobating, for when he began to make dictionaries he included all four verbs, and they have been listed in every considerable dictionary published since, whether in this country or in England.

The leader of the heroic struggle to keep Americanisms out of Britain, in its early stages, was the celebrated William Gifford, editor of "The Quarterly Review." Gifford was a killer in general practice, and his savage assaults on Wordsworth, Shelley, and Keats are still unpleasantly remembered. He was the first magazine editor in history to make the trade pay, and when he died in 1828 he left £25,000 and was buried in Westminster Abbey. One of his major specialties was the villainousness of everything American, from politics to table manners and from theology to speechways. Among the allegations that he either made himself or permitted his contributors to make were these: (*a*) that the Americans employed naked colored women to wait upon them at table, (*b*) that they kidnapped Scotsmen, Irishmen, Hollanders, and Welshmen and sold them into slavery, and (*c*) that they were planning to repudiate the English language altogether, and adopt Hebrew in its place. This last charge, as it flew from tongue to tongue, acquired variorum readings. One of them made the new American language an Indian dialect, another made it Greek, and a third was to the effect that the people of Britain would be forced to acquire Greek, thus leaving English to the wicked will of the barbaric Yankees. It all sounds idiotic today, but in 1814 it was taken quite seriously by many Englishmen. Gifford was a tyrannical editor and so vastly enjoyed slashing his contributors' copy that Southey once denounced him as "a butcherly review-gelder." But anything that was against the dam-yankee passed his eye unscathed, and he piled up accusations in a manner so shameless that "The North American Review" was moved to protest that if the tirade went on it would "turn into bitterness the last drops of good-will towards England that exist in the United States."

In the early Twenties of that century there was some amelioration, and when Gifford retired from the "Quarterly" in 1824, voices that were almost conciliatory began to be heard. They heaped praises on Niagara Falls, found something to commend in Cooper's "Spy," and even had kind words for the speed and luxuriousness of American canalboats. But my most diligent researches have failed to unearth anything complimentary to the American language. It continued to be treated as a grotesque and immoral gibberish, full of uncouth terms and at war with all the canons of English. Every British traveller who came to these shores between the War of 1812 and the Civil War had something to say about the neologisms his ears and eyes encountered on his tour, and nearly all were constrained to deplore them. Captain Basil Hall, who was here in 1827 and 1828, went about in a palpitating daze, confounded and outraged by the signs on American places of business. *Clothing Store* he interpreted after long thought, and *Flour and Feed Store* after prayer and soul-searching, but what on earth was a *Leather and Finding Store?* Captain Thomas Hamilton, who followed five years later, found it impossible to penetrate to "the precise import" of *Dry-Goods Store,* and when he encountered an establishment offering *Hollow Ware, Spiders, and Fire-Dogs* he gave up in despair.

Hall was not one to take it lying down. He decided to call upon Noah Webster, whose American Dictionary of the English Language had just come out, to find out what the Yankees meant by using the mother tongue so cruelly. Webster shocked him by arguing stoutly that "his countrymen had not only a right to adopt new words, but were obliged to modify the language to suit the novelty of the circumstances, geographical and political, in which they were placed." The great lexicographer "who taught millions to spell but not one to sin" went on to observe judicially that it was "quite impossible to stop the progress of language—it is like the course of the Mississippi, the motion of which, at times, is scarcely perceptible; yet even then it possesses a momentum quite irresistible. Words and expressions will be forced into use in spite of all the exertions of all the writers in the world."

"But surely," persisted Hall, "such innovations are to be deprecated?"

"I don't think that," replied old Noah. "If a word becomes universally current in America, where English is spoken, why should it not take its station in the language?"

"Because," declared Hall with magnificent pertinacity, "there are words enough already."

This heroic dogma is still heard in England, where even native novelties are commonly opposed violently, and not infrequently strangled at birth. There seems to be, in the modern Englishman, very little of that ecstasy in word-making which so prodigiously engrossed his Elizabethan forebears. Shakespeare alone probably put more new words into circulation than all the English writers since Carlyle, and they were much better ones. The ideal over there today is not picturesque and exhilarating utterance, but correct and reassuring utterance, and one of its inevitable fruits is that bow-wow jargon which Sir Arthur Quiller-Couch describes in "On the Art of Writing" as "the medium through which boards of government, county councils, syndicates, committees, commercial firms, express the processes as well as the conclusions of their thought, and so voice the reason of their being." It is, at its worst, at least in accord with what are taken to be the principles of English grammar, and at its best it shows excellent manners and even a kind of mellifluous elegance; indeed, the English, taking one with another, may be said to write much better than we do—at all events by the standards of the schoolmaster. But what they write is seldom animated by anything properly describable as bounce. It lacks novelty, variety, audacity. There is little juice in it. The reader confronted by it is treated politely and lulled pleasantly, but he seldom enjoys the enchantment of surprise. That diligent search for new and racy locutions which occupied so much of the work day of Walt Whitman and William Dean Howells alike, and is practised so assiduously by scores of saucy Andersons and Hemingways, Sandburgs and Saroyans today, is carried on across the ocean by only a few extravagant eccentrics, virtually all of whom—for example, James Joyce and Ezra Pound—are non- and even anti-Englishmen. The hundred-per-cent English writers, save when they stoop to conscious wickedness, seldom depart very far from the jargon of Quiller-Couch. It is by no means a monopoly of the classes he named, nor is it reserved for solemn occasions. I find it also in my favorite English weekly, the "News of the World," which is devoted principally to sports, the theatres, and the more scabrous varieties of crime, and is probably a far better mirror of England than the "Times." When the "News of the World" reports the downfall of a rural dean or a raid on a Mayfair night club, the thing is done in a style so tight and brittle that nothing to match it is discoverable in this country, at least outside the pages of "The Homiletic Review." "When we want to freshen our speech," Mrs. Virginia Woolf was lately saying, "we borrow from American—*poppycock, rambunctious, flip-flop, booster, good mixer.* All the expressive, ugly, vigorous slang which creeps into use among us, first in talk, later in writing, comes from across the Atlantic."

But whether slang or something better, it always encounters opposition—sometimes merely sullen, but at other times extremely violent. At more or less regular intervals, war upon the invasion is declared formally, and there ensues a long uproar, with the papers full of choleric letters to the editor. One such sharpening of activity was loosed early in 1933, when the chief constable of Wallasey, a suburb of Liverpool, reported in alarm that his policemen were being called *cops* by the tougher youngsters of the place, and otherwise insulted with blasphemies picked up from American movies. "*Oh-yeahs,*" he said, "are frequent in answer to charges, and we are promised *shoots-up in the burg* [*sic*] and threatened to be *bumped off*." Half the amateur publicists who took a hand in the discussion which followed advocated using the cat on the offenders, and the other half demanded that American movies be barred from England as intolerable public menaces, like cattle infected with foot-and-mouth disease. As usual, the debate ended in philological futilities. Was *oh yeah* actually English, even bad English, insane English? Or was it only an American borrowing from one of the dialects of the savage Red Indians, or maybe from Polish, Pennsylvania Dutch, Gullah, Yiddish, or some other such godless and anti-British lingo? No matter! *Oh yeah* continues to flourish from the Lizard to Unst, and with it *cop* flourishes too. The latter, in fact, has swept upward from the level of bad boys baiting constables to that of bishops following their transcendental occasions. Even before the chief constable of Wallasey sounded his cry of "Wolf!" a right reverend father in God had been charged before the Farnham (Surrey) magistrates with applying *speed-cop* on a public road to a member of the *mobile police*. Overhauled in his car, so the testimony went, he had demanded, "Are you a *speed-cop?*" His Lordship denied with some heat that he had used the term, or anything else so unseemly, but the magistrates apparently concluded that he must have let it slip, for they took a serious view of his very modest adventure in speeding, fined him £10, and suspended his driving license for three months. I give his name and dignities as a warning to lesser evildoers. He was the Right Reverend Cyril Henry Gelding-Bird, D.D. (Oxon.), Assistant Bishop of Guildford and Archdeacon of Dorking, and a man previously unknown to the police.

Whenever an Americanism comes publicly into question in England, there are efforts to track down its etymology, and sometimes the theories offered are extremely bizarre. In January, 1935, for example, the London "Morning Post" opened its columns to a furious and fantastic discussion of the verb-phrase, *to get his goat*. I content myself with one of the explanations: "Among the Negroes in Harlem it is the custom for each household to keep a goat to act as general scavenger. Occasionally one man will steal another's goat, and the household débris then accumulates to the general annoyance." The truth is that *to get his goat* seems to be of French origin, and in the form of *prendre sa chèvre,* philological genealogists have traced it back to the year 1585. But whatever is strange and upsetting is put down, in England, to the hellish ingenuity of Americans—save, of course, when genuine Americanisms are claimed as really English. This last happens often enough to give what may be called a cockeyed aspect to the perennial pother. In 1934 even the learned Dr. C. T. Onions, one of the editors of the great Oxford Dictionary, succumbed to the madness by offering to find in the dictionary any alleged Americanism that a reporter for the London "Evening News" could name. The reporter began discreetly with *fresh* (in the sense of *saucy*), *to figure* (in the sense of *to believe* or *conclude*), and *to grill* (in the sense of *to question*), and Dr. Onions duly found them all. But when the reporter proceeded to *bunkum,* the learned editor had to forget conveniently that its progenitor was the thoroughly American *buncombe,* when *rake-off* followed he had to admit that the earliest example in the dictionary was from an American work, and when *boloney* and *nerts* were hurled at him he blew up with a bang.

Here, of course, Dr. Onions and his interlocutor ended on the level of slang, but there is no telling where they would be if they could be translated to the year 2036. *Boloney,* like *to belittle,* has the imprimatur of an eminent tribune of the people, and is quite as respectable, philologically speaking, as *buncombe, gerrymander, pork barrel, filibuster, carpetbagger, gag rule,* or *on the fence*. All these came into American from the argot of politics, and got only frowns from the schoolmarm, but they are all quite sound American today, and most of them have gone into English. As for *nerts,* it seems to be but one more member of an endless dynasty of euphemisms, beginning with *zounds* and coming down to *son-of-a-gun, gee,* and *darn*. *Darn,* like *nerts,* is an

Americanism, and Dr. Louise Pound has demonstrated that it descends from *eternal,* which first turned into *tarnal* and then lost its tail and borrowed the head of *damn.* I have heard a bishop use it freely in private discourse, with a waggish sprinkling of actual *damns. Son-of-a-gun* is now so feeble and harmless that the Italians in America use it as a satirical designation for native Americans, who seem to them to fall far behind the Italian talent for profanity and objurgation. It is, I believe, a just criticism. Some time ago I was engaged by a magazine to do an article on American and English swearwords. After two or three attempts I had to give it up, for I found that neither branch of our ancient Frisian tongue could show anything worthy of serious consideration. The antinomians of England stick to two or three banal obscenities, one of which, *bloody,* is obscene only formally, and we Americans seldom get beyond variations of *hell* and *damn.* A single Neapolitan boatman could swear down the whole population of Anglo-Saxondom.

Bloody is perfectly innocuous in the United States, and it may be innocuous in England also on some near tomorrow—or even more disreputable than it is today. There is no predicting the social career of words. Dr. Leonard Bloomfield says that even "our word *whore,* cognate with the Latin *carus* (dear), must have been at one time a polite substitute for some term now lost." Prophecy fails just as dismally when propriety does not come into question. Shakespeare's numerous attempts to introduce new words, some of them his own inventions and others borrowed from the slang of the Bankside, failed almost as often as they succeeded. He found ready takers for *courtship, lonely, sportive, multitudinous, hubbub* and *bump,* but his audiences would have none of *definement,* in the sense of description, or of *citizen* as an adjective, and both seem strange and uncouth to us today, though all the others are as familiar and as decorous as *cat* or *rat.* When John Marston used *strenuous* in 1599 it was attacked by Ben Jonson as barbarous, but a dozen years later it had got into Chapman's Homer, and in 1670 it was being used by Milton. It remained perfectly respectable until 1900, when Theodore Roosevelt announced the Strenuous Life. Both the idea and the term struck the American fancy, and in a little while the latter passed into slang, and was worn so threadbare that all persons of careful speech sickened of it. To this day it carries a faintly ridiculous connotation, and is seldom used seriously. But by 1975 it may be restored to the dignity of *psychopath* or *homoousian*. No one can say yes with any confidence, and no one can say no. "Even the greatest purist," observes Robert Lynd, "does not object to the inclusion of *bogus* in a literary English vocabulary, though a hundred years ago it was an American slang word meaning an apparatus for coining false money. *Carpetbagger* and *bunkum* are other American slang words that have naturalized themselves in English speech, and *mob* is an example of English slang that was once as vulgar as *photo*."

Three Americanisms borrowed by English to one Briticism come into American! The true score, I suspect, is even more favorable to the Yankee as word-maker. Down to 1820, according to Sir William Craigie, the trans-Atlantic trade in neologisms ran mainly westward, but then it began to shift, and today it is very heavily eastward. It would be difficult to recall a dozen British inventions that have entered the common American vocabulary since the First World War, but the number of Americanisms taken into English must run to hundreds, and perhaps even to thousands. The American movie and talkie, of course, have been responsible for the introduction of many of them, but there is something beyond that, and something more fundamental. They are adopted in England simply because England has nothing to offer in competition with them—that is, nothing so apt or pungent, nothing so good. His Lordship of Guildford did not apply *speed-cop* to that *mobile policeman* as a voluntary act of subversion, born of a desire to shock and insult the realm; he let it slip for the single reason that it was an irresistibly apposite and satisfying term. And so with all the other Americanisms that challenge and consume their British congeners. They win fairly on palpable points and by every rule of the game. Confronted by the same novelty, whether in object or in situation, the Americans always manage to fetch up a name for it that not only describes it but also illuminates it, whereas the English, since the Elizabethan stimulant oozed out of them, have been content merely to catalogue it. There was a brilliant exemplification of the two approaches in the early days of railways. The English, having to name the wedge-shaped fender that was put in front of the first locomotives, called it a *plough,* which was almost exactly what it was, but the Americans gave it the bold and racy appellation of *cow-catcher*. For the casting which guides the wheels from one rail to another the English coined the depressingly obvious name of *crossing-plate;* the Americans, setting their imaginations free, called it a *frog*. The same sharp contrast appears every time there is a call for a new word today. The American *movie* is obviously much better than the English *cinema;* it is even better English. So is *radio* better than *wireless,* though it may be Latin, and *job-holder* better than *public servant,* though it is surely literal enough, and *shock absorber* vastly better than *anti-bounce clip,* and *highball* than *whisky and soda,* and *bouncer* than *chucker-out,* and *chain store* than *multiple shop,* and *string bean* than *French bean,* and *union suit* than *combination*. Confronting the immensely American *rubberneck,* Dr. J. Y. T. Greig of Newcastle could only exclaim "one of the best words ever coined!" And in the face of *lounge lizard,* Horace Annesley Vachell fell silent like Sir Isaac Newton on the seashore, overwhelmed by the solemn grandeur of the linguistic universe.

One finds in current American all the characters and tendencies that marked the rich English of Shakespeare's time—an eager borrowing of neologisms from other languages, a bold and often very ingenious use of metaphor, and a fine disdain of the barricades separating the parts of speech. The making of new words is not carried on only, or even principally, to fill gaps in the vocabulary; indeed, one may well agree with Captain Hall that "there are words enough already." It is carried on because there survives in the American something that seems to have faded out of the Englishman: an innocent joy in word-making for its own sake, a voluptuous delight in the vigor and elasticity of the language. The search for the *mot juste* is an enterprise that is altogether too pedantic for him; he much prefers to solve his problem by non-Euclidian devices. *Hoosegow* was certainly not necessary when it appeared, for we already had a large repertory of synonyms for *jail*. But when the word precipitated itself from the Spanish *juzgado* somewhere along the Rio Grande it won quick currency, and in a little while it was on the march through the country, and soon or late, I suppose, it will produce its inevitable clipped forms, *hoose* and *gow,* and its attendant adjective and verb. *Corral,* which entered by the same route in the Forties of the last century, had hatched a verb before the Civil War, and that verb, according to Webster's New International (1934) now has four separate and distinct meanings. *Bummer,* coming in from the German, is now clipped to *bum,* and is not only noun, verb, and adjective but also adverb. *Buncombe,* borrowed by the English as *bunkum,* has bred *bunco* and *bunk* at home, both of which rove the parts of speech in a loose and easy way, and the last of which has issue in the harsh verb *to debunk,* still under heavy fire in England.

The impact of such lawless novelties upon the more staid English of the motherland is terrific. The more they are denounced as heathen and outlandish, the quicker they get into circulation. Nor do they prosper only on the level of the vulgate, and among careless speakers. There are constant complaints in the English newspapers about their appearance in the parliamentary debates, and even in discourses from the sacred desk, and they begin to show themselves also in *belles lettres,* despite the English dislike of new ways of writing. Their progress, in fact, is so widespread and so insidious that they often pop up in the diatribes that revile them; the Englishman, conquered at last, can no longer protest against Americanisms without using them. Moreover, they are now supported actively by a definitely pro-American party of writers and scholars, and though it is still small in numbers, at least compared to the patriot band, it shows some distinguished names. The late Robert Bridges, Poet Laureate, was an active member of it, and among its other adherents are Wyndham Lewis, Edward Shanks, Richard Aldington, and Sir John Foster Fraser. Sir William Craigie, perhaps the first of living lexicographers, is so greatly interested in the American form of English that he has spent the years since 1925 in a scientific examination of it, and will presently begin the publication of an elaborate dictionary. If only because of the greater weight of the population behind it, it seems destined to usurp the natural leadership of British English, and to determine the general course of the language hereafter. But its chief advantage in this struggle is really not the numerical one, but the fact that its daring experiments and iconoclasms lie in the grand tradition of English, and are signs of its incurable normalcy and abounding vigor.

How far it will move away from the theorizing of grammarians and the policing of schoolmarms remains to be seen. They still make valiant efforts to curb its wayward spirit, but with gradually diminishing success. When, a few years ago, the late Sterling A. Leonard of the University of Wisconsin submitted a long series of their admonitions to a committee of educated Americans, including many philologians, he found that opinion was against them on that high level almost as decidedly as it was on lower ones. His judges favored scores of forms that the school grammars and popular handbooks of usage still condemn. Since then a more direct attack upon the conservative position has been made by Dr. Robert C. Pooley of the same university. He shows that some of the rules laid down with most assurance by pedants have no support in either history or logic, and are constantly violated by writers of unquestionable authority. There have even been rumblings of revolt in the conservative camp. The late George Philip Krapp of Columbia, who was surely anything but a radical, was of the opinion that English would undergo profound changes in the United States, and that many of them would be of such a character that its very grammatical structure would be shaken. Dr. George O. Curme of Northwestern University is another eminent grammarian who warns his colleagues that the rules they cherish have no genuine authority, and must be overhauled from time to time. Once they steel themselves to that sacrifice of their professional dignity, he says, "it will give a thrill to English-speaking students to discover that the English language does not belong to the schoolteacher but belongs to them, and that its future destiny will soon rest entirely in their hands."

Dr. Curme is always careful to think and speak of American as no more than a variation of English. But it must be obvious that, in late years, the tail has begun a vigorous wagging of the dog. "The facts that we ought to realize," says Edward Shanks to his fellow Britons, "and that we ignore when we talk loftily about Americanisms, are that America is making a formidable contribution to the development of our language, and that all our attempts to reject that contribution will in the long run be vain."

TECHNICAL DISCUSSION

1. Why does the author begin with a brief story about the word *bluff?*

2. Prepare a list, fully stated, of the author's judgments about the good qualities of American English.

3. Why does the author italicize the words he writes about?

4. Find several judgments about the English attitude toward Americanisms.

5. The author keeps a good balance between judgment and data. Point out some of the judgments and their data. Find, if you can, some unsupported judgments.

TOPICS FOR PAPERS

1. Write a paper that sets forth and defines the special vocabulary of any occupation or activity that you know: railroading, baseball, sawmilling, flying, etc.

2. Spend a half hour or so looking into the *Oxford English Dictionary.* Select a word that interests you, such as *gentle, housewife, boycott,* and write an essay that presents informally what you find in the dictionary about the word. If you wish, write about several words.

3. Go to the library for a book on slang. Write an essay on your discoveries.

4. Write an essay on the types of information one can find in an ordinary collegiate dictionary. Illustrate fully.

5. Write an essay on current campus language.

6. Write an essay on the shades of meaning that words convey.

7. Write a review of a book on language or thought (Hayakawa, *Language in Action;* Arnold, *The Folklore of Capitalism;* Chase, *The Tyranny of Words;* Dewey, *How We Think;* Piaget, *The Language and Thought of the Child*).

The Polkadot Gang

JOHN BARTLOW MARTIN

The bartender in the neighborhood tavern was "fixing to serve drinks" just before midnight, he related later at the inquest, when the two young holdup men came in with guns in their hands. They were just children. One guarded the patrons, Mr. and Mrs. Richard Nicholas, who had come in for a nightcap to celebrate Mrs. Nicholas'

"The Polkadot Gang." From *Harper's Magazine,* September, 1943. Reprinted by permission of the author and *Harper's Magazine.*

birthday. The other holdup man went round the bar to the bartender, Fred Gross, and told him it was a stickup.

Gross later recalled that he told the bandit to go ahead and take the money. But, "He pushed me around the corner and he started at me first. I said, 'What do you want?' and he hit me across the head with the gun butt . . . he said, 'Gimme money,' and I gave him ten dollars and two fives. He knocked me also with a club or something, and he went over to the cash register, cleaned that out."

Meanwhile two other members of the gang had been looting the adjoining liquor store. Now they came into the tavern. All four hoodlums were calm and methodical although three of them looked scarcely twenty years old. The leader, Eugene Guzy, was thirty-five. He was dissatisfied with the hundred-odd dollars they had collected. He and his partner were moving again toward the bartender, Gross, who was dazed by the beating he had received, when the door opened and Officer Walter Storm came in. Storm stood six feet one inch and weighed two hundred and ten. He was thirty-three years old and had been on the Chicago police force a little less than eight years. He had just come off duty and was on his way home, having worked from 4 P.M. till midnight.

As he entered Gross yelled a warning, "Walter, it's a stickup." The bandit leader Guzy turned and Storm drew his gun and, Gross told the Coroner's jury later, "the gun was six feet from this fellow when Walter Storm started to shooting and the other fellow started to shooting, and that's the end of this."

The bandit leader's three companions lost little time in fleeing when the shooting began. One of them, curly-haired Nick Gianos, nineteen years old, described the evening in this way: "We went out and we stuck up the joint, and one of my friends got shot, and one of the officers got shot. And I seen that happen. And I waited to see them both fall and I run out to the car."

Another, Leo Piscopo, who was twenty-one and who had been one of the two who held up the liquor store, said he entered the tavern proper and started to frisk the customers just as the "bartender hollered 'It is a holdup' and the girl started screaming, and then I looked up. . . . I saw both Eugene and Officer Storm start to draw. . . . I didn't see the shooting. . . . By that time I had gone and the rest of us were gone."

Both Officer Storm and the bandit leader Guzy emptied their guns; both were killed. Guzy was shot in the abdomen and Storm in the left chest. Their bodies lay only a few feet apart, the detectives discovered when they arrived at 12:08 A.M. About thirty-six hours later, on July 7, 1942, the first arrest was made, that of a hefty girl who had been living with Leo Piscopo and had been in the car in which he escaped after the shooting. The roundup of the gang continued for several weeks until ten young men, plus the girl and the dead man, were involved. Three of the young men and the girl were convicted of murder. One of the others was placed on probation. The rest were imprisoned.

Together, they comprised a gang of young stickup experts. None but the leader was over twenty-five and all but three were under twenty-one. Working in various combinations, they had perpetrated more than fifty armed robberies in Chicago over a period of several months during 1942, taking an estimated $10,000 and climaxing their career with murder. They became known as the Polkadot Gang because of the blue polkadot bandannas they sometimes wore as masks. They specialized in tavern holdups, but they also raided other places and they were not above strong-arming a watchman to get his gun. Most of them had police records and records as juvenile offenders.

Much has been written recently about juvenile delinquency, particularly during the war. It may be interesting to inquire into the backgrounds of these young outlaws. How did they get that way?

2

Without exception, the young hoodlums lived at the time of their arrest in an area which has one of the highest rates of juvenile delinquency in Chicago. The Racine Avenue police district is bounded on the east by the Chicago River and railroad tracks, on the south by Kinzie Street and the tracks, on the north by Bloomingdale Avenue, on the west by Damen Avenue. It is some fourteen blocks long and about twelve blocks wide. It lies nearly a mile back of the flashy false lake front of the city; from its alleys you can look up at the spires of the Gold Coast where the wealthy dwell. Of a summer evening young wives sit on the unpainted front steps of tenements and flirt with the street-corner gangs; shadows are heavy, for the street lights are widely spaced, and the enormous storage tanks of the gas company, red-rimmed with warning lights, loom darkly above the river beyond the tracks. Refuse litters the alleys and the streets—broken bottles, waste paper, garbage, the offal of a poverty-ridden city community. More than one strong-arm robbery and rape has been committed in the dark gangways between the tenements. One police officer has said that "90 per cent of the kids in this district go wrong" and, though this estimate is probably more apocryphal than accurate, the officer knows his district. He adds, "We got everything in this district—old-time alky cookers, stickup men, kid hoods that throw bricks at the peddlers, syndicate big-shots, and rape all the time."

Forty years ago the overcrowded population was made up of Swedes, Germans, and Irish, and their children were delinquent; when they moved away, toward the outer periphery of the city, their children stayed out of trouble. And the virus remained to infect those of the Italians and Greeks and Poles who replaced them.

Wars do not raise the juvenile delinquency rate here. (Indeed, war absorbs youths into industry or the Army and keeps them too busy to get into trouble; it enables fathers to make living wages in war industries instead of staying on relief.) Even economic depressions have little effect. Nor can any consistent correlation be shown between the incidence of broken homes and juvenile delinquency. Frequently a child from a good home goes wrong while his brothers and sisters and parents are upstanding citizens.

All this suggests that subtle factors of personality and family and social relationships are involved, and that perhaps the district itself is to blame.

The district is adjacent to the Loop, the city's business center. Heavy industry is close by, crowding in on the deteriorating residences. There are a few "family factories," operated in the home by Mama and Papa who are teaching the kids to make brooms. Most of the residents are laborers, rather than white-collar workers. Housing conditions are bad, poverty is common, sexual relations are inclined to be casual or loose, perhaps owing to overcrowded living arrangements. The children's playgrounds are the streets and alleys and the roofs of sheds. Their homes may not be ideal but they enjoy themselves hugely. Their thrills come from hopping dangerous rides on speeding trucks, from throwing stones at peddlers and plundering their fruit carts, from pilfering vegetables at sidewalk markets, from leaping onto trains in the yards and heaving coal off the moving cars, from, ultimately, committing petty thieveries and jack-rolling drunks and stealing fast cars and pulling stickups.

Their heroes are the big-shot criminals of the district. "What can you expect?" says the policeman. "These kids see the big shot stickup men, the big-time hoods, all duked up, with fancy clothes and fancy women and fancy cars. What can you expect?"

The Polkadot Gang was composed of boys led by an older man with a penitentiary record. They came from a group of about twenty youngsters who for years had hung together at Aberdeen and Erie Streets. For a long time they were too young to be permitted in the pool room there so they simply hung about on the corner.

Their pastimes were those of any juvenile street-corner gang in the Racine Avenue District. Sometimes they went down to the teeming Oak Street beach and burglarized parked cars and sold the stolen goods to neighborhood "fences." (These are the local Fagins; they buy "hot" merchandise from the children and, if the youngsters show promise, encourage them to steal.) Growing up, the Aberdeen and Erie bunch dropped truancy and petty pilfering and sought thrills by jack-rolling drunks, that is, luring or guiding drunks into dark gangways and robbing them. At this time the boys were perhaps fifteen.

A little later they would cruise around the district at night in a stolen or borrowed car. Bored, looking for something to do, they might drive over to the Gold Coast where the swells lived; here if they spotted a car parked in a dark block they would stop and strip it of tires and battery and radio. Or they would raise the hood, wire round the ignition, break a window, climb into the car, and clout it.

Some of the boys needed the money but all needed the thrills. When you were a kid you snitched fruit from the grocer's bins and if he chased you, that was an added thrill; when you grew up you heisted taverns, and if the squad chased you that too was a bonus.

The old bunch at Aberdeen and Erie did not remain compact;

some of them simply drifted away and kept out of trouble. The Army got others. But eight of them became involved with the group of criminals known as the Polkadot Gang. In all there were twelve in the gang—eight from Aberdeen and Erie Streets; and also the elder brother of one of them, and a girl who called herself Sharleen O'Neill and said she came from Texas, and a flashy young sport named Tony Moskal who had a criminal record in several States, and the leader of the gang, an older criminal named Eugene Guzy.

Strictly speaking, the Polkadot Gang was not a gang at all. A gang generally is tightly organized; it has recognized leaders and rigid discipline. The Polkadot crowd were different—a loose federation of young hoodlums bound together by ties of friendship and normal social intercourse and the added incentive of mutual protection. They were perhaps midway between a group of young no-goods hanging about a street corner and an outfit of disciplined professional criminals.

3

First, the boys themselves. They varied in intelligence and energy but, in one way or another, the old Racine district mark was on them all.

One of them was Frank Kamick. His correct name was Frank De Pisa and he was called Chico. His father was Italian, his mother Polish, his stepfather Polish. He was born in Chicago January 29, 1922. His father died a year after Frank's birth and his mother married Stanley Kamick. An Adult Probation Department investigator for the Criminal Court reported in 1942, "Defendant [Frank Kamick] says he had to shift for himself ever since he was eleven years old—that his mother is a very heavy drinker and did not seem to care for him. Defendant says his stepfather was a steady worker, but quit his job now because of his wife's drinking and he has started to drink also. This was verified by defendant's mother-in-law."

Frank attended St. Dominick Parochial School at 815 Sedgwick Street from the first to the fifth grades, transferred for two grades to the Edward Jenner Public School, then graduated from St. Dominick's in 1936, when he was fourteen. He attended Wells High School at Augusta and Ashland Avenues for a year and a half. About this time he started getting into trouble. He was transferred to the Montefiore School, where incorrigibles are sent, but he remained there only six months, withdrawing "to go to work."

He had already been in trouble. He was arrested June 29, 1937, with another boy for stealing two bicycles in Winnetka, a wealthy lake-shore suburb about sixteen miles north of Chicago. Again, he and another boy were brought in to the station for stealing; when the juvenile officer questioned them they both wept. The other boy said he wanted to be a printer when he grew up. But Frank Kamick didn't know what he wanted to be.

He always "hung on the street." Every now and then a cruising squad would stop and ask him what he was up to. He never had much money but somehow he usually managed to have a car. Though good-looking and husky and red-haired, he was not notably popular with girls.

On June 15, 1938, he was arrested with four other boys for larceny of a motorcycle and two cars which they allegedly were caught stripping. He was placed under special supervision by the Juvenile Court until October 6, 1938, and was ordered to remain at home with his parents. How successful this home treatment was is indicated by the fact that the case was "continued generally until June 1, 1939, when same was closed, as defendant was over seventeen years old and was now serving a term of nine months in the County Jail." He had been arrested on March 1, 1939, for auto larceny and three charges of burglary. His conviction was for petty larceny.

Frank was now lost to the juvenile authorities. He kept getting into trouble with the police. His Boys' Court record shows that he was arrested on April 1, 1940, and convicted of petty larceny, was sentenced to thirty days in the County Jail; that he was arrested September 30, 1940, as disorderly and placed under one year's supervision of the Holy Name Society.

Automobiles were his downfall time and again. As early as May of 1937, when he still was getting involved with juvenile authorities, he was fined five dollars and costs for disorderly conduct, and the records show that the arresting officers were from the Stolen Auto Section. He was arrested February 20, 1941, and convicted of tampering with an automobile and sentenced to thirty days in the House of Correction and fined one dollar. Several times he was convicted of failing to have vehicle licenses; sometimes this is the only charge that police can make stick against a man whom they suspect of driving a stolen car. Two burglary charges were filed against him and stricken off with leave to reinstate in May of 1939. He was charged with disorderly conduct December 10, 1941.

Frank Kamick never had much of a job. He didn't work at all in 1942. Earlier, he had worked a month as a laborer and quit; he had also worked at odd jobs and peddled fruit and vegetables from a truck. In his application for probation he described himself as "able to do labor." But he was intelligent. When examined by the Institute of Juvenile Research in 1938, he was 16 years 6 months old but on the Haggerty Intelligence Test he scored a mental age of 17 years 7 months and was graded as having "superior intelligence."

Sometime in the midst of all this, he married and got away from the home where his mother drank excessively. By the time he was arrested as a member of the Polkadot Gang he had a baby nineteen months old and his wife was pregnant again. They lived in a five-room flat on the first floor of a two-storey frame double dwelling at 651 North Carpenter Street. Although this is in the heart of the Racine Avenue district, the home was "nicely furnished and kept immaculately clean" by Kamick's twenty-year-old wife, Clara. She went "on relief" after his arrest in 1942 during the Polkadot roundup.

Armed robbery is the crime to which the kid hoodlums graduate. It requires nerve, daring; its thrill is that of grocery-store pilfering multiplied a thousandfold. To go into, say, a crowded tavern and, with drawn gun, to terrorize the customers, vault the bar, loot the till, slug the bartender, swagger out, roar away in a fast car, elude a seventy-five-miles-an-hour police pursuit—that is something for a Racine District boy. Frank Kamick was twenty years old when he was arrested as a member of the Polkadot Gang. (A policeman says it was Frank who fired the gang's sawed-off shotgun accidentally during a holdup; the sawed-off shotgun is a murderous affair, wholly inaccurate at any range much over twenty feet and almost impossible to control, since its barrel is cut off just above the breech; stickup gangs use it exclusively to intimidate victims and they carry revolvers to do their shooting with.)

Kamick was charged with participating in three separate Polkadot Gang robberies. In two he was accompanied only by recent graduates of the old bunch from Aberdeen and Erie, but in the other his companions included two of the mob's big shots—Leo Piscopo and Leo's girl friend, Sharleen O'Neill. In all three cases Kamick's partners were imprisoned for terms ranging from one to ten years to one to life. Kamick was placed on probation for five years. (He was involved in a curious aftermath of the Polkadot Gang's depredations: Two young men, one without any prior criminal record, were convicted of a stickup and, though innocent, served seven months in the penitentiary before Kamick confessed that the Polkadot Gang was guilty.)

4

The other seven in the Gang were named Americo Girardi (dubbed "Mammy" by the Gang), Salvatore Termini, Alphonse Cozzi, Joseph Chirello, George De Pasquale, Nick Gianos (known as the Greek), and Joe Piscopo (Leo's kid brother). It is possible that Joe, who was seventeen years old, was indirectly responsible for the formation of the Polkadot Gang. In June, 1942, Joe was in trouble and needed some money. His big brother Leo, who didn't hang round with the punk kids at Aberdeen and Erie, wanted to help his young brother out. And Leo had something else on his mind: Sharleen O'Neill. But we will come to that presently.

The family histories of these seven are not identical by any means. If Frank Kamick came from an unfortunate home, "Mammy" Girardi did not. Kamick's mother drank excessively and his father was dead; Girardi simply was a retarded child of a good family. He was not particularly bright in school and frequently a truant; he was a loud-mouthed braggart, with ambitions to be a tough guy. In 1942 he worked for the Yellow Taxicab Company for six months, making a good record and quitting about the time the Polkadot Gang was formed. He had had a number of minor brushes with the police but was not so deeply involved but that his application for probation could be endorsed by a doctor, an undertaker, and a priest. For his participation in Polkadot jobs he was given two concurrent sentences: one to twenty years and one year to life.

Girardi's pal in the Gang was Salvatore Termini, a boy of twenty-two. He had managed to keep pretty clear of the police but had been a persistent truant in school and had been declared "incorrigible" by a priest of the district. The Termini family had walked through the valley of tough luck during the depression years and had been on relief since 1931. One day Salvatore went for a ride with some of the boys from the old bunch, including Mammy Girardi, his pal. Those who tell of it say that Termini did not know where the crowd was going now that they had guns, nor that by this time they had joined the Polkadot Gang. On that ride they held up a gasoline station owned by Fred Gloor at 7200 West Higgins, getting seventy dollars in cash and merchandise. It was Termini's first job and for it he went to Joliet to serve a term of one year to life.

Like Termini, Alphonse Cozzi hadn't much of a criminal background, but he probably had a worse start in life than anybody else in the Gang. He was a dull boy with the lowest I.Q. in Grade School 57. He stayed at home a great deal, unlike the more adventurous boys, and simply sat in the five-room flat, without "any ambitions or intention to advance in any endeavor." His schooling was over when he was sixteen. On August 28, 1941, he was sentenced to six months in the House of Correction for auto tampering. He hadn't been out for many months before he was caught in the Polkadot roundup and was on his way to the penitentiary.

Cozzi's partner in two of the Polkadot stickups was Joe Chirello. He had been kicked around almost since his birth, living in orphanages and foster homes after his mother was committed to a mental institution. In 1942 she was still there; his father's whereabouts was unknown, and his two big brothers were in the Army. Joe grew up tough but he had no criminal record except two pickups for disorderly conduct. On June 19, 1942, he was married to an attractive girl of sixteen and moved north, out of the Racine Avenue district, into a hotel in a fairly good apartment area. The girl's parents helped them with money and the honeymoon was serene; then the police got him for his participation in the Polkadot Gang. In the ten days before his wedding he had participated in two stickups and he was given concurrent sentences of from one year to life.

George De Pasquale had been a tough kid all his life, a charter member of the old bunch at Aberdeen and Erie. He had been arrested and charged with theft when he was thirteen years old. None of the others in the family was ever in trouble. At one time the police picked up one of his brothers. His mother hurried to the station, the police recall, and said: "Let him go. It's George you want. He's the only one of my kids that's no good."

One of George's pals in that thirteen-year-old theft job was Nick Gianos. Nick was fourteen then. By 1942, when he was nineteen and George was eighteen, both were members of the Polkadot Gang. Nick's parents were thoroughly respectable, the hard-working proprietors of a South Side restaurant, but their boy had started getting into trouble early and kept right on. Nick stood well with the Polkadot leaders and participated in many of the stickups. He was along one night in June, 1942, when the Gang stuck up three taverns in succession, with the police trailing them from one job to another.

These seven were the rank and file of the Gang. The moving forces behind the Gang were Leo Piscopo and his girl friend Sharleen O'Neill, Tony Moskal, and Gene Guzy, the leader.

5

Tony Moskal was twenty-five years old, a little older, a little tougher, a little flashier, a little more experienced criminally than the boys who hung round the south end of the district at Aberdeen and Erie. He was never one of them. His father was a respectable tavern keeper in a business district at 831 Ashland Avenue, and Tony's stamping ground was in that neighborhood. Tony lived with his parents over the tavern in a new building that was far from slummy. Although he had a good home he refused to stay in it, sleeping out in cars or in the homes of other youths. As a child he had everything. His parents were kind to him. Tony was tall and dark and slender and good-looking; he always had a new Ford and expensive pin-stripe suits and plenty of pretty girls. He had no need of money. Yet he was a thief, a burglar, and an armed bandit from the time he was seventeen years old. And before that he had a record in Juvenile Court and in Boys' Court.

He had been arrested January 17, 1934, and had admitted the theft and stripping of cars. He served ninety days and was scarcely at liberty before he was charged with auto larceny at Geneva, Illinois, and was sent to Joliet for from one to five years.

It may have been there that he met Eugene Guzy, who later was to lead him back to the penitentiary for murder. Moskal was received at Joliet October 5, 1935; six weeks later Guzy was sentenced to Joliet to serve one year to life on four robbery charges.

Moskal was discharged from prison at the expiration of his sentence on July 4, 1938. His prison record is not available but it should be noted that though he was a first-time offender he was forced to serve more than three years of his one-to-five-year sentence.

He had been out almost a year to the day when he was picked up for investigation and found to be working for his father in the tavern. A month later, August 8, 1939, he was arrested near there by police who charged that he had broken a window in a parked car. He apparently was discharged but was picked up repeatedly after that. He was held for investigation in a shooting but was not identified; he was put on probation for auto tampering; he was investigated on a variety of complaints. Apparently these arrests became annoying and Tony left Chicago, for he was next heard of in Bowling Green, Kentucky, where on November 25, 1940, he was charged with grand larceny and the possession of burglary tools. It is said that he was engaged there in hijacking slot machines.

Tony apparently extricated himself from his Kentucky difficulties because by December, 1940, he was back in Chicago "without visible means of support." After that, arrests followed with monotonous regularity until the Polkadot Gang was formed.

The organization of the Gang did not occur until Eugene Guzy appeared on the scene and, as the police believe, came round to the Moskal tavern to look up Tony. Guzy was thirty-five years old and had never had anything to do with the bunch at Aberdeen and Erie. A laborer, larceny man, punch-press operator, and armed robber, Guzy had a record dating back to 1931, when he had served thirty days in the House of Correction. He was a burglar by 1933 and when he was arrested at that time it was noted that he hadn't worked for three years and that he walked with a limp. He was married but apparently it had been no great success, for his wife had signed a complaint against him the afternoon of October 20, 1934. They were separated in 1935, she said later, but she saw him an hour before he was killed in the tavern holdup in 1942.

The police had long been suspicious of Guzy and finally, in 1935, they made something stick on him: arrested with six other men, three of whom had previous records, and charged with six armed robberies, he was convicted on four counts November 11, 1935, and went to Joliet to serve a term of from one year to life. He was paroled March 29, 1940.

When he came out, the police think, he looked up Tony Moskal, whom he probably met while in prison. The Moskal tavern was in the center of the district, where Guzy used to hang out. Both Tony and Guzy had records; both had served time. Guzy was thirty-five years old with nearly a decade of experience with the police behind him. Moskal was ten years younger but he had had a lot of experience also.

Meanwhile Moskal met Leo Piscopo in Guy's Crystal Tap on Ogden Avenue, one of the few modern, clean, respectable taverns in the district. This place is not a hoodlum hangout. When he met Moskal there, Leo Piscopo was living with his parents, his sister, and his younger brother, Joe, in a five-room flat in an old brick building the family owned on Erie Street. His father worked hard, Leo also was a working man, and he had not been in serious trouble. He had been in the hands of the police a number of times but his jams had not been serious.

But at the time Moskal met him at the Crystal Tap Leo had a heart interest: Sharleen O'Neill. Virtually nothing is known of her. She was hard-boiled, fat, twenty-two years old, and said she was from Texas. Her true name may have been Barbara Reynolds. When Leo met her she was working as a waitress in a white-tile hamburger place on Ogden Avenue a short distance from the Crystal Tap. She and Leo found an apartment for themselves up on the North Side. Sharleen had plenty of nerve and when Moskal appeared on the scene, she and Leo were doubtless open to a proposition.

Thereafter it was like tumbling down a row of blocks. Leo's brother Joe came to him in trouble. Joe is said to have hung out with the other boys at Aberdeen and Erie, but his difficulties had resulted in no more than a five-dollar fine for disorderly conduct and an eight-dollar fine for speeding. But in June, 1942, he was questioned in connection with two robberies of grocery stores. He was in a jam, he needed money to get out, and he didn't have it. His big brother Leo, who had nothing to do with the boys at Aberdeen and Erie, would help him.

Here was Joe needing money, here were Leo and Sharleen not exactly satisfied with life. At this juncture Leo meets Tony Moskal, who has an acquaintance named Eugene Guzy who is looking for action. Joe's money trouble crystallized the Polkadot Gang.

Leo apparently was now galvanized into action. Kid brother Joe had friends and the Gang was recruited from the old bunch at Aberdeen and Erie. Some of them had drifted away; now they returned. Joe Chirello brought the girl he was about to marry to the Crystal Tap to meet the boys. Smart red-haired Frank Kamick, who had found time to get married and father a child in the midst of his many arrests for petty thefts, now came back to the fold. So did stupid Mammy Girardi, who bragged about his pitifully few arrests and wanted to be a big shot sought for murder; and his friend Salvatore Termini, who joined the Gang and got sent up for his first job. And Al Cozzi, with the lowest I.Q. in School 57; and Nick the Greek Gianos; and George De Pasquale, who had grown up tough—they all gathered now, with a big shot to lead them: Gene Guzy, who had done four years and four months for armed robbery.

They started out "to make some robberies," as Leo Piscopo later phrased it. They made a wave of them. Then, one day in late June or early July, some of them were driving out to the western suburbs to go horseback riding—a favorite sport with many Chicago hoodlums when the money starts rolling in from stickups—and they stopped for a beer at the tavern at 5143 West North Avenue. They looked the place over and decided it would be a good spot to rob. Sharleen cased it, as she cased many of their jobs, wearing a blond wig as a disguise over her red-brown hair. So they met in Guy's place on Ogden Street the night of July 5th and Nick the Greek Gianos, Leo Piscopo, Tony Moskal, Gene Guzy, and Sharleen O'Neill made the robbery. But Officer Storm interrupted it and he shot Guzy dead and was himself killed. The others fled.

A few blocks away these others grew curious about what had happened to Guzy and the copper. So they sent Sharleen back to look things over. She went into the tavern and bent over the two bodies; she really was interested only in her big-shot friend, Gene Guzy, but she couldn't help seeing that both men were dead or dying, their bodies lay so close together. Having satisfied her curiosity, she walked through the crowd of curious spectators, escaping perhaps two minutes before the police arrived, and took a street car back to the Racine Avenue district, where she met the other three survivors, Leo Piscopo and Moskal and Gianos, at Guy's Crystal Tap on Ogden Avenue. (Sharleen was what the police call a standup guy; long after some of the men had confessed she refused to talk.) They rode round awhile and got something to eat and met De Pasquale, who had missed his appointment with murder by a half-hour.

That morning the five of them drove to New Buffalo, Michigan, and stayed overnight. The next afternoon Nick and Sharleen and Leo came back and she went to the apartment on the North Side to get some clothes so that they could return to Michigan. But officers were waiting in her apartment and arrested her. They found Leo and his brother cruising in a car nearby. These two had left Nick downtown; when they did not pick him up by 5:30 he told the coroner's jury, "I knew they were stuck, that they got caught. And then I went to the hotel, and then from there I went also to pick up my girl, and then we were going to get married. And we went to a show that night. . . . So we left the show and come back at the hotel, and Officer Gazzola pinched me."

The roundup of the other members of the Gang followed. It had taken not quite twenty years of life at Aberdeen and Erie, in the heart of Chicago's slum, to prepare the boys for their career as members of the Polkadot Gang. The corporate life, if it may be so described, of the gang had lasted barely four weeks. The total take of the gang had come to about $10,000, which, among twelve people, meant $833 apiece. In addition to the sentences for armed robbery and grand larceny already listed, Sharleen got twenty years and Leo Piscopo thirty-five years and Tony Moskal fourteen years and Nick Gianos fourteen years, all for murder. Joe Piscopo got from one to ten years for grand larceny in two stickups. Gene Guzy's entry on the blotter was closed out forever. His life and Officer Storm's canceled out.

TECHNICAL DISCUSSION

1. How does the author attempt to capture interest at the start of his essay?

2. What is the intention of the last paragraph in the first section of the essay?

3. Study the first four paragraphs in the second section as a series of judgments with little support. Does it seem to you that the author should have "backed up" these judgments? Does the remainder of the section contain enough factual material to balance the judgments in the first part?

4. What is the purpose of the third section of the essay? Is the purpose stated in the first paragraph of this section?

5. Why did the author spend so much time and space on Frank Kamick?

6. Is the fourth section a continuation of the third? Explain your answer.

7. What is the purpose of the fifth section? Does the purpose change with the line "Thereafter it was like tumbling down a row of blocks"?

8. Write a topical outline of this essay.

TOPICS FOR PAPERS

1. A case history of a normal young man (girl): yourself.

2. A study of the "gang" you ran around with while in high school: personalities, activities, etc.

3. An escapade.

4. A study of your social environment: your home town, your farm community, your living conditions at school, etc.

The Woman M.D.

CHARLOTTE HUGHES

A girl on hospital ambulance service learns a lot about the nature of man that is outside the experience of a philosophy professor. She discovers that the Bowery tramp whose head she sews up in a precinct station is more grateful than any other patient she will ever have if she lives to practice until she is 80. She decides this when he looks her

"The Woman M.D." From The New York *Times* Magazine, February 16, 1941. Reprinted by permission of the author and The New York *Times*.

direct in the eyes, with plenty of hard-boiled cops around to discourage a display of emotion, and says with profound and sober sincerity, "If you ever get into trouble, I want to be there to help."

She discovers that the dirtier people are, the better they are able to withstand infection. She finds out that it is safe to mend a strong, unwashed derelict on the sidewalk, but that a recently bathed college boy or any more tender sample of humanity ought to be taken to an emergency room where things are sterile. She learns that Chinese never complain of pain and wait until they are almost dying before they call an ambulance. And she is shocked to discover that people who ought to know better don't hesitate to call out an ambulance as a practical joke.

There is a lot for one young woman to face in a few months on "the bus." She faces just as much throughout her career as a man does. Yet for some reason the Army has passed the women by in lining up the medical profession for defense. The men are to have Army ratings and a definite role. The women want to be included and think that they, as well as anybody, can do emergency work among civilians, the main victims of modern warfare. Not having been asked, they are annoyed.

So the 7,500 women doctors all over the country have filled out questionnaires telling what each could do in her community in an emergency. Based on the answers, a card catalogue will soon be in the hands of the Surgeon General at Washington.

The Surgeon General can be sure that, whenever he puts his faith in a woman doctor, he is trusting an exceptionally proficient and conscientious person. It would be practically impossible to find a slipshod woman doctor. The few women who manage to survive the merciless process of elimination have to be more than average good. For that process of elimination is about ten times as fierce for women as it is for men.

Most medical schools in the country take women on a ratio up to one girl to ten men, never above that ratio. Harvard, and Jefferson in Philadelphia, are the only major colleges that still refuse women altogether. In the 1938-39 session there were 1,144 women in accredited medical schools.

Girls like medical school. After the first grim moment in anatomy, when a cadaver is cut up and the girls think the men wonder why women have to be present, things go smoothly. Testy professors sometimes make remarks about how women weren't allowed when they went to medical school, but it is all good natured.

The weeding-out process really begins to clamp down on girls when it comes to getting a hospital interneship. Hospital boards are full of plain and fancy reasons why they can't take women. Of 6,790 interneships approved by the A. M. A. in 1939, there were only 277 open to women, and only 167 were occupied by women. Beginnings of a survey for 1940 show that the number has jumped considerably.

One reason why the opposition is slowly melting is that women have shown themselves to be fearless and capable internes. A New York hospital that serves one of the toughest and most varied districts in the world appointed its first woman interne ten years ago. She had a lot more to put up with than the girls at that hospital face now.

At first the men internes wouldn't speak to her, said she looked frail and hoped she wouldn't last. She showed them, and in a few weeks had the men standing up for her like so many Sir Galahads. But it was the enlightened ambulance driver who took her under his wing from the beginning and showed her how to fill out various forms. He also told sidewalk crowds what was what.

"Looka da noice," somebody was sure to say. "Wy'nt the horspital send a doctah?"

"She ain't no noice, she's a soigen. Cantcha read the sign on the cap?" the driver would fume.

This girl went out into the cold, choppy harbor, shivering in the icy wind, to see seamen taken sick on voyage. She plowed through the thick odor of dime-a-night flop houses to find the poor soul who had crawled in where it was warm to die.

The Tombs Prison, one of the grimmest assignments on any hospital beat, was a regular point of call. Nights when the Tombs doctors are off duty the girl, or man, who happens to be "on the bus" has to answer calls put through when a drug addict acts up. The first woman to answer these calls made fast friends with the guards and set a good precedent. It was comforting to have a friendly guard there when a prisoner nearly crazy for want of a hypodermic made for her and her bag of dope.

Sometimes things are a little gruesome and stomach-raising even to a girl who has schooled herself to expect the worst. In the middle of a lovely blue morning last Summer the girl on the bus was called to an El station, and when she got to the platform she found a grinning cop and no patient. The cop was grinning because he thought for once he had something to make his level-headed interne friend quail. He had.

"Where's the patient, Mike?" the girl asked.

"Right over there in that suitcase," the cop said. "You have to pronounce it dead."

Girl internes and residents look cool, capable and attractive in the white coat and skirt that they wear, and with their hair tied close to their heads they manage to look appealing without the use of make-up. The residents and internes at the New York Infirmary for Women and Children, all girls (the hospital is run entirely by women) look like a group of college girls, except that they are a little older—between 25 and 30.

The resident in surgery is a slight Chinese girl with lively shoe-button eyes who wishes there were more emergency work to do. The senior interne in obstetrics has handled 150 deliveries alone and hopes to chalk up 200 before her term is up. The internes get $25 a month, the residents $45. They live on that, too—few get money from home. So they are experts at having fun in New York, and dressing themselves, on pennies. They have one or two good outfits among them, and when anybody has a date everybody else contributes gayly to the costume. None of them would dream of leaving medicine and surgery for something easier and more lucrative.

Girl internes say they have no more ardent admirers in the world than their men patients, who apparently work up a feeling of wonder, approval and gallantry toward them. Men from the fish market and the docks have marveled at the tender treatment they have received at the hands of the women who have sewed them up. "That light touch sure is okay," they remark.

The roughnecks of the Bowery treated the first woman ambulance surgeon of their neighborhood with downright chivalry. Around 1900 she spent a year chasing to gunshot wounds and the remains of street fights with brickbats in a horse-drawn ambulance. When her year was up the men in the neighborhood passed the hat and presented her with a large engraved testimonial in flowery, if not altogether grammatical, language. They kept it pure and took no money from people with police records, saloon keepers or proprietors of questionable establishments.

Most women doctors, when they set up private practices (which isn't more difficult for a woman than for a man) go in for obstetrics, pediatrics or gynecology, so naturally have no men patients. And some women flatly refuse men patients because men bore them. Men are plain sissies when it comes to standing pain, these women say, and a man with the slightest ache thinks he is going to die. That makes him a dull and ornery patient.

Some take men because the men insist upon it. Usually the women in the family come first, and the men follow out of sheer admiration for the way their womenfolk have been treated. Some of the older women doctors with general practices have whole families, having delivered the mothers first of their babies. The children, male and female, keep right on coming, and so do the husbands.

Older women doctors, who did the pioneering, are inclined to have chips on their shoulders about discrimination against women. The younger women are not.

Women doctors can't understand why anybody should think that surgery is no job for a woman.

"I suppose most people think surgery is like being a butcher," said one young woman surgeon, "but there is very little blood; there shouldn't be any. You may not know it, but your insides are really beautiful. I think surgery is nearer dressmaking; you clip with scissors and you sew with a needle. It is a very delicate business, and small quick hands are an asset."

Men doctors give women grudging approval. But there seems to be very little cooperation between men and women when it comes to referring patients to each other. Women usually refer their patients to other women if they have to, men send theirs to other men. There is quite a lot of jealousy on this score.

This jealousy shows itself on hospital staffs where men and women work side by side. It is a rare woman who gets a top job on a hospital staff, and these coveted hospital jobs carry no pay. So you have to be full of an evangelical enthusiasm to get to be a successful woman doctor. Also you have to have a very fine brain.

TECHNICAL DISCUSSION

1. Why does the author begin with the series of remarks that we find in the first and second paragraphs?
2. Some of the author's judgments are supported. Find two or three and classify the type of data used to support them.
3. Find a series of judgments that are unsupported. Do you question the author's right to make them? Explain.
4. Write a topical outline of the essay.

TOPICS FOR PAPERS

1. Training of nurses.
2. The woman in the law school.
3. The woman engineer.
4. The career woman *versus* the housewife.
5. Economic discrimination against women workers.

Tools and the Hand

WILSON FOLLETT

> "Those poor fellows aloft in the freezing blast were working with spanners on nuts . . . they were dealing with great weights and an infinite complexity of gear. . . . I watched them with anguish and admiration, thinking 'that is real glory; man is doing nothing finer than that anywhere; it passes unnoticed and the men who are aloft will neither be praised nor thanked; yet what a feat it is.' I went home, wondering why the deeds of work are not heeded, while the deeds of sport fill the headlines."
>
> —JOHN MASEFIELD

It is my good fortune to live in a countryside where hand tools still persist for many a use that, in the modern world at large, is more and more relegated to machines. Good hand tools are, for that reason, generally cherished, and the niceties of their idiom well understood by old and young. The explanation of this regional conservatism—lag, a

"Tools and the Hand." From *The Atlantic Monthly*, April, 1942. Reprinted by permission of the author and *The Atlantic Monthly*.

sociologist would call it—is that our characteristic transactions are on a small, highly individualized scale, the scale of the hundred-acre or "one-man" dairy farm, without the possible margin of profit that would support such overhead as mechanization always involves.

When one of our framed barns needs a ten-by-twelve structural timber replaced, there can be no question of inviting some town contractor to put in a stick from Georgia or Oregon, already saddled with the tolls of a unionized lumber crew, power dragsaws, caterpillar tractors, a sawmill, a long haul by railroad or freighter, several short hauls by truck, and four selling profits. Instead, some old fellow, very likely nearer eighty than seventy, goes into the wood lot with measurements penciled on a spruce chip in his overalls pocket, picks his hemlock, drops it with the aid of a boy on the other end of the crosscut saw (which he has filed and set himself), trims the trunk, with adz or broadaxe hews it to shape where it lies, works the mortises in it with auger and chisel, "twitches" (i.e., hauls) it with the farm's yoked oxen or team of horses, and finally—with the aid of building jacks and perhaps an ingenious arrangement of tackle in lieu of the many hands that make light work—"slips it in." (That piece of understatement is the only locution ever heard from our one-man contractors for an operation that demands the utmost niceties of engineering skill; an operation in which everything must be exactly right from beginning to end if the whole is not to be exactly wrong.)

When that old fellow's lifework is done the past beneficiaries of it gather at the auction and compete for the tools with which he did it; and the result, always a little mystifying to city visitors who have come on the chance of picking up antiques, is that these tools fetch a good deal more than they cost him new. The bids are not made primarily *in memoriam,* out of sentimental piety. What coaxes the dollars out of our tight-buttoned pockets is the belief that we are buying some residue of the merit that was worked into the tools by the hands that laid them down.

And that is a perfectly true belief. For the relation between man and tool is a reciprocal one. The well-designed tool will subtly train and reëducate the hand that uses it, but hardly more than the hand in its turn will modify the tool. The quality of workmanship seems to impress itself upon the substance of cold steel, gradually improving or impairing its constitution. Some obscure kind of polarization or ionization seems gradually to take place in the very particles of the cutting edge, until its temper is matched to the temperament of the user. This phenomenon, indefinable but observable, explains why every skilled hand worker possesses at least a few cutting tools that he will lend only with great reluctance—tools that no silent borrower can help himself to without the owner's knowing it the moment he starts to use them again. It also explains why he insists upon sharpening his tools himself. Such a workman, when at last his eyesight becomes too impaired to trust, will keep his edged tools in shape by a delicate combination of touch and the sound of contact with grindstone or oilstone or file. Experience has taught him that the apparently keener edge produced by someone else will not hold up under his kind of stroke. It is harder to grind a tool to another's muscular habits than to perceive a match flame in bright sunshine.

This whole fine interaction between implement and man is experienced in a typical enough way by anyone who has learned to use a grass scythe with moderate proficiency. It is possible, of course, to pick up the rudiments of the swing and of the all-important footwork by studying someone who is, as we say, "a good man on the crooked stick." But every learner finds that the real niceties of scything, the differences between a feat of main strength and an effortless art, are taught by the crooked stick itself—its balance, the adjustment of the handles to his own height, the distribution of weight and leverage between snath and blade. Submit yourself to the genius of the implement, and it swings itself and you, like the enchanted broom of the sorcerer's apprentice. There you have the tool as teacher. You meet the tool as pupil when you undertake to grind a blade that someone else has been grinding for his own use. The first edge you put on it may gladden your critical eye and fill you with pride, but after a few minutes' scything you will think the grass is fence wire. The other fellow has ground his different personality into it; it has become tuned to his habit, his touch. You will have to put it through all of three or four sharpenings to make it yours.

The complete woodsman makes acquaintance with a brand-new axe—and what a calamity he makes of having ever to get one!—by putting it, directly after helving, on the grindstone. He does this, not to make it sharper, but to familiarize himself with its temper and to work out any warp in the metal or inequality between its sides. On an occasion when time pressed I saw such a woodsman forgo this initial process of teaching his blade something of himself while learning something of it; and his second stroke, which had to go through a hemlock knot charged with frost, took out a half-moon of steel that included a good third of one cutting edge. (It was a double-bitted axe.) He looked at it mournfully and said: "I *knew* I ought to have ground it. I mistrusted the two sides weren't even. They almost never are." His self-punishment was drastic, even for his kind of rugged moralist. He made himself use the other edge for two winters after that one.

Kitchen utensils, too, I hear it testified, receive in the course of time an impress that makes them invaluable and irreplaceable. A giver of loaves who cooks with a locally famous versatility and originality—also with incredible ease—makes daily use of tools from two gifted cooks of other generations, one born in 1838, one in 1859. She avers that one of the old mixing spoons, with bowl worn down to the shape of the gibbous moon and maple handle lathe-turned with a sculptor's regard for the nature of the human hand, can impart more about the knack of beating cake batter than all the teachers of cookery in all the seminaries. When she tries to make shift with one of its modern counterparts she finds that the new handle was designed for the eye only, or perhaps for the convenience of automatic machinery; until she can get someone to whittle half the wood out of it and sandpaper it to the contour of the old one it cramps her hand and presently lames it.

The proverb about the new broom that sweeps clean may have been true when it was coined, but it is hopelessly false of today's brooms, which never sweep clean until taught to by discipline and much wear.

There is, in short, no tool like an old tool.

2

A chronic distress of the latter-day Jack-of-all-trades—and he still exists in legions—is the dearth of small hand tools fit to replace the old ones when they are finally worn out or ground away. More and more he has to depend on implements with so little character of their own that they will take no impress from his, or so short-lived that they have to be thrown away before he can get them broken in. This deficiency of an age teeming with improvements is the more maddening because it exists side by side with very remarkable advances in the science of metallurgy. But hardly anyone finds it to his advantage in these days to make and sell small things except in great volume; everything seems to be sacrificed to "turnover," to "repeat orders." The result is that instruments once bought for a lifetime are now bought for a year, and those once good for a year have to be replaced for the single job. Whence the needle that (unless you can get it from England) will not sew, the razor blade that will not shave, the carving knife that will only haggle, and the new half-inch bitt that bends under a pressure not quite sufficient to make it penetrate. Whence, too, the replacement of the water-cooled grindstone with a geared, high-speed bench grinder that removes twenty times the metal it ought and burns the temper out of what is left. Whence, finally, a national junk pile that is bound to be one of the future wonders of archaeology; it has already created a well-nigh insoluble problem of disposal, and at a time when everyone concerned with the military defense of the nation is having nightmares over threatened shortages of essential metals.

Consider the trifling matter of files—which is not so trifling if you reflect that every kind of wood saw in the world, whether operated by hand or by power, whether used for lumber or for fuel, is constantly dependent on files for its maintenance in service. My wagon-building grandfather, who renewed a lot of saws between 1860 and 1910, used to keep a running biography of every file he used. It was in the form of notches on the wooden handle, one notch for every saw filed. The handle was always uncommonly large—he had turned it on his own lathe to fit his own hand—and the notches were so fine and close that to count them was a test of eyesight. For the best files of that period the notches ran all the way down one side of the handle, around the end, all the way up the other side, and part way down on a second circuit. The occasional file that took him only half or two-thirds of the way down the first side was a "bad one"; it left him disgusted and nursing a grievance. The proportion of bad ones, he noticed, was greatly on the increase toward the end of his working life. Today, after all our discoveries in technology and in the face of national advertising in which the file manufacturers claim scientifically rigid standardization and make almost religious protestations about keeping faith with the public, any man who takes care of his own saws would gladly pay a fivefold price for the worst "bad one" my grandfather ever laid eyes on.

The moral seems fairly plain. For every improvement in the collective, machine-turned, mass-producing aspects of workmanship we have paid something out of the individual, hand-turned, made-to-order aspects. The questions in my mind are such as these: Can we afford this price? Do we really have to pay it? In the long run does not industry itself need, as a permanent part of the national background and atmosphere, the man who can turn his hand to anything and whose animating ideal is the best work he can do with the best tools he can get? In the end can any number of factory inspections, however rigid, be a competent substitute for the all-round artisan's self-judgment—for individual conscience? Is it truly a good thing for the future of American housebuilding, furniture, shipbuilding, aircraft, dynamos, radio sets, tractors, textile machinery, ordnance, and so on, that we should ask the amateur mechanic, the Jack-of-all-trades, the farmer and his boy, to make shift with screwdrivers that turn in their handles, planes with adjustment screws that cross-thread after a few turns, and cutting tools that, if they will accept an edge at all, will not hold it? Can we suppose for a minute that these two things have nothing to do with each other, and that we can bypass integrity in the small affairs and yet collect its benefits in the great ones?

In lieu of undertaking direct answers to these questions I will cite two representative circumstances that have, for those who want to see it, a bearing on the answers:—

(1) The personnel executives of industries under a necessity of rapid expansion in the interest of national defense have taken to assuring us almost with one voice that their mainstay among the hordes of new learners is the youngster from the farm—the boy who has grown up with assorted tools, done miscellaneous tinkering from as far back as he can remember, and rooted himself in the habit of taking every difficulty as an invitation to his faculty of contrivance.

(2) The officers of a military engineering detachment consider under official instruction the problem of replacing quickly a bombed bridge

over a small river with heavily forested banks. The first thing they are taught is that the time has gone by when it could be expected that a regiment of the United States Army would include enough able axemen to supply the makings of such a bridge from timber felled on the spot. Their best procedure will be, if you please, to demolish some sound building in the vicinity, say a ruggedly framed barn, and haul its girders to the site.

Maybe the axemanship is really not there any more; maybe it is still there and the military higher-ups can't believe it or find it. The truth must be one or the other. Either seems deeply shocking. Also, it brings up the interesting question how far a nation can get toward the winning of a war or any other crucial struggle of the present by trading on its past virtue—the virtue, say, of those excellent hewers of wood, our grandfathers.

3

There are, to be sure, a good many Americans who refuse to be at all shocked by evidences that all-round manual competence is on the wane. As a rule they are the ones whose acquaintance with hand tools is restricted to implements designed for propelling a ball or landing a game fish. Their very definition of progress is the conquest of nature, the conquest of leisure. In the fact that machines increase while hand tools diminish they read the news that sweat and blisters and fatigue become all the time less necessary to the conduct of the world's work; and, unable to conceive that any rational person will coarsen his body with avoidable toil, they find this news worth celebrating. In every laborer who takes off his overalls, in every process that is translated from a pick-and-shovel basis to the pushing of buttons, the adjustment of levers, and the reading of dials, they perceive a net gain for civilization.

With all respect for Mr. Stuart Chase and other panegyrists of the power age, the labor-saving device, I believe they are rushing the pace of evolution and ignoring some deep, permanent needs of the animal man. We happen to be pretty effective machines ourselves, and it is self-evident from the way we are constituted that these machines are designed to do work. They have to do it to keep in what is significantly called "working order." The unworked body starves for work as the unfed body starves for food. One proof is the gratuitous rigors undertaken to get Mount Everest climbed or a mile run one-fifth of a second faster. Proof of a left-handed sort is also discoverable in the woman of the all-electric, completely mechanized ultramodern kitchen, who finds herself with the leisure to contract a fine assortment of the new nervous and psychic diseases while standing around waiting for automatic appliances to do their stuff.

What is forgotten or conveniently ignored by those who are always bemoaning the foot-pounds of energy wasted by walking upstairs or lifting a flatiron or hand-feeding a steam boiler is the simple primary fact that *we have the energy*. Our only conspicuous modern way of wasting energy is by not using it. The sedentary American is notoriously losing his teeth on a labor-saving diet, his legs and his lungs on labor-saving developments in transportation; and the medicos who look him over in great numbers in connection with military service find a deplorable recent softening of his whole body, significantly accompanied by losses of mental toughness and elasticity. We congratulate each other on the release from tools and toil, lapse into a lopsided life that is bound to result in jumpy nerves and jangled wits, and then try to cure each other's ills by psychiatric methods, when all that is needed

. . . is not to sit still
Or frowst with a book by the fire;
But to take a large hoe and a shovel also,
And dig till you gently perspire.

What the times call for is another *Past and Present,* a new Carlyle's new affirmation of the dignity of labor—real, regular labor that uses the body for what it is good for and tires it enough to teach it what a supreme luxury is earned rest.

However, no one outside of a few faddists and fanatics can seriously be expected to pray for the daily bread of hard labor just because he knows it is indispensable to a balanced diet. The real argument for a pick-and-shovel technique of living is not the therapeutic one, but the very argument commonly urged in favor of the machine-and-kilowatt technique: to wit, the argument from efficiency. For there is more than one kind of efficiency, and nearly every enhancement of one kind is at the expense of some other. In agriculture, for instance, a corporal's guard with machinery can produce the tonnage of food that would require, with hand methods, an army—but *not on the same acreage*. To save man-hours that we think important we waste land that we think unimportant. Let the density of population pass a certain point and you arrive at a reversal of values, of necessities. A thousand back-yard garden plots worked by a thousand men with hoes will then be incomparably more efficient than their combined area tractor-worked as a unit by a small crew.

Some days ago, with my two favorite implements of destruction, axe and bush scythe, I tore into a partly swampy corner of land that, as I found by the tree rings, had been neglected for some twenty years. It is potentially a fine calf pasture—which, indeed, it had been a generation ago, on the affidavit of rotted posts and rusted wire. Now, the "efficient" way to reclaim this corner was to pick a morning of exactly the right conditions and burn it out—the same "efficient" method our hard-pressed forefathers used on a hundred years' supply of the fifty-inch pines that would be worth almost anything to us if we had them today. Well, it happens that my household had long sighed to have a tamarack growing within sight of the buildings. There had been but one such of any size, and that had been felled by the Big Blow of 1938. Inching my way into this jungle by the laborious method of clearing a few square rods at a time and piling the brush, I soon came upon a perfect young thirty-foot tamarack at the centre of a clump of scrub pines, where no one would ever have seen it if I had efficiently summoned fire to do my work for me.

Saving that tree to flourish in the open and become more beloved with every season and every inch of its growth—that seems incomparably more important than the alternative saving of myself, my hours and strength; more important to more persons, and for a far longer time.

4

And then, when we elect to save ourselves there is always the pertinent, usually unanswerable question, What for?

The man who discreetly thins a wood lot and turns the surplus trees into firewood has the inestimable advantage of knowing perfectly well that in a variety of small ways he is making the world better. He is improving a bit of forest, whether as future timber or just as present trees. He is creating comfort out of nature's waste. He is building up his own bodily strength and skill. He is having a good time; for virtually all such work is done by men who love it. And, following a practice as cordially approved by every department of local and national government as by his own common sense, he is basking in the good conscience of the good citizen. Imagine that by buying his fuel he saves his time for such white-collar pursuits as are supposed to be worth saving it for—specifically, the mental pursuits, such as participating in refined converse with his fellow time-savers on what the world is coming to, or plaguing his mind about what other people ought to do to be saved, or inventing one more labor-saving contrivance, or reading the *Critique of Pure Reason,* or shaping this essay. Can he then enjoy anything like the same assurance that his use of time will make the world better?

The work of our hands being so self-evidently good so much of the time, and that of our heads generally so dubious even when it is not palpably indifferent or bad, it seems rather wonderful that any creature should have the hardihood to stake the whole meaning of his existence on brain work alone.

Abroad in the land spreads a strange assumption that there is something peculiarly, preëminently cultural in leisure and its fruits—in superior articulacy, the wider diffusion of luxuries and refinements, the release of the mind from practical exigencies, the resulting appetite for generalizations and abstractions, the quest of amusement, and above all the dedication of more and more individuals to art and science and theoretic reflection. But culture, by any definition worth talking about, is the whole sum of a people's arts of living; and of these its necessary work is by all odds the greatest item. Culture is not ornament: it is workmanship, which is integrity. Any man who looks down upon himself or another as a disinherited expatriate from culture because he has to work with his hands instead of his head is truly to be pitied, but not for the reason he imagines. He has already shown that he has little head to work with.

What in the world was ever more integral with the deepest meanings of culture than the conception, the evolution, the canon and tradition, of any basic tool? Consider, for example, what a profoundly, thrillingly original deed of the mind, what a really epic feat of synthesis, was performed by the unsung inventor to whom it first occurred to put the knife, the wedge, and the sledgehammer together into the one tool that we call the axe. It is a simple-seeming tool—now that we have it; its existence is what we glibly call inevitable; not to have it is, for us, unthinkable. But imagine your way back, back, and back into that shadowy prehistoric time before any living being had conceived the possibility. Does its existence seem one of the inevitable things *now?* Is it not, rather, one of the miraculous things? From a point an hour or an instant before it has come into the world can you regard it as a simple tool? Is it not the having it at all that has suddenly become almost unthinkable?

From this point grope your way forward and forward again and survey a little of what this axe has done in human history—the difference it has made to man's environment and hence to man, the part it has played in his taming of the wild, the probabilities of where he would find himself today without it. As an incorporation of sheer mind-stuff the invention of gunpowder is not to be compared with it, for that was accident. As a determining factor in man's tenancy of his habitat throughout the ages, gunpowder with all its extensions and applications may be trivial beside the axe, though it seem otherwise at certain violent hours of history. In relatively modern times and on our own continent some other unsung genius of cultural history hits upon the now standard retrocurved helve, and at last the tool is consummated, its dynamic efficiency instantly doubled by the inspired union of knife, wedge, hammer with the potent principle of the lever. What that the mind has ever been able to accomplish in the realm of abstractions is so difficult or so improbable before the fact, so unarguable a ministry to need, or so tremendous in its effect upon the life of the race? Yet there are those who take such things for granted and patronize them as representing a rudimentary, childish, ignoble cunning.

Nor is this all. The axe is a tool with a very eminent educative and disciplinary power. There is a code for its use, a complicated set of rules and prohibitions enforced by penalties—the same rules and the same penalties for all users everywhere. Axemanship is, in that, not unlike seamanship. A vessel will certainly kill you in the end if you do not handle it just so, and for that reason it must be dealt with by men whose fidelity to its requirements is so trained into them that their training will take automatic hold when they are tottering from fatigue or paralyzed with terror or running a fever. You have to respect the axe just so, or it will admonish you—and about the mildest admonition it knows anything about is an amputated finger. There are half a hundred specific niceties of precaution that you have to observe as inflexible laws. They govern the position of your hands in splitting, that of your feet in chopping or hewing, the way you carry the tool, what you do with it between strokes, the allowances you make for different kinds of wood, for knots, for invisible decay, for hard frost, for wet hands or mittens, for brush, for bystanders.

If a man is a sheer wizard of the axe, he can habitually short-cut some of these laws and perhaps get away with it indefinitely. Almost anybody can temporize with them a little at times when he is fresh and feeling fine and his strokes are going to a split hair where he wants them. But the unwritten law exists to protect the axeman from his own fallibility—from carelessness and the virtuoso's cockiness, from a stumble, from numbing cold and the fatigue that sneaks up like a thief an hour before sunset. The high incidence of missing digits and of lamed and one-armed men in every wooded region says that the only real surety is to observe the letter of the law always—to behave as if all the conditions were chronically against you. The really finished axeman is distinguished from the novice, not only by his chips, but by the chances he forbids himself ever to take.

For my part, I think it salutary for every mother's son of us to deal with at least one thing that, because he has a wholesome fear of it, will hold him up to this sort of mark. I cannot believe that the moral stature of the race, or even of its best, has as yet quite outgrown the profit of some such self-discipline. Whatever uniformly enforces it for a great number is a cult, which is to say a section of culture. And, in the way of all genuine culture, it is no departmentalized and irrelevant mastery, like a parlor trick, but an impregnation of the whole man, like the grain in wood.

I, for a trifling instance, never pick up an axe without remembering that it means something to me to keep "these ten toes upon my hands" because I hope and intend to put in several thousand hours of my declining years playing, or playing at, the sonatas of Beethoven. These also are, if you like, a cult, a discipline, and the bond of a great sodality. What I deplore, not to say resent, is the vapid assumption that such an employment of time and tissue has a cultural significance above or alien to that of the varieties of manual work throughout which I shall, if provident and lucky, have preserved the necessary quota of fingers. What I presume to possess cultural significance is the meaning that Beethoven can have to us from the wood lot, the furrow, and the lathe; likewise the sustenance that at desk or typewriter, easel or keyboard, we draw from the work we have done and store up for the work we have yet to do.

TECHNICAL DISCUSSION

1. The author does not have a central judgment in this essay or a series of judgments, but he has a purpose which unifies the essay and which springs from a principle of life that he holds. What is the purpose? What is the principle? Perhaps the title will give you a clue to each.
2. Find several of the unsupported judgments made by the author and be ready to discuss in class the experiences the author might have had in mind as he wrote.
3. Some of the author's judgments are supported. Find two or three of them and their supporting data.
4. What is the general topic of the second section? Pick out the important judgments in this section.
5. What is the general topic of the third section? Pick out the important judgments in it. Explain the presence of the story about the tamarack tree.
6. What is the topic of the last section? Does the material here have any direct bearing on the author's purpose and on the principle of life that may be said to actuate him?

TOPICS FOR PAPERS

1. Do some research on a definition of culture; then write an essay in which you (a) define culture and (b) come to some conclusions about the culture of your community.
2. If you know a Jack-of-all-trades, write a character description of him, putting considerable emphasis on his tools, his work, and the values life holds for him. If possible, talk to him about his work and ideas.
3. Do you have any work or activity that satisfies a "muscle hunger" in you, a need to do something that requires physical skill and strength? If

so, write an essay in which you describe one of the times you performed such an act, treating your subject with attention to the details of the act and your emotional and philosophical responses as you performed it. Perhaps it was only a long walk you hungered for, or a climb up a mountain. Perhaps you felt impelled to make a piece of furniture or a model ship. Perhaps you tore down the motor of your car and put it together again.

In Praise of E. B. White, Realist

CLIFTON FADIMAN

It has been remarked—ever since Van Wyck Brooks pointed it out some decades ago—that the superior American writer often becomes famous, wealthy, influential, even more skillful, but only rarely becomes mature. Maturity still makes us uneasy. It is not irrelevant that the middle-aged heroes of the whisky advertisements have obviously been selected by virtue of their betrayal of no sign of any thought process whatsoever behind their photogenic distinction. Many of our writers find growing up not merely difficult but socially and emotionally unrewarding. Those who do insist on developing whether their readers like it or not are freaks.

E. B. White is such a freak.

He is also one of the most useful political thinkers in this country.

He is also one of the finest living writers of prose in this country.

This triad of statements will embarrass Mr. White, who not only writes as if he were a modest man—that's merely a trick—but actually is one. It may possibly arouse skepticism or even irritation in many others, including those who admire Mr. White for certain qualities that are as delightful as they are relatively unimportant. Agreed, he has the charm of a dozen Irishmen. He is a master of light verse. His sketches of country living are humorous and poetical. He is fey. He is whimsical. He is funny. He is beautifully absurd. Because he is all these things there is some danger that he will be considered a minor writer. I use the word danger advisedly. Thoreau was put down, is still being put down, as a "nature writer" and an eccentric. The truth is that we have not yet caught up with Thoreau, and unless we do so

"In Praise of E. B. White, Realist." From The New York *Times* Book Review, June 10, 1945. Reprinted by permission of the author and The New York *Times* Book Review.

our democracy, which is identical with the globe's democracy, is by so much the more in peril.

In using the solemn word *major* I run some risk of alienating people, including the subject of this essay. Nevertheless, I will use the word *major*. E. B. White is a major writer. He is a major writer because his ideas and sentiments are large and basic and because, within the limitations of his chosen style and form, he writes about them perfectly.

In these remarks (intended not as a critical essay but merely as a longish advertisement constructed to induce you to buy a few of Mr. White's ideas) I propose to write about him as if he were major.

In the early years of *The New Yorker* magazine, edited then, now, and let us hope forever by the nonpareil Harold Ross, E. B. White contributed excellent light verse and various prose oddments. For about ten years prior to 1938 he wrote or rewrote the first page (Notes and Comment) each week. For several years thereafter he wrote small essays for *Harper's* magazine under the heading One Man's Meat, and is now back on Notes and Comment again. He has published a couple of books of light verse: "Quo Vadimus" (amusing sketches); "Is Sex Necessary?" (with James Thurber), still funny and still reasonably wise; "Every Day Is Saturday," a collection of *The New Yorker* pieces, and "One Man's Meat," mainly from the pages of *Harper's*. During the approximately twenty years covered by the publication of these frail-appearing volumes he has grown from a paragrapher to a writer, from a light-fingered original humorist to a light-giving original thinker. That *The New Yorker,* which is primarily a magazine of entertainment, should have been his seminary and his graduate school is a tribute to the flexibility and vision of its editor. What hath Ross wrought?

A sentence or so back I spoke of Mr. White as an original thinker. I do not mean that you will find much that is "new" in him. I mean only that his mind naturally works from origins. His most casual remarks, and most of them are quite casual, come out of a sense not only of where man is but of what he started from. They are almost always based, though rarely explicitly, on an original, that is, fundamental, proposition which mankind when it is rational accepts as true. I have been casting about for a good short example of this kind of thinking and believe I will start with this one:

> Clubs, fraternities, nations—these are the beloved barriers in the way of a workable world; these will have to surrender some of their rights and some of their ribs. A "fraternity" is the antithesis of *fraternity*. The first (that is, the order or organization) is predicated on the idea of exclusion; the second (that is, the abstract thing) is based on a feeling of total equality. Anyone who remembers back to his fraternity days at college recalls the enthusiasts in his group, the rabid members, both old and young, who were obsessed with the mystical charm of membership in their particular order. They were usually men who were incapable of genuine brotherhood or at least unaware of its implications. Fraternity begins when the exclusion formula is found to be distasteful. The effect of any organization of a social and brotherly nature is to strengthen rather than to diminish the lines which divide people into classes; the effect of states and nations is the same, and eventually these lines will have to be softened; these powers will have to be generalized. It is written on the wall that this is so. I'm not inventing it, I'm just copying it off the wall.

It is my contention that this is original reflection. It goes back to an original abstract idea accepted by mankind when mankind is thinking rationally—the idea of fraternity. It demonstrates that college fraternities represent the opposite of this idea. The "practical" proof, if you must have one, of the soundness of the reasoning is that this paragraph is quoted as one of the basic arguments in the recent program of educational reorganization drawn up by a committee of Amherst College teachers. As a result it is probable that fraternities will be abolished at Amherst. The plain fact of the matter is that, if all college men could think, the mere attentive reading by them of Mr. White's half-dozen sentences would result in the immediate abolition of all fraternities, which in turn would constitute a radical step away from infantilism.

Mr. White is a very useful writer because he is an abstract thinker who does not write abstractly. His base is always a generalization, which is what makes him more than a journalist; but the development is always concrete. Here is an example: In October, 1940, he wrote a semi-joshing, semi-indignant piece on the design of the American motor-car. In the course of it he said, "The ultimate goal of automobile designers is to produce a car into whose driving seat the operator will sink without a trace." After enlarging on that nice (and true) point he went on to state: "The public's passive acceptance of this strange vehicle is disheartening, as is the acceptance by other peoples of the strange modern governments which are destroying them in a dulcet fashion. I think there will some day be an awakening of a rude sort, just as there will some day inevitably be a union of democracies, after many millions have died for the treacherous design of nationalism."

Now the parallel between the design of the motor-car and the "treacherous design of nationalism" (read fascism) is more than a piece of wit. In the first place it is based on a true relationship: in both cases "the operator will sink without a trace." But underlying Mr. White's concrete statements are certain unmentioned abstract ideas: first, that liberty is a good; second, that passive acceptance, as against rational reflection, is an evil. For me this is philosophy quite in the Greek sense.

Philosophy is a calm vision of the whole, journalism an excited perception of the part. Mr. White once wrote that he liked the radio comments of the late Hendrik Willem Van Loon on the day's events "because he has made them seem like a part of a whole, not like an isolated moment in time." This is profoundly true, and it is just as true that if radio commentators in general dared to talk about the events of the day as part of a whole the network officials would in unison shriek, "controversial." The result is that rational reflection is for the most part barred from the air. We get "forums" instead.

One of the results of having a vision of the whole is that Mr. White is forced to see the part for exactly what it is. If it is part of something big he sees that. (Remember the comment on college fraternities.) If it is part of something little he sees that. If the part is so small as to be almost nothing he cannot help seeing that too.

In July, 1938, he wrote, "It must have been two years ago that I attended a television demonstration at which it was shown beyond reasonable doubt that a person sitting in one room could observe the nonsense in another." Now this too is more than a witty and perfectly constructed sentence. It actually is a complete summary of all that is fundamentally important about television. Note that Mr. White does not say that it is not pleasant to observe nonsense. On the contrary, he knows, as we all do, that nonsense may be very pleasant, indeed, and interesting and even mildly necessary. But nonsense is small. The implication of the sentence is that television is small. It is small when it relays the contortions of a blues singer twenty feet into another room. It is exactly as small (though vastly more dreadful) when it relays the antics of diplomats ten thousand miles if the antics say no more than does the blues singer. Mr. White has his eye on the ends; the big network giants have their eye on the means. This is quite proper, because the size of the eyes involved is exactly proportioned to what they are interested in observing.

Television is only a small part of our national activity; but it is part of the mainspring of that activity, which is accumulation. Mr. White, even in his very early days, never lost sight of the design of that mainspring and of the basic fact that the accumulator, living under whatever system of government, is a slave. I offer two diverting samples (but all Mr. White's diversions, remember, seek rather than escape the center). 'Way back in *The New Yorker* of May 26, 1928, he printed this small quip:

A life insurance man told us of a remarkable business migration which took place in Madison Square recently. He said that one division of the Metropolitan Life moved en masse from one building to another, across the connecting bridge. At 2:30 the one hundred clerks ceased work and got up from their desks. At 2:41 the first desk was upended by a porter. At 3:35 the whole works had been transferred to the other building and electricians were installing the telephones. At 3:36 the clerks sat down and took up their duties. "And didn't any of the clerks escape?" we asked. But it was the wrong question.

It was, of course, the right question. It is we who have been giving the wrong answers.

Which leads to another brief entry, of May 13, 1933:

Mr. Edward A. Filene, the merchant of New England, told the alumni of Columbia University that we all want the same thing. "We all want some arrangement by which more people will be enabled to buy more things." Do we? That is a fair question to ask, because the cumulative goal of "more things" has remained almost unchallenged in all the long palaver of industrial recovery. A little research among the writings of another New Englander, who long ago turned out a passable essay on economy, reveals a more amusing, possibly a more sound, ideal. "The mass of men," he wrote, "lead lives of quiet desperation." And then, you will recall, he told of being present at the auction of a deacon's effects and of noticing, among the innumerable odds and ends representing the accumulation of a lifetime of endeavor, a dried tapeworm.

Thoreau remembered the tapeworm; White remembers the tapeworm; most of the rest of us merely manufacture the tapeworm.

He who remembers the tapeworm is the only crucially valuable commentator on American life. When Knute Rockne died, for instance, the nation gave way to an orgasm of grief, and President Hoover sent a eulogistic message. Mr. White (this was in 1931) uttered the one piercing comment on this national event. He said of it that Knute Rockne "was in the big money, and that was why Hoover happened to know about him." He then said the proper and human thing: "We see nothing wrong in the President's expressing grief over the loss of a beloved football coach, but," he went on, finally giving us the insight that marks the thinker and the critic of civilization, "from the diplomatic angle it seems to leave out certain other deceased members of college faculties, men who worked with undergraduates in groups other than groups of eleven. In our unofficial capacity, therefore, we take this opportunity to express the nation's grief in the death of all the other upright members of college faculties who died during the past year. We are sorry we don't know their names."

The point I should like to make about Mr. White's attitude is that it is not the attitude of an amiable, educated young man with high ideals. It is the attitude of a realist. His whimsical remarks are not sweet, though they are sweetly put; each one grasps a truth, holds it fast, exhibits it for all to see. That is why I have called this advertisement "E. B. White, Realist." His wit is realistic, his humor is realistic and, of course, his fantasy is realistic. It is, for example, the stock market reports that are fantastic, whereas it is Mr. White who is realistic in saying, "If a man wants to buy wheat, let him buy wheat and let the wheat be delivered to his door."

The spur of Mr. White's realism is the fact that he has the eye of a poet, a poet being a man who sees through things. Having the eye of a poet he is intensely aware of the unreality of our taken-for-granted environment. He is aware of the millions of substitutes for ideas, the millions of substitutes for emotions, the millions of substitutes for human beings. Out of this awareness the sweet and bitter of his prose continually well.

Perhaps I can make this clear by a personal reminiscence. About two weeks ago I passed an average American day. In the course of it the following minor things occurred:

1. I received a bill for my quarterly dues—which I gladly paid—from the American Federation of Radio Artists. But I am not a radio "artist," and neither are 99.9 per cent of my colleagues "artists." I am a radio worker, my status being that of employee.

2. I lunched with an amiable publisher, a valued friend, who suggested to me four ideas for books which he said would prove popular. They would have, too; but it never occurred to him that a book should come out of a writer's mind and heart rather than out of a publisher's inventive powers.

3. I noticed an advertisement for toffee showing two American soldiers, candy bar in hand, riding hell-for-leather in a jeep. The caption read: "When the going gets tough, it's Blank's Toffee." The writer of the advertisement and the readers of it were apparently unaware that the statement was pure madness.

4. A placard in a hotel lobby attracted my attention. It informed me that a well-known band was returning to entertain the hotel's clientele "by command." It is obvious that nobody at all commanded the engagement of the band, and even if anybody did, the band would not play better or worse for that reason.

5. Returning home, I found a well-written letter from the alumni committee of my alma mater, urging me to contribute money. The money was to be used for seven clearly listed purposes. Not one of these purposes had anything whatsoever to do with the proper education of young men, although my college was founded for that purpose and, so far as I can see, should not be used for any other.

I have drawn up this list of items (selecting these five from a much larger day's bag) to indicate that, for the most part we live in a world whose connection with reality is of the frailest. The average man, one of whom is speaking to you, functions on a level, observes on a level, entertains himself on a level, noticeably remote from what is real. It is not that we lie to each other; it is that we think we are speaking truth. This is the essence of lunacy.

It is the accepted, conventional, respectable lunacy that Mr. White sees and writes about, as did Swift and every other important satirist that ever lived. But he has more opportunity and vaster scope, because our lunacy is more extensive, more ramified and more attractively disguised.

The greatest of our lunacies can, however, be put with extreme simplicity. It is that humankind is fairly well determined to commit suicide. (We are doing it gradually, of course, the two German Wars against Mankind being merely the first steps.) This is the larger lunacy that has engaged the attention of E. B. White, realist, during the last two or three years and has impelled him to write the words which I for one believe entitle him to be called one of the most useful political thinkers in this country.

If you will write *The New Yorker,* 25 West Forty-third Street, New York City, and ask for a reprint of certain editorials, they will probably send you one. It is called "World Government and Peace" and is the work of a humorous writer and paragrapher, E. B. White. Perhaps I can give you the gist of it.

Mr. White grasped his central idea some time ago, long before Wendell Willkie gave it so dramatic an elaboration. On May 2, 1931, meditating on the popularity of Father Coughlin, he wrote:

We happen to be in a small way on the other side of the fence from Father Coughlin on all his points; but we must confess, after reading the statistics about his audience, that being on the other side of the fence from him is like standing all alone in the middle of a million-acre field. What an impressive thing it is! Talking against internationalism over the radio is like talking against rain in a rainstorm: the radio has made internationalism a fact, it has made boundaries look so silly that we wonder how mapmakers can draw maps without laughing; yet there stands Father Coughlin in front of the microphone, his voice reaching well up into Canada, his voice reaching well down into Mexico, his voice leaping national boundaries as lightly as a rabbit—there he stands, saying that internationalism will be our ruin, and getting millions of letters saying he is right.

That was fourteen years ago. Since then, by dint of using his mind, Mr. White has come a long way. He is now the most persuasive (I do not say systematic or exhaustive) American analyst of the lunacy that is nationalism and the sanity that is world law. Mind you, he is no "idealist"; he knows what the product (peace) is, he knows how much we must pay for it, and he knows what will happen if we do not buy.

Let's take a concrete problem that is bothering many of us, the problem of an international police force. Here are one long and one short White paragraph on the subject, dated May 15, 1943:

Dr. Gallup, the asker, has asked people whether they favor an international police force, and three out of four have said they do. That is very nice. It is also quite misleading. Asking a man whether he wants an international police force is like asking him whether he wants the Rockettes. Of course he does, but the question is not whether he thinks the Rockettes are a good idea but whether he knows what is in back of them, making them effective; in short, whether he is in earnest about the girls and willing to give up time and money to build a stage big enough to hold them, hire an orchestra loud enough to accompany them, buy costumes rich enough to adorn them, and in general sustain an organization orderly enough to give them meaning and make them click. Dr. Gallup should ask his question again, this time adding, "And you people realize, of course, that a police force is no good if simply used as a threat to strengthen agreements between independent powers, that to have meaning it must be the certified agent of the law, that to have law we must first have a constitutional world society, and that to achieve that each nation must say good-bye to its own freedom of action and to its long-established custom of doing as it damn well pleases. *Now* how many of you want an international police force?"

Here's one hand up, Dr. Gallup.

In other words, the disease is sovereignty; the cure is justice based on world law. As Mr. White puts it, "We are informed, almost hourly, that a new world order is in the making, yet most of the talk is of policy and almost none of the talk is of law." The law must be planetary, thinks White (echoing, by the way, a large number of other thinkers, including Jesus) and our devotion to it must be planetary also. As the realist puts it, "If somebody were to discover rubber plantations on Mars, a world government would not only be a prime necessity, it would be a damn cinch."

Apparently we are waiting for the discovery of those rubber plantations on Mars, and, to pass the time while waiting, we are killing each other noisily, torturing each other insanely, and, worst of all, fooling ourselves fatuously. We talk of joint action but we do not know what the term means. History (perhaps we can remember some quite recent history such as Trieste and Poland) shrieks at us that as long as the world is run on the principle of national sovereignty, there will never be any tendency toward joint action until it is too late. "Therefore, the problem is not how to make force available for joint action, but how to make world government available so that action won't have to be joint."

I offer a final quotation from Mr. White, realist. The date is Feb. 24 of this year.

> The delegates to San Francisco have the most astonishing job that has ever been dumped into the laps of a few individuals. On what sort of rabbit they pull from the hat hang the lives of most of us, and of our sons and daughters. If they put on their spectacles and look down their noses and come up with the same old bunny, we shall very likely all hang separately—nation against nation, power against power, defense against defense, people (reluctantly) against people (reluctantly). If they manage to bring the United Nations out of the bag, full blown, with constitutional authority and a federal structure having popular meaning, popular backing, and an overall authority greater than the authority of any one member or any combination of members, we might well be started up a new road.
>
> The pattern of life is plain enough. The world shrinks. It will eventually be unified. What remains to be seen (through eyes that now bug out with mortal terror) is whether the last chapter will be written in blood or in Quink.

Who's crazy? Mr. White, a quiet, rather unimposing man, a mere writer, a humorist who makes a living writing for a small local magazine? Or the diplomats who are going through exactly the same motions that have produced wars for four thousand years? Is it possible that Mr. White and those like him are correct—and the big, busy men with their big, teeming, idea-empty portfolios wrong? Is it possible that Willkie was right—and that Eden and Molotoff and Stettinius are wrong? Is it possible that T. V. Soong (as Mr. White reported) said the only truly realistic thing at San Francisco when he announced flatly that in the cause of world peace China was willing to give up some of her sovereignty?

Of course Mr. White is not a practical man. He doesn't make much money and he will never be a Senator. He is—let's be brutal—just a poet. But I seem to remember a sentence he once wrote that stays with me: "A despot doesn't fear eloquent writers preaching freedom—he fears a drunken poet who may crack a joke that will take hold."

Mr. White is now engaged in cracking some remarkable jokes. Who knows? Perhaps they will take hold. If not, we have a choice before us. We may choose war or slavery. Being a strong, courageous, energetic people we will choose war. But the odd part of it is that after we have done so, we will find that we have also chosen slavery.

Read Mr. White and see why.

TECHNICAL DISCUSSION

1. Find the major judgments Fadiman makes about White. Point out supporting materials.
2. Find judgments Fadiman makes about people and life in general. Point out supporting materials.
3. Are the ideas Fadiman has about people and life in general related to the ideas about White? Explain.
4. Find paragraphs that consist almost wholly of judgment.
5. Find statements about White's writing techniques. Point out the illustrations that Fadiman uses to make the techniques clear.
6. Find Fadiman's definition of "original thinking." How does Fadiman make his meaning clear?

TOPICS FOR PAPERS

1. Study the advertisements in popular magazines and write a paper describing the world the advertisers seem to have in mind for us. Describe, also, your reactions to that world, defending or attacking its values.
2. Read Thoreau's *Walden* and write a paper in which you establish Thoreau's major conclusions and come to conclusions of your own about your life if you lived it on the principles Thoreau held.

3. Read one of White's books and write an essay in which you state his fundamental judgments and in which, by using appropriate quotations, you demonstrate that he made those judgments.

4. Write a paper in which you apply one of White's judgments (or Fadiman's) to your community. Can you find evidence that White is correct or not?

5. Write a paper in which you discuss fraternities (or nations) in relation to the charge that they are not true brotherhoods. Draw on your experience in so far as you can. Draw also on what you can find written about them, for instance, Vincent Sheean's story of his college days in *Personal History* (Wendell Willkie's *One World*).

How to Mark a Book

MORTIMER J. ADLER

You know you have to read "between the lines" to get the most out of anything. I want to persuade you to do something equally important in the course of your reading. I want to persuade you to "write between the lines." Unless you do, you are not likely to do the most efficient kind of reading.

I contend, quite bluntly, that marking up a book is not an act of mutilation but of love.

You shouldn't mark up a book which isn't yours. Librarians (or your friends) who lend you books expect you to keep them clean, and you should. If you decide that I am right about the usefulness of marking books, you will have to buy them. Most of the world's great books are available today, in reprint editions, at less than a dollar.

There are two ways in which one can own a book. The first is the property right you establish by paying for it, just as you pay for clothes and furniture. But this act of purchase is only the prelude to possession. Full ownership comes only when you have made it a part of yourself, and the best way to make yourself a part of it is by writing in it. An illustration may make the point clear. You buy a beefsteak and transfer it from the butcher's icebox to your own. But you do not own the beefsteak in the most important sense until you consume it

"How to Mark a Book." From *The Saturday Review of Literature,* July 6, 1940. Reprinted by permission of the author, *The Saturday Review of Literature,* and *The Reader's Digest.*

and get it into your bloodstream. I am arguing that books, too, must be absorbed in your bloodstream to do you any good.

Confusion about what it means to *own* a book leads people to a false reverence for paper, binding, and type—a respect for the physical thing—the craft of the printer rather than the genius of the author. They forget that it is possible for a man to acquire the idea, to possess the beauty, which a great book contains, without staking his claim by pasting his bookplate inside the cover. Having a fine library doesn't prove that its owner has a mind enriched by books; it proves nothing more than that he, his father, or his wife, was rich enough to buy them.

There are three kinds of book owners. The first has all the standard sets and best-sellers—unread, untouched. (This deluded individual owns woodpulp and ink, not books.) The second has a great many books—a few of them read through, most of them dipped into, but all of them as clean and shiny as the day they were bought. (This person would probably like to make books his own, but is restrained by a false respect for their physical appearance.) The third has a few books or many—every one of them dog-eared and dilapidated, shaken and loosened by continual use, marked and scribbled in from front to back. (This man owns books.)

Is it false respect, you may ask, to preserve intact and unblemished a beautifully printed book, an elegantly bound edition? Of course not. I'd no more scribble all over a first edition of "Paradise Lost" than I'd give my baby a set of crayons and an original Rembrandt! I wouldn't mark up a painting or a statue. Its soul, so to speak, is inseparable from its body. And the beauty of a rare edition or of a richly manufactured volume is like that of a painting or a statue.

But the soul of a book *can* be separated from its body. A book is more like the score of a piece of music than it is like a painting. No great musician confuses a symphony with the printed sheets of music. Arturo Toscanini reveres Brahms, but Toscanini's score of the C-minor Symphony is so thoroughly marked up that no one but the maestro himself can read it. The reason why a great conductor makes notations on his musical scores—marks them up again and again each time he returns to study them—is the reason why you should mark your books. If your respect for magnificent binding or typography gets in the way, buy yourself a cheap edition and pay your respects to the author.

Why is marking up a book indispensable to reading? First, it keeps you awake. (And I don't mean merely conscious; I mean wide awake.) In the second place, reading, if it is active, is thinking, and thinking tends to express itself in words, spoken or written. The marked book is usually the thought-through book. Finally, writing helps you remember the thoughts you had, or the thoughts the author expressed. Let me develop these three points.

If reading is to accomplish anything more than passing time, it must be active. You can't let your eyes glide across the lines of a book and come up with an understanding of what you have read. Now an ordinary piece of light fiction, like, say, "Gone with the Wind," doesn't require the most active kind of reading. The books you read for pleasure can be read in a state of relaxation, and nothing is lost. But a great book, rich in ideas and beauty, a book that raises and tries to answer great fundamental questions, demands the most active reading of which you are capable. You don't absorb the ideas of John Dewey the way you absorb the crooning of Mr. Vallee. You have to reach for them. That you cannot do while you're asleep.

If, when you've finished reading a book, the pages are filled with your notes, you know that you read actively. The most famous *active* reader of great books I know is President Hutchins, of the University of Chicago. He also has the hardest schedule of business activities of any man I know. He invariably reads with a pencil, and sometimes, when he picks up a book and pencil in the evening, he finds himself, instead of making intelligent notes, drawing what he calls "caviar factories" on the margins. When that happens, he puts the book down. He knows he's too tired to read, and he's just wasting time.

But, you may ask, why is writing necessary? Well, the physical act of writing, with your own hand, brings words and sentences more sharply before your mind and preserves them better in your memory. To set down your reaction to important words and sentences you have read, and the questions they have raised in your mind, is to preserve those reactions and sharpen those questions.

Even if you wrote on a scratch pad, and threw the paper away when you had finished writing, your grasp of the book would be surer. But you don't have to throw the paper away. The margins (top and bottom, as well as side), the end-papers, the very space between the lines, are all available. They aren't sacred. And, best of all, your marks and notes become an integral part of the book and stay there forever. You can pick up the book the following week or year, and there are all your points of agreement, disagreement, doubt, and inquiry. It's like resuming an interrupted conversation with the advantage of being able to pick up where you left off.

And that is exactly what reading a book should be: a conversation between you and the author. Presumably he knows more about the subject than you do; naturally, you'll have the proper humility as you approach him. But don't let anybody tell you that a reader is supposed to be solely on the receiving end. Understanding is a two-way operation; learning doesn't consist in being an empty receptacle. The learner has to question himself and question the teacher. He even has to argue with the teacher, once he understands what the teacher is saying. And marking a book is literally an expression of your differences, or agreements of opinion, with the author.

There are all kinds of devices for marking a book intelligently and fruitfully. Here's the way I do it:

1. *Underlining:* of major points, of important or forceful statements.

2. *Vertical lines at the margin:* to emphasize a statement already underlined.

3. *Star, asterisk, or other doo-dad at the margin:* to be used sparingly, to emphasize the ten or twenty most important statements in the book. (You may want to fold the bottom corner of each page on which you use such marks. It won't hurt the sturdy paper on which most modern books are printed, and you will be able to take the book off the shelf at any time and, by opening it at the folded-corner page, refresh your recollection of the book.)

4. *Numbers in the margin:* to indicate the sequence of points the author makes in developing a single argument.

5. *Numbers of other pages in the margin:* to indicate where else in the book the author made points relevant to the point marked; to tie up the ideas in a book, which, though they may be separated by many pages, belong together.

6. *Circling of key words or phrases.*

7. *Writing in the margin, or at the top or bottom of the page, for the sake of:* recording questions (and perhaps answers) which a passage raised in your mind; reducing a complicated discussion to a simple statement; recording the sequence of major points right through the books. I use the end-papers at the back of the book to make a personal index of the author's points in the order of their appearance.

The front end-papers are, to me, the most important. Some people reserve them for a fancy bookplate. I reserve them for fancy thinking. After I have finished reading the book and making my personal index on the back end-papers, I turn to the front and try to outline the book, not page by page, or point by point (I've already done that at the back), but as an integrated structure, with a basic unity and an order of parts. This outline is, to me, the measure of my understanding of the work.

If you're a die-hard anti-book-marker, you may object that the margins, the space between the lines, and the end-papers don't give you room enough. All right. How about using a scratch pad slightly smaller than the page-size of the book—so that the edges of the sheets won't protrude? Make your index, outlines, and even your notes on the pad, and then insert these sheets permanently inside the front and back covers of the book.

Or, you may say that this business of marking books is going to slow up your reading. It probably will. That's one of the reasons for doing it. Most of us have been taken in by the notion that speed of reading is a measure of our intelligence. There is no such thing as the right speed for intelligent reading. Some things should be read quickly and effortlessly, and some should be read slowly and even laboriously. The sign of intelligence in reading is the ability to read different things differently according to their worth. In the case of good books, the point is not to see how many of them you can get through, but rather how many can get through you—how many you can make your own. A few friends are better than a thousand acquaintances. If this be your aim, as it should be, you will not be impatient if it takes more time and effort to read a great book than it does a newspaper.

You may have one final objection to marking books. You can't lend them to your friends because nobody else can read them without being distracted by your notes. Furthermore, you won't want to lend them because a marked copy is a kind of intellectual diary, and lending it is almost like giving your mind away.

If your friend wishes to read your "Plutarch's Lives," "Shakespeare," or "The Federalist Papers," tell him gently but firmly to buy a copy. You will lend him your car or your coat—but your books are as much a part of you as your head or your heart.

TECHNICAL DISCUSSION

1. This essay is interesting because it combines thematic and informative writing. Find the dividing line between the two types.
2. Is the thematic section given to one central theme? to several? to unsupported themes? Analyze the section for evidence to support your answer.
3. Which of the types of informative writing that we discussed in Chapter 2 does the author use?
4. Do the last four paragraphs of the essay revert to the thematic purpose of the author? Explain.

TOPICS FOR PAPERS

1. A review of *How to Read a Book,* by Mortimer J. Adler.
2. An intimate essay about your favorite reading.
3. A general process story of what happens in the library system between the time when the student goes in to get a book and the time he walks out with it. Use "color" to lighten the story of the process.

Appendix
Library Research and Documentation

LIBRARY RESEARCH AND DOCUMENTATION

PART of the work of the undergraduate is the term report, or research paper. Students may have as many as four or five such reports to do in one term. Beyond question research is not easy, but it is not as hard as the inexperienced freshman may think when he hears his older friends on the campus agonizing over reports written in the past or faced in the future. The individual steps of research are simple. It is when the researcher skips them or performs them in a slipshod way that he winds trouble upon trouble. The one general mental preparation the student should make is to swear to begin his paper as soon as the assignment has been given and to take every step of it correctly the first time. There will be more leisure for dancing and conversation over cokes if that oath is made and kept; and there will be the solid fun that goes with a genuinely creative act, for good research is creation of a high order.

The term report is a special problem that the student works out alone, generally in the library, in addition to the regular class assignments. The report has two chief aims: to present the facts and conclusions of the problem and to show, by documentation, the sources of every fact and opinion that the student himself did not originate. Though the report should deal with a subject of interest to the student, it is written with some degree of objectivity and with strict attention to form. Library skill is a necessary element in the student's equipment; and as documentation is an adjunct of library research, the techniques of the footnote and bibliography and of the integration of source material are also part of the student's equipment. The purpose of this appendix is to give the student enough of this equipment so that he can write creditable term reports. We shall begin with subjects for research.

SUBJECTS FOR RESEARCH

Everything is a subject for research. Look at the first object that meets your eyes: the typewriter, a pencil, the etching over your desk, electric light bulbs. Anyone can spend a great part of his life finding facts and making judgments about these objects, if they interest him. Only rarely, however, do the facts about such things interest the professor. He wants his students to dig into subjects that expand their knowledge and develop their skills in relation to the course he is teaching. He may even tell his students what their topics are to be. If he is teaching Roman history, he will want topics under that heading. If he is teaching soil conservation, he will want topics under that heading. Students therefore expect guidance in the choice of a topic.

The alert freshman may wonder just what good his research can do the world. It isn't likely that it will add much in the way of undiscovered fact. This need not worry him if he will look at the research as designed to add to *his* stock of knowledge. If he does it well, he cannot fail to improve his understanding of life and his skill in handling intellectual problems. There is also an even chance he will read something that will set his spirit aflame with a curiosity strong enough to last the rest of his days. He may in solving one problem arouse interests that will take him literally down the Mackenzie River or figuratively anywhere the mind can go. There is also a fair chance that part of the paper can be original. Some possibilities of originality are the following: Suppose a contemporary novelist comes out with a novel on a social theme. The student can do library research to find out what sociologists and historians have said about the social theme and then put the novelist in his setting, correcting, criticizing, approving, or comparing. Suppose the student has been taking a course in farm management. He can look up the facts and principles as they apply to the farms and crops in his locality and then use the library materials as the basis of a study of his own or a neighbor's farm. Suppose the student is taking a course in nutrition. The food habits of any given locality, or boarding house, studied in the light of what the student can find out about nutrition would make an interesting and partly original paper.

Students who have a completely free choice of subject and who cannot, even so, settle on a topic may find the following list suggestive enough to help them. It is a general list and should give a clue to something of interest.

Salmon conservation
Ceramics
Soil erosion
Laces
The Pulitzer prizes
Great women
Labor unions
County government
Art
Sheep raising
Slavery
Superstition
The forest ranger
Great dams
Highway engineering
Mental telepathy
Circus life
Election campaign issues
National parks
Public health
Game laws
Indian treaties
Exploration
Nylon
Homesteading
Indian reservations
Colorado and statehood
Forest fires
Seaweeds
Weather
The grasshopper
Mass production
Radio advertising
Wild flowers
Native desert animals
The last ice-age
Mountain climbing
Installment buying
Railroads
Malnutrition
Cotton
Fire departments
Captains of industry
American cities
Political leaders
Wagnerian sources
Mexican social patterns
Williamsburg, Virginia
Naval history of the Great Lakes
Coal by-products
Paper
Soy beans
Pine tree diseases
Period furniture

After the student has in mind his general subject, his next problem is to make the subject specific—that is, to give it limits determined by the required length of the paper and by the facilities for study. The rule is to select a topic which can be adequately treated within the assigned limits. A rambling, vague development of a huge subject is pointless; and so is a development which gets only part of a topic. The paper must be whole, and wholly done; therefore the student has to divide his general subject into its natural segments. Suppose we assume the general subject is exploration. The topic might be the preparations made by Lewis and Clark for their western journey; or it might be the instruments of sea navigation used during the fifteenth century; or the obstacles attendant to climbing Mount St. Elias; or Magellan's last day alive. Each of these topics is integral. Each constitutes a whole. Let us assume, for another example, that the general subject is public health. Obviously it, like exploration, cannot be treated in two to five thousand words. It must be cut into topics: the legal position of compulsory vaccination of public school students; the methods of preventing bubonic plague in seaport towns; the training required of a school nurse; the economics of a municipal dental clinic. A method of narrowing broad subjects is to ask questions for which answers are wanted. Of the subject wild flowers we might ask the following questions: Which geographic area do we want to study? What are the annuals of that area? The perennials? What are the seasons when the blooms appear? At what altitudes do the plants grow? Each of these questions could serve as the basis for a whole paper, or several of them could be used. It doesn't take much imagination to ask questions when we are faced with a broad subject; and the questions provide a focus for reading, making intelligent study possible. The narrowing also provides emotional security for the young researcher. Knowing precisely what it is he wants to do, he approaches the library directly and makes measured progress.

THE LIBRARY

Research divides itself, speaking broadly, into two main activities: (1) discovery of new facts by exploration in the laboratory or elsewhere and (2) putting old facts into new combinations. Most researchers, of course, use both, with one or the other emphasized. For the student the first will be familiar through his science work, and the second through his library reading. Both are important, but the present nature of undergraduate college education puts a heavy emphasis on the library.

The library is primarily a repository of written material, a storehouse of man's records. It is, in addition, a highly complicated mechanism for making use of the records. Because of the complication, the research worker must know a minimum of library technique in order to work effectively; and the student, therefore, needs some instruction in library system and procedure.

After his specific topic is determined, the student makes his bibliography, or list of readings from which he is to gather his facts. He will find in the library three great sources of the items on his list:

1. General references and prepared bibliographies
2. The card catalogue
3. Periodical guides

General References and Prepared Bibliographies. The young researcher should probably go to the general references for his start. These range from popular encyclopedias and dictionaries to highly specialized reference works, which are usually located together in the library. Librarians will tell the inquiring student where they are found, if he does not already know. Every field of knowledge has its special encyclopedias and dictionaries, and the student must not overlook them; but he ordinarily first uses the general sets, such as the *Encyclopaedia Britannica,* and there gets his first wide view of his subject. Often he will find at the conclusion of each article a list of books on the subject. This list he will copy.

The general reference section of the library will also contain books of bibliographies on a great many subjects. It may be that the student can find in these all the references he needs for his whole study.

The following is a short, alphabetized list of general references and bibliographical aids found, at least in part, in every good library. The list is itself a "bibliography," and its form is rigorous as to detail. Such detail is an essential part of the information the researcher includes with his report.

Bibliographic Index: A Cumulative Bibliography of Bibliographies, 1883 to date. New York: Wilson, 1938—.

Book Review Digest, 1905 to date. New York: Wilson, 1906—.

Cambridge Bibliography of English Literature. Ed. by F. W. Bateson. New York: Macmillan, 1941. 4 vols.

Cambridge History of American Literature. Ed. by William Peterfield Trent, *et al*. New York: Putnam, 1917-1921. 3 vols. Reprint ed. 1933. 3 vols.

Cambridge History of English Literature. Ed. by A. W. Ward and A. R. Waller. New York: Putnam, 1907-1927. 14 vols.

Chambers Biographical Dictionary. New ed. Philadelphia: Lippincott, 1935.

Dictionary of American Biography. Ed. by Allen Johnson and Dumas Malone. New York: Scribner, 1928-1937. 20 vols. plus index vol.

Dictionary of National Biography. Ed. by Leslie Stephen and Sidney Lee. London: Oxford University Press, 1885, 1937. 24 vols.

Education Index: A cumulative Author and Subject Index to a Selected List of Educational Periodicals, Books and Pamphlets, 1929 to date. New York: Wilson, 1932–. 3 vols.

Encyclopaedia Britannica: A New Survey of Universal Knowledge. 14th ed. New York: Encyclopaedia Britannica, Inc., 1929. 24 vols.

Encyclopedia of the Social Sciences. Ed. by E. R. A. Seligman and Alvin Johnson. New York: Macmillan, 1930-1935. 15 vols.

Hammond, C. S. and Co. *New World Loose Leaf Atlas*. New York: Hammond, 1936.

Mudge, Isadore G. *Guide to Reference Books*. 6th ed. Chicago: American Library Assn., 1936. Supplement, 1939.

New Standard Dictionary. New York: Funk & Wagnalls, 1913. Plate revision, 1938.

New Standard Encyclopedia of Art. New York: Garden City Publishing Co., 1939.

Oxford English Dictionary. Ed. by A. H. Murray, *et al*. Oxford: Clarendon Press, 1888-1933. 10 vols. and Supplement. Corrected reissue, 1933. 12 vols. and Supplement.

The Oxford History of Music. 2 ed. Oxford: Clarendon Press, 1929-1934. 7 vols.

Palgrave, H. I. *Palgrave's Dictionary of Political Economy*. Ed. by Henry Higgs. London: Macmillan, 1923-1926. 2 vols.

Roget, Peter M. *Roget's International Thesaurus of English Words and Phrases.* Revised ed. by C. O. S. Mawson. New York: Crowell, 1932.

Sayre, Wallace Stanley. *Your Government:* An Outline for Every American Citizen. 3 ed. New York: Barnes & Noble, 1935.

Shores, Louis. *Basic Reference Books:* An Introduction to the Evaluation, Study, and Use of Reference Materials. 2 ed. Chicago: American Library Assn., 1939.

Spalding's Official Athletic Almanac, 1893 to date. New York: American Sports Publishing Co., 1893—.

Webster's New International Dictionary. 2 ed. Springfield, Mass.: Merriam, 1934.

Who's Who, 1848 to date [Living Englishmen]. London: A. and C. Black, 1849—.

Who's Who in America, 1899/1900 to date. Chicago: A. N. Marquis Company, 1899—.

World Almanac and Book of Facts, 1866 to date. New York: World-Telegram, 1866—.

Card Catalogue. The second of the three great sources of bibliographical material is the library card catalogue, a filing system in which is listed, alphabetically, on small cards, every book the library has on its shelves, each book on its own card. The catalogue is so ingeniously arranged that a student who knows nothing about the writers in the field he is studying may in a short time have an armful of valuable books about it.

Should the student know the names of the authors, he looks for their books under those names. Should he know the titles, he looks under titles—according to alphabetical arrangement, of course. But if he knows neither authors nor titles, he looks under the subject heading; and if he is wise, he will try several headings should the first one fail. For instance, if he wants books on games, he should try "games." If that fails, he should try "recreation," "sports," "playground activities," etc., until he does find the cards listing the books. When the right subject card is discovered, there will be found behind it in a group all the cards listing titles in the library on that subject.

✱
+
ND3359 **Sullivan,** *Sir* **Edward,** *bart.*, 1852–1928.
.B7S8 The Book of Kells, described by Sir Edward Sullivan, bart., and illustrated with t· enty-four plates in colours. London, New York [etc.] "The " ltd., 1914.

v, 34 p. xxiv mount

Each plate accom descriptive letterpress.

1. Book of K mina- tion of books a Studio.

Library

FOR HOME USE

CALL NUMBER
COPY WORDS OR SYMBOLS OVER NUMBER
✱ +
ND 3359
B7S8

AUTHOR Sullivan Edward
TITLE The Book of Kells
BORROWER (PRINT) Edna
ADDRESS (PRINT) NUMBER 91
VOLUME OR YEAR
ACC.
COP.

READING ROOM USE FOR TWO HOURS

FORM A3

AUTHOR Sullivan, Edward

TITLE The Book of Kells.

DO NOT WRITE IN THIS SPACE

CALL NUMBER
COPY WORDS OR SYMBOLS OVER NUMBER
✱ +
ND 3359
.B7S8

VOLUME OR YEAR

COP ACC.

BORROWER'S NAME (PRINT) Edna Harris

ADDRESS (PRINT) 918 Foster Ave. SCHOOL: Educ.

BOROUGH: Brooklyn CITY: N.Y. TEL. Ma 6-2145

NO BOOKS ISSUED WITHOUT BURSAR'S RECEIPT
USE A SEPARATE SLIP FOR EACH TITLE

113-200M-136

FILL OUT A CALL SLIP

Often the books are listed under two subject headings. The student may find "see also" cards, which will give related titles, again in the appropriate alphabetical place in the catalogue. It may be seen from this that almost every book in the library is listed three times in the catalogue—invariably twice and frequently five or six times: by author, by title, by subject heading. Each listing is an individual card in its proper alphabetical spot.

All this makes the problem of finding book titles relatively easy. One finds the card catalogue, usually in a prominent place near the loan desk. He searches through it for author cards, title cards, or subject cards. He fills out a "call slip," found nearby, and presents it to the attendant at the loan desk. If the book is not in use or on reserve, the student receives it shortly. The information put on the call slip is generally the call number of the book—a number that indicates the place on the shelves where the book is kept, the author, the title, and the student's name and address. The call number should be copied exactly and with any symbols accompanying it; otherwise much time may be wasted in a futile hunt. As a final point, the student should know the library rules for the use of its books.

The illustrations of catalogue card and call slips above are typical. The first is an author card, the second is a call slip for a book to be used at home, and the third is a call slip for a book to be used in the library.

Periodical Guides. The last of the three chief sources of bibliographical items in every library is that which gives the key to periodical and newspaper material. Unless the student knows how to use the magazine and newspaper files that exist everywhere, they are for him barricaded highways to successful scholarship.

Adequate libraries always have files of magazines. The important articles in them are indexed, and the most useful of the indexes are the following:

Poole's Index to Periodical Literature, 1802-1906. Boston: Houghton, Mifflin and Company, 1882-1908. 7 vols.

The Readers' Guide to Periodical Literature, 1900 to date. New York: H. W. Wilson Company, 1905—.

International Index to Periodicals, 1907 to date. New York: H. W. Wilson Company, 1913—.

The student who wants to use the periodical files for source material should find the section of the library that contains them. Somewhere in the vicinity he will find the periodical indexes.

Poole's Index lists articles, mainly in general literature, of the nineteenth century under subject and title.

The Readers' Guide is a more satisfactory tool because it is contemporary and lists all of the important articles appearing in well over a hundred magazines. The listing is made alphabetically, under subject; author; and for fiction, drama, etc., under title. *The Readers' Guide* is therefore somewhat like the library card catalogue in arrangement. The entries are highly abbreviated and are meaningless unless the student can translate them. The key to the abbreviations appears in the front of each volume and the entries can be checked there. Typical entries are such as these:

Subject entry, "see" reference
CROP insurance. See Insurance, Agricultural

Subject entry
INSURANCE, Agricultural
Crop insurance. R. Clapper. il R of Rs 94:30-4 N '36

Author entry
Clapper, Raymond
Crop insurance. R of Rs 94:30-4 N '36

Title entry
BITTER passion; story. See Flandrau, G. C.

Translated, the information in the first three items above is this: On the general subject of crop insurance Raymond Clapper has an article appearing in the *Review of Reviews,* volume 94, pages 30 to 34, November, 1936, entitled "Crop Insurance."

The Readers' Guide is cumulative—that is, new volumes appear at regular intervals and later are amalgamated and bound in volumes representing longer periods of time, generally one to two years.

The *International Index* lists titles on more technical subjects than does *The Readers' Guide.* The articles are available in the language of the country where they are published. The listings are made under subject and author.

Two of the more specialized indexes, of which there are several, are the following:

Annual Magazine Subject Index, 1907 to date. Boston: F. W. Faxton Company, 1908—.

The Industrial Arts Index, 1913 to date. New York: H. W. Wilson Company, 1913—.

The first of these lists articles, English and American, on art, travel, and history. The second follows the specialty indicated by its name: business, trade, and engineering.

A point to remember is that every magazine provides indexes for itself at the completion of its "volume," a sequence of issues bound together. If we lack any other guide, this index is a sensible way to get at material.

After the student gets a list of articles on his topic, he refers to the check-list of magazines in the library to discover which are available. As he is ready to read, he fills out call slips and presents them to the attendant, or he goes to the open shelves and finds the volumes himself. As a rule magazines must be read in the library. The risk of losing material that can never be replaced requires this restriction.

Some libraries keep files of newspapers; but few newspapers are indexed, and the student who wants material from them of a local nature must thumb through back issues. If the material is of national or international scope, there is aid. *The New York Times Index,* 1913 to date, and *The Official Index to the* [London] *Times,* 1914 to date, are kept in many libraries, making it possible to find the exact dates of events since 1913. With the date, the student can go to his local paper and quickly get from the files the issues he wants, for national and international news events appear in papers on the date, or near it, of occurrence. These indexes, like those for magazines, are kept up to date by supplements, later issued as bound volumes, or by regularly appearing supplements that do not need amalgamating.

The student who has gone through the library, carefully exploiting all its resources—general references, card catalogue, and periodical guides—should have in his possession a considerable list of books and articles on his topic. This list is sometimes called a "working bibliography." Each item is on a card and will look somewhat as follows:

Subject	Theodore Dreiser
Author	Cargill, Oscar
Title	Intellectual America
Publisher and date	New York: The Macmillan Company, 1941
Library call number	PS88 .C37
Part of book applying to the subject	Chapter II, Section 3, "American Naturalism," pages 107-127

READING

By the time the student is ready for serious and sustained reading he can probably make a rough outline which divides his topic into sections. With this outline in mind he can read to fill it in with details. If he has themes to support, he looks for supporting data. If he is writing informatively, he looks for the facts. If he does not yet know which purpose is to control his material, he examines everything until he does know. In any event, he reads to fill in the rough divisions of his topic with material. Without these divisions, he may toil unnecessarily through profitless books. If his discoveries require that he revise his outline, naturally he does so.

The student should not attempt to read every reference word for word. The experienced reader looks through chapter headings for hints concerning subject matter. He uses the index. He skims until he hits a vein that needs careful working; then he digs into it. Once he finds material, he gathers it, item by item, on cards. If he quotes his source directly, he uses quotation marks—*invariably!* The card is checked immediately for accuracy; and a complete bibliographical notation, including page number, is written on it. The card is then given a heading that indicates the place in the outline where the material is to be used. Should the student wish to comment on the material, he may use another card, appropriately referring to the earlier one; or he may use space, if any, on the first. He should label his comment in some way so that later he does not confuse it with material copied or summarized from his readings. Whenever his readings suggest an idea, he should write it down at once. He will otherwise lose much that comes from himself by way of analysis and criticism, for the original stimulus that brought the idea may never be repeated.

The following illustrates a note card:

Subject	Theodore Dreiser Sources of his novels
Notes (Summarized)	*An American Tragedy* is drawn largely from the New York *World* account of the Chester Gilette-Grace Brown murder and subsequent trial. Much of it is copied, even to punctuation. Some of it is changed only slightly. p. 111 *The Financier* and *The Titan* use material taken from newspaper accounts of "the notorious Charles Yerkes." p.112
Source	Cargill, Oscar. *Intellectual America*. New York: The Macmillan Company, 1941

WRITING

Documentation. Writing a research paper offers no new difficulties to the student except for the formal requirements of documentation. The student knows if he is writing an informative or thematic paper and how to do each, but he may be puzzled by the intricacies of footnotes and bibliographies.

Footnotes. The chief occasions for using footnotes are the following: to put before the reader material that is not a unified part of the text itself; to give the source of all direct quotations which are not common knowledge; and to acknowledge the source of details that are borrowed from another person.

If the writer could make in his text a complete acknowledgment of everything borrowed, he would not need footnotes; but it seldom happens that he can, for the details of annotation quickly overload the text and put too great a strain on the reader. The footnote device is the solution.

The mechanics of the footnote vary, but the description that follows is of a typical system.

Footnotes, as illustrated in the pages of text reproduced with this chapter, go at the bottom of the page where they originate. Because the margins of every page are kept the same size, the more footnotes used the sooner the text is broken off to supply room. A mark is drawn, or typed, part of the way across the page, from the left toward the center, between the text and the footnotes. This prevents confusion. The lines in each footnote item are single-spaced, but the space between each item is doubled, or at least made a bit larger than a single space. This provides for easier reading. Each footnote begins with a number that corresponds with the number previously used *just after* the material in the text that is to be documented. The sequence of numbers generally begins anew on each page. The sequence may run through a whole chapter.

If a bibliography accompanies the paper, the footnote form is slightly different from what it would be if there were no bibliography. The first reference to a given source, furthermore, differs from all the succeeding references to the same source. The first is called the *primary* reference. The succeeding references are called *secondary.*

Most student papers will have a bibliography, and the primary footnotes for a book will contain the following types of material:

1. Name of author or authors;
2. Title (underlined in typed or hand-written manuscript to show italics), edition if more than one, editor, translator if any;
3. Page or pages from which material is taken, volume number if the source contains more than one.

The following are typical entries:

[1] John Gallishaw, *Twenty Problems of the Fiction Writer,* p. 72.

[2] Paul Hollister, "Walt Disney," *1941 Essay Annual,* ed. by Erich A. Walter, pp. 201-219.

[3] John A. Hayward and George C. Hazleton, *The Reports of the Circuit Court of the District of Columbia,* Vol. 2, p. 87.

[4] W. B. Yeats, *Letters to the New Island,* ed. with introduction and notes by H. Reynolds, p. 20.

[5] Frank Aydelotte, *English and Engineering,* 4th ed., p. 12.

The primary forms for the footnotes that refer to articles in magazines or to such bulletins and pamphlets as are published serially will contain the following types of material:

1. Name of author if any;
2. Title of the article (in quotation marks);
3. Name of magazine or serial (underlined in typed or hand-written manuscript to show italics);
4. Volume or serial number;
5. Date (in parentheses);
6. Page or pages from which material is taken.

The following are typical entries:

[1] R. Clapper, "Crop Insurance," *Review of Reviews,* XCIV (November, 1936), p. 32.

[2] Cary Byers, "The Future Strength of Germany," *Harper's Magazine,* CXC (December, 1944), pp. 48-57.

[3] Francis Densmore, *Pawnee Music,* Bureau of American Ethnology Bulletin No. 93 (1929), p. 10.

[4] *Mammals of New Mexico,* North America Fauna No. 53, U. S. Dept. Agr. Biol. Survey (1931), p. 345.

Newspaper footnote entries contain all the information necessary for rapid location of the source indicated. Typical entries are such as these:

[1] "Argentina Quits Hemisphere Group," New York *Sun,* January 10, 1945, p. 14.

[2] "The President Must Lead," Editorial, New York *Times,* January 9, 1945, p. 18.

[3] Orville Prescott, "Books of the Times," New York *Times,* January 9, 1945, p. 17.

Footnote entries that refer to such source material as interviews, lectures, and letters contain enough data to identify them. The entries below are typical:

[1] From a class lecture by Dr. Walter Brownson, October 11, 1944.

[2] Statement by Dr. James Reeves, personal interview.

Footnote references to standard editions of literary, classical, and religious works use a short form. In reference to plays such words as "act," "scene," and "line" may be omitted, leaving only capital roman numerals for acts, lower case roman numerals for scenes, and arabic numerals for lines. The following are illustrative footnote references to plays and classical and religious works:

[1] Jonson, *Volpone; or, The Fox,* I, iv, 19-24.

[2] Keats, "Ode to a Nightingale," lines 51-55.

[3] Acts 6:4.

[4] Dante, *Inferno,* Canto X.

When the paper is not accompanied by a bibliography, the primary form of book entries includes all the information as directed above and in addition the place of publication, the publisher, and the date of publication. The additional items are enclosed in parentheses. Note the following:

[1] John Gallishaw, *Twenty Problems of the Fiction Writer* (New York: G. P. Putnam's Sons, 1929), p. 72.

[2] Franz Alexander, *Our Age of Unreason* (Philadelphia: J. B. Lippincott Company, 1942), pp. 197-198.

The primary forms are used only once for each source named. After the complete citation has been made, secondary forms are used in order to save time and space. Some of them and their uses are the following:

When a footnote reference is the same as the last one preceding except for the page number, we simply write

[6] *Ibid.,* p. 117.

If the page is the same, the abbreviation *Ibid.* (for *ibidem,* in the same place) is sufficient. The page number is omitted. The *Ibid.,* and any other such word or phrase, is underlined in typed or hand-written manuscript to show italics.

When the footnote reference is the same as one already used, but when others have come between the first and succeeding entries, we write the following:

[8] Gallishaw, *Twenty Problems,* p. 84.

[9] Clapper, "Crop Insurance," p. 34.

Some writers use the abbreviated phrase *op. cit.* (in the work cited) instead of the title, but only when no other books or articles by the author have been used in the research.

[8] Gallishaw, *op. cit.,* p. 84.

Bibliography. The bibliography is a list of the written sources of the materials presented in the study. Unless the list is very long, all the items may be arranged in one alphabetical column; but if the list is long, the items may be divided by sub-topics or by some such artificial classification as books, periodicals, and general references. The arrangement of the details within each item should be consistent with standard practice, both in the order of presentation of the details and in punctuation. We should treat each item as an abbreviated sentence exactly parallel in structure to all the other items. Double authorship, edition numbers, anonymity, or editorship should cause no trouble. The bibliography of general references, on page 411, and that which follows below contain enough examples for study. Standard forms for bibliographical items follow (Note that in bibliographies the author's last name comes first):

BOOK

Chase, Stuart. *The Tyranny of Words.* New York: Harcourt, Brace and Company, 1938.

MAGAZINE ARTICLE

Clapper, R. "Crop Insurance." *Review of Reviews,* XCIV (November, 1936), 30-34.

ANONYMOUS MAGAZINE ARTICLE

"The Presidency." *Time,* XLV (January 15, 1945), 17.

NEWSPAPER ARTICLE

New York *Times* (December 1, 1941), 4.

CHAPTER IN BOOK

Brooks, Van Wyck. "Longfellow in Cambridge." *The Flowering of New England,* Chapter VIII. Modern Library Edition. New York: Modern Library, 1941.

It frequently happens that a professor, with good reason, uses a system of documentation that belongs to his special field. There are several such. The student who is asked to follow such a system will of course get the necessary instruction and use it in his paper.

The information given here on documentation is only a start on the subject. No better place to continue the study can be found than the student's own observation as he reads documented material. He will find many things to add to his repertoire. As a guide in interpreting some of the abbreviations he will run into, the following list is offered:

bibl.	bibliography
cf.	compare
et al.	and others
f., ff.	and the following page(s)
l., ll.	line(s)
loc. cit.	in the place cited
MS.	manuscript
op. cit.	in the work cited
passim	here and there
tr.	translator
vol.	volume
vs., vss.	verse(s)

Exercises

A. Select a topic for a research paper and as quickly as possible hand to the teacher the following:

1. An exact statement of the subject after you have narrowed it—Ants: How They Find Their Way About; There Was Fun To Be Had on the Old Oregon Trail;
2. Two or three working bibliography cards, at least one of which cites a periodical source if any are to be used;
3. Two or three filled in note cards;
4. A preliminary topical outline of what the paper will cover.

B. Finish the research paper started in Exercise A, using appropriate documentation. Study as models the specimen pages below.

C. Read "The Cattleman's Frontier, 1845-1867," page 428, studying it for its footnote techniques. You will find that the form varies slightly from that which you have just learned. Be ready to explain the items, to point out the variation, and to ask questions about anything you do not understand.

D. Read "The Evidence on 'O. K.,'" page 444, for an illustration of research writing that does not use footnote documentation. Be ready to explain the author's method of citing his sources and to defend or attack it.

Specimen Page from a Research Paper

It is said of Hippolyte Adolphe Taine that he claimed only to have co-ordinated and systematized the scientific method latent in Sainte-Beuve.[1] A comparison of Taine with Cousin, however, will reveal that the latter probably had considerable influence. Cousin and Taine have decided similarities.[2] There seems little doubt, though, that Taine's ability to generalize, as exemplified in his *History of English Literature,* 1863, caused more commotion in the literary world than did either Cousin or Sainte-Beuve. The *History of English Literature,* especially the "Introduction," is now generally thought to be too rigidly limited by its principle, but it was and still is influential.

Taine was a scientific positivist, believing that the basis of knowledge is scientific fact gained from a minute analysis of phenomena. Genuine history, he believed,

> is brought into existence only when the historian begins to unravel . . . the living man, toiling, impassioned, entrenched in his customs, with his voice and features, his gestures and his dress, distinct and complete as he from whom we have just parted in the street.[3]

Taine found three primal mainsprings of human action: race, surroundings, and epoch. Race was for him the same as for Herder. Epoch, as for Cousin, was to be explained in terms of a master idea. Surroundings included the natural and the sociological. Man, Taine said,

> is not alone in the world; nature surrounds him and his fellow men surround him; accidental and secondary tendencies come to place themselves on his primitive tendencies, and physical or social circumstances disturb or confirm the character committed to their charge.[4]

Again, this time concerning social interrelationships, Taine said that there is a law of mutual dependence:

> A civilization forms a body, and its parts are connected with each other like the parts of an organic body.[5]

When there is a change in one of the organs of an animal, all the organs

---

[1] Irving Babbitt, *Masters of French Criticism,* p. 218.
[2] See Cousin's *History,* p. 168.
[3] H. A. Taine, *History of English Literature,* tr. N. Van Laun, p. 2.
[4] *Ibid.,* p. 14.
[5] *Ibid.,* p. 22.

Specimen Bibliography: Wildlife Conservation

Audubon, J. J. *The Birds of America.* Philadelphia: J. B. Chevalier, 1840-1847. 7 vols.

Conservation of Wildlife, Hearings before Select Comm. on Conservation of Wildlife Resources, House Rep., 76th Cong., 3rd Sess., Washington, D.C., 1940.

Courtney, W. B. "Unhappy Hunting Grounds." *Collier's,* XCII (November 4, 1933), 20+.

Darling, J. M. "Save Our Game! Provide Reservations, Stop Useless Swamp Drainage." *Scientific American,* CLIII (September, 1935), 117-19.

Ditmars, R. L. *The Reptile Book.* New York: Doubleday, Doran & Co., 1935.

Elliott, H. W. *Fur-Seal Fisheries of Alaska.* Doc. 175, House of Rep., 54th Cong., 1896.

Ely, Alfred, Anthony, H. E., and Carpenter, R. M. *North American Big Game.* New York: C. Scribner's Sons, 1939.

Forbush, E. H. *Useful Birds and their Protection.* Boston: State Board of Agr., 1905.

"Game Situation." *Canadian Forum,* XII (May, 1933), 285.

Grinnell, J. "A Way to 'Bring Back' the Native Bighorn to the Yosemite." *Sierra Club Bulletin,* XX (1935), 28-31.

Henderson, Junius. *The Practical Value of Birds.* New York: Macmillan Co., 1934.

Hornaday, W. T. *Our Vanishing Wild Life: Its Extermination and Preservation.* New York: C. Scribner's Sons, 1913.

Knowles, Mrs. J. E. "Montana Slaughters Antelope." *Nature Magazine,* XXVIII (December, 1936), 362.

Lewis, Meriwether. *Original Journals of the Lewis and Clark Expedition, 1804-1806, etc.* Ed. by Reuben G. Thwaites. New York: Dodd, Mead & Co., 1904-1905. 8 vols.

Nelson, E. W. *Wild Animals of North America.* Washington: National Geographic Society, 1930.

Pearson, T. G. *Adventures in Bird Protection.* New York: D. Appleton-Century Co., 1937.

Skinner, M. P. *Bears in the Yellowstone.* Chicago: A. C. McClurg & Co., 1925.

"Wild-Fowl Situation." *Bird Lore,* XXXV (November, 1933), 357.

ILLUSTRATIVE RESEARCH PAPERS

The Cattleman's Frontier, 1845-1867

ERNEST STAPLES OSGOOD

In 1830, more than two hundred years after the first white man had made a clearing in the forest about him and in so doing had created that most significant of boundaries, the American frontier, the westernmost point in the area of continuous settlement was still less than halfway across the continent. According to the census of that year, the area containing more than two inhabitants to the square mile extended almost as far west as the western border of the young state of Missouri. Here, where the Missouri River coming down from the north bends sharply eastward on its way to the Mississippi, the frontier had paused, and twenty-five years were to elapse before the line of compact settlement advanced much beyond that point. To the rear, north and south, the wings of the frontier line bent far back toward the east and, as the center halted at the bend of the Missouri, the flanks, pivoting on that point, swung slowly westward during the succeeding decades, and new states were formed in the upper Mississippi Valley and in the lower South.

Although the western advance had paused in Missouri, the visitor to the town of Independence, established in 1831 at the apex of this salient, would have found nothing but movement and activity about him. Through its streets and on the river close by, there passed the whole pageantry of the frontier. Here, at the gateway to half a continent, an observer could, as the years went by, mark the emergence of the "Far West," as hunter and trail maker, trapper and trader, home seeker and gold seeker moved out along the western trails into those regions of which the average American was but dimly conscious and about which he knew next to nothing.

The river was a roadway of exploration. Up its lonely reaches had moved the keel boats of Lewis and Clark, a quarter of a century before the founding of the town. Seven years later, the Astorians, whose experiences were to be made familiar to the reading public by the pen of Washington Irving, passed by on their way to the mouth of the Columbia. Then on a day in the spring of 1819, the roving Indian gazed in wonder at a strange monster of smoke and noise moving upstream without any apparent effort on the part of those directing its course. Major Stephen Long and his party on the steamboat *Western Engineer* were on their way to the mouth of the Platte River. From there, in the following spring, they began their journey overland to the heads of the Platte, the Arkansas, and the Red. On his return, Long confirmed the opinions of other travelers that the country beyond the Missouri could never be utilized by white men, but must ever remain the home of the wild tribes who roamed over those frightful and terrifying wastes. For a half-century thereafter the Great American Desert was a fixed idea in the minds of most Americans.

Beyond these "steppes of Tartary," far up in the mountains, the "brigades" of the fur companies and the lonely trapper were busy expanding the great fur trade, which reached its height during the thirties. From the remote north country, where the Missouri and its tributaries head deep in the heart of the Rocky Mountains, they came, their keel boats laden with great bales of peltry for the St. Louis market. Each spring, when the water was high, the inhabitants of Independence turned out to see the steamboat of the American Fur Company, bound for Fort Union, the company's post located at the mouth of the Yellowstone, a thousand miles upstream. As the stories of the "mountain men" circulated around the border settlements and as the journals of explorer and traveler found their way into print, the topography and general character of the mountain regions, hundreds of miles to the west, were known long before the intervening country that began at the outskirts of the Missouri towns was anything more than a name.

This region between the settlements and the mountains, the last area of continental United States to become familiar to the average American, went under the general name of the Indian country. Here was a country, stretching all the way from the Red River to the Canadian boundary, which seemed destined by a kind Providence to provide a permanent home for the Indian. Here he might live undisturbed, freed from the pressure of the westward-moving pioneer, who would never, it was believed at the time, settle in that semi-arid, treeless country where all efforts at agriculture must surely fail. In the western section, on the High Plains and in the mountains, the wild tribes might roam as of old, following the great herds of buffalo upon which their whole tribal existence was based. In the eastern section, close to the Missouri River, room could be provided for the more civilized or the weaker tribes of the eastern United States, who were impeding the advance of the north and south wings of the frontier.

All through the thirties the Federal Government was busy negotiating treaties with these eastern tribes, treaties by which they surrendered their old tribal homes for reservations beyond the western border. When persuasion and solemn promises of undisturbed and perpetual possession failed, force was used, for the western Jacksonian democracy, then in the saddle in Washington, had little patience with humanitarians who demanded that the Indian problem be solved on the basis of abstract justice. Up the Missouri River on steamboats chartered by the government, or along the rough frontier roads of the southwest, the remnants of once powerful tribes moved under military guard to their new homes. Across the border, the new reservations formed an unbroken front from the Mexican boundary at the Red River to the northwestern corner of Missouri. North of Missouri, the tribes of the upper Mississippi were pushed back during the same period, thus clearing the way for the settlement of southern Wisconsin and eastern Iowa.

However permanent and satisfactory this solution of the Indian question might appear to the pioneer farmer and the eastern statesman, the visitor to Independence would soon discover that Indian isolation was the most temporary of expedients. While the treaties were still being negotiated, the wagons of the Santa Fé traders were cutting deeper and deeper the tracks that led out of the streets of Independence, over the sun-baked plains of the Cimarron and the Arkansas, across the Mexican border to the ancient Spanish city where Yankee trade goods could be sold at immense profit. This trade, which flourished during the thirties, quickened the life of the Missouri towns, increased the interest that the border was taking in the Southwest and, incidentally, contributed much to the knowledge of the country over which the trail ran.

Before the close of the thirties there were signs of a new movement among the crowds that thronged the streets of the Missouri settlements. In the remote Northwest, beyond the barrier of the Rockies, the American trapper was making contact with the Canadian fur trader in the valleys of the Columbia and its tributaries. Mountain men talked of Oregon, the richest fur country of all, of likely routes thither, and of the necessity for American effort in that region unless it were to become the exclusive domain of the Canadians. In 1832, several parties of fur traders and explorers were outfitting at Independence for the Columbia River. The trail that they took led across the trackless Indian country of the Platte at Grand Island, up that river and its tributary, the Sweetwater, until at last it topped the low divide that separates the waters of the Missouri system from those of the Columbia and the Colorado. Here was South Pass, discovered ten years before by the fur trader, Ashley, a low, grassy divide over which wagons might be drawn with little difficulty. There were no wagon tracks in the year 1832 when Bonneville and Sublette and Wyeth went through, but behind them there was to follow a multitude beneath whose feet rose the dust of the greatest of all frontier roads, the Oregon Trail.

In the history of the westward movement, the missionary has seldom been far behind the explorer and the fur trader, sometimes, indeed, he has led them. In 1834 two Methodist missionaries had established themselves in the valley of the Willamette, a tributary of the Columbia, near Fort Vancouver, where Dr. John McLoughlin ruled benignly over his vassals, white and red, in the interests of the great Hudson's Bay Company. Two years later Dr. Marcus Whitman, sent out by the American Board of Commissioners for Foreign Missions, began his work further up the Columbia in central Oregon. Eastward, over the mountains, in the valley of the Bitter Root, the Jesuits had established themselves by 1840 under the leadership of Father De Smet.

The fertility of the soil was of slight importance to the fur trader. The missionary, however, had a good eye for land, for those Indian converts who could be induced to settle down to farming in the neighborhood of the mission were likely to stay Christianized. In their reports the missionaries were as enthusiastic over the rich land of the Willamette as they were over the prospect of saving souls. Here was land that equaled, if it did not surpass, the best that the prairie region of Illinois could offer. As this news spread, farmers began to think and talk of Oregon and the way thither. By 1843 the movement of the homeseeker out over the Oregon Trail had begun, a movement that in a few years increased to thousands and built up a new American commonwealth on the shores of the Pacific. Long lines of wagons passed through the dusty streets of Independence, and in the crowd that swarmed around them, the talk was no longer of fur and Indian trade but of land, of crops, of climate, and of the fortunes in the fertile soil of Oregon awaiting those who would brave the long march and all its attendant dangers.

Two hundred miles upstream, where the Missouri is joined by the Platte, another group was gathering in the fall of 1846. In their winter quarters on the western edge of the new state of Iowa, the Mormons were laying their plans for the coming spring. They had despaired of finding a home in the States, for wherever they had settled, their neighbors had coveted their land, envied their prosperity, and disapproved of their way of life. Somewhere beyond the plains and mountains lay the Promised Land. Before the close of the next year, they had found it in the valley of the Great Salt Lake.

Then in the next year came the news that was to set the whole frontier in motion. Eastward along the trail to the border settlements, across the country to the crowded cities of the seaboard and on beyond the seas sped the magic word that was to bring a whole world flocking westward—gold! The discovery of a few nuggets in a California millrace was destined to fill the harbor of the Golden Gate with a forest of masts, to make the Isthmus of Panama a highway for the nations, and to crowd the Oregon Trail with an army of adventurers, who would find no rest until the weary miles had been traversed and they stood at last in that fabulous land of gold by the blue waters of the Pacific.

When the emigrant bound for Oregon or California turned his back on the Missouri settlements and struck out along the westward trail, his condition was not unlike that of the traveler sailing out of an eastern seaport on a trans-atlantic journey. Beyond the narrow wagon track a vast waste stretched away on every side to the far horizon, its swells and hollows as lacking in identity as the crests and troughs of the Atlantic rollers. Herds of buffalo and great bands of antelope, seemingly as multitudinous as the fish of the sea, moved over the face of these great solitudes. It seemed unlikely that man would ever be more than a wayfarer in these wastes. Only the roving Indian, the occasional trapper, and the little garrisons at the trading posts strung out along the trail served to dispel such illusions. The myth of the American Desert, so long a part of the American's stock of ideas about his country, had its origin as much in the impression resulting from such solitary vastness as in any evidence of the sterility of the soil or the rigors of the climate. Men accustomed to the companionship of woods and streams, of green meadows and uplands, of familiar hills and limited horizons, found nothing hospitable in the leagues of brown grass, nothing familiar in the monotony of rolling plain or wind-scarred butte.

Into this great solitude rode the cattleman. From the ranches of Texas and New Mexico he pushed his way northward across the lands of the Indian nations to the railroad that had begun to bridge this waste. The desire for new pastures and markets sent him further and further north, until his herds met and mingled with other herds drifting down out of the northern valleys. It was the range cattleman who broke the spell; who made these great areas his own; who, in his search for grass, crossed every divide, rode into every coulee, and swam every stream. The solitude of the desert passed, and men began to realize that this, our last frontier, was not a barrier between the river settlements and the mining communities in the mountains but an area valuable in itself, where men might live and prosper.

The cattle business of the High Plains began as a result of the necessities of the emigrants along the Oregon Trail, and the earliest herds were brought together to meet that demand. The westward trek of thousands to Oregon and California in the two decades before the Civil War stirred into new activity the far-western trading posts, which had languished following the boom period of the fur trade. The rather scattered, nebulous population of the fur country began to drift down into the trail when it became apparent that money could be made out of the western-bound pioneer, who was a ready customer up to the limits of his resources. In these unfamiliar wastes, where nature appeared so strange and formidable to his unaccustomed eyes, he was eager to accept assistance from anyone more experienced than he. By the time he began his journey up the North Platte, his animals were footsore and weak and his stock of food was running low. It was a strong and well-equipped outfit indeed that was not anxious to bargain for such aid and comfort as those along the trail were able to furnish.

Nor were the traders who were finding favorable locations along the trail loath to gain all they could from these necessitous travelers. Flour, coffee, bacon, powder, and shot were always in demand. Sometimes the emigrant lacked these essentials because of ill-advised provisioning at the outset, sometimes he was the victim of wandering bands of Indians who held up trains and exacted tribute. Flour, brought down by packhorse from the Oregon settlements, sold for one hundred dollars a hundredweight on the trail.[1] As early as 1845 Fort Bridger had become one of the chief entrepôts of this trade. Hither the mountaineers had resorted for years to trade their season's supply of hides and Indian articles for flour, pork, spirits, powder, lead, blankets, butcherknives, hats, ready-made clothes, coffee, and sugar.[2] Such posts merely had to enlarge their stocks in these articles to meet the emigrant's demands.

But the traders soon found ways of making money other than by selling these standard supplies of the posts. Three new economic activities sprang up along the trail, each of them the result of utilizing the local natural advantages and resources and each of them a part of the business of transportation rather than supply. These were the operation of bridges and ferries, the furnishing of forage, and the exchanging of fresh for worn-down work cattle.

It was not long after the western migration had begun before bridges or ferries were established at the more difficult stream crossings. At strategically located points on the North Platte, the Sweetwater, and the Green rivers, ferrymen were prepared to take the emi-

[1] Joel Palmer, "Journal of Travels over the Rocky Mountains, 1845-46," *Early Western Travels* (Cleveland, 1906), edited by R. G. Thwaites, XXX, p. 86 *et seq.*

[2] *Ibid.*, pp. 74-75.

grant and his team across for a toll.[3] These ferries became natural trading points, and here road ranches, often the property of the ferryman, sprang up.

With every year of travel over the emigrant road, it became more and more difficult to find sufficient grazing ground for the animals. As a result, there developed a market for hay. Temporary posts, consisting of a tent and a corral set up along the trail to catch the season's trade, were soon converted into more substantial ranches. Their owners began to put up the wild hay that grew along the streams and were prepared to supply forage to the motive power of the emigrant trains at thirty-five cents to a dollar and a half a hundredweight. A small garden patch on the side might prove profitable, when potatoes brought five cents apiece during the emigrant season. Such establishments usually consisted of an adobe house, often a dwelling and store combined, a few stock corrals made out of the cottonwoods that bordered every stream, and a haystack.[4] These road ranches, the product of the emigrant trade, were the first ranches of the northern ranges.

The need of the travelers for fresh work stock and the profits to be made out of such a trade induced many of the traders to go into the cattle business. One fat and well-conditioned work steer might be exchanged for two worn down and foot-sore ones. Dairy cattle, driven along with the trains, appeared less valuable on the Sweetwater than they did in Missouri, and many a family cow, unused to the hardship that such a journey imposed, was destined never to reach the green valleys of the Willamette but was traded off for ten dollars or a little flour.[5]

[3] The toll bridge over the North Platte, twenty miles west of Fort Laramie, which cost $5,000 to build, took in $40,000 in tolls during the single season of 1853. A five-gallon keg of whiskey was sufficient to pay a toll charge of $125.00 on a train of nineteen wagons crossing the Platte at this point. "Autobiography of William K. Sloan," *Annals of Wyoming* (Cheyenne), IV, 246, July, 1926.

[4] Diary kept by Silas L. Hopper, "Nebraska City to California, April-August, 1863," *Annals of Wyoming,* III, p. 117, Oct., 1925. Gen. Sherman on his trip west in 1866 wrote back to Rawlins that "these ranches consist usually of a store, a house, a corral, and a big pile of hay for sale . . . you are never out of sight of train or ranch." Sherman to Rawlins, Aug. 21, 1866, *House Ex. Doc.* No. 23, 39 Cong., Sess. 2, p. 5.

[5] Sometimes this loose stock amounted to a considerable band. The good price for beef at the California mines induced some herdsmen to essay the long drive with a beef herd. Greeley notes such a herd from southwestern Missouri. Horace Greeley, *Overland Journey* (New York, 1860), p. 72.

The early herds of the northern ranges were the product of such trade. Captain Richard Grant, trading along the road from Fort Hall, had a herd of six hundred in 1856.[6] Horace Greeley, on his way to Salt Lake three years later, found this business thriving along Black's Fork and Ham's Fork of the Green River. Here he found "several old mountaineers, who have large herds of cattle which they are rapidly increasing by a lucrative traffic with the emigrants, who are compelled to exchange their tired, gaunt oxen and steers for fresh ones on almost any terms. R. D., whose tent we passed last evening, is said to have six or eight hundred head; and, knowing the country perfectly, finds no difficulty in keeping them through summer and winter by frequently shifting them from place to place over a circuit of thirty or forty miles. J. R., who has been here some twenty odd years, began with little or nothing and had quietly accumulated some fifty horses, three or four hundred head of neat cattle, three squaws, and any number of half-breed children. He is said to be worth $75,000."[7] These were Wyoming's first cattlemen.

As the forage along the trail became scarce from constant cropping, the more enterprising herdsmen drove their cattle north into the sheltered valleys of the upper Missouri in what later became western Montana, their wintering places being the Beaverhead, the Stinking Water (later the Ruby), and the Deer Lodge valleys. The value of this region as a stock-raising country had been demonstrated by the Jesuit fathers at the St. Ignatius Mission, located on the Clark's Fork of the Columbia. Here under their tutelage, the Flatheads had settled down to a more or less civilized existence and by 1858 had developed so far in the arts of farming and animal husbandry that they were sowing three hundred acres to wheat and were herding on the adjacent hillsides and in the neighboring valleys over a thousand head of fine stock.[8]

Had it not been for the Mormon war of 1857-1858, the Jesuits and

[6] Granville Stuart, *Forty Years on the Frontier* (Cleveland, 1925), II, p. 97.

[7] Greeley, 195. This entry was made while Greeley was at Fort Bridger. The J. R. referred to may have been J. B.—Jim Bridger.

[8] Report of Lieutenant B. F. Ficklin to Major F. J. Porter, April 15, 1858, in Annual Report of the Secretary of War, 1859, *House Ex. Doc.* No. 2, 35 Cong., Sess. 2, Vol. II, pt. 2, p. 70. Major John Owen had in 1850 purchased the buildings of St. Mary's Mission on the Bitter Root River from the Jesuits. This mission had been established nine years before by Father De Smet. Owen established a trading post here that he

their Indian converts might have remained undisturbed for another decade. When, however, the elders of the Mormon church issued an edict in February, 1857, ordering the Gentiles within the Mormon territory to leave forthwith, the isolation of the mountain regions north of the trail was destroyed. During the years previous to 1857, many enterprising merchants from the Missouri river towns had brought out loads of goods and had set up in business in the Mormon settlements. This trade had proved enormously profitable and considerable sums had been invested in the business. The order to evacuate Mormon territory left these merchants with no alternative than that of immediately disposing of their stocks as best they could. Many of them traded off their remaining merchandise for the cattle of the Mormons at ruinous figures and hurried out of the territory before their enterprising customers could recover the purchase price by stampeding the herd. Some headed for California where the mining communities offered a safe market. Others drove northward to the posts along the trail.[9] Here traffic had stopped when the rumors of burned freight trains and massacred emigrants sped eastward. The traders, seeing their custom diminish and fearing the ravages of the Saints and their Indian allies, sought refuge in the mountains until the storm blew over. Into the valleys of western Montana straggled the herds of the traders and of those who had been expelled from Utah.

Neither the protection afforded by the army of General Albert Sidney Johnson sent out to quell the rebellion, nor the market for beef, which the presence of this force created, was sufficient to tempt the traders to come down out of the northern valleys. In December, 1857, a small detail from Johnson's forces was sent north to contract for beef with these fugitive cattlemen. The report of the commander of this beef-buying expedition gives a good picture of the situation in the upper Missouri country, the cradle of the stock-growing industry of Montana.

called Fort Owen. When the early cattlemen entered the valley from the south, they found Owen cultivating a considerable plot of ground and pasturing stock that he had bought of the Catholic fathers. Paul C. Phillips, *The Journals and Letters of John Owen* (New York, 1927).

[9] Sloan, "Autobiography," *op. cit.,* 260-263. Sloan was engaged in this trade with the Mormons. He had a store at Provo and was driven out along with the other Gentiles in the Territory in 1857. He estimated the total Gentile population at about three hundred in Salt Lake and not more than fifty in the rest of the Territory.

After experiencing great difficulty in crossing the snow-choked divide that separated the headwaters of the Missouri from those of the Snake, the party got down into the upper Missouri country.

After getting on the head waters of the Missouri, the snow entirely disappeared. On the fourth, our rations were exhausted, but I was not uneasy, as I expected to arrive soon at the Beaver Head, a point on the Jefferson Fork of the Missouri, fifty miles above the Three Forks of the Missouri, and one hundred east of the Mormon settlement on Salmon River, a popular wintering ground of the mountaineers, on account of their stock.

To my surprise, on arriving at Beaver Head, I found all the evidences of the mountaineers having left recently, and hastily, and taken the trail in the direction of Flathead Valley. . . .

On the 10th, overtook the camp of Mr. Herriford, where I obtained a supply of beef, and learned from him that about December first they had heard of the burning of the supply trains by the Mormons, and of threats uttered by the Mormons at Salmon river fork, against the mountaineers at Beaver Head. Fearing for the safety of their stock, they had started for the Flathead valley, as a more distant and secure point.

At the Deer's Lodge, overtook another party of mountaineers, with whom I made a contract for the delivery of three hundred head of beef-cattle, by April 16th, at ten dollars per hundred [weight], also to bring down about one hundred head of horses. Afterwards proceeded down the Flathead valley, where I could have a contract for two hundred head of cattle, but their fear of the Mormons was so great that no price would induce them to undertake to deliver them here. Several were making preparations to move their stock to Fort Walla-Walla this spring, in order to be beyond the reach of the Mormons. . . .

I spent several days at St. Ignatius mission (situated on one of the branches of Clark's Fork of the Columbia, on forty-seventh parallel) established by the Catholics, for the benefit of the Flatheads, Pend d'Oreilles, and Hootenais [*sic*].

. . . Under the direction of the priests they are improving rapidly in agriculture. This year they will sow about three hundred bushels of wheat; they raise large quantities of vegetables, especially potatoes, cabbage, and beets.

Their horses are superior to all other Indian horses, in size and power of endurance. The tribe, about sixty lodges, owns about one thousand head of cattle.

As it was impossible to buy stock in Flathead valley, on conditions contemplated in my instructions, on March 3rd I started for Deer Lodge, expecting to start immediately on my arrival with what stock I had contracted for at that place.

The contractors refused to deliver their beef at this place [Fort Scott, Utah] but offered to deliver it there [Deer Lodge Valley] as they were afraid of being robbed by the Mormons on the road.

Buying a few animals, to replace those lost, started on March 12th to return, . . .

The new grass was beginning to grow finely before I started on Jefferson fork; contrary to my expectation and information I had received from the oldest mountaineers, found snow in the mountains, between Missouri and Snake rivers, from three to six feet deep for a distance of twelve miles. . . .[10]

The Mormon danger was, however, only temporary, and in the following year the trade along the trail was as brisk as ever. The sojourn of the traders in the mountain valleys had given them much information of the grazing resources of the upper Missouri country and had established a practical route from the trail to that region. Later, when gold was discovered in western Montana, the trail over which the traders fled with their herds became the chief connection between the mining towns of Montana and the great central route of transcontinental travel.

In addition to these herds of the traders, which had had their origin in the trade along the emigrant trail, there were the train-cattle or "bull-teams" of the freighting companies, which supplied the army on the plains, brought out the Indian annuity goods, and furnished the mining camps in the mountains with the necessities of life and equipment for the mines.[11] These trains of thirty or more wagons to a unit, each wagon with its six yoke of oxen, creaked their way across the plains in an endless procession. Thousands of head of these work animals were wintered by their owners in favorable spots along the trail. In the winter of 1857-1858, the firm of Russell, Majors, and Wadell wintered fifteen thousand head on a range that extended

10 Ficklin Report, *op. cit.,* 69-70. See M. L. Wilson, "Early Montana Agriculture," *Proceedings of the Mississippi Valley Historical Association,* 1918, IX, 429-440; also Conrad Kohrs, "A Veteran's Experience in the Western Cattle Trade," *Breeder's Gazette* (Chicago), Dec. 18, 1912, pp. 1328-29.

11 Frederic L. Paxson, *History of the American Frontier,* p. 462.

southward from the trail for a distance of over two hundred miles.[12] This range was far enough east so that the Mormon danger was not felt.

The experience of the early cattlemen along the trail and in the mountains of western Montana had demonstrated the practicability of wintering stock on the northern ranges a full decade before the Texas longhorn put in his appearance. Any further expansion in this pioneer industry beyond the point already described had to wait on the development of new local markets.

The discovery of gold in the Rocky Mountains, coincident with the Mormon outbreak and the scattering of the herds into the mountain valleys, created just such a market. In the autumn of 1858 gold was discovered some two hundred miles south of the Oregon Trail on the upper waters of the South Platte. By the next spring, the plains were alive with the Pike's Peak gold rush. The old trail was crowded, and to the south other thousands of gold seekers were making new trails across the unfamiliar brown wastes to where rise the eastern escarpments of the Rockies. The oxen used for this new trek were turned out to graze on the plains at the foot of the mountains, while their owners hurried on up the canyons to the diggings. For the more thrifty, ranches were established where cattle could be boarded for a dollar and a half a month.[13]

Here was a local market, which must be supplied, and which, in the fever of the gold rush, was not inclined to haggle over the price. The winter of 1858-1859 saw twenty-five thousand people at the Colorado mines or on the road, and beef of any kind or quality was at a premium. "From that time to the present," commented the *Rocky Mountain News* in retrospect twelve years later, "the Denver market has been supplied exclusively the year around with beef from the neighboring plains."[14] Train cattle and the stock of the gold seekers were used to start the ranches that began to grow up along the South Platte. In 1861 Iliff, destined to become the first "cattle king" of the northern ranges, was supplying the Colorado mining towns with beef

[12] *Annual Report of the Commissioner of Agriculture*, 1870, pp. 303-309.
[13] Greeley, *op. cit.*, p. 115.
[14] The *Rocky Mountain News* (Denver), quoted in the *National Live Stock Journal* (Chicago), I, p. 71, Nov., 1870.

from a herd that ranged up and down the South Platte for a distance of seventy-five miles or more.[15]

In another region the stimulus of this new and insistent market was being felt. Close to the southern borders of Colorado Territory, small communities of Mexicans had settled along the upper Rio Grande and its tributaries. Here they developed a system of stock growing perfectly adapted to their physical environment, a system that the cattle growers of the High Plains were never able to duplicate because of the inadaptability of eastern-made land laws. "They hold their lands," wrote one observer, "without title and in accordance with their own customs. The land along the streams, being the only land that can be cultivated, each man holds so many varas or yards front on the stream and extending back at right angles with the stream to the bluff or as far as water can be carried by ditches for irrigation. The rest of the land is open to all as pasture and worthless for any other purpose. By this system of survey, each man has an equal use of water and bottom land, whether he cultivates three varas or one hundred, and all would be willing to pay for the land cultivated if they could take it in the *shape* they now hold it. The survey and sale of this land in regular sections would probably drive out the present population, while it might fail to bring in an equally industrious one."[16]

Cattle from these ranches found a ready sale in the Colorado towns, and thus the first connection between the southern stock-growing areas and the northern ranges was established, a connection that was to grow in magnitude until it constituted one of the most distinctive features of the "cow country."

The "busted" gold seekers of the Pike's Peak rush had scattered by 1862. Some had limped back to the border settlements to form an outer crust of plains-wise folk along the Kansas and Nebraska frontier; some drifted into the freighting business on the trails or took to ranching along the Platte or on the upper reaches of the Arkansas; some followed the rumor of gold to the north and became denizens of the roaring mining camps of the Clearwater and Salmon rivers. To the east, across the Bitter Root Range, some of the herdsmen who had

[15] Dr. Henry Latham, *Trans-Missouri Stock Raising; the Pasture Lands of North America* (Omaha, 1871), p. 41.

[16] Report of the Surveyor-General of Colorado, Utah, Nevada, and Idaho in the *Annual Report of the Commissioner of the General Land Office*, 1864, p. 80.

fled from the Mormon danger were finding pay dirt in the Deer Lodge Valley.[17] News of these strikes filtered into the camps to the west and south. In 1862 a wave of prospectors rolled through the western passes, and by 1865 Bannock, Virginia City, and Helena were all on the map.

The solitary prospector might live off the country. As he worked from one mountain gulch to another, the bands of elk, blacktail, and mountain sheep furnished him with his chief food staple. Groups of miners, for whom the season had not been successful, often wintered in some likely hunting country and not uncommonly got through the winter on a bill of fare of "meat straight." Gathered in the mining camps by the thousand, however, they must be fed, and all the necessities of life, save what the country could supply, must be freighted in.

Here was a market for the Montana stock grower, who soon found that taking gold dust from the miners in exchange for beef was almost as profitable and far more certain than getting it from the placers. Even a poor worn-down ox might bring one hundred dollars in gold when its owner auctioned it off to the Sunday crowd of miners in the street of Virginia City where beef sold on the butcher's block at twenty-five cents a pound.[18]

Such prices as these and the free pastures in the mountain valleys induced many of the new arrivals to engage in stock raising. A demand was thus created for stock cattle, which was felt in Oregon, California, on the Platte, in the border settlements of Kansas and Missouri, and even in Texas. As early as 1866, Nelson Story came up over the Bozeman Trail to the Gallatin Valley with a herd of six hundred Texas longhorns that he had picked up in Dallas.[19]

The number of cattle in the vicinity of the mines increased rapidly. By 1868, five years after the settlement of Virginia City, the assessors of the nine counties of Montana listed 10,714 oxen and 18,801 cows and calves. Four years later, although the number of oxen had fallen off, because of the practice of using mules and horses for freighting, the number of stock cattle had risen to over 75,000.[20] In Deer Lodge

[17] Stuart, I, pp. 132-156.

[18] Kohrs, p. 1328.

[19] A. L. Stone, *Following the Old Trails* (Missoula, 1913), p. 212.

[20] Annual reports of the auditor and treasurer of Montana Territory, Helena, 1860-1872.

County, the center of the new industry, cattle had become so numerous that the need for regulating the winter range was felt. The fact that the Federal Government possessed the sole power to legislate for the public domain did not prevent the Montana territorial legislature in 1866 from passing a law giving the county commissioners of Deer Lodge County power to define what should be summer grass land in the county and prohibiting stock owners from pasturing their stock on winter grass land, unless they owned the same.[21] Although this law was repealed the next year, it is significant, for it illustrates how soon after the establishment of the stock-growing industry in a given area, the problem arose of conserving the free grazing of the public domain. As we shall see, neither the stockman nor the government was able to solve the problem.

The settlement of a large mining population in the mountains, the resulting increase in traffic across the plains, and the building of the Union Pacific, all occuring between 1860 and 1870, rudely disturbed the Indian isolation of the preceding decade. The Indian hostilities that ensued forced the Government to give more attention to the military problem of the plains, and resulted in the establishment of forts to protect the new communities and the various lines of overland communication. These new army posts created additional local markets where good prices were paid for beef. In 1871, the newly established post at Cheyenne, Fort D. A. Russell, was paying a contract price of eight dollars and thirty-five cents a hundredweight to the cattlemen along the Platte.[22] Much of the trade for the early ranchers of Wyoming centered around these forts, where quantities of hay for the cavalry mounts and beef for the men, two commodities that the locality was prepared to supply, were needed.

In 1867 the rails of the Union Pacific penetrated Wyoming. The work gangs who laid the rails and the horde of hangers-on who constituted those ephemeral towns at the rail head must be fed. Buffalo, brought down by such hired men of the railroad as Buffalo Bill, helped to meet this demand, but the cattle of the Wyoming ranchman

21 *Laws of Montana Territory,* 1866, Sess. 2, p. 35. This law, which was an invasion of the power of the Federal Government over the public domain, was repealed at the next session. *Laws of Montana Territory,* 1866, Sess. 3, p. 83.

22 Letter of T. H. Durbin in *Letters from Old Friends and Members of the Wyoming Stock Growers Association* (Cheyenne, 1923), p. 45.

found as ready a market along this first transcontinental railroad as they had found along the old emigrant trail.

Thus, by the close of the sixties, there existed in the northern section of the High Plains and in the adjacent mountain valleys, herds of considerable size, recruited from the stock of the emigrant and gold seeker, from the work animals of the freighting companies, from the Mormon herds, and from the herds of Oregon and California. Their owners were making good profits in supplying the local market of mining camp, section crew, and military post. The possibility of expanding their herds so as to utilize to the full the enormous pastoral resources on every hand depended upon a supply of cheap cattle that could be used for stocking the empty ranges and upon a connection with the eastern market.

The inhabitants of the brash little towns on the Union Pacific were conscious that they were living along one of the great highways of the world's commerce. They speculated on the wealth of the rich cargoes from the Orient, borne eastward by long lines of freight cars. Local newspapers noted in their columns the passing of especially valuable trainloads of tea and silk from China or ore from the mines, and commented upon the fact that fortunes were rolling by their very doors every day. Out on the Laramie Plains and along the tributaries of the Platte a less romantic way freight was developing, far more essential to the well-being of these communities and of the railroad that served them. The passing of the first stock train bound for the Chicago market meant that the utilization of these northern ranges had begun in earnest.

The Evidence on "O. K."

ALLEN WALKER READ

When you first look at the vast quantity of writing on the origin of "O. K.," you find a wilderness of claims and counter-claims. But when you discard the hearsay evidence, the unfounded speculation, and the misread manuscripts, you get a reasonable pattern of historical development. I am able to present here the earliest documentary evi-

"The Evidence on *'O. K.'*" From *The Saturday Review of Literature,* July 19, 1941
Reprinted by permission of *The Saturday Review of Literature.*

dence; first, however, it is necessary to dispose of four alleged instances that arise from misinterpreted manuscripts.

The earliest of these is dated December 8, 1565. The letters O. K. are said to occur at the end of the will of Thomas Cumberland, a lorimer of London, entered in the Archdeaconry Court registers. It is unreasonable to suppose that "O. K." as we know it could have lain dormant for nearly three hundred years. The finder of it, as he says in *Notes and Queries* for June 10, 1911, did not think that the letters were the initials of the scrivener, but some such explanation must be the case. Another alleged instance comes from the year 1757, but an examination of the manuscript shows that it is not "O. K." at all but an ill-written "Att.," standing for "Attestation" or "Attested by" at the end of a document. For many years faith has been put in an instance of 1790, from the records of Summer County, Tennessee, with this entry: "Andrew Jackson, Esq., proved a Bill of Sale from Hugh McGary to Gaspar Mansker, for a Negro man, which was O. K." But an investigator has examined this manuscript, as he writes in *American Speech* for April, 1941, and finds that the "O. K." is clearly "O. R.," standing for "Order Recorded." Finally, an alleged instance of 1815 has recently turned up in the diary of a Boston businessman, William Richardson. The marks have the appearance of a small "o k," without periods, interlined at a blotted place in the manuscript; but they do not fit into the sense well and are out of tone with the other parts of the text. All things considered, we can consign the instances of 1565, 1757, 1790, and 1815 to the same limbo.

The story begins, then, in the Spring of 1840, and is closely bound up with the political situation in New York City. The Democratic Party was intent on re-electing Martin Van Buren for a second term, and they kept up interest, particularly in the radical Locofoco branch, by means of a set of social clubs. On March 11, 1840, the Locofoco newspaper, the New York *New Era,* listed the clubs as follows—the Butt Enders, the Tammany Temple, the Indomitables, the Huge Paws (named for their symbol, a muscular arm grasping a hammer), the Van Buren Association, and the Simon Pures. Twelve days later a new club made its first public appearance by an announcement of a meeting to be held March 24, 1840. This was "The Democratic O. K. Club," and the name marks the first appearance of "O. K."

The meaning of the name was held a secret, in keeping with political practices of the time. The meteoric rise of the "Know-Nothing" party a few years later was based on a similar secrecy, with oaths not to reveal its mysteries. As we shall see later, this "O. K. Club" was named after "Old Kinderhook," the birthplace of Martin Van Buren, near Albany. In papers of the time Van Buren was referred to in such terms as "the magician of Kinderhook," "your cunning Kinderhook Fox," and "the Kinderhook pony." Later in the year, after Van Buren was defeated, a Whig banner carried this inscription:

K. K. K. K. K.
KINDERHOOK KANDIDATE KANT
KOME IT KWITE

The Charter election in New York was to be held April 14, 1840, and the preceding weeks contained much political flurry. The Whigs arranged for a meeting at the Masonic Hall on March 27, to discuss the pending Registry Bill, which they favored. The Locofocos were angered by the announcement, addressed to "citizens of New York, without distinction of party," for it was obviously a Whig affair. The *New Era,* therefore, on the morning of the day of the meeting published a paragraph that was a veiled incitement to riot and disturbance. The heading contained the letters "O. K." in large type, and as the meaning was a secret, they were a cabalistic device to mystify the opposition.

At this meeting on March 27 the Locofocos used "O. K." as a watchword. According to the New York *Times* of March 28, p. 2c: "The *war cry* of the Locofocos was O. K., the two letters paraded at the head of the article in the *Era,* to which we have referred. 'Down with the Whigs, boys, O. K.,' was the shout of these poor, deluded men. We have not words to express our abhorrence of the charlatans who fomented the disturbance." The New York *Morning Herald,* March 28, was more restrained in writing: "About 500 stout strapping men, many of them with sticks, . . . marched three and three, noiselessly and orderly. The word O. K. was passed from mouth to mouth, a cheer was given, and they rushed into the Hall and upstairs, like a torrent." The New York *Daily Express* in its report, March 28, p. 2b, also mentioned the slogan: "The gang of rioters headed by Custom House officers, and a Locofoco Street Inspector, rushed through the lower hall, shouting the watchword of the New Era, 'O K,' and attacked the persons on the stairs." It will be noted that the expression "O. K." is here definitely attributed to the *New Era,* and by finding the first instance in that paper we are very near the beginning. The New York *Times* on April 10, p. 2c, referred to the *New Era* as "the brazen organ of the O K boys." The newness of "O. K." is further supported by a sentence from the New York *American,* March 28, p. 2c: "This band of the *'Old Butt-Enders,'* reorganized under the new cognomen of *the O. K. club,* seemed to consider the invitation of the New Era as sufficient authority for violence and outrage."

The Whigs would not long put up with this secret Locofoco slogan, and in the next few weeks they satirically attributed many meanings to it. First in the field was the *Morning Herald,* March 30, p. 2a, with this paragraph:

> THE O. K. CLUB—O. K. LITERATURE.—This gang of loafers and litterateurs, who broke in upon the Whigs at Masonic Hall on Friday evening last, and kicked up the row there, are said to number 1,000 bravos, being the picked men of the old "huge paws"—"butt enders"—"roarers," and "ball rollers." The origin of their name, O. K., is curious and characteristic. A few years ago, some person accused Amos Kendall to General Jackson, of being no better than he should be. "Let me examine the papers," said the old hero, "I'll soon tell whether Mr. Kendall is right or wrong." The General did so and found every thing right. "Tie up them papers," said the General. They were tied up. "Mark on them, 'O. K.,'" continued the General. O. K. was marked upon them. "By the eternal," said the good old General, taking his pipe from his mouth, "Amos is *Ole Kurrek* (all correct) and no mistake," blowing the smoke up the chimney's cheek. After this the character of Amos was established on the rock of Gibraltar. Harvard College, on hearing of this event, was thrown into extacies, and made the General an LL. D., which he is to this day.
>
> The O. K.'s are now the most original and learned Locofoco club of the day. Their arguments are the most convincing test logicians ever invented.

As this has more spice than is usual among newspapers of the time, it may be from the pen of James Gordon Bennett himself. Without question it is purely satirical, pouring scorn on the "grand old man" of the Democratic party, then in retirement at the Hermitage; and thus the connection of Jackson with "O. K." is a fabrication out of whole cloth.

This same explanation appeared in the N. Y. *Commercial Advertiser* three days later, April 2, p. 2b: "'O. K.'—The meaning of these mysterious letters, the power of which, when exerted, is so fatal to the peace and harmony of the city, is a question of grave deliberation in certain quarters. We are not proficients in cabalistic puzzles; but it is asserted that these constituted the endorsement of General Jackson upon papers that he had examined and found right—thus, O. K.—*Oll Korrect.*" This paragraph appeared also in the N. Y. *Spectator,* April 6, p. 1b, and was reprinted in the Albany *Advertiser* and thence taken into the N. Y. *Daily Express,* April 7, p. 2a. Thus it gained wide publicity.

Other papers made sportive explanations, such as that of the *Daily Express* on April 2, p. 2c: "'O. K.'—Many are puzzled to know the definition of these mysterious letters. It is Arabic, reads backwards, and means *kicked out*—of Masonic Hall." When the Democrats were soundly defeated in an election in Connecticut, the same paper reported (April 11, p. 2c): "'O. K.'—The wicked Whigs have put a new definition to these strange initials. They translate them now *Old Connecticut.*" The *Times* of April 13, p. 2a, echoed: "Last and most approved version.—O. K. OLD KONNECTICUT!!!" Another Whig version soon current was "Out of 'Kash,' Out of 'Kredit,' Out of 'Karacter,' and Out of 'Klothes.'" Some months later a Congressman from Illinois on the floor of the House of Representatives offered the interpretation "Orful Kalamity."

Bennett continued his chaffing in the *Morning Herald* of April 1, p. 2c:

O. K.

NEW YORK, Mar. 27, 1840

MR. BENETT:

SIR: You have taken the leborty (*sic passim*) to Slander us most publickly in this mornings paper. the O. K. Institute which you hav so falsley repsented was established for our own pleasure and enjoyment and was never intended for sich a d - - - d Rascale as your self

A MEMBER

which you was mean enought to pursenate

ANSWER—I cry you mercy, O. K. I have no wish to depreciate from the high reputation of so erudite a Society. Nor shall I ever interfere with your amusements in knocking down people. Col. Webb and you may enjoy a monopoly of that business.—*Ed. Herald.*

The use of "K. O." in the sense of "kicked out" must have been unusually galling to the Locofocos. It formed a headline in the N. Y. *Times* of April 6, p. 2b:

K. O.

KICKED OUT

The K O system is working admirably. It was first put in operation at Masonic Hall on Friday night, March 27th, where the bullying O K's, who attempted to disturb and break up a peaceable meeting of citizens were KICKED OUT.

And in referring to the Tammany mayor the next day, p. 2b, they added "K. H. O." in black boldface type, evidently meaning "Kick Him Out." When a Locofoco vote canvasser was expelled from a hotel, they said (April 9, p. 2b) that "Van Buren's Janizary was K O of the kitchen."

The Locofocos were obliged to meet this barrage of ridicule in some fashion. They could best neutralize the scorn by blandly accepting the "oll korrect" story, and thus offset the "K. O." headlines by "O. K." headlines of their own. Therefore the *New Era* on April 9 and 10 accepted the meaning suggested by the Whigs and launched the expression into its present-day usage. At a meeting of the Democratic voters of the 12th Ward on April 9, as reported in the *New Era* of April 11th, p. 3d, they adopted this resolution: "Resolved, We will say to Martin Van Buren, O. K., you can remain at the white house for another four years." The Whig papers soon followed suit, and on April 14 both the *Times* (p. 2d) and the *Morning Courier* (p. 2c), reporting good news from Ohio, had the headline, "CLEVELAND, O. K.!!" Illustrative of the new usage is this passage from the *Morning Herald* of April 21, p. 2d: "The Brigadier soon reached the Battery, reviewed his Brigade, found 'all the whiskers put in' and pronounced every thing O. K. As soon as the Irish rebels heard of this movement, they flung away their shelelahs, and was K. O. in no time."

Meanwhile the O. K. Club continued to put "O. K." on their banners as they marched in parades and torchlight processions, and an "O. K. Ball" was held. The report of one procession, in the *Daily Express,* April 11, p. 2c, makes the point of the newness of "O. K.": "We observed in the Tammany Procession 'the Butt Enders,' 'Indomitables,' and 'Huge Paws,' with the same banners they had last spring. The O. K. concern was the only novelty." In this same procession, according to the *New Era* of April 21, p. 2a, one of the banners had on it "a huge Cabbage mounted upon legs, singing out O. K. to General Harrison, and chasing him like a racer." Even as late as May 8 the Locofocos still regarded "O. K." as their special cabalistic property.

Late in May, "O. K." had so far passed into general usage that the Locofocos felt free to divulge its original significance. The following, from the *New Era* of May 27, p. 2f, is the passage that reveals the "Old Kinderhook" signification, before "all correct" supplanted it:

> JACKSON BREAST PIN. We acknowledge the receipt of a very pretty gold Pin, representing the "old white hat with a crape" such as is worn by the hero of New Orleans, and having upon it the (to the "Whigs") very frightful letters O. K., significant of the birth-place of Martin Van Buren, old Kinderhook, as also the rallying word of the Democracy of the late election, "all correct." It can be purchased at Mr. P. L. Fierty's, 486 Pearl street. Those who wear them should bear in mind that it will require their most strenuous exertions between this and autumn, to make all things O. K.

The first instance I have found of the use of "O. K." by anyone outside New York City is that of a correspondent in Montpelier, Vermont, in a letter dated April 20, 1840. As printed in the N. Y. *New Era,* April 27, p. 2a, he promised to bring about "the redemption of our State from British Whiggery next fall! Will you not say 'O. K.'? Go ahead!" As the presidential campaign grew hot in the fall of 1840, the expression "O. K." swept over the entire country, reaching Ohio, for instance, early in September. Examples showing the historical continuity in succeeding decades are provided in Thornton's *American Glossary* (1912). It was popularized in England at least as early as the 1880's; and according to the recollections of the English scholar A. G. Bradley, it was originally taken over by "Artemus Ward," who was received in London in 1866 with great acclaim.

On the basis of the documentary evidence here presented, the many ingenious etymologies that have been put forward, such as the ten assembled by Mencken in his *American Language* (4th ed.; 1936), must be thrown out of court. In the tracing of word history nothing can take the place of specific historical citations. These are now available for "O. K."

Index

INDEX